Wit's Pilgrimage

For Andrew Pitcairn-Hill

Wit's Pilgrimage

Drama and the Social Impact of Education in Early Modern England

Darryll Grantley

University of Kent

Ashgate

Aldershot • Burlington USA • Singapore • Sydney

Published by
Ashgate Publishing Limited
Gower House
Aldershot
Hants GU11 3HR
England

Ashgate Publishing Company
131 Main Street
Burlington
Vermont 05401 – 5600
USA

*PR
658
.E48
G73
2000*

Ashgate website: http://www.ashgate.com

British Library Cataloguing-in-Publication Data

Grantley, Darryll
  Wit's Pilgrimage: drama and the social impact of education in early modern England
  1. Theater and society – England – History – 16th century
  2. Theater and society – England – History – 17th century
  3. Education – Social aspects – England – History – 16th century
  4. Education – Social aspects – England – History – 17th century
  5. England – Civilization – 16th century
  6. England – Civilization – 17th century
  I. Title
  306.4'84'0942'0903

US Library of Congress Cataloging-in-Publication Data

The Library of Congress Control Number is pre-assigned as: 00–104299

ISBN 0 7546 0167 6

This book is printed on acid free paper

Printed in Great Britain by Athenaeum Press Ltd, Gateshead, Tyne & Wear.

Contents

Illustrations

Acknowledgements

I am grateful for the help given to me in various ways by Christopher Baugh, Peter Brown, Gavin Carver, Hugh Cunningham, Alison Finlay, Roger Lockyer, Kate McLuskie, David Shaw, Jim Tatum, Nina Taunton and Sue Wiseman. I would like to acknowledge the assistance of Mr Paul Pollak, archivist of the King's School, Canterbury, Dr Jan Piggott, archivist of Dulwich College, and the librarians of Gray's Inn, the University of Kent, and the British Library. The encouragement and advice of the two commissioning editors with whom I worked, Rachel Lynch and Erika Gaffney is much appreciated. The valuable comments and criticisms of the anonymous reader for Ashgate helped to improve the final product by the elimination of several errors and much clumsy writing. Sue Sherwood and Cat Fergusson gave considerable help with the preparation of copy, while the assistance of Ruth Peters and Kirsten Weissenberg at Ashgate was very important. Finally, my thanks are due to Marion O'Connor, a conversation with whom several years ago about the drama of the Inns of Court proved to be the genesis of this project.

CHAPTER ONE

Introduction

It is not long, since the goodlyest graces of the most–noble
Commonwealthes vpon Earth, Eloquence in speech, and Ciuility in
manners, arriued in these remote parts of the world: it was a happy
reuolution of the heauens, and worthy to be chronicled in an English
Liuy, when Tibers flowed into the Thames; Athens remoued to London;
pure Italy, and fine Greece planted themselues in England; Apollo with
his delicate troupe of Muses, forsooke his old mountaines, and riuers; and
frequented a new Parnassus, and an other Helicon, nothinge inferiour to
the olde, when they were most solemnely haunted of diuine wittes, that
taught Rhetoricque to speake with applause, and Poetry to sing with
admiration.[1]

This is how Gabriel Harvey in 1593 described the coming of the new learning
and its impact on England in the course of the sixteenth century. What is
immediately apparent from the quotation is Harvey's awareness of the novelty
of the educational and cultural changes he is describing, and the sense of a
social revolution. He revealingly chooses to foreground the issue of social
behaviour, citing first the two 'goodlyest graces' of eloquence in speech and
civility in manners. The change in manners is something which is frequently
remarked upon in the period. Harvey's view of the phenomenon is a very
positive one, perhaps understandably so as he was himself a beneficiary of the
educational system that gave him the opportunity for substantial social
mobility, and he was a notorious social climber. The social implications of the
refinement of manners were not always viewed in such a favourable light,
however. Robert Greene's *Quip for an Upstart Courtier* of 1592, for example,
discusses the issue of behaviour and social mobility in rather different terms:

if the one altered his nature, & became either indued with learning or
valour he might be a gentleman, or if the other degenerated from his
auntient vertues hee might be heald a pesaunt.
(C1ʳ)

. . .

the worlds are changde and men are growne to more wit, and their
mindes to aspyre after more honourable thoughts, they were Dunces in
diebus illis, they had not the true vse of gentility, and therefore they liued
meanly and died obscurely, but now mens capacities are refined, time

hath set a new edge on gentleme[n]s humors and they shew them as they
should be, not like gluttons as their fathers did in chines of beef and alms
to the pore, but in veluets, sattins, cloth of gold, pearle, yea perle lace.
(C2^v)

Greene's attitude to self-fashioning in this text is satirical; the picture of social
change is conservative and infused with regret. The statement here is part of a
debate between a figure called Velvet breeches, a new style of courtier who
expresses the sensibilities of the new age, and another called Cloth breeches
who gives voice to a nostalgia for an idealized earlier age of fixed hierarchies
and certainties. Velvet breeches is an Italian, signifying the importation of
Italianate styles and behaviour to the Court, with all the emphasis on
refinement of manners which that entailed.

        Of course, the phenomena around which this debate circulates are part
of a larger process of cultural change that has religious, political and economic
ramifications, and constitutes something of a social revolution in the years
from the early sixteenth century to the Civil War. Most of the dimensions of
this have been explored elsewhere and are, in any case, beyond the scope of
this study.[2] However, the passages cited point to one particular social aspect of
the transformation that was taking place in the period, and which had profound
implications for the culture of the nation in both its formal (or institutional) and
its informal aspects. Significant in this are not simply changes in behaviour or
even attitudes to it, but the actual role and function of social behaviour as a
means of signalling social identity and rank, or membership of particular social
groups. There was an increasing trend to place an ever greater emphasis on
matters such as manners, customs and ordinary behaviour.[3] The political,
religious and economic developments which had accompanied the Tudor
ascendancy were bringing to the fore many men whose claim to elite status did
not repose automatically on birth or long-held family estates. Though the speed
and extent of change should not be overstated, and the profound conservatism
of early modern English society needs to be recognized, it is apparent that new
means were emerging through which social identity could be defined. The
relative absence of established means of social definition of the 'new' men
encouraged a greater recourse to more immediately accessible modes of social
self-definition. Dress was one of these, and complaining references to the
extravagance of dress, as well as to transgressions against the sumptuary laws
of the period are legion. Another was behaviour and social accomplishment.[4]
These and other factors would eventually lead to a growing corporate sense of
identity on the part of the elite, even though considerable divergences remained
between the various groups that composed it.

Education

Centrally involved in this process was another phenomenon of the period, the substantial expansion of educational provision in the country. Education operated both to effect material social change and perhaps more particularly to influence social attitudes in a number of ways, and its institutionalization at a national level served to consolidate this impact throughout the sixteenth century and into the seventeenth. In the preface to *The Civil Conversation*, George Pettie's 1581 translation of a work of the Italian Stephano Guazzo (*La Civil Conversatione*), learning is put significantly above dress and other external factors in determining gentility:

> you see that it is Learning which accomplisheth a Gentleman, and the want of it which blemisheth hym and that neither comlinesse of personage, neither gaynesse of garments, neither any exteriour Ornamentes are to be compared to the lineamentes of Learning, without which, though a man shake the feather after the best fashion, and take vpon hym neuer so bygly, he shall neuer be accounted of amongst the wyse, nor neuer be filed on the roale of ryght and sufficient Gentlemen. (2ʳ)

It was a fact well understood and discussed, particularly by humanist advocates of aristocratic education, that education was closely connected to economic advancement by paving the way to office in the expanding civil service. Thomas Elyot's powerfully influential text, *The Governor* of 1531, is perhaps the most prominent but far from the sole example of this awareness. The development of education as a tool for advancement or the maintenance of privilege involved both the acquisition of formally learned skills and a more unofficial dimension which took the form of the refinement of behaviour. In the early years of the seventeenth century, this unofficial education even came in for some satiric comment in John Earle's *Microcosmography* (first published in 1628) that describes a young man at university in the following terms: 'His Father sent him thither, because he heard there were the best Fencing and Dancing Schooles, from these he ha's his Education, from his Tutor the oversight' and: 'His maine loytering is in the Library, where he studies Armes and *Bookes of Honour*, and turnes Gentleman-Critick in Pedigrees' (1633, H8ʳ⁻ᵛ, H9ʳ).[5] For the established elite (to whom these manuals are ostensibly addressed) it was a matter of preserving their sense of separateness and distinctness against the increasing challenges to their position from the 'new men' who were availing themselves of the opportunities offered by political and economic changes in the realm. But to these men the prescriptions for elite manners, accomplishment and behaviour were of equal, if not greater, importance as sources of instruction on how to fashion their social identities to suit the ranks to which they were aspiring. Frank Whigham has observed that: 'the corpus of Renaissance courtesy literature began to develop at a time when an exclusive sense of aristocratic identity . . . was being stolen, or at least encroached upon, by a horde of young men not born to it' (1984, 5).

The prescriptions for refined behaviour were not only a product of the emergence of ideas of social polish as a *sine qua non* of elite status, but went hand in hand with the increasing advocacy of education on the part of the humanist philosophers. In *The Governor* Elyot includes and encourages all the traditional noble accomplishments, but he goes on to warn:

> These persones that so moche contemne lernyng, that they wolde that gentilmens children shulde haue no parte or very litle therof: but rather shulde spende their youth alway (I say not onely in huntynge and haukynge, whiche moderately vsed as solaces ought to be, I intende nat to disprayse) but in those ydle pastymes whiche for the vice that is therin, the commaundement of the prince, and the vniuersal consent of the people expressed in statutes & lawes do prohibite.
> (Book I, XII, 44ʳ/F4ʳ)

Elyot is referring to gambling, but his sideswipe at those who place too much emphasis on the traditional accomplishments is also clear.[6] This points to the fact that some distinction can be made in the courtesy texts between their promotion of chivalric sporting pursuits and their prescriptions for social behaviour. Traditional upper-class recreational activities and the accomplishments which were seen as associated with them, such as hunting skills, dancing and horsemanship, were beginning to be regarded in some quarters as problematic when they were embraced exclusively as the definitive markers of aristocratic identity. This was because they could sometimes impede a pursuit of other aspects of education that were becoming in many respects more important. The other dimensions of self-improvement – the refinement of behaviour and the acquisition of skills appropriate for professional life through formal learning – went less problematically together.

Drama

The role and function of drama in education have a direct relevance to the development of skills in social behaviour. In his philosophical text of 1605, *The Advancement of Learning*, Francis Bacon relates a story to illustrate the exercise of specific faculties developed through education:

And it is not amisse to obserue also, how small and meane faculties gotten by Education, yet when the[y] fall vnto greate men or great matters, doe work great and important effects: whereof we see a notable example in *Tacitus* of two Stage-plaiers, *Percennius* and *Vibulenus*, who by their facultie of playing, put the *Pannonian* armies into an extreame tumulte and combustion. For there arising a mutinie amongst them, vpon the death of Augustus Caesar, Blæsus the lieutenant had committed some of the Mutiners which were suddenly rescued: whereupon Vibulenus got to be heard speake, which he did in this manner, *These poore innocent wretches, appointed to cruel death, you haue restored to behould the light. But who shall restore my brother to me, or life vnto my brother? that was sent hither in message from the legions of Germany, to treat of the common Cause, and he hath murdered him this last night by some of his fencers & ruffians, that he hath about him for his executioners vpon Soldiours: Answer Blæsus, what is done with his body: the mortallest Enemies doe not deny buriall: when I haue performed my last duties to the Corpes with kisses, with teares, command me to be slaine besides him, so that these my fellowes for our good meaning, and our true hearts to the Legions, may haue leaue to bury vs.* With which speeche he put the army into an infinite fury and uprore, whereas truth was he had no brother, neyther was there any such matter, but hee plaide it meerely as if he had beene vpon the stage.
(Book 2, Ss2ᵛ–Ss3ᵛ)

Bacon recognizes clearly the value of performance skills in the matter of social command, and he is not alone in doing so. In 1601 another writer, Thomas Wright, in *The Passions of the Mind in General* also commented on the importance of behaviour in social life, and looked to players to provide models:

Looke upon other men appassionat, how they demeane themselves in passions, and observe what and how they speake in mirthe, sadnesse, ire, fear, hope &c, What motions are stirring in the eyes, hands, bodie &c. And then leave the excesse and exorbitant levitie and other defects, and keepe the manner corrected with a prudent mediocritie. And this may be marked in the stageplayers who act excellently; for as the perfection of their exercise consisteth of imitation of others, so they that imitate best, act best.
(163)

There is repeated stress in the period on the value of the drama in the acquisition of skills, not only of rhetorical projection, but more generally the achievement of a social 'presence'. The prominence of drama in social pedagogy was an early feature of the educational revolution, and one that will be further discussed in the chapters that follow. This function is enhanced by the perception that, in many contexts, courtly and otherwise, the line distinguishing professional from social skills is a very blurred one indeed.

The relationship between education and drama is complex and not unproblematic, not least because of the institutional structures that evolved to accommodate each activity. It is a relationship, however, which contributes important perspectives on the ways in which drama functioned within its society and it encompassed a number of aspects. These included: education as a prominent motif in the aristocratically patronized drama of the sixteenth century, educational institutions as venues of drama, the contribution of the academy to the evolution of public modes of drama, education and the playwrights, education and the audience, and the representations of learning and social behaviour on the public stage.

The university curriculum itself in the sixteenth and seventeenth centuries was increasingly shaped in ways that both encouraged the role of the arts in the formation of gentlemen and promoted the performative aspects of the learning process. Religious changes in the early sixteenth century had resulted in the strengthening of the faculty of Arts in the Tudor university, and the predominance of the faculty in the university in terms of size. Humanist ideas began to shape the content of degree studies, and fostered the study of subjects that would be of self-evident relevance to the development of the theatre culture of the late sixteenth and the seventeenth centuries. The study of classical languages and literatures was promoted, and other subjects were introduced, as the idea took root that a complete education involved a mastery of all areas of knowledge. In his proposal for a college for gentlemen, *Queen Elizabeth's Academy* (1572), Sir Humphrey Gilbert proposed that modern languages and history were suitable topics of study for the educated man, and he proposed to have in his academy teachers of French, Italian, Spanish and German (7). The libraries of students in the period also show a strong commitment to the study of history, and in the early sixteenth century the first chairs of history were established at both English universities. Oral performance was built into the educational process in the form of the system of disputations, academic exercises in which students debated before their peers and teachers. These exercises became increasingly literary, with a stress on eloquence and 'wit,' and gave the students the opportunity to exercise styles of rhetoric.[7]

Significant in the impact of the educational system on the emerging public drama is the collection of colleges known as the Inns of Court, most especially during the sixteenth-century segment of its history. Together the Inns composed an elite educational institution in a period when education was beginning to have a prominent function in the processes of change and mobility. Though they were termed 'the third university of England', and were ostensibly concerned with legal training, they were far more than this. Usually taking students who had already passed through the universities, they were for many a type of cultural and political finishing school. On the one hand the Inns were valued for their capacity to provide social skills and accomplishment, while on the other they were regarded as providing the best vocational preparation for high public office. They enjoyed close connections with the Court and government, particularly under the patronage of Lord Burghley. The Inns were thus centrally placed in the process of forging the new elite, from a range which encompassed at one end the sons of the aristocracy and at the other those of wealthy tradesmen. Perhaps most significant of all was the fact of their location in London at a time when the capital was becoming ever more the hub of national life, especially as a residential establishment housing a large number of educated young men with powerful connections and frequently considerable ambition. These same factors, which strengthened the agency of the Inns in social change, also gave them prominence in the cultural history of the period. As a residential educational community they constituted a centre not only of political and religious debate, but also of cultural production and particularly of consumption. For all these reasons and more, they are one of the more important points of focus for a consideration of the theatrical culture of the period.

If the theatre history of the period cannot be fully understood without reference to the broader culture, the extraordinary developments which took place in early modern drama are an indispensable part of any consideration of that culture. Raymond Williams has remarked with reference to the English Renaissance: 'It was above all in drama that the otherwise general processes of change in conceptions of the self and society are articulated and realized' (1981, 146–7). It was not simply that drama was an intensely social medium, but also that its production involved the presence of dedicated theatres, which together constituted an economic as well as a cultural institution in the life of the capital.

One of the social phenomena in the period with the most immediate relevance to the place of the drama in society, and its ideological voice, was the emergence of an ever-widening divide between elite and popular culture. This has been described by the social historian James Sharpe, referring to cultural developments extending over a somewhat longer period, in the following terms:

> In 1550, or thereabouts, popular culture, it has been claimed, was everybody's culture: the elite might participate in a learned culture as well, but the cultural forms and attitudes of the masses, their sports, belief systems and so on would be shared by the aristocracy and the remainder of the upper classes. Yet by 1800 the elite had withdrawn from the culture of the people, and had developed a distinctive culture (or perhaps number of cultures) of their own. The new concepts of aristocratic behaviour, and the growth of bourgeois susceptibilities, which came some time after them, made members of the elite unwilling, perhaps even

unable, to participate in the robust pastimes, the indecorous ceremonies, and the superstitious customs of the lower orders. . . . this was part of a far-reaching change in the general intellectual climate: for the present, it is enough to note that from 1650, participation in popular culture by a member of the elite was likely to be an attempt to reinforce popularity, an adventure or a precursor of what a later age was to know as slumming. (1987, 285–6)

Peter Burke has advanced a distinction between a 'great tradition' of culture transmitted by such official cultural institutions as schools and universities, and a 'little tradition,' maintained in the lives of the unlettered, that he identifies as 'folksongs and folk tales, devotional images and marriage chests, mystery plays and farces, broadside ballads and chapbooks, and above all, festivals such as Christmas, New Year, Carnival, May and Midsummer' (1978, 24). He points out that the withdrawal of the nobility from popular culture came about in the early modern period, and cites the fact that Sidney found *Chevy Chase* to have a 'rude style' and that Puttenham's *Artes of English Poesie* of 1581 makes an explicit distinction between 'vulgar poesie' created by the 'instinct of nature' and 'artificial poesie' created by the educated (ibid., 277).

Many modern evaluations of the early modern drama situate the commercial drama of the early modern period, and particularly that of the public theatres, squarely within the realm of popular culture, largely on the basis of its technically broad availability. This is a view that has been taken of earlier drama as well, and David Bevington's description of the Tudor interlude drama follows very much this line:

Popular theater must be one that played to country as well as to town, to lower and middle classes as well as to the gentry, developing thereby a drama for many tastes and for a wide range of opinion on ethical, religious and political questions. Such distinctions are needed if we are to find the professional precursors of Marlowe and Shakespeare. Their theater was a truly national one and might be expected to owe much to its own history as an institution. (1962, 8)

Michael Hattaway, in his examination of a later range of plays from the early modern commercial repertoire, selected on the basis of their acceptability to a wide audience, has this to say about them: 'The popularity of these plays . . . is a function of their appeal to the whole spectrum of Elizabethan society . . . Plays and players "the abstract and brief chronicles of the time" were, like sermons (their rivals in entertainment), important components of mass culture' (1982, 1). Raymond Williams also defined the popular nature of this theatre on the basis of the extent of its contemporary consumption, but also because of the linguistic range that it encompassed:

Making its way in popular rather than primarily aristocratic theatres, it drew heavily on those arts of visual representation (in both acting and scene) which had been central in popular pre-literate culture. It included, in one part of its range, highly abstract or formal argument, in the vocabulary of the highly educated, as well as elements of formal verse, in received and closely structured forms. But it included also, in diverse as well as some regular relations with these, the everyday language and speech-forms of war, politics, business and trades, as well as the wide vocabulary and speech-forms (including the 'vulgar' speech-forms) of everyday popular discourse.
(1981, 154–5)

However, the various ways in which there continued to be cultural intersections between the early modern theatre and the various processes and structures of education would inevitably have a complicating effect on both the position of drama in the culture and its representations of that culture. The position of drama in early modern society and its status as a cultural discourse, were increasingly complex and affected by the contrasts and conflicts between its literary dimensions on the one hand and the undeniably popular elements of the medium on the other. This was further compounded by attitudes to the commercial nature of the enterprise, Puritan disquiet about the putative moral effects of theatre, and the abiding concerns about the principle of representation on the part of a society in which the reinforcement of its hierarchical structures depended precisely on display and self-representation. The nature of the product itself also adds to this difficulty, perhaps to a greater extent than any other art form, written or unwritten.

The comparisons and contrasts made available by the existence of relatively more exclusive performance locations such as coterie theatres, or private, domestic playing contexts, as well as theatrical activity at Court, also contribute to the idea of public theatre fare as popular culture. The more open availability of the public theatre drama reinforces the notion that it more or less evenly represented the whole culture. The difficulty here resides in the looseness of the term 'popular', and particularly the basis on which it reposes. Despite his own radical position, Williams's analysis smacks strongly of 'golden age' ideas. While Hattaway's definition is to some extent useful in distinguishing drama which was conceived and produced for the public stage from that which was destined for more exclusive contexts, such as Court theatres, it is perhaps going too far to consider the public theatre plays as fully fledged components of 'mass culture'. Relevant here is a question posed by another scholar, in relation to drama of a slightly earlier period:

How far can supposedly popular plays be seen as reflecting 'popular' attitudes, if by the latter one means the attitudes of the social ranks below

the Court gentry and the urban patriciates? Can such plays be seen as
reflecting a 'national' or regional culture distinct from that of the Court?
Or do they rather represent elite conceptions of what a popular audience
would or should wish to see and hear?
(Walker, 1991, 25)

What is remarkable about the developments in the sixteenth century – apart
from the emergence of dedicated venues for drama – is the effective narrowing
of the range of modes of theatre and the emergence of one dominant mode of
play on the public stage (albeit with various inflections of genre). The
performance cultures and contexts of especially the early part of the century
yield a striking array of modes of drama or drama-related activity in the
culture, including dramatic games and semi-dramatic sequences as part of
festivity in various community and institutional contexts, the episodic
arrangements of the cycle plays, place and scaffold drama, and allegorical and
semi-allegorical plays geared to itinerant production. These forms were all
determined by the particular functions and material circumstances of the plays.
By the end of the century, one strain had become dominant, and it is not
insignificant that what was to prevail on the commercial stage was a form
which had originated in the elite patronized drama of the hall, modified by
academic models. Given that the entire history of the early modern commercial
stage from the building of the first dedicated theatre to the suppression by the
Puritan authorities in 1642 was only around seventy years, it is arguable that
the drama as a whole never quite freed itself from assumptions that
underpinned its elite origins.

　　　While it is true that the repertoire of plays on the public commercial
stage in its heyday was wide, and that this included plays aimed at popular
audiences, there is considerable significance in the distinctions frequently made
by playwrights as well as commentators on the theatre between different types
of audiences. The idea that the socially inferior members of the audience are
only capable of 'shows' and spectacle is a commonly repeated observation, as
in Jonson's reference in the prologue to the Court performance of *The Staple of
News* to the 'vulgar sort / Of Nut-crackers, that onely come for sight' (6–8), or
the (oddly-punctuated) comment in the epilogue to Thomas Heywood's *The
Brazen Age*:

> All we haue done we aime at your content,
> Striuing to illustrate things not knowne to all,
> In which the learned can onely censure right:
> The rest we craue, whom we vnlettered call,
> Rather to attend then iudge: for more then sight
> We seeke to please. The vnderstanding eare
> (L3^v)

Furthermore, the generic variation within the single mode of theatre that dominated the early modern public stage continued to exhibit a strong strand of neoclassical ideas and conventions that were the preserves of precisely those educational institutions which were also instrumental in culturally defining the elite. Genre is never innocent of ideological implications; genre and form dispose towards certain ways of seeing and are inscribed from the outset with particular social values. It is also to a large extent self-perpetuating, setting up conventions of representation that form models for works created subsequently.

The broad evolution of theatrical culture in the sixteenth century might thus be seen in terms of its shift into specific cultural spaces. On the one hand, what took place in the century was a relative de-theatricalization of the broader culture in terms of both geographical and social range, despite the continuation of a great deal of provincial playing. On the other, theatrical representation was not only a product of the ways in which elite culture was changing, but actually formed an essential part of that culture. At the very top of the hierarchy the dramatization of power had always been part of the way that power was actually constituted and exercised but, if anything, that process was appropriated by the broader elite in the course of the century. In using a theatrical metaphor in the early part of the century to describe the exercise of royal power, Thomas More implicitly recognized the power relations in the specific type of theatrical production to which he was referring:

> And so they said that these matters bee Kynges games, as it were stage plays, and for the more part plaied vpon scafoldes. In which pore men be but lokers on and thei th' wise be, will medle no further. For they that sometyme step vp and play with them, when they cannot play their parts, they disorder the play and do themself no good.
> (Sylvester, 1963, 81)

If the association of drama with education has implications for the position it occupies on the spectrum of culture from the popular to the elite, it also impacts on the ways in which it functions socially. This is particularly relevant to the question of whether early modern drama operates to contain dissent or contributes to the subversion of the ideological basis of the social and political status quo. The debate on the drama, led on the side of those advocating its radical and subversive function by Jonathan Dollimore, with Stephen Greenblatt being the most prominent of those scholars arguing for its conservative and containing role, was at its most vigorous in the mid-1980s.[8] However, there have been challenges to the defined oppositions in terms of which the debate is constituted. Discussing a somewhat different but related area of cultural activity in the period, popular festivity, Leah Marcus has remarked that:

By comparison with courtly and ecclesiastical ceremonial, the old calendar customs were highly volatile. Before the seventeenth century, they had sometimes been countenanced or even promoted by the official hierarchy; but just as often, they had been suppressed as an immoral threat to the social order. Their equivocal status has survived into the present.
(1986, 1)

Greg Walker has made a similar point about Tudor interlude drama:

The great hall plays of the early Tudor period do not fit readily into this subversive-or-supportive antithesis. They appear both to have endorsed political authority by praising and applauding their patrons *and* to have engaged with it in complex and genuine negotiations over the use of that authority (and the power wielded) for concrete political ends. They could also confront their royal and noble audiences with often quite brutal criticisms seemingly with impunity.
(1998, 51–2)

In respect of the drama of the commercial stage, Theodore Leinwand has described the opposing positions of the debate in the following terms: 'We read, on one hand, of legitimation, surveillance, domination, appropriation, and control and, on the other, of destabilization, contestation, opposition, and autonomy' (1990, 477). He goes on to argue that this strict binarism oversimplifies the situation, and he has called for a more complex view of structures of power in the drama. He bases his discussion on the constable figure in Shakespeare's plays who is 'pulled upward by the emulation of his betters and his willingness to enforce their laws', but who is equally 'weighted down by coarseness, foolishness, his body and his countermeanings' (481). Leinwand goes on to argue that the binary contrasts in views of the exercise of power break down in the operation of the law. Though the law did not subvert power, it was capable of being used by those within the popular strata for their own ends. A little more recently, Jean Howard recognized the space for both orthodoxy and contestation:

it does not seem to me true that these texts always served established power, whether one defines established power as the monarchy, the aristocracy, the Anglican Church, or the male sex . . . the drama enacted ideological contestation *as much as* it mirrored or reproduced anything that one could call the dominant ideology of a single class, class faction, or sex.
(1992, 7, my emphasis)

In 1994 Kathleen McLuskie contributed the view that there are difficulties in 'locating the professional dramatists in an opposition between elite and popular culture.'[9]

The issue of education is pre-eminently one that would tend to introduce ambiguities into the operation of, especially, social power. Education was part of the official culture. The broader educational system was organized by and for the benefit of the state, though in many cases schools were locally patronized. What is more, education had a significant input into the formation of social identity; it offered the possibility of clear distinctions between a refined and cultivated elite, and an ignorant rabble. However, on the other hand, it was available in varying measures to a relatively broad band of the population, and many from the lower end of the social spectrum were alive to the possibilities it offered for social mobility, initially far more so than the elite in the perceptions of some early commentators.[10] What is more, it was patently clear to Humanist writers that ability and aptitude did not divide along class lines, and the availability of education was instrumental in pointing up this fact. These contradictory ways in which education related to the social hierarchy would, because of the interconnections between drama and education, add to the complexities of the ways that the drama related to this hierarchy. The fact that the drama was a written form with classical antecedents and had an established place in the formal culture of the educational institutions, yet in other forms was also a commercial product on sale to a broad public, contributes to the difficulties in respect of its cultural place and its relation to official ideology. It also affects the ways in which the playwrights viewed, or at least represented their audiences, the terms in which they flattered them or otherwise, and in which the playwrights saw themselves.

CHAPTER TWO

'Ornaments to the City': the emergence of national institutions

If it is a truism that English society experienced a widespread and profound transformation in the course of the sixteenth century, among the ways in which this is most clearly manifest are on the one hand those developments which took place in the provision of education, and on the other the changes in the theatrical culture of the nation. In both areas of activity, the process of change ecompassed both material and organizational structures, and the 'content' of their products. The system of education was completely transformed during the period, and for its part the theatrical culture of England at the end of the century was scarcely identifiable with the situation that had prevailed at its beginning. Also noteworthy are the remarkable parallels that can be discerned between the developments in these two areas of cultural activity. While the drama saw the emergence of dedicated buildings in the last quarter of the century, there was also a substantial increase in college and school building as a result of state and private investment. The impulse towards secularization in both areas was a consequence of the changes not only in religious politics, but also in the social role of each within the culture. Both became, in the course of the century, increasingly subject to state influence as they developed into national institutions of some importance, albeit that the state was neither monolithic nor always uniform in its policies. As such, they were both part of a trend towards the centralization of English culture in the capital.[1] The development of London as a centre of theatrical enterprise coincided with the substantial increase in importance of the Inns of Court as an educational and cultural institution, and the establishment of elite schools in and around the capital.[2] The existence of a commercial theatre culture housed in dedicated buildings was determined by very similar social changes and conditions which propelled major educational institutions into an enhanced role in national and cultural life.[3] The growth in cultural prominence of education on the one hand and theatre on the other, not only takes place in curiously close juxtaposition, but in a way which makes each a touchstone of political and cultural change.

It is scarcely meaningful to talk of a 'system' of education at the outset of the sixteenth century, such was the diversity and lack of connection between those individuals, bodies or institutions providing instruction at various levels. The field of education extended from the very basic and informally organized dame schools, or private tutors at one end to the highly formalized settings of the universities and Inns of Court at the other. While this diversity persisted to some extent through the changes that took place in the course of the sixteenth century, what had emerged by the end of it was a considerable amount of formal organization, involving a substantial degree of state regulation and control. From early in the century, humanist thought gave education a central place in the new conceptions of society. Though it was never formally organized as a national programme, particularly after the Reformation an educational system of sorts started to emerge, with a fairly coherent ideology. Both the government and prominent Protestants (often as patrons at a local level) took a hand in establishing new schools or colleges, or refounding existing establishments along secular lines. The Tudor administration was very conscious of the need for educated public servants as the range and complexity of government activity grew (Cooper, 1983, 44; Jordan, 1970, 225). In the early sixteenth century, educated and talented laymen began to replace clergy in high political office (Stone, 1984, 673). The government pursued a sustained policy of educational expansion throughout the century from the 1530s, so that writing in 1577, William Harrison remarked: 'there are not many corporate towns now under the Queen's dominion that have not one grammar school at the least' (83). The government now involved itself to a considerable extent in the organization of education. One feature of this, following Henry VIII's assumption of control of the church, was the re-establishment of cathedral schools as grammar schools (Cressy, 1975, 6). At least eighteen schools which were founded or re-established between 1535 and 1547 name Henry as their benefactor. Another instance of government intervention was the imposition of a uniform grammar book, as part of a programme to replace the monastic practices in schooling (Orme, 1973, 256–71).[4] The administrations under Henry's successors followed the policy of establishing schools even more vigorously; of the 51 schools endowed in Edward's reign, 27 attribute their establishment to the King and at least 136 schools were founded by royal endowment in Elizabeth's reign between the middle and the end of the century (Cressy, 1975, 5).

.   As in the case of the various arrangements for the provision of education, the range of activities that might fall under the description of 'theatrical', 'representational' or 'celebratory' are multifarious at the start of the century. This diversity is manifest at one social extreme in the quasi-dramatic activities of village festivals, and at the other in the refined entertainments at Court or in academic contexts. If it is hard to talk of one educational culture, the notion of a single theatrical culture is equally problematic. Just as the nation's education in the period underwent a process of systemization which increased the power of central government over its provision and organization, the main thrust of developments in drama was towards a diminution in provincial, community endeavours and their substantial replacement by a commercial theatre that was not only based in London, but was under a form of central government regulation, albeit fraught with many complexities. This involved the relative de-theatricalization of grassroots popular culture, a phenomenon that occurred for a variety of political and socio-economic reasons, apart from the most obvious factor of religious change. The decline to extinction of the cycle plays was almost complete in the sixteenth century, many having their final productions in the 1570s, such as the plays of Chester (1575), York (1572), Chelmsford (1576?), Wakefield (1576?) and Coventry (1579). Harold Gardiner in the 1940s claimed that official opposition to the plays was 'the true and practically sole cause of the cessation of the medieval religious stage' (1946, xiii). However, the fact is that several cycles were abandoned before the break with Rome, so that the process of decline was underway before any religious or centrally based political opposition was present as a factor. Conversely, some cycles lasted until very late in the century and even beyond it. More recent work on urban communities suggests a more complex set of circumstances operating in the processes of change in the sixteenth century. Certainly, the force of discouragement on the part of powerful Protestant reformers cannot be discounted, and must be considered a significant factor, but several economic and social factors such as economic turbulence in provincial towns, the weakening of gilds, and the emergence of a new Protestant individualism also had a major part to play.[5]

The logocentrism of Protestantism and its tendency to promote literacy also underpinned the thrust towards education. Archbishop Grindal's efforts to cultivate an educated ministry are illustrated by his promotion of 'prophesyings'. This is a particularly Protestant phenomenon which is related to the insistence on scriptural study. It is worth noting that, in the course of the century, the universities broadened their role from initially training only the clerical elite to educating virtually the whole ministry of the Church of England (MacCulloch, 1990, 115; Collinson, 1988, 45–6). Matthew Hutton's observations on the Creed Play – that it would be enjoyed by the 'ignorant sort' and that 'the learned will mislike it' – both proceed from the Protestant preoccupation with educational seriousness, and indicate the implications of this attitude for the drama (*REED: York*, 353). Whereas the urban drama had made available religious teaching through images and visually-presented narratives to a literate and non-literate population alike, Protestant teaching relied more on the word, with a concomitantly heavier emphasis on education. In discussing the secularization and 'sacralisation' of towns in the sixteenth century, Patrick Collinson notes that 'the town became self-consciously a godly commonwealth, its symbolic and mimetic codes replaced by a literally articulated, didactic religious discipline' (1988, 55).

The dramatic and semi-dramatic festivals in rural communities also suffered a decline in the course of the sixteenth century along with other aspects of local community culture. In his long historical poem, *The Second Part of Albion's England* written near the end of the century, William Warner laments the passing of morris dancing, Robin Hood Plays, and other such festivals in terms which betray an awareness of the significance of these activities in defining a cultural identity (as indeed they did) (1589, P4^v). Their decline is a measure of the profound transformation that took place in English culture in the course of the sixteenth century. Perhaps more fatal to small community festivities and folk drama than official prohibitions was the suppression of religious gilds, but religious objections and institutional changes were far from constituting the only determinants of the decline. Another, perhaps more material factor which was both indicative of and to some extent a determinant of the change in social ethos, is the movement towards enclosure and engrossing in many rural communities. The decline of local festivals is thus symptomatic of a far more wide-reaching change than simply that of religious ideology. It is in some ways indicative of the interaction between economic and social changes in sixteenth-century communities and the advent of Protestantism, both factors promoting the tendency towards the privatization of culture.

If both educational institutions and theatrical companies came to enjoy a far greater degree of individual and state patronage than ever before, this had important implications for their place in the national culture. The effects of the changes in the course of the century were such as to propel both the developing system of education and the emerging London theatrical culture to the status of national institutions, however problematically the latter may have been viewed (especially initially) by some contemporaries. In the case of the emerging system of education, this development consisted not just in the centralizing effects of an increased government involvement in its direction, such as the imposition of the universal Latin grammar, and the control of universities through statesmen-chancellors, but also in the growth in size and significance of the Inns of Court in the capital. The parallel process in the commercial theatre was the combination of a focus of theatrical culture on London with a progressive extension of not only Court interest in, but also state involvement with, the business of theatrical activity. This may have had its detrimental effects, and may have produced problems for writers and performers in the theatre, though the system of control remained inconsistent, somewhat haphazard and lacking in fully effective formal mechanisms of policing. It was also subject to conflicts between different figures and bodies of authority, state and local.[6] Nonetheless, the fact of increased state regulation did implicitly recognize the status of theatre as a cultural institution of undoubted, if contentious significance.

Another feature shared by the system of education and the theatrical culture of the period was the fact that both activities extended, in various ways, across almost the entire social spectrum. The developing educational system catered, albeit in divergent ways and in vastly different measure, to people of a large range of social ranks. As S. P. Anglin has noted: 'Any school might contain at the top of its social scale the sons of one or two baronets, knights or gentlemen of the county and at the bottom the sons of small shopkeepers and craftsmen' (985, 116).

This diversity of participation had its counterpart in the theatrical culture too. Dramatic activity was recognizably a feature of many forms of community celebration in the sixteenth century, those communities extending across the range of social rank from rural villages to the royal Court. It was thus in some measure part of the culture of all sectors of society, and if this society was progressively 'de-theatricalized' in the course of the century as much community festival declined, the emergent commercial theatre aimed at and succeeded in attracting a broad social base of attendance. The classroom of the late sixteenth century was one place of social juxtapositions, and the commercial theatre was another. Although in neither case does this involve mixing of classes on an equal basis, this breadth of social embrace nonetheless contributed to the importance of both areas of cultural activity as national institutions. The fact that both enjoyed the participation of hugely divergent levels of society, most particularly as consumers, places any institutional and structural developments connected with these forms of endeavour firmly in the centre of social change. To a far greater extent than ever before, people of different ranks shared the locations dedicated to education and those dedicated to the presentation of drama, and what is significant is the way in which social participation – or attitudes to it – in these areas of culture developed and changed in the course of the sixteenth and seventeenth centuries.

The developing educational system had a complex and enduring relationship with the emerging institution of theatre; the connections between the two areas of activity take many forms and are sustained throughout the early modern period, however problematically at times. A feature they share is the fact of their ambiguous relationship with the phenomenon of social mobility and perceptions of social identity in what was a strongly hierarchical society. Despite the nominal breadth of reach of both the system of education and the commercial theatre in terms of consumption and client base, neither has a straightforward role in the processes of social change. As the educational system had a more immediately active and wide-ranging role in this social formation, and because it forms a highly relevant part of the social backdrop to the development of theatre in the period, this will be considered first.

The expansion of education in the sixteenth century was of self-evident agency in the process of social mobility. For many boys of plebeian origins, schools were the first step in the acquisition of an education which gave opportunities for social advance in church careers. Laud, the Archbishop of Canterbury was a clothier's son, Harsnett, the Archbishop of York was a baker's son, Corbet, the Bishop of Norwich, was a gardener's son and there were other many instances of social mobility through education (Lawson and Silver, 1973, 117, 136–40). Henry VIII's chief bishops were all men who had risen from the lesser gentry and yeomanry: William Warham, John Fisher, Richard Cox, Cuthbert Tunstall, Hugh Oldham, Hugh Latimer, and Thomas Cranmer (Simon, 1966, 65). The most politically powerful men in the realm under Henry VIII came up by the same route; Thomas Wolsey was the son of an Ipswich burgess, and Thomas Cromwell was also of common parentage (Simon, 1966, 65, 100).

There was a clear attempt on the part of some educational reformers to extend access to education as a form of social improvement, and there was at the very least a consciousness on the part of many of the need to make provision for the poor.[7] However, the increased availability of learning also served to underscore both the existing, and the evolving social polarities. Though humanist thinkers and writers played a significant role in advocating and promoting education in the sixteenth century, the basis of their ideas was conservative in respect of social organization and hierarchy. While the emphasis in humanist discourses on education and society was usually on the well-being of the realm, the audience addressed is invariably a gentle one and the privileged status and position of this group, far from being called into question, is usually seen as essential to the welfare of the commonwealth. Elyot's *Governor* is one of the most significant of the humanist essays on education. It was clearly so regarded in the period, as it went to eight editions in the fifty years following its publication in 1531.[8] In this text Elyot advocated a humanist education for the aristocracy in order to benefit both individual members of the class and society as a whole. Plans for academies to educate the children of gentlemen were proposed at various times by Sir Nicholas Bacon and Sir Humphrey Gilbert. Luis Vives, Roger Ascham and other humanist educational theorists of the early and middle part of the sixteenth century also tend to view the matter of education from the point of view of the noble elite. Both Elyot and Ascham (in *The Schoolmaster*) deplore the neglect of education by the nobility, because they view the consequence of this as being the erosion of the power and position of the established elite in favour of the children of 'mean men'.[9] A later theorist, Richard Mulcaster, adopts a more liberal perspective. He was writing in the last decades of the century when there had been a considerable increase in the use of public educational facilities, and perhaps it is for this reason that he, as a public schoolmaster himself, adopts a somewhat different position.[10] Like Ascham and Elyot he argues from the point of view of the good of the whole commonwealth but, while stopping short of advocating a universal system of education, he actively supports the idea of making education available to people of all ranks (and even to girls, at least at elementary level). Mulcaster argues that some people, irrespective of social rank, are endowed with extraordinary intellectual qualities (1581, 145). He points out that the country would suffer if education were confined to particular sectors of the population: 'If all riche be excluded, abilitie will snuffe, if all poore be restrained, then will towardnesse repine. If abilitie set out some riche by priuate purses for priuate preferment: towardnesse will commende some poore to publicke prouision for publicke seruice' (1581, 138). He also appears to advocate a sort of platonic meritocracy:

> Plato in his wished common weale, and his defining of natural dignities, appointeth his degrees and honors, where nature deserueth by abilitie & worth, not where fortune freindeth by byrth and boldnes though where both do ioyne singularitie in nature and successe in fortune, there be some rare ieuell. Hereupon I conclude, that as it is necessary to preuent a great number for the quantitie thereof: so it is more then necessarie to prouide in the necessarie number for the qualitie thereof.
> (1581, 138)

However, Mulcaster considers the question as a social theorist with a broad overview of his society. As suggested above, his conception of education proceeds from the perspective of the requirements of the state, something he had in common with many other humanists. He too, therefore, ultimately comes down against a universal (or too extensive) provision of education, citing the danger of the overproduction of educated men: 'To haue so many gasping for preferment, as no goulfe hath stoore enough to suffise, and to let them rome helples, whom nothing else can helpe, how can it be but that such shifters must needes shake the verie strongest piller in the state where they liue, and loyter without liuing?' (1581, 134). Mulcaster goes on to argue also that there are evident dangers in the acquisition of learning by the non-gentle, and it is liable to become 'a bootie to corruption, where the professours neede offereth wrongful violence to the liberalitie of the thing' (1581, 146). This idea is related to a concern expressed in an interlude written a few years earlier than Mulcaster's publication, Thomas Lupton's 1578 play *All for Money*, about the subservience of learning to material gain in an age of materialism: 'Manie doe embrace and studie me dayly / But will you knowe why, and also to what ende, / Forsooth for great liuing, and also for money' (127–9).

Whereas other markers of social class were various and sometimes not very clearly defined, the sort of classical education acquired in the grammar schools and particularly the universities was unequivocal in imparting the sophistication that naturally placed those who had it within the class of gentry.

The values which informed this sort of education were elitist, and the fact of having acquired them was in itself empowering. The dichotomy that emerged in education was one that was to be an enduring and significant factor in the development and preservation of the English class system. Classical education was for those who were, or were on their way to becoming, gentlemen, while useful and mechanical skills were for those who would work with their hands (Kearney, 1970, 118; Lawson and Silver, 1973, 144–5). In the case of the universities, scholars lived in communities and increasingly so during the course of the century, so that a sense of social cohesion and class identity was arguably contributed to by the cultural imprinting of the educational process. Conversely, the attention paid to ranking in the universities underlined social stratification even within these circumscribed and privileged contexts.

Grammar schools were endowed not only by the Crown, but by private individuals as well, particularly from 1560 onwards. That there was strong middle and upper class interest in them is suggested by the large number of bequests to and endowment of schools by individual members of these classes, particularly in the provinces (Lawson and Silver, 1973, 105–7; Cressy, 1975, 8; Simon, 1966, 232–3). In London patronage tended to be corporate, and the merchant elite of the city were also generous in their endowment of schools (Jordan, 1970, 225–6). Although grammar schools had been conceived for a wide social range and generally intended for able children of poorer families, frequently declaring this objective in their endowments, they rapidly became dominated by the more prosperous classes. Gentry families soon developed a strong interest in education and were to exercise a considerable influence over grammar schools through control of governing bodies and powers to appoint masters, and they reaped benefits from these schools substantially in excess of their contribution to them (Simon, 1966, 361, 372). At the refounding of the King's School, Canterbury in 1540, Cranmer had some difficulty in insisting on the provision for poor boys. He complained of the other commissioners that they: 'would have none admitted, but Sons, or younger brethren of Gentlemen. As for other Husband-mens Children, they were more meet . . . for the Plough and to be Artificers, than to occupy the place of the learned sort. So that they wished none else to put to School but only Gentlemens Children' (Strype, 1694, Bk. I, 89). Their exclusiveness may have been exacerbated by the fact that the statutes of some grammar schools required that boys be able to read and write before admission (Charlton, 1965, 98–9). For admission to Shrewsbury School, to which many of the leading families of Shropshire and North Wales sent their sons, a boy had to be able to read, to write his name, to 'have his accidence without the book' and to have a certain amount of Latin (Fisher, 1889, 42). This was clearly something that was more within the capacity of better off households to achieve. In Holgate's and St Peter's schools in York, founded in 1546 and 1557 respectively, the range included the sons of Northern gentry, clergy, officials and wealthy families (Palliser, 1982, 105). The nobility and upper gentry, who had customarily had their children educated by private tutor, began in the course of the century to send them to schools as urged by humanist educationalists.

The grammar schools were able to contribute to the general level of literacy without substantially undermining the social divisions of sixteenth century society because a fairly common phenomenon was for poorer boys to complete just a few years of schooling and then to leave to find employment. There was relatively little by way of scholarship funds to aid the sons of the poor to remain in school (Simon, 1966, 373). Poor pupils frequently dropped out of school for economic reasons and went to do apprenticeships (Anglin, 1985, 39; Carlisle, 1818, Vol. 2, 578–81). Robert Crowley, writing in 1548, complained:

> what menchyldrene of good hope in the liberall sciences and other honeste qualities (wherof this realme hath great lacke) haue ben compelled to fal to handycrafts and come to daye labour to sustayne theyr parents decrepet age and miserable pouertie: what frowarde and stoubourn children haue herby shaken of the yoke of godly chastisement rennyng hedlonge into all kyndes of wickednes and finally garnished galowe trees.
> (Bi^{r-v})

The status of grammar schools varied as well. Winchester, founded in 1387 and Eton, founded in 1440, emerged very early as front runners among schools. It was to Eton that Bess of Hardwick sent her sons. Shrewsbury was another to gain prominence and counted both Philip Sidney and Fulke Greville among its pupils in the sixteenth century (Charlton, 1965, 97). A school that was centrally important in the development of school drama, particularly in relation to the Court, was St Paul's, which quickly became an educational institution of considerable prominence in the capital. St Paul's was a product of both philosophical developments and social changes. After John Colet had left Oxford to become Dean of St Paul's, he founded the school in 1508 to put into practice his radical ideas for the new learning, and chose as its governors the Company of Mercers rather than a religious institution. The school rapidly became fashionable among the elite and received the sons of important statesmen and courtiers (Wilson, 1978, 72–3). It also had a prominent part to play in the theatrical culture of the capital, and as such had strong connections with the Court. In terms of its role in the culture, St Paul's is thus a significant example of the means of transmission of new ideas, the various social forces shaping the new cultural institutions of the realm and the material structures by which the elite domination over cultural production was established and maintained.

Fig. 1: The King's School, Canterbury.
By permission of the Headmaster and Governors of the King's School

Expansion also occurred at the universities in the sixteenth century. Many new colleges were endowed at the two universities and both institutions saw a large increase in numbers (Curtis, 1959, 35–7). It was particularly from the mid-century onwards that the substantial growth in attendance becomes evident. From the 1560s students started coming to the universities in increasing numbers and admissions rose from 300 per year in the first half of the century to 700 per year in the second. This reached a peak in the 1580s when the total number of students at the two universities was around 3000 (Stone, 1974, 17; Cressy, 1975, 6; Lawson and Silver, 1973, 126). The Tudor administration was very aware of the significance of the argument which Thomas Elyot was making about the importance of education for those charged with the administration of the realm, and perceived the need for educated public servants as the range and complexity of government activity grew (Cooper, 1983, 44; Jordan, 1970, 225). In the early sixteenth century, educated and talented laymen began to replace clergy in high political office (Stone, 1984, 673). Along with the considerable royal endowment of grammar schools, the central administration invested in higher education with the establishment of Regius professorships at Oxford and Cambridge in 1540 and the generous endowment of Trinity College in 1547 (Cressy, 1973, 6). The provision of scholarships was also part of what amounted to an educational programme on the part of the government. The policy does seem to have succeeded in providing a greater supply of men with higher education for public service, to judge from the increasing numbers of parliamentarians recorded as having attended an institution of higher education as the century wore on.[11]

The huge growth in public education provision in the sixteenth century provided the nobility with a viable alternative to the private, domestic contexts in which their sons had traditionally been educated. Though the majority of peers in the sixteenth century continued to be educated at home by private tutors, it is a notable feature of the period that increasing numbers of gentry and nobility began to attend schools set up for public education.[12] Similarly, the universities and the Inns of Court experienced a growing influx of gentry from the mid-century onwards (Stone 1964, 41–80; Stone, 1965, 687–92; Stone, 1974, 27–8). If university education had not been much valued by the aristocracy in the early years of the sixteenth century, it is clear that, towards the latter half of the century, the effect of exhortations of the humanists and the changing perceptions about the sources of wealth and status and power in the state made the gentry and aristocracy substantially more aware of the importance of education for their children, and these classes began to make use of the universities in greater numbers (Hexter, 1950, 1–20; Stone, 1965, 688; Stone, 1984, 264). The landed gentry and the aristocracy in the middle of the sixteenth century were attracted by the capacity of the college system of the universities to provide a disciplined and protective environment for their children while permitting them to acquire the education for which they increasingly perceived the need. The university might even be regarded as a substitute for the earlier practice of sending children from noble households to other such households for purposes of social education and the acquisition of social skills, a practice which largely died out in the sixteenth century. Many even used their influence and patronage to acquire for their own sons college places originally intended for poorer students. William Harrison commented in his *Description of England* (1577) of universities:

> They were erected by their founders at the first, onelie for poore mens sons, whose parents were not able to bring them vp vnto learning: but now they haue the least benefit of them, by reason the rich doo so incroch vpon them. And so farre hath this inconuenience spread it selfe, that it is in my time an hard matter for a poore mans child to come by a felowship (though he be neuer so good a scholer, & woorthie of that roome).
> (1577/87, 77)

There is also some evidence of the dropping out of poor students from universities because of the difficulty of sustaining the financial burden (O'Day, 1982, 91). Another motive that has been imputed to the gentry for sending their children to university is that it was a conspicuous form of consumption (Charlton, 1965, 149–50). Certainly, the luxuriousness of accommodations increased in the course of the century, despite the inevitably more crowded conditions, and the colleges were in some ways privileged societies (Mallet, 1924, 142; Curtis, 1959, 36). When they were used as finishing schools, the qualifications which universities provided were considered less important than the social training they provided, and a far lower percentage of gentle entrants to universities actually took degrees than their non-gentle counterparts who were seeking passports to advancement (O'Day, 1982, 104–5).

Apart from increasingly coming to serve the needs of the existing nobility and upper gentry, universities provided new members to the ruling elite (Curtis, 1959, 266–7). Though social distinctions were largely maintained, a degree of social contact between the rising sons of 'mean men' and the students from elite backgrounds was inevitable. By 1622, Henry Peacham felt it necessary to advise gently born students at the universities: 'For the companions of your recreation, consort your selfe with Gentlemen of your owne ranke and qualitie: for that friendship is best contenting and lasting. To be ouer free and familiar with inferiors argues a baseness of spirit, and begetteth contempt' (39–40/G2^{r-v}). A university education was a means by which the prospective 'new men' so keenly promoted by Henry VIII's administration could equip themselves to get their feet on the ladder of political advancement. It should be stressed that the objective of these students of humble origin was not to challenge the structure of hierarchy, but to improve their place in it. That the universities were increasingly highly valued by the rising classes as a means of social advancement is indicated by the fact that about half the undergraduates between the 1570s and 1630s were sons of tradesmen or the like. Even for poor children, attendance at university was not impossible and humanist thinkers did not exclude them from their theories of education and society (Caspari, 1954, 11–13). Even though the scholarships that were available came to be monopolized by the better off, it was also possible to work one's way through university as a 'servitor' or 'sizar', a servant to a wealthier student. This became a common practice, and such students might work as attendants to dons as well. The continuance of substantial numbers of plebeian students at the universities might be ascribed to this practice, since the enlarged entry of wealthy gentry increased the availability of study through these means.

The emergence of the Inns of Court as a highly elite institution in the sixteenth century was another important factor in the contribution of the educational institutions to the maintenance of the social hierarchy. The law was considered an eminently appropriate area of study for the gentry and nobility, since it concerned itself with legislation and therefore with government. Erasmus remarked that in England there was no surer means to advancement than the law, since it was from the profession of law that the greater part of the new nobility was drawn (Allen, 1922, Vol. 4, 17). The anonymous writer of *The Institution of a Gentleman* in 1555 recommends:

> And for because that equitye and iustyce do strengthen euery estate of men, and causeth them to floryshe in a commune wealth, it is therefore a verye meete offyce for a Gentlemanne to be called to the mynystracion of the lawes, and so accordinge to hys knowledge therin too proceade in the degrees of the same, by the whyche he maye becomme a defender of Justyce.
> (D4^v)

As they provided the highest levels of training in the law, the Inns became the most expensive and prestigious institutions of tertiary education in the country during the sixteenth century. They had for some time been a significant means for the advancement of families of middling rank and many men rose to considerable wealth and power through their legal training.[13] But the Inns also straddled the elite classes; with the development of interest in education on the part of the landed gentry and nobility in the latter half of the sixteenth century an increasing number of young noblemen went to the Inns. In the case of the rising gentry, part of reason for the increase in numbers attending the Inns in the period might be ascribed to a desire to acquire the social cachet that went with membership (Charlton, 1965, 186). Helped by the geographical location in London, there was also a strong relationship with the Court and government, which further increased the prestige of the institution.

The contradictions surrounding the role of education in social mobility are manifest in its implications for the hierarchies of rank and power in early modern England. On the one hand the relative openness of the system, and the opportunities it provided for social advancement, posed an apparent challenge to the position of the landed elite. The contemporary awareness of these implications is present in the exhortations of Elyot and others to the elite not to allow the children of 'mean men' to usurp their position. On the other hand, effective social mobility through education was largely restricted to a few who went on to university and who were mostly the sons of established or economically rising families in any case. Schooling was nominally open, and socially broad-ranging in its intake, but ultimately its full benefits were restricted to a circumscribed section of the population. In the end it thus came to furnish a means by which the social hierarchy was reinforced, rather than fundamentally challenged. Because education is a process of formation, the privileged access of the elite to education gave them a greater chance to acquire accomplishments, such as a command of rhetoric or familiarity with the classics, which reflected on personal identity. This allowed elite identity to be demonstrated as residing in superior personal qualities, rather than being just a matter of wealth, power or birth. In an age that was both competitive and in which identity politics played a significant part, this was a weighty advantage. The expansion in the availability of education also served to strengthen the ranks of the elite by the addition of able men who saw their own interests best served precisely by the maintenance of a structure of hierarchy in which they had the opportunity to improve their own position.

The increased production of educated men had an economic dimension as well. Though such men were needed by the administration and society, they were not necessarily required in the numbers which were being produced. It was not easy or even perhaps possible to fine-tune educational provision to social requirements. The religious changes meant that there was a diminution in the number of jobs available in the Church, and the overproduction of graduates led to a considerable degree of discontent.[14] In *The Puritan*, a play dating from 1606, a beleaguered graduate, George Pye-boord complains:

> As touching my Profession; the multiplicity of Scholars, hatcht and nourisht in the idle calms of Peace makes 'em like Fishes, one devour another, and the Community of Learning has so plaid upon Affections, that thereby almost religion is come to Phantasie, and discredited by being too much spoken of – in so many and mean Mouths myself being a Scholar and a Graduate, have no other comfort by my Learning, but the

Affection of my words, to know how Scholar-like to name what I want,
and can call my self a Beggar in both Greek and Latin.
(1.1.pp. 7–8/A4ʳ–A4ᵛ)

This element of scholarly discontent would inevitably have a significant impact
on the way in which those intellectuals who had a hand in shaping public
cultural discourse represented their society. This was eminently true of the
playwrights of the period, whose social position was at best ill-defined. A
discussion of this will be pursued in Chapter 4.

This context of a society in which education was increasingly being
seen as a valuable social currency is highly pertinent to the development of the
theatre as a cultural institution. The status of the theatre and those who worked
in it is also fraught with problems. The work of actors and dramatists often
brought them into contact with the elite and even the Court, but they were
practitioners of what was often regarded as a dubious trade. Questions arose
surrounding the legitimacy of what were sometimes seen as excessive social
aspirations on the part of actors and playwrights in the commercial theatre.
Another area of complexity related to the position of drama as a written form
with literary antecedents and dimensions, but one which largely operated in
open, non-exclusive contexts, and therefore posed a challenge to accepted
notions about the relationship between different levels of discourse and social
hierarchy. The system of education is relevant to these issues both in terms of
its own apparent address to the status quo and questions surrounding social
mobility, and in the relationship between the drama and the process of
education. The institutional dimensions of these issues will be addressed here,
and (insofar as they are detachable) the conceptual in later chapters.

The influx of gentry into the capital gave rise to a substantial
development of luxury trades in London.[15] The commercial theatre which
developed with the growth of the capital might be viewed as one variety of
these luxury trades (as could, in some respects, the schools in and around
London). In his *Apology for Actors* of 1612, Thomas Heywood argues that the
theatre is a natural contributor to the status of London as a capital city, and he
views it in terms of social hierarchy:

Now if you aske me why were not the Theaters as gorgeously built in
other Cities of *Italy* as *Rome*? And why are not Play-houses maintained
as well in other Cities of *England*, as *London*? my answere is: it is not
meet euery meane Esquire should carry the part belonging to the
Nobility, or for a Noble-man to vsurpe the estate of a Prince. *Rome* was a
Metropolis a place whither all the nations knowne under the Sunne,
resorted: so is *London*, and being to receiue all Estates, all Princes, all

Nations, therefore to affoord them all choyce of pastimes, sports, and recreations.
(C2^r)

...

First, playing is an ornament to the Citty, which strangers of all Nations, repairing hither, report of in their Countries, beholding them here with some admiration: for what variety of entertainment can there be in any Citty of Christendome, more then in *London*?
(F3^r)[16]

The status of 'commercial' (or at least not directly community generated) drama and those who wrote, mounted and performed it, was subject to a range of factors in which some change is discernible over time, but all of which continued to operate in some measure throughout the period. In the Elizabethan period at least, plays and players were accorded a degree of importance by the fact of their being part of a process by which the prestige of the nobles who were their patrons was enhanced.[17] To some extent, too, the status of the early playing companies was guaranteed by the very social structure that privileged the noblemen. The prestige which companies gained from the association with noble patrons frequently translated into material advantage. Suzanne Westfall's analysis of the *Northumberland Household Book*, the account book of the household of the Earl of Northumberland, shows higher payments to the troupes of patrons with higher status, and to those whose patrons have a particular relationship with the Earl (1991, 132, see also 101, 105). The reception of acting troupes in towns was also influenced by the distinction of their associations. The recollection of R. Willis, as a septuagenarian in the 1630s, of attending a play in his youth in the middle years of the previous century, includes a description of the factors determining such a reception (*Mount Tabor, or Private Exercises of a Penitent Sinner*):

> In the City of Gloucester the manner is (as I think it is in other like corporations) that when Players of Enterludes come to towne, they first attend the Mayor to enforme him what noble-mans servants they are, and so to get a licence for their publike playing; and if the Mayore like the Actors, or would show respect to their Lord and Master, he appoints them to play their first play before himselfe and the Aldermen and common Counsell of the City; and that is called the Mayors play, where every one that will comes in without money, the Mayor giving the players a reward as hee thinks fit to shew respect unto them.
> (*REED: Cumberland, Westmoreland, Gloucestershire*, 362–3)

The discriminations made in the latter part of this observation seem to have been current throughout the realm.[18]

However, the relationship between the status of acting companies and the status of players and the acting profession is at best an oblique one. Even in the case of the pre-1570s itinerant troupes, the relative detachment of companies from their patrons' households, and their visible pursuit of a gainmaking activity complicated this. It was, in fact, with the fully-fledged development of the theatre as a commercial enterprise that the business of playmaking afforded opportunities for social mobility to those working in it. Some actors, most notably perhaps Edward Alleyn, acquired substantial wealth by means of their profession, and the theatre as business enterprise might be seen as making a contribution to the climate of social mobility in the period. However, Alleyn's success was unusual, and it was far from consistently true that the theatre provided a substantial living.[19] What is perhaps more important in terms of contemporary social attitudes is how the wealth of actors was perceived, though comments on this matter unfortunately most often come from satirical or antitheatrical sources which imposes an inevitable bias on the attitudes expressed. Such a piece is *Ratsey's Ghost*, dating from 1605, in which players are described in the following terms: 'whom Fortune hath so wel fauored that what by penny-sparing and long practise of playing, are growne so wealthy, that they haue expected to be knighted, or at least to be coniunct in authority, and to sit with men of great worship on the Bench of Justice.' Ratsey goes on to advise the country player with whom he has fallen in to get to London: 'and when thou feelest thy purse well lined, buy the some place of Lordship in the Country, that growing weary of playing, thy mony may there bring thee to dignitie and reputation'. The player replies that he has heard 'of some that haue gone to London very meanly, and haue come in time to be exceedingly wealthy' (A4ᵛ–B1ʳ). In *A Groatsworth of Wit* (1592) Robert Greene creates a satirical portrait of a prosperous member of the acting profession:

> What is your profession, sayd Roberto? Truely sir, said he, I am a player. A Player, quoth Roberto, I tooke you rather for a gentleman of great liuing; for if by outward habit men should be censured, I tell you, you would be taken for a substantiall man. So am I where I dwell (quoth the player) reputed able at my proper cost, to build a Windmill. What though the worlde once went hard with mee, when I was faine to carrie my playing Fardle a footebacke; Tempora mutantur: I know you know the meaning of it better than I, but thus conster it, it is otherwise now; for my very share in playing apparrell will not be solde for two hundred pounds. (D4ᵛ)

Forty years later than this, a less satirical view of London players is to be found in Thomas Nabbes's *Covent Garden* of 1632:

> *Dobson*: But tell me *Ralph*, are those Players the ragged fellowes that
> were at our house last *Christmas*, that borrowed the red blanket off my
> bed to make their major a gowne; and had the great pot–lid for *Guy of
> Warwicks* Buckler?
> *Ralph*: No, *Dobson*; they are men of credit, whose actions are beheld by
> everyone, and allow'd for the most part with commendations. They make
> no yearely Progresse with the *Anatomy* of a Sumpter-horse, laden with
> the sweepings of *Long-lane* in a dead Vacation, and purchas'd at the
> exchange of their owne whole Wardrobes.
> (B1 ᵛ–B2ʳ)

Ironically perhaps, the perceptions of the rise to wealth of actors actually
presented an impediment to their social acceptability within the
commonwealth. The players' access to fine apparel through their profession,
and arguably their ability to ape the manners of their social superiors, was a
source of unease. This was in the context of widespread perceptions
(particularly among the elite) of intense social aspiration by people of all
ranks.[20] This was more particularly true, perhaps, in the early seventeenth
century, but as early as 1555 the writer of *The Institution of a Gentleman*
remarked, in his epistle to Lord Fitzwater preceding the work:

> And when I consydered that handycraft men in these dayes doo stande
> much in the estimacion of their degrees, and seke both the maintenaunce
> and profyt of al those that be mecaniques like them selues, the Shomaker
> striuinge with the Currier, thᵉ Currier with the Tanner, the Butcher with
> the Grasier, the Chaundeler wyth the Cooke, eche one hauinge with the
> other a great debate for the vpholding of his occupacyon, fearing leste by
> neclygence, or ouersight, hys facultie myghte decaye.
> (A2ᵛ–A3ʳ)

Especially with the advent of the institutionalized London theatre, the situation
of the social status of actors (and the business of playing) became complicated
by the very fact of the nakedly commercial nature of the enterprise. In other
non-commercial contexts in the sixteenth century, drama had been a cultural
activity which had enjoyed some prestige, at least in civic terms. The mounting
of cycle and other plays in the provincial cities which staged them was part of
an enhancement of the status of those cities.[21] Gilds were expected to
contribute pageants to the greater glory of the community. In a sense
membership of the gild, and thereby indirectly the community itself was
signalled and recognized through contribution to patronage of the plays.
Admission to crafts was generally marked by, and conditional upon,
recognition of the individual's obligation to pay pageant money. It was not
simply the status of whole communities that could be enhanced by theatrical
production, however. Towns were not simply a collection of individuals, but

were constituted in economic, social and cultural terms, by a range of component bodies. Particularly in the highly stratified society of the sixteenth century however, the means by which attachment and relatedness were signified also helped to define status. Mervyn James has remarked: 'Urban societies, no less than landed aristocratic societies, constituted communities of honour, and were therefore intensely competitive in their internal structure' (1986, 35). Since the plays were forms of display directed at the community as a whole, they constituted effective signifiers of social standing. James points out that the plays owned by individual gilds functioned as status symbols which, sold by gilds declining in economic power and bought by those in the ascendant, came to express changes in the social body (1986, 37–8). In the case of the amateur actors in the gild plays, their position in the commonwealth was regulated by their professional status within the gild structure. With the advent of the London commercial theatre, the status of the professional players was not subject to the normal trade hierarchies of the livery companies. However, in a profession or trade which in many ways is characteristic of venture capitalism, there are curious echoes of similar principles to those that prevailed in the livery companies. The most successful of the commercial playing companies, the King's Men, maintained its dominance partly through being run on lines that recall the spirit of those companies.[22] Though the acting profession did not enjoy gild affiliation, the fact that this company maintained its principle of being co-owned by its sharers could possibly be seen to reflect the co-operative values of the trade gilds. This principle would have involved the attachment of status to professional activity particularly, say, in the relationship of sharers to hirelings.

Other contexts of playing which continued to survive also present a contrast with the public theatre, most notably the academic stage. In *Hamlet*, Polonius declares himself to have been an actor in his youth while he was at university, and mentions his prowess with some pride.[23] That his remark on the activity of acting is put into the mouth of a senior courtier (albeit a rather silly one) might perhaps be construed as a subtle attempt on Shakespeare's part to enhance the respectability of his art, but more realistically the credibility of Polonius's enthusiasm is based on the fact that his activities were entirely academic and devoid of any contamination by commercial considerations. Given the use of dramatic activity in educational contexts to develop rhetorical skill and the refinement of manners, and the drama's association with elite patronage, the problem with the commercial theatres was that they brought this prized cultural activity into the marketplace and therefore into the realm of non-gentle trades. The commercialism of the enterprise of theatre would sit most uncomfortably with the idea of a form of cultural production which had pretensions to learning. In his *Gull's Horn Book* of 1609 Thomas Dekker, though himself a playwright in the public theatre, presents a satiric view of the marketing of art in the theatre:

> The Theater is your Poet's Royal-Exchange, vpon which, their Muses (thᵗ are now turnd to Merchants) meeting, barter away that light commodity of words for a lighter ware than words. *Plaudites* and the Breath of the great Beast, which (like the threatnings of two Cowards) vanish all into aire. *Plaiers* and their *Factors*, who put away the stuffe, and make the best of it they possibly can (as indeed tis their parts to doe) your Gallant, your Courtier and your Capten, had wont to be your soundest paymaisters, and I thinke are still the surest chapmen: and these by meanes that their heades are well stockt, deale vpo[n] this comical freight by the grosse: when your *Groundling*, and *Gallery Commoner* buyes his sport by the penny, and like a *Hagler*, is glad to vtter it againe by retailing.
> (27–8)

Similarly, in Sonnet 110 Shakespeare apparently laments his activities as both actor and playwright because it involved his selling himself: 'Alas, 'tis true. I have gone here and there / And made myself a motley to the view, / Gored mine own thoughts, sold cheap what is most dear' (1–3). The social dimensions of this commodification of art and learning are also suggested in Richard Lovelace's satire, 'On Sanazar's being honoured', in *Lucasta* (his collection published posthumously in 1659):

> Vandall ore-runners, Goths in literature
> Ploughmen that would *Parnassus* new manure;
> Ringers of Verse that All-in chime,
> And toll the changes upon every Rhime.
> A Mercer now by th'yard does measure ore
> An Ode which was but by the foot before
> Deals you an Ell of Epigram, and swears
> It is the strongest and the finest Wears.
> (83) [24]

The playing companies in the late sixteenth and the seventeenth centuries were less and less able to avail themselves of the fiction of connection to noble households. The fact of playing for money with no other strongly entrenched allegiances or obligations, placed actors in a position outside the accepted status structure and made them – in the view of some – a danger to that structure. Andrew Gurr has summed up both the challenges and the anomalies associated with them:

> The authorities were frightened of the companies of players. Their travelling habits made them comparable to vagabonds. Their freedom to

roam the country was menacing. They might carry infection from the outside world in ideas as well as the plague. They attracted large crowds and their insistence on being paid for their work of 'play' made them dangerous as well as seductive. Behind all those threats there was the strangeness of their counterfeiting, their imitations of reality. . . The Shakespearian sharer-led company was anomalous for its time in its democratic social and political organization. It was a threat to order and authority. That gives a sharp edge to the prime paradox in all this history, that the survival and the growing prosperity of such companies, the King's Men above all, was due almost entirely to the support and consistent protection given them by the highest authority in the land.
(1996, 9)

Stephen Gosson raised the question of the status of actors in his *Plays Confuted in Five Actions* which appeared in 1582:

Most of the Players haue bene eyther men of occupations, which they haue forsaken to lyue by playing, or common minstrels, or trayned vp from theire childehoode to this abhominable exercise & haue now no other way to gete their liuinge. A common weale is likened to the body, whose head is the prince, in the bodie: if any part be idle, by participation the damage redoundeth to the whole, if any refuse to doe theire duetie, though they be base, as the guttes, the gall, the bladder, how daungerous it is both to the bodie, and to the heade, euerie man is able to coniecture.
(G6^v)

An objection to the mercenary aspects of acting is also expressed in an account of Roman actors by Robert Greene (who can by no means, however, be taken as a disinterested observer of the acting profession) in *Francesco's Fortunes, Or the Second Part of Never too Late* (1590):

Thus continued this facultie famous, till couetousnesse crept into the qualitie, and that meane men greedie of gaines did fall to practise the acting of such Playes, and in the Theater presented their Comedies but to such onely, as rewarded them well for their paines: when thus Comedians grewe to bee mercinaries, then men of accompt left to practise such pastimes, and disdained to haue their honors blemisht with the staine of such base and vile gaines.
(B4^v)

If the fact of being in 'trade' was one complication in the status of actors, another was that they were often perceived to be able, because of their access to expensive dress, to present themselves in a social light which did not match their substance. This became a basis of satirical attacks on them. Stephen Gosson in his 1579 tract, *The School of Abuse*, was outraged that this phenomenon was to be found even in the lowest category of actor, the hireling:

Ouerlashing in apparel is so common a fault, that the very hyerlings of some of our Players, which stand at reuersion of vi.s by the weeke, iet vnder Gentlemens noses in sutes of silke, exercising themselues too prating on the stage, & common scoffing when they come abrode, where they look askance ouer the shoulder at euery man, of whom the Sunday before they begged an almes.
(C6^r/23^r)

Gosson's allegation may have proceeded from a Puritan antitheatricalist position, but it is corroborated in *The Stage-Players Complaint* a good sixty years later (a text much more sympathetic to the theatre) in which two actors reminisce:

> *Quick*: Oh, the times, when wee vapoured the streets like Courtiers.
> *Light*: A pritty comparison! like Courtiers indeed; for I thinke our pockets were as empty as the proudest of them.
> (3)

Fame was another factor in the influence and status of actors. It is likely that the virulence of the satirical remarks made by Puritans and others against players was partly fuelled by their perception of the high profile which actors inevitably enjoyed within the society, since these comments frequently made reference to the overweening pride of players. In the academic play, *The Second Return from Parnassus* dating from around the turn of the century, the actor 'Kempe' says to the scholars Philomusus and Studioso:

> But be merry my lads, you haue happened vpon the most excellent vocation in the world: for money, they come North and South to bring it to our playhouse, and for honour, who of more report than *Dick Burbage & Will Kempe*? Hee's not counted a Gentleman that knows not *Dick Burbage & Wil Kemp*, there's not a country wench that can dance Sellengers Round but can talk of *Dick Bur-bage* and *Will Kempe*.
> (1788–95)

A comment by Samuel Rowlands in *Epigrams* (no. 30), published in 1600, about the comic actor, Dick Tarlton, also suggests the influential power of fame:

> When *Tarlton* clown'd it in a pleasant vaine
> With conceites did good opinion gaine
> Vpon the stage, his merry humours slop.
> Clownes knew the Clowne, by his great clownish slop
> But now th'are gull'd, for present fashion sayes,
> *Dick Tarltons* part, Gentlemens breeches plaies:

In euery streete where any *Gallant* goes,
The swagg'ring Sloppe, is *Tarltons* clownish hose.
(C2^v)

However, by 1628 John Earle in his *Microcosmography* points to a residual
paradox in the actor's reputation, despite some increase in the profession's
status by this time: 'His profession ha's in it a kind of contradiction, for none is
more dislik'd, and yet none more applauded, and hee ha's this misfortune of
some Scholler, too much witte makes him a foole' (1633, H2^{r-v}).

Their access to the trappings of elite status, while supposedly lacking
the substance which went with that appearance was perhaps one of the
profoundest sources of social discomfort with regard to actors. The problem
with their being 'copper-lace gentlemen' was made all the more acute by the
fact of the uncertainty as to precisely what that elite substance actually
consisted of. Though several attacks on actors focus on their pretensions in
terms of apparel, their access to the trappings of gentry also extended to their
command of gentle manners. Earle also remarks of the actor: 'Hee do's not
only personate on the Stage, but sometime in the Street: for he is mask'd still in
the habite of a Gentleman. His parts finde him oathes and good words, which
he keepes for his use and Discourse, and makes shew with them of a
fashionable companion' (1633, H2^v) .

The polish of actors was naturally a product of their training and
profession.[25] The terms 'mimics' and 'apes' are frequent terms of abuse for
players and this lies somewhat at the heart of the problem about drama. On the
one hand, the illegitimacy of actors' pretensions was often referred to in terms
of their mimicry of gentle speech and manners. On the other hand, the
uncomfortable fact was that it was frequently through a process of mimicry in
drama that 'audacity' and social competence were legitimately taught in
educational contexts. Thomas Heywood, in his *Apology for Actors*, makes a
claim that the social performance of a cultivated man is at least as important as
the substance:

> *Tully* in his booke *ad Caium Herennium*; requires fiue things in an
> Orator, *Inuention, Disposition, Eloquution, Memory*, and *Pronuntiation*,
> yet all are imperfect without the sixt, which is *Action*: for be his inuention
> neuer so fluent and exquisite, his disposition and order neuer so
> composed and formall, his eloquence, and elaborate phrases neuer so
> material and pithy, his memory neuer so firme & retentiue, his
> pronuntiation neuer so musicall and plausiue, yet without a comely and
> elegant gesture, a gratious and bewitching kinde of action, a naturall and
> a familiar motion of the head, the hand, the body, and a moderate and fit
> countenance sutable to all the rest, I hold the rest as nothing. A deliuery
> & sweet action[n] is the glosse & beauty of any discourse that belongs to
> a scholler. And this is the action behoouefull in any that profess that

quality, not to vse any impudent or forced motion in any part of the body, no rough, or other violent gesture, nor on the contrary, to stand like a stiffe starcht man, but to qualifie euery thing according to the nature of the person personated: for in oueracting tricks, and toyling too much in the anticke habit of humors, men of the ripest desert, greatest opinions, and best reputations, may break into the most violent absurdities. (C4ʳ)

The question of education and its relation to social mobility and position intersects significantly with the status of playmaking, the status of actors, and the relation between playwrights and players. This is especially apparent in the conflicts between the dignity of writing as an educated activity and the 'trade' aspects of the theatre business.[26] The litany of complaint starts not long after the establishment of the commercial theatre. Stephen Gosson expresses his repentance for his own time as a playwright in the following terms in his *School of Abuse* of 1579: 'I haue sinned, and am sorry for my fault: hee runnes farre that neuer turnes, better late then neuer. I gaue my self to that exercise in hope to thriue but I burnt one candle to seek another, and lost bothe my time and my trauell, when I had done' (24ᵛ/C7 ᵛ).[27] This is a view shared by more than one disgruntled writer for the stage. Writing a few years later in 1586, Anthony Munday (under the pseudonym of Anglo-phile Eutheo) says in *A Second and Third Blast of Retreat from Plays and Theatres*: 'I confesse that ere this I haue bene a great affecter of that vaine art of Plaie-making, insomuch that I haue thought no time so wel bestowed, as when my wits were exercised in the inuention of those follies' (49–50).

At the beginning of the seventeenth century Henry Crosse, in a tract called *Virtue's Commonwealth*, refers – in order to discredit it – not only to the actors' acquisition of wealth but also to the illegitimate striving for status which accompanied it:

> What true glory can they iustly merit, that are praised by the witlesse and braine-sicke multitude? And as these copper–lace gentleymen growe riche, purchase lands by adulterous Playes, & not a fewe of them vsurers and extortioners, which they exhaust out of the purses of their haunters, so they are puft vp in such pride and selfe-loue, as they enuie their equalles, and scorne their inferiours.
> (1603, Q1ʳ)

Where the learning of writers for the stage is employed to the profit of players, it is seen by Crosse as prostitution:

> it were further to be wished, that those admired wittes of this age, Tragædians, and Comœdians, that garnish Theaters with their inuentions,

would spend their wittes in more profitable studies, and leaue off to
maintaine those Anticks, and Puppets, that speake out of their mouthes:
for it is a pittie such noble giftes, should be so basely imployed, as to
prostitute their ingenious labours to inrich such buckerome gentlemen.
And much better it were indeed they had nor wit, nor learning at all, then
to spend it in such vanitie, to the dishonour of God, and corrupting of the
Common-wealth.
(ibid., Q3^v)

Samuel Rowlands in *The Letting of Humours Blood* (1600) sees the theatre as
an activity inappropriate to the dignity of learning:

I would haue *Poets* proue more taller men:
... yours consist's in Wits choyce rare inuention,
Will you stand spending your inuentions treasure,
To teach Stage parrats speake for pennie pleasure,
While you your selues like musick sounding Lutes
Fretted and strunge, gaine them their silken sutes
(A3^r)

It is likely that playwrights like Gosson who had turned from the stage through
religious conviction, or (as in Greene's case) had lost their appeal to the public
and the players, would be more inclined to dredge up an antipathy to actors on
whatever grounds. However, this sense of social and intellectual debasement in
writing for the stage is to be found in other writers, often going hand in hand
with the abuse of actors. This occurred during a period in which the status of
some actors was becoming enhanced by the fact of fame or (in the case those
of the King's Company) the developments in the organization of their business,
such as the sharer system. This arrangement gave the shares in the company a
certain professional position, which even extended to enabling them to take on
apprentices (Gurr, 1996, 97–100). The theatrical profession in general had,
even by 1586, attained sufficient status in the eyes of some for the writer on
heraldry Sir John Ferne (admittedly not a very exclusive analyst) to include in
his *Blazon of Gentry* as an occupation whose members were worthy of the
grant of arms, 'the arte and skill of Playes, practised in Theaters, and exposed
to the spectacle of multitudes' (74–5).[28] As Muriel Bradbrook has pointed out,
the *poetomachia* around the turn of the century pursued, among other issues,
the question of whether learned playwrights had the right to feel superior to
their actor employers (1962, 88). Most playwrights made no objection to
having to do the work they did and if, as in Shakespeare's case, they ranged
themselves with the actors, it is likely to have proceeded partly from a
recognition of commercial realities, and partly from a due regard for the
player's art.[29]

Some actors and others associated with the theatre actually did seek and obtain grants of arms, including Alleyn and Shakespeare (Hosking, 1952, 228–9; Schoenbaum, 1977, 227–31). It is perhaps a testimony to the values of the age that Shakespeare was, as the Victorian scholar J. O. Halliwell concluded, more concerned about the establishment of his status in society through pursuit of means and dignities, than he was about the fate of his plays (cited in Schoenbaum, 1977, 220). What is inescapable is the acute awareness of the issue of status on the part of those who worked in the theatre industry, and the uncertainty of their own status. Edward Alleyn was one of the most spectacular examples of social mobility among actors. In his family the social ascent started with his father whose rank was recorded as a 'yeoman' and who bought an inn. Alleyn was able, as the result of his successful career on the stage, to buy a manor house and a substantial amount of other property, to sustain several aristocratic social connections, and to marry the daughter of John Donne, the Dean of St Paul's (Hosking, 1952, 227). However, besides his renown as an actor, his most enduring claim to fame is his founding of an educational institution, the College of God's Gift (later Dulwich College) in 1619.[30] It is perhaps not surprising that many men who had risen from humble beginnings through their education were themselves disposed to be patrons of education. Such men included Thomas Wolsey, William Warham, John Fisher, Richard Cox, Cuthbert Tunstall, Hugh Oldham, Hugh Latimer, Thomas Cranmer; all these were patrons of scholars, founders or supporters of schools and colleges and men keenly interested in humanist ideas (Simon, 1966, 65).[31] It is arguable that these charitable deeds are not entirely selfless, and that they are in large part designed to redound to the glory of the benefactors themselves. That these benefactions should have taken the particular form of educational endowments might, in the case of those who rose to prominence in the church and state, be ascribed to their recognition of their debt to the educational system. However, there is also the matter of the social dimensions of education, and its association with gentility and social accomplishment. Alleyn appears to have had a strong interest in an upward social trajectory, including his socially advantageous marriage, and it is obvious that his benefaction was very much part of this.[32] To found an institution, the work of which was to produce the very quality of gentility in the form of learning and the refinement of manners, would establish a claim to gentle status that went beyond the material fact of wealth to the essence of the condition itself.

Both the increased provision of education and the new profession of commercial theatre made social mobility available, a fact which suggests that the effect of both was likely to present challenges to the existing social hierarchy. In reality however, despite the fact that both these developing institutions exhibited structures which facilitated a radical questioning of the mystification of rank in early modern English society, they also worked in quite the opposite direction. In many respects the position of the elite, and the system of hierarchy and deference which validated that position, were actually strengthened by these emerging institutions. The circumstances that brought about this state of affairs were not a result of a calculated ideological programme, but rather the consequence of a range of factors, material and political. The ultimate outcome was, however, to contribute to the battery of institutional structures which propped up the deference society in the period.

The parallels between the developments that took place within the fields of education and of theatrical culture in the course of the sixteenth century are remarkable. The political and social developments in the course of the century did not put paid entirely to the diversity of the range of activities that constituted the national provision of education. Nor did they fully manage to curb the various forms of the nation's theatrical culture. What they did do, however, was permit the rise to cultural centrality and dominance of certain institutionalized structures which became pre-eminent in terms of power and influence. The regulation of education and the theatre by the state and the *de facto* involvement of both with social and cultural politics contributed further to the status of their most significant structures – major schools, universities and Inns of Court in the case of the one, the London theatres in the case of the other – as collectively constituting national institutions, something which is itself of importance here. Their role in moulding values and attitudes gave them a powerful influence over social ideology. Though increasingly less direct, the relationship between the world of education – most particularly the Inns of Court – and the world of the theatre was a further dimension to this complex relationship which helped to influence the nature of early modern theatre, its modes of representation, its conventions, and the assumptions which underlay its products and to sustain them until the closure of the theatres.

CHAPTER THREE

'Good behaviour and audacitye': drama, education and the quality of gentility

You a Gentleman? that's a good Jest i'faith; can a Scholar be a
Gentleman – when a Gentleman will not be a scholar? (*The Puritan*
[1606], Act 3, p. 32)

An anonymous 1579 tract, *Civil and Uncivil Life*, takes the form of a dialogue between two young gentlemen, Vincent and Vallentine, in which the matter is raised of the comparative merits of town over country life for gentlemen. Vincent describes to his friend the sort of companions and neighbours he has in the country: 'They are our honest neighbours, Yeomen of the Countrey, and good honest fellowes, dwellers there about: as Grasiers, Butchers, Farmers, Drouers, Carpenters, Carriers, Taylors, & such like men, very honest and good companions.' Vallentine responds: 'And so I thinke, but not for you beeing a Gentleman: For as their resort vnto your house shal giue them occasion to learne some point of ciuillity, and curtesie, so your conuersinge with them will make you taste of their bluntnes and rusticitie, which wil very euill become a man of your calling.' He then goes on to describe the London gentry: 'the most liue in Court or Cittie among the better sorte, you should euer finde company there, fit for your estate and condicion: I meane Noble and Gentlemen' (H4^v).

A number of attitudes are exhibited in the tract that can be related to a range of social, economic and cultural developments in the sixteenth century. Firstly, in advocating Vincent's detachment from the company of his 'honest neighbours', Vallentine's argument implies both the erosion of local social attachments and patterns of economic obligation on the part of the gentry and nobility, and a resultant sharpening of the divisions between popular and elite culture. Secondly, his urging his friend to go and live among gentlemen in the 'Court or Cittie' points to the increasing centralization of English culture in the century: the growth of London in cultural and economic prominence and the concomitant relative decline in importance of provincial communities as centres of social focus and cultural production. Thirdly, and perhaps most significantly indicative of the social changes in the period, Vallentine exhorts his friend to acquire 'point[s] of ciuillity' and to avoid 'bluntnes and rusticitie.' In advocating the mechanisms of self-fashioning and acquisition of social skills, Vallentine's argument promotes the notion that the basis of gentility lies in behaviour. It also recognizes the emergence of a group which perceives its cohesion as residing in shared values and standards of social comportment, including modes of speech.[1]

The role of the formal structures of education in catering to this social requirement was increasingly important as education was secularized. As the role of schools and universities changed from providing primarily for those destined for clerical careers towards embracing a broader role in the teaching of skills, the matter of social accomplishment as an aspect of education gained in significance. The influx of the children of the elite into the schools and universities from the middle of the sixteenth century onwards is likely to have contributed to this shift in emphasis, but the social dimension of education would clearly have been important to those who were aspiring to gentle status as well.

The debates in the period about what constituted nobility had a significant effect on thinking about education. The relative absence of England's engagement in foreign warfare had caused the military source of honours to dry up, and the humanist discourses on rank and honour tended to link the idea of the virtue that was considered the basis of nobility with a fitness to govern acquired through education. Influences from Italy contributed strongly to these ideas, facilitated by a tide of translations. Castiglione's *Il Cortegiano* of 1528 was known in England from early in the century but became more widely popular after Sir Thomas Hoby's translation in 1561, and was followed by a number of other translations of Italian treatises on nobility and courtliness, as well as other texts modelled on them.[2] Central to the Italian ideas of nobility was the notion of refinement, and the new definitions of honour in English humanist thought went hand in hand with an increasing interest in 'manners'. The anonymous writer of *A Discourse of the Common Weal* (1581) relates manners to fitness to govern, and tellingly connects this with education: 'Tell me what counsell can be perfecte, what common weale can be ordered and vpright wheare none of the rulers or counsailers haue studied anie philosophie, and specially that parte that teachethe of maners?' (27–8).

The notion of self-improvement as a way to merit the title of 'gentleman' was also a product of a gathering perception that other (more material) means of marking the distinction were being gradually eroded, compromised or at least complicated. The writer of the 1555 courtesy text *The Institution of a Gentleman*, which was aimed at providing a model for gentle self-education, argues in his epistle to Lord Fitzwater that precedes the main body of the text:

> noble men descended of approued gentrye, knowen to be the offsprynge
> of worthy ancitours and Gentlemen, ought to buylde gentry vp agayne,

which is (for trothe) sore decayed, & falne to great ruine: wherby suche corruption of maners hathe taken place, that almost the name of gentry is quenched, and handycrafte men haue obtayned the tytle of honour, though (in dede) of them selues they can chalenge no greater worthynes then th^t spade brought vnto their late fathers: but finding few & feble tenauntes in th^t house of worthy fame, these base sorte of men haue easely entred therin, & at this daye doo beare those armes which were geuen vnto old gentry, as perpetual remembrance of their worthy dedes. (A3^{r-v})

The increase in gentry attendance at the universities can be ascribed to the desire for material and political advancement, or simply the confirmation or enhancement of personal status, encouraged by the proliferation of these humanist ideas (Charlton, 1965, 137–8; Kearney, 1970, 26–7). What this most importantly represents, however, is the institutionalization of processes of social induction and the formation of social identity, which had hitherto been a matter for elite private households.

It was significant that graduates had an almost automatic access to gentle status, as was noted by Sir Thomas Smith in *De Republica Anglorum* of 1584:

For whosoever studieth the lawes of the realme, who studieth in the universities, who professeth liberall sciences, and to be shorte, who can live idly and without manuall labour, and will beare the port, charge and countenaunce of a gentleman, he shall be called master, for that is the title which men give to esquires and other gentlemen, and shall be taken for a gentleman. (72)

This might in part be explained by the fact that a degree equipped young men for occupations which were deemed gentle. However, another important dimension to this is the contribution of higher education to the very quality of gentility. George Pettie, in the preface to his 1581 translation of Guazzo's courtesy tract, *The Civil Conversation*, urged gentlemen: 'neuer deny your selues to be Schollers, neuer be ashamed to shewe your learnyng, confesse it, professe it, imbrace it, honor it: for it is it which honoureth you, it is only it which maketh you men, it is onely it whiche maketh you Gentlemen' (Preface 2^r).

Education is seen also in terms of a commodity to be possessed, the ownership of which reflects on the possessor. In his educational manual, *The Petty School* of 1587, Francis Clement remarked: 'how highly soeuer a man should be aduaunced ether in th^e honour of princely dignitie, or by the glory of triumphant victory, all this yet were to little purpose, vnles the high renowme, & wonderfull fame of learning had vndertaken also to repose the same in her golden coffers of perpetuall registrie' (C8^v). The use by especially noble families of the universities for the training of youth in social skills is illustrated by the fact that many young men from these families attended university without bothering to take degrees.[3] The social training that formed part of the experience of university education was derived from both official and informal quarters. The formal educational programmes of the universities placed a strong emphasis on the development of rhetorical skills, which contributed to the refinement of speech. The assignment of older students as mentors to younger ones encompassed not only academic but social and disciplinary guidance, and this was enhanced by the collegiate structure. More informally, schools of dancing and fencing made instruction in these aristocratic skills available to students.[4]

It was not simply in membership of exclusive communities through which social education was acquired in the universities, however. Another important source of this was the growing influence of courtesy literature, which can be defined as a category of prescriptive texts on behaviour and morals. That students at Oxford and Cambridge tended to own a range of these texts is indicated by the wills of students who died while pursuing their studies. These wills give details of the private libraries left by students, and they suggest the popularity of works on gentle accomplishments (Curtis, 1959, 136). The texts owned by students included Castiglione's *Courtier*, Elyot's *Governor*, and Guazzo's *Civil Conversation*. These publications sought to provide instruction in the codes of behaviour and values that were appropriate to a gentleman, and the self-consciousness which becomes apparent in this process of codifying behaviour and values is revealing, particularly as this emerged in a period of considerable social change and upheaval. Between 1540 and 1640 there was a large increase in the numbers entering the professions, and a considerable rise in the status of professions (Brooks, 1994, 113–40). A substantial growth took place in the size and wealth of the landed class, partly as a result of the confiscation and redistribution of church property. There was also a boom in the birthrate of this class in relation to the rest of the population, even though the population as a whole doubled between 1500 and 1620. This helped to promote eighty years of social mobility within the elite, on a scale never previously experienced (Stone, 1966, 22–46; Stone, 1972, 72–6). Alongside these socially destabilizing factors may be ranged the fact that elite identity as signalled by behaviour was, because of the widespread availability of courtesy literature, no longer required to have been inculcated from birth, but could be acquired by study in adulthood (Whigham, 1984, 6; Mason, 1935, 23–57, 113–43). Thus a not insignificant dimension of gentility was *acting* gentle.[5] Another was the adherence to a code of values which was understood and accepted by a group that was increasingly coming to identify itself through these shared values.[6] It is clear that it was not just 'new men' who needed to learn these social codes, but also the established gentry for whom it was no longer sufficient to define their status either through birth or material means such as land.[7] The exhortations of Vallentine to his friend Vincent in *Civil and Uncivil Life* recognize this situation acutely.[8]

Education became a way of reconciling two opposing views of gentle status, one that associated it with intrinsic qualities of superiority, and the other that recognized the acquirability of the attributes which were associated with rank. In the theories of Richard Mulcaster, the most ostensibly egalitarian of sixteenth-century educational theorists, the role of education is to develop the possibilities of the elite body to project an impression of inherent superiority.[9] He placed particular emphasis on the training of the body. The greater part of his 1581 tract, *Positions*, is given over to describing various forms of physical activity: 'lowd speaking, singing, lowd reading, talking, laughing, weeping, holding the breath, dawnsing, wrastling, fencing and scourging the top' and also 'ball games, walking, running, leaping, swimming, riding, hunting, and shooting' (54). In the *Elementary* which appeared the following year, the implications of bodily superiority become clear:

> In the bodie theie require, that it be able for strength, and health to abide exercise the preseruer of the[m] both: that it be of good proportion and correspondent to the minde for trauell in studie, & if it maie be, to haue it personable withall, bycause personablenesse is an allurement to obedience, a gracious deliuerer of anie inward vertew, & somtime was estemed a thing most worthie of the principall seat. Was not *Saul* noted in his election to be king, to haue bene taller and more personable, the[n] the rest of the peple? Did not *Thalestris* the *Amason* Quene half contemn *Alexander* the great: when she saw his person to be of no great shew, whose name was so renouned, as the report thereof did cause hir com to se him? Did not *Euripides* saie & *Porphyrie* vpon his word, that a bodie of presence is best worthie to rule?
> (1582, 16)[10]

Exercises that developed a poise and command, and which had been the province of domestic contexts of elite education, were now part of a public educational process that, in its more elevated sectors, was geared to producing a corpus of educated people who could run the country and the professions, and who had a shared system of social attitudes, behaviour, speech and values. The educational institutions had a prominent role in providing such a common code of behaviour and mode of speech and thought for an elite increasingly diverse in its social origins. In this context, Mulcaster's advocacy of exercises takes on a very particular function. By the sixteenth century chivalric accomplishments did not *in themselves* create a nobleman, though such activities were seen as appropriate to his social position: they had by this time become additional to the man rather than a *sine qua non*. In Mulcaster's scheme they, and exercises like them, become essential in equipping the body with fitness for elite status. He goes on to reveal the real purpose of these exercises:

> And as those qualities, which I haue set out for the generall traine in their perfection being best compassed by them, may verie well beseeme a gentlemanly minde: so may the exercises without all exception: either to make a healthfull bodie, seeing our mould is all one: or to prepare them for seruice, wherein their vse is more. Is it not for a gentleman to vse the chase and hunt? doth their place reproue them if they haue skill to daunce? Is the skill in sitting of an horse no honour at home, no helpe abroad? Is the vse of their weapon with choice, for their calling, any blemish vnto them? for all these and what else beside, there is furniture for them, if they do but looke backe: and the rather for them, bycause in deede those greate exercises be most proper to such persons, and not for the meaner.
> (*Positions*, 197–8)

The educated body thus displays an apparently natural or inherent superiority. In Mulcaster's conception of education of the elite, those 'greate exercises' are no longer either for martial ends, or (as they had more latterly become) simply a recreational end in themselves, but have the specific purpose of *shaping* social identity through bodily development. The process is analogous to Foucault's analysis of the operation of power in terms of its 'capillary form of existence, the point where power reaches into the very grain of individuals, touches their bodies and inserts itself into their actions and attitudes, their discourses, learning processes and everyday lives' (1980, 39). It is also related to Castiglione's notion of *sprezzatura* described in *Il Cortegiano* as the appearance of nonchalance in the performance of accomplishments which, in fact, require rigorous training to master. The idea, in the translation by Sir Thomas Hoby of 1561 (as *The Courtier*), is expressed as follows:

> But I, imagynyng with my self oftentymes how this grace commeth, leauing a part such as haue it from aboue, fynd one rule that is most general whych in thys part (me thynk) taketh place in al thynges belongyng to man in worde or deede aboue all other. And that is to eschew as much as a man may, & as a sharp and daungerous rock, *Affectation* or curiosity & (to speak a new word) to vse in euery thyng a certain *Reckelesness*, to couer art withall, & seeme whatsoeuer he doth & sayeth to do it wythout pain, & (as it were) not myndyng it.
> (C2^r)

This is part of the 'magicality' of elite status which is the aspect of power that depends on signification.[11] One scholar (A. S. Golding) has argued that 'the upper classes appeared fit to rule to the degree that they showed themselves to

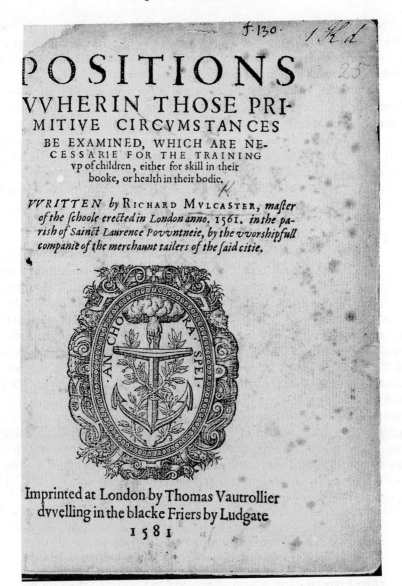

POSITIONS

VVHERIN THOSE PRI-
MITIVE CIRCVMSTANCES

BE EXAMINED, WHICH ARE NE-
CESSARIE FOR THE TRAINING
vp of children, either for skill in their
booke, or health in their bodie.

VVRITTEN by RICHARD MVLCASTER, *maſter
of the ſchoole erected in London anno.* 1561. *in the pa-
riſh of Sainct Laurence Povvntneie, by the vvorſhipfull
companie of the merchaunt tailers of the ſaid citie.*

Imprinted at London by Thomas Vautrollier
dvvelling in the blacke Friers by Ludgate
1581

Fig. 2: Title page of Mulcaster's *Positions* (British Library Shelfmark C.175.L.10)
By permission of the British Library

be free of the domination of the humours' (1984, 75–6). Perhaps the most important implication of this is that the pedagogical interest of Mulcaster and others in the body was precisely for the purpose of placing a distance between social identity and the reality of bodily existence.

A parallel process to the development of the body was the cultivation of competence in speech as a means of signifying rank. An anthropological argument which is relevant to the processes of social change in the period is Pierre Bourdieu's analysis of the relationship between language and class (1991, 81–9), and particularly the following observation: 'Language is a body technique, and specifically linguistic, especially phonetic, competence is a dimension of bodily lexis in which one's whole relation to the social world, and one's socially informed relation to the world, are expressed' (1984, 86). The aspect of formal education which had possibly the most relevance to the refinement of manners and social competence was the study of rhetoric. At all levels – the schools, universities and Inns, this formed a significant part of the curriculum. Richard Mulcaster even suggested that: 'We do attribute to[o] much to toungues . . . and esteeme it more honorable to speak finely, then to reason wisely' (*Positions*, 242). Mulcaster is not referring here specifically to educated accents, but the educational historian, Joan Simon has suggested that early modern grammar schools contributed to a development of the uniform speech of the educated class (1966, 364–5).[12] It is possibly of some relevance that the term 'polite' in the abstract sense of 'polished, refined, elegant' is recorded by the *Oxford English Dictionary* as first occurring in 1501.[13] Another early instance occurs in Elyot's *Governor* in which he urges (of the women detailed to take care of noblemen's children): 'that they speke none englisshe but that, which is cleane, polite, perfectly and articulately pronounced, omitting no lettre or sillable as folisshe women often times do of a wantonnesse, wherby diuers noble men, and gentilmennes chyldren (as I do at this daye knowe) haue attained corrupte and foule pronuntiation' (19ᵛ).[14] The importance of grace of speech is also emphasized in *The Courtier*:

> And this do I saie as well of writing as of speaking, wherein certayne thinges are requisite that are not necessary in wrytyng, as a good voyce, not to[o] subtyll or soft, as in a woman: not yet so boysterous and rought, as in one of the Countrey, but shrill, clere sweete and wel framed with a prompt pronunciation & with fitte maners and gestures, which (in my minde) consiste in certain mocions of al the body not affected nor forced, but tempered wᵗ a manerly countenance and wᵗ a mouing of the eyes, that may geue a grace & accord with the words, & (as much as he can) signifie also wᵗ gestures the entent & affection of the speaker. (4ʳ)

The social value of eloquence is emphasized in Nicholas Ling's *Wit's Commonwealth* of 1597: 'Great men ought to be considerate in theyr speech, and to be eloquent in sententious words, of another phrase then that of the vulgar sort, or else be silent wanting the vertue of eloquence' (51^v). That social education is a matter of learning codes, is sometimes made very explicit. *The Court of Civil Courtesy* (translated by S. R. Gent from the Italian in 1577) is subtitled: 'Fitly furnished with a pleasant porte of stately phrases and pithie precepts: assembled in the behalfe of all younge Gentlemen, and others, that are desirous to frame ther behauiour according to their estates, at all times and all companies. Therby to purchase worthy prayse, of their inferiours: and estimation and credite amonge theyr betters.' This text goes on, indeed, to provide a range of verbal formulae suitable for employment in a number of social situations.[15] The anonymous tract, *The School of Good Manners* dedicated to the young Edward Harington in 1595 gives a detailed account of bodily and facial gestures and manner of speaking as part of a programme of refining behaviour (A1^r–C3^r).

In his *Little Book of Good Manners for Children*, Erasmus declared: 'Let others paint on their escutcheons, lions, eagles, bulls, leopards. Those are the possessors of true nobility who can use on their coats of arms ideas which they have thoroughly learned from the liberal arts' (quoted in Watson, 1908, 105–6).[16] If education enabled individuals to acquire the values, manners and modes of speech that were coming to constitute the outward signs of membership of the gentle class, then drama also had a significant part to play in inculcating a sense of what defined elite identity. Drama, as practice and as a cultural product, intersects most particularly with those aspects of education, both informal and formal, that are concerned with social refinement – the consumption of courtesy literature by students in the institutions of higher education, and the teaching of rhetoric at all levels.[17] Drama emerged very readily and naturally from the educational activities which took place in schools, particularly as a result of the new ideas about education that were becoming current at the time.[18] Humanist thinkers were concerned to improve the methods of teaching Latin and in the connections between new teaching methods and dramatic activity, the name of Nicholas Udall stands out. In the same year in which he was appointed headmaster of Eton, Udall published his *Flowers for Latin Speaking*, a school textbook that essentially incorporated the new ideas in education. This book, the success of which kept it in use for about fifty years, sought to inculcate proficiency in Latin through exercises based on dramatic dialogues from Terence (Edgerton, 1965, 31). Its publication embodies a number of tendencies present at this time. Apart from exemplifying an aspect of humanist pedagogical methodology, it also places an emphasis on eloquence and linguistic accomplishment as the goal of education, and puts drama at the centre of this endeavour.[19] The practice became sufficiently

commonplace by the early years of the seventeenth century for Jonson to put
the following Puritan objection in the mouth of one of the gossips in *The Staple
of News* of 1626:

> *I would haue ne'er a cunning* Schoole-Master *in* England. *I meane a*
> Cunning-Man, *a* Schoole-Master; *that is a* Coniurour, *or a* Poet, *or that
> had any acquaintance with a* Poet. *They make all their schollers* Play-
> boyes! *Is't not a fine sight, to see all our children made* Enterluders? *Doe
> wee pay our money for this? wee send them to learne their* Grammar, *and
> their* Terence, *and they learne their* play-books? *well, they talke, we shall
> haue no more Parliaments (God bless vs) but an' wee haue, I hope,*
> Zeale-of-the-land Buzy, *and my Gossip,* Rabby Trouble-truth *will start
> vp, and see we shall haue painfull good Ministers to keepe Schoole, and
> Catechise our youth, and not teach 'hem to speake* Playes, *and act* Fables
> *of false newes, in this manner, to the super-uexation of Towne and
> Countrey, with a wanion.*
> (Act 3 intermean, ll. 44–56)

The place of drama in the educational process, at least in the more important
institutions, has implications for its place in the general culture as well.
Bourdieu has observed: 'The educational system defines non-curricular general
culture, negatively at least, by delimiting within the dominant culture, the area
of what it puts into its syllabuses and controls by its examinations' (1984, 23).
The role of especially the more prominent grammar schools in developing a
refinement of manners, eloquence and social skills in their pupils is something
which should be emphasized here since, as will be argued, it is central to the
function of drama within the schools and, reciprocally, the influence of the
schools on the forms and conventions of the drama. Thomas Elyot stressed the
importance of refined behaviour in self-presentation: 'It is also where a man
speakethe courtaisely, with a swete speche or countenance: wherewith the
herers (as it were with a delicate odour) be refresshed, and alured to loue hym,
in whom is this most delectable qualitie' (1531, 114^v–15^r). It was not only in
the exercise of Latin, but in the teaching of eloquence, verbal and gestural
refinement, and a general confidence and nobility of manner and behaviour,
that drama was considered a useful educational tool, and was sometimes
tolerated for this reason even when regarded as an otherwise inferior art.

In educational theory, the question of the didactic role of drama in the
period is complicated by two major factors. One is the problem of religious
contention and contemporary perceptions about the use of drama in advancing
particular perspectives in the debate. Another is the problem of
antitheatricalism. This had a number of points of departure but, since the
impulse behind it was overwhelmingly Puritan, the main thrust concerned its
moral effects. This inevitably impinged upon the drama's social position as a

mode of discourse, but in addition to and complementing this there was also suspicion in some quarters about its status as a 'debased' art form. While some humanists like Martin Bucer are enthusiastic in their championship of the educational use of theatre, others were more doubtful.[20] Vives adopts a neo-platonic position in placing drama within the category of corrupt arts, though in his theatrical story, *The Fable of Man*, he counters this by representing acting as a divine skill precisely because of the capacity for transformation (Barish, 1981, 110–11).[21] For his part, Roger Ascham is concerned about the 'meanness' of the matter of Plautus and Terence.[22] However, despite their reservations about moral effects, educational theorists like Ascham and Vives recognize the value of drama in training for rhetorical skills, and Ascham advocates the comedies of Terence and Plautus among the books that are to be used for the learning of eloquence.[23]

Notable here is an implicit detachment of the acquisition of competence in social performance from issues of religious morality – something which would be of significance for the development of drama in the period. This is echoed too in *The Advancement of Learning* where Francis Bacon argues for skill in social performance as the key to successful participation in society, without making any reference to a requirement for morality:

> And therefore whatsoeuer want a man hath, he must see, that he pretend the vertue that shadoweth it, as if he be *Dull*, he must affect *Grauitie*, if a *Cowarde*, *Mildenesse*, and so the rest: for the second, a man must frame some probable cause why he should not doe his best, and why he should dissemble his abilities: and for that purpose must vse to dissemble those abilities, which are notorious in him to giue colour that his true wants are but industries and dissimulations: for *Confidence* it is the last but the surest remedie: namely to depresse and seeme to despise whatsoeuer a man cannot attaine, obseruing the good principle of the Marchantes, who endeuour to raise the price of their owne commodities, and to beate down the price of others.
> (99^v/ Cc4^v)

In actual educational practice, the importance of drama seems less equivocal than it might appear in the theoretical discussions by humanist writers. William Malim's *Consuetudinary* (c. 1560) which documented teaching methods at Eton, stressed the pedagogical value of drama for the development of verbal and gestural skills (Maxwell Lyte, 1911, 154). In 1557, John Bale wrote approvingly in his *Scriptorum Illustrium* of Ralph Radcliff's use of drama for improving the eloquence and elegance of speech of his boys:

> Ibi solitus est quotannis simul iucunda & honesta plebi edere spectacula, cum ob iuuentutis, suae fidei & institutioni commissae, inutilem pudorem

exuendum; tum ad formandum os tenerum et balbutiens, quo clare, eleganter & distincte uerba eloqui & effari consuesceret.
(700)

(There he was accustomed each year to mount shows before the public that were at once delightful and respectable, not only to banish the unprofitable bashfulness of the youth who had been committed to his trust and instruction, but at the same time to train the tender and stammering voice, whereby it would grow accustomed to speak and express words clearly, elegantly and distinctly.)

At the re-establishment of Westminster School in 1560, the statutes incorporate plays as educational exercises:

In order that young people may spend Christmas time more profitably, and may gain a better familiarity with graceful gesture and pronounciation, we enact that every year, within twelve days after Christmas, or subsequently, at the Dean's direction, the Head-Master and the Under-Master should jointly see that one play in Latin be acted either privately or publicly; the master of the choristers another, in English, either comedy or tragedy, by the scolars and choristers in Hall. If they fail in this duty, a fine of ten shillings is to be imposed on the party whose negligence is the cause of the omission.
(Forshall, 1884, 468)

The fact that Westminster incorporates the production of plays within its charter gives some indication of the importance which drama had in particularly the schools catering to the elite. Richard Mulcaster promoted play acting at Merchant Taylors to teach 'good behaviour and audacity' (Ellis, 1800, Pt I, 419–21, 511–12, 603–4). The attention to genteel accomplishments in Mulcaster's educational programme is recorded by one of his pupils, Sir James Whitelocke, in his recollections of his schooldays:

His care was also to encreas my skill in musique, in whiche I was brought up by dayly exercise in it, as in singing and playing upon instruments, and yeerly he presented sum playes to the court, in whiche his scholers wear only actors, and I on among them, and by that meanes taughte them good behaviour and audacitye.
(*Liber Famelicus*, 12)

Thomas Elyot had urged the careful selection of plays to accord with the elite's conception of itself: 'The nexte lesson wolde be some quicke and mery diologes elect out of Luciane whiche be without ribawdry or to moche skorning, for either of them is exactly to be eschewed specially for a noble man, the one anoyeng the soule, the other his estimation concernyng his grauitie' (1531, 31^r).

The drama in schools was often promoted by particular individuals who had an interest in the activity. In his school in Hitchin (the school of George Chapman), Ralph Radclif is recorded by Bale as producing plays of which he himself was the author.[24] Thomas Ashton, when appointed as the first headmaster of Shrewsbury School, introduced drama in the school from the outset. The Statutes of Shrewsbury School provided that 'Everie Thursdaie the Schollers of the first forme before they goo to plaie shall for exercise declame and plaie one acte of a comedie'.[25] Among pupils at the school were Sir Philip Sidney and Fulke Greville, Lord Brooke. Even before Udall's appointment, the study of Terence was introduced to Westminster School (the school of Ben Jonson) by Alexander Nowell as an exercise in eloquence, and the annual play became an established tradition in the school (Sargeaunt, 1898, 48–9). Udall's appointment to Eton and Westminster followed dramatic work for royalty, while Ashton's work on urban drama preceded his appointment as headmaster of Shrewsbury (and he continued to be active in town drama during his headmastership).[26]

The educational value of the drama, and most particularly in inculcating appropriate styles of comportment is suggested by a statute of St John's College, Cambridge, drawn up 1544–5 which recognized the contribution of plays to the learning regime of students:

> on the eves of festivals during the four short vacations these students shall not waste [their] time in idleness and games, but they should be occupied in composing poems, letters, or speeches; in the reading of Greek poets, orators, or historians; or in the putting on of dialogues, comedies, or tragedies according to the will and assignment or order of the reader of humanities and other examiners.
> (*REED: Cambridge* 132, trans. 1113)

The statutes of Queen's College in 1558–9 go further in defining the value of these activities in refining behaviour:

> And lest our youth, trained perhaps in other respects, remain crude in pronounciation and gesture and unpolished, we wish the professor of the Greek language and also the examiner to be responsible for putting on two comedies or tragedies every year between the twentieth day of December and the beginning of Lent.
> (*REED: Cambridge* 205, trans. 1130)

Earlier Queen's College ordinances even indicate punishments for non–participation by students.[27] The value placed on drama as a serious area of endeavour at the universities is revealed, too, by the fact that as early as 1512,

Oxford granted a certain Edward Watson a degree in grammar on condition of his composing a dramatic comedy (which could thus possibly be regarded as the first *de facto* degree in drama from an English academic institution).[28] The connection between rhetorical training in the universities and their dramatic activity is clearly made in John Leland's *Poetic Encomia* of 1522-3 to Stephen Gardiner: 'And since you show bright colours of polished rhetoric to the schools, / The highest crown wreathes [your] hair. / And since the learned play depends upon you, the learned producer, / Then the crown for comedy [is] brought forth by your stages' (*REED: Cambridge* 94–5, trans. 1105).

The perceived importance of plays in the broader programme of social education at the universities gave them a position of some privilege which afforded them a protection not always enjoyed by other forms of dramatic endeavour in a period where substantial suspicion of the stage existed. In 1584 the Earl of Leicester, defending university plays declared himself 'accepting them as commendable and great furderances of Learning [and] do wish them in any wise to be continued at set times and increased, and the youth of the Universitye by good meanes to be incouraged in the decent and frequent setting forth of them' (Wood, 1796, Vol. 2, 222).

Universities in the sixteenth century, like the large noble households or the Court, composed communities which were both producers and consumers of cultural products. University halls were very much like household halls and shared many of their characteristics in their social arrangements. They were internally very hierarchical socially, while recognizing their own position within the elite culture. From the 1550s onwards both gentlemen commoners and plebeians on scholarships began increasingly to lodge in colleges (Sharpe, 1987, Ch. 10; McConica, 1986, 1–68). This strengthened the collegiate system and the identity of the colleges as communities. In their consumption of drama too, the universities echoed the arrangements found in noble households and performances of plays were often accompanied by banqueting (Boas, 1914, 25).

Dramatic production was also a factor in the presentation of the corporate identity of academic communities. The academic stage was not an inconsiderable element in the enhancement of the status of the universities as institutions of privilege and prominence in the realm. An illustration of the special advantages which they enjoyed is a letter of the 28 January 1594 from the Head and Fellows of Trinity College, Cambridge to Lord Burghley asking to borrow robes from the collection in the Tower:

> Whereas we intend for the exercise of yonge gentlemen and scholers in
> our Colledge, to sett forth certain Comœdies and one Tragœdie. There
> being in that Tragœdie sondry personages of greatest astate, to be

represented in Auncient princely attire, which is no where to be had but
within the office of the Roabes at the Tower.
(*REED: Cambridge* 355)

The lending of apparel for plays as a manifestation of the special links between
the universities and the centre of power is something which occurs on a
number of occasions during the later sixteenth century. This is illustrated by a
letter, written between 1553 and 1556 by three members of the Privy Council
to Sir Thomas Cawerden, the Master of the Revels, to request the loan of suits
of apparel for the performance of a 'learnyd tragedy' which the fellows and
scholars of New College, Oxford, intended to mount at Christmas (Feuillerat,
1914, 96–7). The vestments for *Ajax Flagellifer*, planned for the Queen's
entertainment at Cambridge in 1564 were also 'brought from London and
remote parts' (*REED: Cambridge* 238 trans. 1138). The records of St John's
College include payment for the carriage of vestments from London for a play
(*REED: Cambridge* 122). Particularly in view of the signifying power of dress
in the period, the fact of this traffic of apparel between the official organs of
state and the universities might be considered an implicit recognition by the
authorities of the importance of social apprenticeship at the universities and
particularly the role of drama in it.

However, it was particularly what the universities offered by way of
hospitality that reinforced their status. Before the accession of Elizabeth,
dramatic activity had been a private affair, for the entertainment only of
members of the university (Boas, 1914, 89). In the course of the century,
though, the universities were several times hosts to important visitors, and on
each occasion, drama played a major role in the entertainment of these guests.
In 1552/3 a sum of money was laid out by Christ's College 'towardes the
honest enterteynemente of the worshippe of the towne & thuniversitie which
resorted to our colledge to see the plaies there' (*REED: Cambridge* 178). A
visit to Oxford by its chancellor Leicester, accompanied by an ambassador, the
Cardinal de Chatillon, was planned for 1569 and it was proposed to mount *The
Destruction of Thebes* as an entertainment. The visit was evidently cancelled,
though in January 1594/5 Leicester did finally visit (Boas, 1914, 158, 192). On
the occasion of the visit by Albertus Alasco, Prince Palatine of Siradia in
Poland, to Oxford in 1583 two 'theatra' were set up, one at St Mary's for
disputations and the other at Christ Church 'pro ludis theatricis'. The Prince
saw a comedy, William Gager's *Rivales*, and Halliwell's *Dido* (see below). The
visit cost the university the substantial sum of £350 (Wood, 1796, I, 215–18).

The major instances of the universities' playing host were, however, the
royal visits, of which there were three in all under Elizabeth. Cambridge
received the Queen in 1564 and Oxford entertained her in 1566 and later in
1592. The extensiveness of the dramatic offerings on these occasions is

remarkable. In Cambridge four plays were planned, though they could not all be performed during the visit. Oxford in 1566 also projected (and mounted) four plays. All these were planned as part of sojourns of five and seven days respectively, so that dramatic activity was an extremely prominent aspect of the proceedings. The pattern was that learned disputations were held during the day, and plays in the evening. Given that disputations were essentially the work of the university put on display, the plays can be regarded partly in this light, but also as the currency of formal social intercourse between the institutions and their sovereign.[29]

As a mode of discourse by which the universities defined themselves to the crown and nobility, the plays and their production were managed in such a way as to maximize the element of display. Their variety was one aspect of this. Cambridge staged a comedy by Plautus, *Aulularia*, *Dido* a tragedy in Senecan style by Edward Halliwell, a member of the university, a scriptural play in English by Udall, *Ezechias*, and a Latin polemical play *Ajax Flagellifer* that was played to the Queen after her visit (*REED: Cambridge* 230–31, 242, 1142–3). Oxford, at the first visit, presented a Latin comedy in prose, *Marcus Geminus*, and two plays by Oxford men, Richard Edwardes's *Palamon and Arcyte*, an English play based on Chaucer and James Calfhill's Latin tragedy, *Progne*. In addition to demonstrating versatility, care was taken to ensure the representation of the whole institution in both cases. Though some plays were put on by particular colleges, in a number of them players from all colleges were included, notably *Aulularia* and *Ajax Flagellifer* in Cambridge, and *Progne* in Oxford (Boas 93, 97, 105). The magnificence and expense of the productions was also conspicuous. The disappointment provoked by the Queen's initial disinclination to see *Ajax Flagellifer* was partly occasioned by the fact that the trouble and money spent on it had been considerable (*REED: Cambridge* 238, 1138). At Oxford the splendour of the lighting and scenic arrangements for *Palamon and Arcyte* excited comment, and the Queen was reported to have been taken with the magnificence of the scenes for *Progne* (Chambers, 1923, I, 127 note; Boas, 1914, 105). The fact that the performance of *Palamon and Arcyte* went ahead despite an accident which killed three people is testimony to the prominence of drama as a part of the formal proceedings of the visit.

These visits also involved the Office of the Revels, and the events were at once aspects of the life of the universities and events in the life of the Court. The Queen was accompanied by a substantial contingent of courtiers and at one play at which she declined to be present, she offered the consolation that a large number of nobility would attend. While the dignity of the university was to a large extent upheld by the classical nature of the dramatic performances, a certain theatricality of state in the ceremonial proceedings also helped both to give due recognition to the courtliness of the occasions and to exalt the host institutions. In both places the presence of the monarch was made the focus for an elaborate occasion of corporate self–display. In fact, the universities were engaging in a process of theatrical self-representation that bears some comparison to that found in particularly the Jacobean royal masque.[30] The theatrical aspects of the occasions were not confined to the dramatic fare. In Cambridge the hall decorations for the performance of the *Aulularia* were extremely elaborate and the Queen was seated prominently on a red velvet chair, while at the performance of *Palamon and Arcyte* at Christ Church in Oxford a canopied chair was arranged on stage for the Queen (*REED: Cambridge* 233–4; Boas, 1914, 100). In Cambridge, the exclusivity of the occasions was such that only selected members of the colleges were allowed to attend the plays, and in Oxford during the second royal visit, scholars who were not permitted to see the plays were bound under pain of imprisonment not to disrupt the proceedings with 'any outcries or undecent noyses' (*REED*: *Cambridge* 235; Boas, 1914, 253).

If these occasions indicate the importance of drama at significant ceremonial points in the life of the universities and their self-definition as corporate structures of cultural authority in early modern society, what also becomes apparent from the records is the sheer volume of dramatic activity in academic communities. The records reveal play productions in many colleges and the importance of this as a component of university cultural life becomes all the more striking when it is considered that members of the university visited each other's colleges for performances, so increasing the frequency of their exposure to plays. That this was a common occurrence is indicated by statutes of 1573/4 for Gonville and Caius College which make provision for the safeguarding of the college when all its members were out seeing tragedies and comedies at other colleges, and also when there was an influx of people from outside when such activities took place within the college (*REED: Cambridge* 267, 1146).[31]

Of all the educational institutions in the sixteenth century, the one in which drama played the most important role in social education and in establishing the social identity of the institution, was the Inns of Court. As in the case of the universities, aspects of the everyday activities of the Inns were close to the forms of dramatic expression in the plays which they produced. The Readers' Feasts – banquets given at the installation of those newly promoted to the rank of reader – involved a considerable amount of theatricalized ceremony and encompassed both 'solemn-revels' (the ceremonials by which new readers were invested) and 'post-revels' which included dancing and 'Stage-plays' (Dugdale, 1666, 205).[32] The halls used for disputation were also used for revels and plays (Finkelpearl, 1969, 33). Though the revels were largely confined to specific times of year such as Christmas, or special occasions, the mock disputations at the *moots* that were the pedagogical exercises of the Inns were not far removed from the sort of structured rhetorical disputation which one finds in plays such as *Gorboduc*.[33] Other, more specifically cultural accomplishments were an integral part of the activities of these institutions, including literary and musical activities. As well as providing professional training, the Inns of Court functioned as a finishing school for the acquisition of social skills and accomplishments. In the mid-sixteenth-century *Accedens of Armorie*, Gerard Legh points to the combination of professional and social training at the Inns, describing the institution in the following terms:

> A place . . . wherin are th^e store of gentilmen of th^e whole realme, that repaire thither to learne to rule, and obay by law, to yeld their fleece to their prince & comon weale. as also to vse all other exercises of body & minde wherunto nature most aptli serueth, to adorne by speaking, contenance, gesture, & vse of apparel, th^e person of a gentilman, whereby amitie is obtained & continued, th^t gentilman of all countres in ther yong yeres, norished together in one place, with such comely ordre, and dayly conference are knitt by continuall acquainance in such vnitie of minds & maners, as lyghtly neuer after is seuerid, then which is nothing more profitable to the comon weale.
> (1562, 205^r)

Residence at the universities and Inns of Court gave the sons of established landed families coming, as they did, from a variety of regional locations, not only a formal education but a consciousness of their membership of a national ruling class and, importantly, contributed to the cultural homogeneity of that class (Wrightson, 1982, 191–2). They also, naturally, provided an induction for those from other backgrounds into the class they were effectively joining. The fact that a university education was seen as a significant part of the process of making a gentleman was indicated by the fact that the sons of peers had the privilege of taking a degree in three years at Oxford whereas those of lower rank had to serve the full term. In 1591, this privilege was extended to the sons of knights and esquires (Mallet, 1924–7, II, 122). The contribution of drama to the social cohesion and corporate identity of higher educational institutions bears some comparison to the role of the cycle drama in urban communities. As in the case of the urban plays, this encompassed both actual and symbolic corporate and collaborative activity. One striking example of the former is the collaboration of Sackville and Norton in the writing of *Gorboduc* (see below p. 97). The symbolic aspect is exemplified not only by the drama's function in the institutions' presentation of themselves to royalty, but other aspects of revelling as well.

This role of dramatic activities within educational institutions, particularly the higher ones, provides a context for the function of drama as an instrument of self-development, for formal rhetorical training and the inculcation of 'audacitie', and for the acquisition of social *savoir faire*. The roles are complementary, the drama contributing to the skills of the new educated elite, and to its sense of cohesion and the cultivation of its manners. If it was the case at this highly circumscribed level of society that drama was a customary aspect of social and cultural life, the interlude drama was also fulfilling something of this function in a broader context. If theatrical performance helped to articulate social identity institutionally and in terms of community, the drama also worked on a more individual level. Both within the educational institutions, and more widely in society, the drama might be seen to operate as a form of courtesy literature in providing social education. Essential to this was the didactic role of the interlude. With the advent of secularization, what had been a medium primarily of religious instruction was not only turned to engage political and social concerns, but also became in both explicit and implicit ways arguably the most effective means through which refined manners – and what might be termed social identity and consciousness – were inculcated. This was, in many respects, a natural extension of the more narrowly defined role of theatrical exercises in the teaching of rhetoric. As a form of courtesy literature, the drama had the advantage that it could not merely present argument, but also indeed *demonstrate* dress, behaviour, speech and manners, and so models of social identity could be actualized on stage.[34] While most, if not all the interlude drama of the sixteenth century and beyond can be regarded as incorporating implicit instruction in social behaviour, the most striking illustration of the ways in which this shapes the conventions of representation in drama is provided by those plays that most overtly engage the debates about gentility and rank.

The preoccupation of the drama with the question of gentility and its relation to manners can be seen to emerge very early in the secular history of the form, and one of the earliest non-theological issues to surface as a subject of the interlude drama was indeed the debate about the nature of nobility. The debate was a central issue in the courtesy literature of the period. It was fuelled by the anxieties of the existing landed elite on the one hand, and the aspirations of the 'new men' taking advantage of conditions favourable to social mobility on the other. Essentially, the contention was between the idea of nobility of blood, inherited as a member of a noble family, and honour as conferred by the state, or acquired through personal endeavour and the sort of self-improvement constituted by both formal and informal processes of education. It is, in fact, in the drama that this argument finds early articulation as a debate. It constitutes the central issue of two early plays, Henry Medwall's *Fulgens and Lucres*, written for performance in the household of John Morton, Archbishop of Canterbury in about 1497, and *Gentleness and Nobility*, attributed to John Heywood, and printed by Rastell in 1525. The climax of Medwall's play (whose patron had risen to his position through his education – a 'new man') is a debate between two suitors for the hand of the wealthy and noble heiress, Lucres, in which the virtuous Gayus prevails over the nobly born but vain and idle Cornelius. Based on a translation (c. 1460) by John Tiptoft of Buonaccorso da Montemagno's *De Vera Nobilitate*, the play moderates the more extreme positions taken in both the original and the translation. In *Gentleness and Nobility* the whole play is a debate, essentially between a merchant and a knight about who has claim to be called noble, but is complicated by the entry of a ploughman who presents a third perspective. Here the debate is left open, the knight and the merchant having to some extent been united in their opposition to the ploughman, while also accepting some of his moral arguments. The fact that on the one hand these plays are either cast in the form of, or incorporate a debate, and on the other that courtesy literature is generally presented in the form of dialogues, increases the resemblance between these forms.[35] However, the dialogues in the courtesy tracts are, in essence, false debates as there is ultimately no equality of argument. The 'losing' argument is there principally to provide a contrasting justification for the points which the debate has been set up to make, and to give a structure to their expression. This is true too of the debates in *Fulgens and Lucres* and *Gentleness and Nobility*.

The resolution of these debates is less important than the ways in which they manifest the replacement of a theologically based morality by a social agenda. Both make reference to qualities such as charity and virtue, but these are no longer ends in themselves. They become, rather, features of a quality that defines the right to social status and esteem. In both plays the quality of nobility is ultimately tied up with social position and wealth. The argument that wealth enables the possessor to become valuable to the commonwealth might be seen against a backdrop of depopulation and increasing levels of poverty, an economic and social climate which gave rise to passionate polemical literature about these problems. What is of possible relevance to the debate is the fact that, in these economic circumstances, it was London and Bristol merchants who provided 63 per cent of charitable spending between 1480 and 1640, and not the landed gentry, whose capital resources were diminished (Jordan, 1961, 57, 241, 331–2). In *Gentleness and Nobility*, this gives weight to the merchant against the more traditionally established position of the knight. However, there is also the question of wealth as conferring positions of prominence and power, or styles of life appropriate to noble status. In both plays, there is an implicit and uncontested awareness of wealth as a prerequisite of a position of social pre-eminence. In *Fulgens and Lucres* Gayus's essential nobility of character wins him the heiress, thus clinching his entitlement to the wealth he has begun to acquire through 'office and fee' (II, 569).[36] The merchant and the knight in *Gentleness and Nobility* agree on the necessity of means to live the life and exercise the obligations attendant upon noble status. The ploughman's arguments, which are based much more squarely on traditional theological morality, are allowed to contribute an ethical perspective, but not ultimately to permit him a claim to nobility for himself and his class.

However, the greatest significance of these plays for the question of social identity is the connection between moral worth and the refinement of manners, and especially the way in which this determines the forms of the drama. The articulation of the issue goes beyond the explicit debates themselves, and is encoded in the conventions of representation in the plays. In *Fulgens and Lucres* can be found the early appearance of a subplot, which effectively confines and contains the focus of the narrative concerning the servants, called simply A and B. The rivalry of the two servants and the comic (and obscene) game involved in their wooing of the maidservant forms a comic parallel to the debate of Cornelius and Gayus, which is placed at a climactic point. However, in reality, the speeches and actions of the servants occupy the bulk of the play, and they both open and close it. What reduces their involvement to the level of subplot is the particular comic tone of their representation. The game which the servants play in their competition for the maidservant Joan is 'fart-prike-in-cule', a mock-joust with a scatological dimension.[37] There is some irony in the fact that this low–life game echoes parodically a feudal form of elite ritualized conflict, while the more socially elevated protagonists engage instead in a humanistic debate as their form of contest. The debate and its tone unite Gayus and Cornelius, though they are philosophically antagonistic. The persistently scatological language and crude preoccupations of the servants also serve to point up, by means of contrast, the refined manners and values of both elevated protagonists in a way which overrides their differences. The contrast is not essentially a moral one – the servants are not vice figures – but there is a tacit connection suggested between polished manners and moral discriminations. Dramatic form is here developed around the social imperatives to which the drama is responding.

In *Gentleness and Nobility*, there is no subplot as such, but the role of one person of low social rank, the ploughman, is subordinated by dramatic form in a different way. His arguments, besides issuing from the one person who has no realistic claim to noble status, clearly represent an element of devil's advocacy. At one point he even suggests the nobility of animals on the basis of their self-sufficiency, and his assertions never realistically (in contemporary terms) establish a claim for himself. The ploughman's position is compromised by his late arrival into a serious debate, his departure before the end, and his railing tone. The contrast with the 'serious' protagonists is increased when he sets about them with a whip, later saying:

> For, by God, yf he wyll not be content
> To be concludyd by good argument,
> I wyll conclud hym one way, or that I goo,

Or I shall that prove on hys pate, that shall I doo.
(733–6)

His actions bear out the contrast made by the knight later between the genteel behaviour of true gentlemen towards each other, and the 'chydyng, quarrellyng or fyghtyng' (1058) to be found among ranks like carters.

In both these plays, the farcical action and comic perspectives contributed by the figures of low social rank are not only important elements of dramatic interest in what are otherwise simply staged polemics, but contribute to the legitimization of the more highly ranked figures as a class. No matter that there are moral differences between Cornelius and Gayus, or ideological ones between the merchant and the knight, they are in the end united by dramatic tone and focus and the contrasting otherness of the menial classes in respect of the refinement of intellect. It is true that the perspectives of the base figures contribute satirical perspectives on the more elevated protagonists, but this simply serves to underline their own outsider status.

A play which illustrates this clearly, and raises the question of the codes of behaviour and morality appropriate to rank without recourse to an overt debate structure, is *Damon and Pithias* by Richard Edwardes, Master of the Children of the Queen's Chapel. It was performed before the Queen by the Children of the Chapel in the mid-1560s. The eponymous heroes are two young men whose exemplary friendship contrasts with and exposes the corruption of the royal Court into which fortune precipitates them. It is essentially a discourse on Court life, encompassing such issues as flattery, corruption and ambition, but it also engages the moral dimension of gentlemanly behaviour.

There is a moral contrast between elite protagonists, particularly Damon and Pithias on the one hand, and a pair of morally compromised courtiers, Carisophus and Aristippus, on the other. While the friendship of the two heroes is noble and selfless, that of the two courtiers is duplicitous and self-seeking. However, if this provides one set of contrasts, another emerges from the difference in manners between the socially elevated protagonists on the one hand, and on the other the servants and their peers who play a significant part in especially the comic aspects of the narrative. One of these, a rustic figure called Grimme the Collier, is made the mouthpiece of justified moral condemnation of his social superiors, Carisophus and Aristippus, so that in terms of straightforward morality there is no automatic privileging of rank. However, in other ways the capacity for moral superiority is linked to refinement of manners and comportment. Damon's manservant, Stephano, complains of hunger, saying that 'for all your talke of Philosophie / I never heard that a man with wordes could fill his belly' (391–2), at which Damon later comments: 'For trayne up a bondman never to so good a behaviour, / Yet in some poinct of servilitie, he wyll savour: / As this Stephano, trustie to mee his Mayster, lovyng and kinde, / Yet touchyng his belly, a very bondman I him finde' (406–9).

This lower-class incomprehension of higher motives is particularly illustrated later when Gronno, the coarse-mannered hangman detailed to execute Pithias, cannot understand his willingness to sacrifice himself for his friend: 'Here is a mad man: I tell thee, I have a wyfe whom I love well, / And if iche would die for her, could ich weare in Hell: / Wylt thou doo more for a man, then I woulde for a woman?' (78–80). Gronno also expresses pleasure when Pithias is granted new clothes after his reprieve, as this means the executioner is not after all to be denied the cast-off clothes he would have received at Pithias's execution. His motivation is entirely governed by material considerations. This perception of lack of understanding of the disinterestedness of truly genteel behaviour among those who are not essentially gentle is what informs Richard Mulcaster's observation on the different ways in which learning is consumed and used:

> the common man doth learne for necessitie at first, and aduauncement after: the greater personage ought to learne for his credit, and honour, besides necessary vses. For which be gentlemanly qualities, if these be not, to reade, to write, to draw, to sing, to play, to haue language, to haue learning, to haue health, and actiuitie, nay euen to professe Diuinitie, Lawe, Physicke, and any trade else commendable for cunning? Which as gentlemen maye get with most leasure, and best furniture, so maye they execute them without any corruption, where they neede not to craue. (1581, 208)

In drawing a fundamental distinction between the gentle figures and others in terms of their preoccupation with physical appetites and their predisposition to expressing themselves in terms of physical action, the play exemplifies a convention which was informing the principles of social representation to an increasing extent. The allegorical structure of earlier morality drama had been concerned with giving material form to psycho-moral processes, but with the advent of 'historical' or non-allegorical protagonists, a distinction emerged between what might be termed more cerebrally constructed figures, and those whose principal dramatic presence is conceived in terms of their bodily drives. The distinction is in essence a social one. Ascham's discomfiture with the 'meanness' of the matter of Plautus and Terence in the face of their rhetorical excellence, is expressed in terms which articulate an aspiration towards a withdrawal of the cultivated social identity from the corporeal: 'And thus, for matter, both *Plautus* and *Terence*, be like meane painters, that worke by halfes, and be cunning onelie, in making the worst part of the picture, as if one were skilfull in painting the bodie of a naked person, from the nauell downward, but nothing else' (1570, 59^r/R3^r).

Other aspects of the representation of the low life figures in the play involve comedy which derives directly from their low status or social ineptitude. At one point Grimme is being shaved by Jack and Will, servants of the courtiers. His lumpen naïveté allows them to dupe him into thinking he is receiving a luxury shave, with costly lotions – the comedy partly residing in the incongruity of such a situation – and allows them to rob him of his money. Grimme also speaks (mangled) French gained during military service abroad, another 'accomplishment' inappropriate for a collier, a fact remarked on by Jack's comment, 'here is a trimme colier, by this day' (1168).

There is repeated recognition within the play of the value of the study of manners and the exemplary importance of behaviour. This is seen in theatrical terms too. Damon remarks soon after his entry (using an appropriately theatrical metaphor): 'Pithagoras said, that this world was like a Stage, / Wheron many play their partes: the lookers on, the sage / Phylosophers are, saith he, whose parte is to learne / The maners of all Nations, and the good from the bad to discerne' (348–51). This is developed when the corrupt king, Dionysius, is converted to rectitude by the example of the two young men, observing: 'O noble gentlemen, the immortall Gods above, / Hath made you play this Tragidie, I thinke for my behove' (1669–70). Damon and Pithias, too, objectify their behaviour and view it from the outside, particularly in respect of the way it determines their reputation:

> *Pithias*: I shall never aske thee more, my desire is but frindly:
> Doo me this honour, that fame may reporte triumphantly,
> That Pithias, for his friend Damon was contented to die.
> *Damon*: That you were contented for me to die, fame cannot denie,
> Yet fame shall never touch me with such a villanie,
> To reporte that Damon did suffer his friend Pithias, for him giltles to die.
> (1618–23)

If the play promotes superiority of comportment and moral code as defining nobility, it also quite explicitly promotes the value of friendship alongside manners to the cohesion of the elite class. A statement by Damon encapsulates neatly the self-perceptions of an elite founded on an increasingly diverse basis of power, but self-identified through a code of manners and the allegiances which this produced:[38]

> thrise happy are wee
> Whom true love hath joyned in perfect Amytie:
> Which amytie first sprong, without vaunting be it spoken, that is true,

Of likeliness of maners, tooke roote by company, and now is conserved
by vertue.
(318–21)

These plays deliver the arguments on one level, while at the same time
fashioning their dramatic figures and their narratives in such a way as to
furnish another, more tacit form of social education. The drama is not simply
dialogue on theory but has to deal with characters who interact. Drama needs
the dramatic effects of conflict and these plays, in order to represent gentility as
part of a didactic process, require the contrasting presence of ungentle
behaviour. Mode and narrative structure are also complicit in this: dramatic
spaces differentiate social ranks. The discourses on behaviour in the interlude,
whether implicit or explicit, become more complex with the emergence of the
commercial theatre. Here the idea of the drama as an instructive medium is
made more problematic by the fact of a more diverse target audience. The
interludes were also, of course, played to a range of audiences that were
socially heterogeneous. However, their role and the values they articulated
were largely determined by the effects of patronage and touring arrangements
which made elite households the focus of playing companies (Westfall, 1990).

Religious antitheatricalism intensified with the advent of the
commercial theatres, and in the eyes of some polemicists it was only the
capacity of drama to educate that gave it any redeeming features at all. In the
Puritan John Northbrooke's *Treatise Wherein Dicing, Dancing, Vain Plays . . . are
reproved* of c. 1577, plays are damned for their moral effects in entirely
religious terms, but he allows their performance in very specific contexts:

> I thinke it is lawfull for a Scholemaister to practise his schollers to play
> Comedies, obseruing these and the like cautions. First that those
> Comedies which they shall play, be not mixt with any ribaudrie and
> filthie termes and wordes (which corrupt good manners). Secondly, that it
> be for learning and vtterance sake, in Latine, and very seldome in
> Englishe. Thirdly, that they vse not to play commonly, and often, but
> verye rare and seldome. Fourthlye, that they be not pranked and decked
> vp in gorgious and sumptuous apparell in their play. Fiftly, that it be not
> made a common exercise publikely for profit and gaine of mony, but for
> learning and exercise sake.
> (76/L2ᵛ)

Northbrooke thus tolerates drama in extremely limited circumstances and for
the sake of very defined pedagogical objectives.[39]

The drama of the public theatre also, however, maintained strongly
didactic elements.[40] This theatre, though, was rather more profuse in the social
education it made available. The refinement of language was part of a
generalized impulse towards an awareness of the role of the symbolic aspects

of social identity in the process of self–improvement. In the 1555 tract, *Institution of a Gentleman*, the observation is made:

> yea the marchantman thinketh not himselfe well unles he be called on of the worshipful sort of marchants, of whom the handicraftman hath taken example, & loketh to be called maister, whose father and grandfather wer wont to be called goodmen. Thus through the title of maistershippe most men couet to clymbe the steppes of worshippe which title, had wonte to appartaine to gentlemen onely, and men of office & estimacion.
> (Prologue, 1^v–2^r)

Half a century later, the tendency towards the general refinement of speech was a phenomenon recognized by several and seen as a blessing by some, as in Samuel Daniel's *Musophilus* (1599):

> Powre aboue powres, O heauenly *Eloquence*,
> That with the strong reine of commanding words,
> Dost manage, guide, and master th'eminence
> Of mens affections, more then all their swords:
> Shall we not offer to thy excellence
> The richest treasure that our wit affoords?
> Thou that canst do much more with one poor pen
> Then all the powres of princes can effect:
> And draw, diuert, dispose, and fashion men
> Better then force or rigour can direct
> (F2^r)

By the late sixteenth and early seventeenth centuries it had become a widespread practice for men to keep commonplace books, in which they wrote down scraps of verse or other pithy observations which could then be used to lend elegance and sophistication to their conversation. Walter Ong, pointing out that Elizabethan anthologies presented their material not only to be enjoyed, but as materials to be used, goes on to describe the process as follows:

> The conceptual apparatus of 'flowers' and 'collecting' is tied in with the massive tradition of rhetorical invention (which includes poetic invention) running back into classical antiquity and thence to the oral sources of literature. 'Flowers' imply the busy rhetorical 'bee' who goes through the garden (or, at times, the forest) of invention to visit the 'places' (*loci, topoi*) from which 'arguments' are to be extracted.
> (1977, 179)

The commercial theatre was a natural source of such material, and it was simply participating in this culture of collection which was part of the project of self-education of many young men. This educative role was seen positively by those who sought to defend the theatre against the onslaughts of its detractors. In 1612, Thomas Heywood attributes the refinement of language to the instructive effect of the public theatre in the broad range of society, and he uses it in his defence of the stage in *The Apology for Actors*: [41]

> Secondly our *English* tongue, which hath ben the most harsh, vneuen, and broken language of the world, part *Dutch*, part *Irish*, *Saxon*, *Scotch*, *Welsh*, and indeed a gallimaffry of many, but perfect in none, is now by this secondary meanes of playing, continually refined, euery writer striuing in himselfe to adde a new florish vnto it; so that in processe, from the most rude and vnpolisht tongue, it is growne to a most perfect and composed language, and many excellent workes, and elaborate Poems writ in the same, that many Nations grow inamored of our tongue (before despised).
> (F3^r) [42]

He sees the effect of the theatre as extending beyond the linguistic, however, and goes on to argue in the same text for a more profound cultural effect resulting from its teaching function, citing classical precedent:

> Thes wise men of *Greece* ([s]o called by the Oracle) could by their industry, finde out no neerer or directer course to plant humanity and manners in the hearts of the multitude then to instruct them by moralized mysteries, what vices to auoyd, what vertues to embrace; what enormityes to abandon, what ordinances to obserue: whose liues (being for some speciall endowments in former times honoured) they should admire and follow: whose vicious actions (personated in some licentious liuer) they should despise & shunne: which borne out well by the wisedome of the Poet, as supported by the worth of the Actors, wrought such impression in the hearts of the plebs, that is short space they excelled in ciuility and gouernement, insomuch that from them all the neighbour Nations drew their patternes of Humanity, as well in the establishing of their lawes, as the reformation of their manners.
> (C3^r)

However, for others it was exactly this instructive effect of theatre in the culture that constituted part of its danger to the society. Thomas Nashe's 1589 address 'To the Gentlemen Students of Both Universities' prefacing Robert Greene's *Menaphon*, is trenchant in its attack on not only the easy access to elevated language made available by the drama, but also the (spurious) classical and poetic pretensions of the dramatists who peddle it:

> I am not ignorant how eloquent our gowned age is grown of late; so that euery mechanicall mate abhorreth the English he was borne too, and plucks with a solemne periphrasis, his *vt vales* from the inke-horne: which I impute, not so much to the perfection of Arts, as to the seruile

imitation of vaine glorious Tragedians, who contend not so seriously to
excell in action, as to embowell the cloudes in a speech of comparison,
thinking themselues more then initiated in Poets immortality, if they but
once get *Boreas* by the beard, and the heauenly bull by the dcaw-lap.
(McKerrow, III, 311) [43]

The idea also informs Marston's satirical portrait of a theatre fan in *The
Scourge of Villainy*, published in 1598:

> Now I haue him, that nere of ought did speake
> But when of playes or Plaiers he did treate.
> H'ath made a common-place booke out of plaies,
> And speakes in print, at least what ere he sayes
> Is warranted by Curtaine *plaudeties*,
> If ere you heard him courting *Lesbia's* eyes;
> Say (Curteous Sir), speakes he not mouingly
> From out some new pathetique Tragedie?
> He writes, he railes, he iests, he courts, what not
> And all from out his huge long scraped stock
> Of well penn'd playes.
> (H4^r)

Stephen Gosson, in his *Plays Confuted in Five Actions* which appeared the
following year, launches out similarly: 'Many thinges might bee spoken
against Playes, for the vaine ostentation of a flourishinge wit, brauelie for
satisfieng the[m] that are vnsatiable, largelie for instructing of them that are
vnlearned, plainly: which I haue omitted' (A6^r). Later in the same text he goes
on to question the validity of theatre as a model of manners and behaviour:
'How is it possible that our Playemakers headdes, running through *Genus* and
Species & euery *difference* of lyes, cosenages, baudies, whooredomes, should
prese[n]t vs any *schoolemistres of life, looking glasse of maners* or *Image of
trueth*?' (D5^v). The problem, from his Puritan perspective, was that there was
no control over the nature of the social education being provided by the theatre.
His concern was primarily moral and religious, but the question of the spread
of refinement across the social spectrum is seen as a problem in more secular
and social terms in Samuel Rowlands's *Satire 4* (1600):

> *Melfluuious*, sweete Rose-watred elloquence,
> Thou that hast hunted Barbarisme hence,
> And taught the goodman *Cobbin* at his plow,
> To be as elloquent as Tullie now:
> Who nominicates his Bread and Cheese a name,
> (That doth vntrusse the nature of the same)
> *His stomacke stayer*. How dee like the phrase?
> Are Plowmen simple fellowes now a dayes?

Not so my Maisters: What meanes *Singer* then?
And *Pope* the Clowne, to speake so Boorish, when
They counterfaite the clownes vpon the stage?
Since Country fellowes grow in this same age,
To be so quaint in their new printed speech,
That cloth will now compare with Veluet breech
Let him discourse euen where, and when he dare,
Talke nere so Ynk-horne learnedly and rare.
(D8ʳ)

A few years later, Thomas Dekker also took a sardonic view of the phenomenon in his *Gull's Horn Book* (1607), and in his satirical advice to a gallant, he advises him:

> To conclude, hoord vp the finest play-scraps you can get, vppon whiche your leane wit may most sauourly feede for want of other stuffe, when the *Arcadian* and *Euphuisd* gentlewomen haue their tongues sharpened to set vpon you: that qualitie (next to your shittlecocke) is the onely furniture to a Courtier thats but a new beginer, and is but in his *ABC* of complement.
> (30) [44]

With the exception of Gosson, this can not be seen simply as part of standard Puritan antitheatricalism. In the case of those like Nashe, Marston, Dekker, and Rowlands, whose perspectives were social rather than primarily religious, the problem was that the theatre extended the availability of apparently educated behaviour too widely and too easily. [45]

Dekker's objection relates less to the question of morals than to the possibilities for the development of excess and affectation in behaviour, and this was echoed in the comments of other writers as well. This occurs in some cases when the verbal accomplishments too easily acquired do not form part of general social accomplishment. George Wither satirizes a pretentious lover in the first satire of *Abuses Stripped and Whipped* (1613): 'His *Poetry* is such as he can cul, / From plaies he heard at *Curtaine* or at *Bul*, / And yet is fine coy Mistres *Marry muffe*, / The soonest taken with such broken stuffe' (24). [46] Jonson saw a moral implication in the quality of language use. In his prose essay, *Discoveries* printed in 1641, he argues: 'Wheresoeuer, manners, and fashions are corrupted, Language is. It imitates the publicke riot. The excesse of Feasts, and apparell, are the notes of a sick State; and the wantonnesse of language, of a sick mind' (954–8).

It is clear that both the advocates of the early modern public stage and its detractors identified the theatre's capacity to educate, though they viewed it differently. In both the promotion by the theatre's supporters of its cultural role and its opponents' suspicions about its cultural effects there is implicit the same idea. It is that this is a medium which properly belongs within the realm of elite culture. In the one view the educative function of the theatre enables it to raise cultural standards by bringing the beneficial effects of supposedly elite behaviour and morality into broader currency. In the other, this same process debases refinement and undermines social distinctions by making it available to constituencies in which it is inappropriate. Whatever the eventual composition of audiences of the commercial theatre, the sense was never entirely lost that drama was an activity which, because its production (and, ideally, its consumption) required learning, naturally belonged to the elite.[47] Many complaints about the theatre (those not proceeding from narrowly religious considerations) were based on discomfort provoked by perceptions of the theatre's accommodation of a popular constituency. In the next two chapters these will be examined in respect of the perceptions of playwrights about both their own education and status, and that of their audiences.

CHAPTER FOUR

'Poesies sacred garlands':
education and the playwright

Sweet *poesies* sacred garlands crowne your gentrie:
Which is, of all the faculties on earth,
The most abstract, and perfect; if shee bee
True borne, and nurst with all the sciences.
(Jonson, *Poetaster*, 5.1.17–20)

The commercial drama of the early modern period only gradually gained a degree of recognition as a literary art. The attitudes exhibited by Sir Thomas Bodley when he was assembling his library in 1612, were fairly widespread. Bodley wrote to his librarian, Thomas James:

> I can see no good reason to alter my opinion, for excluding suche bookes, as almanackes, plaies, & an infinit number, that are daily printed, of very vnworthy maters & handlyng, suche as, me thinkes, both the keeper & vnderkeeper should disdaine to seeke out, to deliuer vnto any man. Happely some plaies may be worthy the keeping: but hardly one in fortie. For it is not alike in Englishe plaies, & others of other nations: because they are most esteemed, for learning the languages & many of them compiled, by men of great fame, for wisedome & learning, which is seeldom or neuer seene among vs. Were it so againe, that some litle profit might be reaped (which God knowes is very litle) out of some of our playbookes, the benefit therof will nothing neere conteruaile, the harme that the scandal will bring vnto the Librarie, when it shalbe giuen out, that we stuffe it full of baggage bookes.
> (Wheeler, 1926, 221–2)

In an earlier letter he had remarked:

> There are many idle bookes, & riffe raffes among them, which shall neuer com vnto the Librarie, & I feare me that litle, which you haue done alreadie, will raise a scandal vpon it, when it shall be giuen out, by suche as would disgrace it, that I haue made vp a number, with Almanackes, plaies, & proclamacions: of which I will haue none, but suche as are singular.
> (ibid., 919)

Bodley's fears are less to do with the intrinsic qualities of his library than the risks to its reputation and – by extension – his own. His concerns are to do with the 'scandal' to his name and standing which might be occasioned by the inclusion of the drama and other putatively ephemeral writing because of their perceived lack of intellectual substance and therefore their inappropriateness as the reading matter of a gentleman. There is some irony in the fact that Bodley's attitudes are facilitated precisely by the breadth of literacy in the period and the consequently large production of reading matter of various types.[1] Social and intellectual discriminations between types of written product needed to be made since being literate was not a sufficient distinction in itself.

However, Bodley's rather stock response to the products of the commercial theatre – though it usefully illustrates a connection between erudition and gentlemanly reputation – vastly oversimplifies the situation, and might perhaps be considered to proceed mainly from his zeal to promote the cultural authority of his library by the inclusion of only those genres of writing which uncontroversially enjoyed an intellectual status. It is true that Bodley was not alone in his view, though it is likely that social considerations weighed heavily in his judgement.[2] It was ultimately incontrovertible the drama was a written medium, and *did* possess a literary or poetic dimension, whatever the purposes or locations for which it was written.[3] From the perspective of both its forms and its subject matter, it is self-evident that the institutions of higher education in the realm had, however obliquely, some part in shaping the drama. Quite apart from the rhetorical training that was to be gained there and in the grammar schools, the universities provided the transmission of particular models of writing and ideas which had profound relevance for the production of drama. As the universities and Inns of Court were themselves producers of drama, questions inevitably arise about the relationship (if any) between the academic drama and the commercial. In the period there appears to have been in the minds of those concerned with both types a clear distinction between them. Of the writers for the academic stage, only one – the Cambridge playwright Thomas Randolph – went on to produce drama for the public theatre.[4] Though there is some significance in the fact that the sort of educated men who had written poetry as a pastime in the Jacobean period began turning to playwriting in Charles I's reign, there continued to be a concern among certain men about what they perceived as the lack of intellectual seriousness of the drama. At the publication in 1658 of Jasper Mayne's 1637–8 Blackfriars play, *The City Match*, the publisher outlined the author's attitudes to his own play as follows:

> The Author of this Poem, knowing how hardly the best things protect themselves from censure, had no ambition to make it in this way publique. Holding workes of this light nature to be things which need an

Apology for being written at all. Nor esteeming otherwise of them, than of Masquers, who spangle, and glitter for the time, but tis through a tinsell. As it was meerly out of Obedience that he first wrot it, so when it was made, had it not been commanded from him, it had died upon the place, where it took life.
(Note *To the Reader* prefacing the play)

In some cases, writers who would not otherwise have sought to have their plays performed were forced to do so through economic circumstances. Samuel Daniel protested in a letter of 1604 to his patron, the Earl of Devonshire, that the performance in public of his play *Philotas* was the consequence of an 'indiscreation' on his part and that 'when I shewd it to yor hono^r I was not resolued to haue it acted, nor should it haue bene had not my necessities ouermaistred mee' (Grosart, 1885, Vol. 1, xxiii). Even as late as 1629 the courtier Lodowick Carlell, who wrote plays for the King's Men that were performed at the Blackfriars, remarked that his play *The Deserving Favourite*, which had been performed at Court, was not 'design'd to travell so farre as the common Stage' (Gray, 1905, 35).

The attitudes of university authorities to commercial plays and players illustrate this sense of separation between the cultural pursuit and the commercial product. At Oxford, the Earl of Leicester as Chancellor, commenting on statutes passed in 1584 relating to disorder at the universities, made a distinction between those plays which were offered by travelling players, and the theatrical activities of the students themselves: 'As I . . . thinke the Prohibition of common Stage Players verie requisite, so would I not have it meant thereby that the Tregedies, Comodies, and shews of Exercises of Learning in that kind used to be set forth by Universitye men should be forbedden' (Wood, 1796, Vol. 2, 222). This attitude is further manifest in the policy followed by the authorities at Cambridge who, in the 1580s and 90s, repeatedly paid troupes to leave the town without playing (*REED: Cambridge* 311, 332, 339–43, 348–9, 399–400, 985). They later went further and enforced a ban on performances by professional players within five miles of the university or town centre, a prohibition authorized by a letter from King James in 1603/4 which referred specifically to 'common Plaies, Publique shewes, Enterlud*es*, C<o>modies & tragedies, in the English tongue' (*REED: Cambridge* 395). When Lord Burghley wrote to John Hatcher, the Vice-Chancellor in 1580 to ask permission for Lord Oxford's men to mount in the university plays which had been performed publicly, Hatcher made the excuse of 'ye commencment tyme at hande, which requireth rather dilligence in stodie than dissolutenesse in playes' (*REED: Cambridge* 290–1). What is more, a decree of 1600 forbade students to attend 'bullbaytyng*es*, cockpits, como*n* plaies or vnlawfull games' (*REED: Cambridge* 381).[5]

These attitudes can possibly be better understood in the light of the fact that the universities had a strong tradition of in-house drama themselves. The huge bulk of this drama was formally classical, either the work of Greek and Latin authors, or plays written to conform to these models. That the academic drama was performed largely in the classical languages only helped to underline this. Of the more than one hundred university plays listed by Boas as having been performed between 1520 and 1603 only around a dozen were in English (1914, 386–90).[6] There were clear differences between the nature of the dramatic fare served up at the universities – or at least the huge bulk of it – and the drama of the commercial stage. An exchange between Burghley and another Vice-Chancellor of Cambridge, John Still in 1592–3, makes apparent the university's sense of a clear distinction between the classical drama which they mounted themselves and vernacular plays. It also expresses a discomfort with the idea of scholars performing outside the university, albeit in an exclusive context.[7] Burghley had requested the performance of a comedy in English before the Queen, and Still replied:

> How ready wee are to do any thinge that may tend to her Maiesties pleasure, wee are very desirous by all meanes to testyfy; But how fitt wee shalbe for this that is moued, havinge no practize in this Englishe vaine, and beinge (as wee thinke) nothinge beseeminge our Studen*tes*, espeicially out of the Vniu*er*sity: wee much doubt; And do finde our principale Actors (whome wee haue of purpose called before vs) very vnwillinge to playe in Englishe.
> (*REED: Cambridge* 346–7)

The sense of a dichotomy between academic and commercial drama was not only enduring but was also felt and expressed on the part of the public stage. The Caroline writer, Richard Lovelace says in the prologue to his lost play, *The Scholars* of 1636:

> A Gentleman to give us somewhat new,
> Hath brought up *Oxford* with him to show you;
> Pray be not frighted – Tho the Scæne and Gown's
> The *Universities*, the Wits, the Town's;
> The Lines each honest *Englishman* may speake;
> Yet not mistake his Mother-tonge for *Greeke*,
> For stil twas part of his vow'd Liturgie,
> From learned Comedies *deliver me*!
> Wishing all those that lov'd 'em here asleepe,
> Promising *Scholars*, but no *Scholarship*.
> (*Poems*, 58)

One of the possible reasons for this sense of the discreteness of the academic and public stages may lie in the very fact of the continued existence of the former throughout the period.[8] If academic drama had merely been a forerunner of commercial drama it would have been easier to suggest a transition from one to the other, with all the evolutionary determining influences which that would have involved. As it is, the continuing tradition of plays in Latin and Greek at the universities comes to seem ever more arcane and remote when contrasted with the emerging popular commercial stage. A decline took place in classical studies, and particularly Greek, at the universities in the latter half of the sixteenth century, due principally to economic problems (Bolgar, 1954, 327–8). Despite this, it is worth noting that the stream of classical plays as noted by Boas at the universities shows no substantial signs of diminution (1914, 385–90). However, what might more realistically be argued is that what was more influential was the general academic culture (of which drama was a natural part). The sophistication which learning conferred validated, and indeed increasingly even constituted, the quality of gentility on which claims to social esteem and even material reward were based. That in these academic contexts – the universities, the Inns, and even the major schools – forms of drama figured as important modes of discourse is of inescapable relevance here. In his *Apology for Actors* Thomas Heywood made use of this fact to support his defence of the theatre, asking:

> Do not the Vniuersities, the fountaines and well-springs of all good Arts, Learning and Documents, admit the like in their Colledges? and they (I assure my selfe) are not ignorant of their true vse. In the time of my residence in *Cambridge*, I haue seen Tragedyes, Comedyes, Historyes, Pastorals and Shewes, publickly acted, in which Graduates of good place and reputation, haue bene specially parted.
> (1612, C3^v)

The establishment and maintenance by the academic stage of a classical point of reference becomes more relevant when it is borne in mind that not only was it classical forms and genres which helped to distinguish the commercial drama from the earlier interlude tradition, but that this impulse became ever more important in early modern drama. It is not without significance that the first vernacular plays in the neoclassical genres appeared in academic contexts. Thomas Norton and Thomas Sackville's 1561 Inner Temple play *Gorboduc* doubles as the first extant Senecan tragedy and the first neoclassical history play in the vernacular (having been based on Grafton's *Chronicle* of 1556), as well as being the first play in blank verse to be written in English. *Supposes* by the Gray's Inn man, George Gascoigne, was the first vernacular prose comedy and was acted at the Inn in 1566/7. His *Jocasta* written in collaboration with Francis Kinwelmershe another member of Gray's Inn, dates from 1566. In around 1568 another classical tragedy called *Gismond of Salerne* was produced in the Inner Temple, the collaborative effort of five of its members, later revised by one of them (Robert Wilmot) in 1592 as *Tancred and Gismunda*.[9] The view has tended to prevail that these Inns plays are, in a sense, false starts with little or no relation to the drama that was produced on the commercial stage, especially with the emergence of the playhouses. Sir Philip Sidney's negative comparison of the fare of the public theatres with *Gorboduc*. – in which he complains that the commercial drama deviates from the formal structures found in that play – has helped to sideline Inns of Court drama in the history of theatrical development in the century. However, Sidney was basing his statement on narrow notions of Aristotelian dramaturgical prescription, and he recognized that even *Gorboduc* fell short of these.[10] If the commercial playwrights by and large ignored the narrow rules of classical composition, they nevertheless allowed classical modes to determine their work in broader ways, less clearly defined than the strict rules of form, but no less important in shaping the medium. The Ramist influence on the humanist programme of education, with its stress on accomplishments and the practice of rhetorical skills, was a strong force for the encouragement of the promotion of the humanities and the arts.[11] Since the commercial drama showed itself ready to respond very flexibly to the demands of the market, with the emergence and rise to prominence at various points of genres which responded to popular taste, it is all the more remarkable that the format of commercial plays continued to adhere to the basic structures introduced and maintained in academic contexts, even if it did develop variations on the generic categories cited above.[12] The academy arguably continued to be an essential point of reference for dramatists insofar as it provided models of what the drama was. The drama is one of the more significant ways in which the classical humanist impulse was kept alive in the universities, and transmitted beyond them.

Academic influence was encouraged by the immersion of many of the commercial playwrights themselves in academic culture. What is at issue here is the exposure to a milieu of academic writing and thought, rather than a direct engagement with academic drama, on the part of commercial playwrights who received a university education.[13] The domination of early seventeenth-century drama – at least from a modern critical perspective – by Shakespeare and Jonson, neither of whom received a formal higher education, has also tended to promote a relative disregard of the contribution of higher education to the production of commercial theatre. So too has the perception that what we are concerned with here is a largely popular medium. However, firstly the dominance of Shakespeare was not as clear-cut in the period as his modern reputation would suggest, though he was admittedly part of the most successful of the playing companies and his work was a staple of their repertoire. Secondly, the reality is that the majority of playwrights working in the period had received some higher education. The divisions between those writers for the stage between the opening of the theatres in the 1560s or 1570s and their closure in 1642 who are known to have received a higher education, those who did not, and those for whom there is no information about their education are given below. This is broken down into three periods, the Elizabethan, the Jacobean and the Caroline though some playwrights so evenly straddle more than one period that their placing is fairly arbitrary. Those for whom only one play has been identified are marked with an asterisk. In the Elizabethan period the graduates are Stephen Gosson, Robert Greene, Thomas Lodge, Christopher Marlowe, Thomas Nashe, George Peele and the Court dramatists Thomas Campion, George Ferrers, George Gascoigne, John and Jasper Heywood, and John Lyly. The non-graduates were Thomas Kyd, Anthony Munday, and the Robert Wilsons (younger and elder), while nothing is known of the education of Michael Drayton, Richard Hathway, William Haughton (though it is possible he went to university), Henry Porter or Anthony Wadeson.

Graduates among the Jacobean playwrights are Barnabe Barnes*, Francis Beaumont, Robert Daborne, John Day, John Ford, Thomas Goffe, John Marston, Philip Massinger, Thomas May, Thomas Middleton, Edward Sharpham, John Stephens*, John Webster, Robert Wild* and the Court dramatist Samuel Daniel. Thomas Heywood and Gervase Markham probably went to university, though this cannot absolutely be proven, while Thomas Dekker, William Sampson, Cyril Tourneur and John Fletcher, probably did not.[14] The known non-graduates apart from Jonson and Shakespeare include Robert Armin, Lording Barry*, Henry Chettle, Nathan Field, Samuel* and William Rowley. Nothing is known of the education of Joshua Cooke*, Thomas Drue*, Lewis Machin*, John Mason*, Wentworth Smith, Robert Tailor* or George Wilkins. Though George Chapman's education is not known, it is possible and even likely that he went on to university after school at Hitchin.

Among the Caroline playwrights, Alexander Brome*, Henry Glapthorne, Peter Hausted, William Heminges, Shackerley Marmion, Jasper Mayne, Thomas Nabbes, Thomas Randolph and James Shirley were graduates, as were most of the courtier poets who wrote plays, William Berkeley*, Thomas Carew, William Cavendish, William Davenant, John Denham*, William Killigrew, Richard Lovelace* and John Suckling. Known non-graduate playwrights were Richard Brome and Thomas Rawlins, while nothing is known of the education of Robert Davenport, Lodowick Carlell (though his plays indicate a solid education), Joseph Rutter (though it is likely he had taken a degree or had at least attended university, as he was tutor to the sons of the Earl of Dorset) or Lewis Sharpe*. It is clear that graduates maintained a strong presence among playwrights during the entire period, whether fully as professionals or as amateurs, and they heavily predominated in the Caroline theatre.

If there were playwrights who did not have a background of higher learning, an academic input into the business of producing material for the commercial stage was facilitated by the interconnections between writers. In many ways it is artificial to make a distinction between the 'university wits' as the group of late sixteenth-century university educated playwrights (most notably Greene, Marlowe and Peele) are termed, and those who did not have a university background.[15] What is perhaps most important to note about these men is that the first crop of commercial playwrights were graduates. They were followed by an influx of non-graduate writers in the mid-1590s, before more graduates turned their hand to drama later in the decade (Riggs, 1989, 28). The spread of academic influence from graduates to non-graduate dramatists over the whole period would have been readily mediated by the essentially collaborative culture of dramatic writing. It is usual to regard early modern writing for the commercial stage as by and large a solitary activity, but this ignores the huge amount of collaboration which occurred, much of it between graduates and non-graduates.[16] This did not seem to have been impeded by the sort of academic snobbery revealed in Thomas Nashe's remark in 1589 (probably directed at Kyd, who had been a scrivener or 'noverint') about playwrights who had not had an extensive formal education:

> It is common practise now a dayes amongst a sort of shifting companions, that runne through euery Art and thriue by none, to leaue the trade of *Nouerint*, whereto they were borne, and busie themselues with the indeuours of Art, that could scarcely Latinize their neck verse if they should haue need; yet English *Seneca* read by Candlelight yeelds many good sentences.
> ('To the Gentlemen Students' in McKerrow, 1904, III, 315)

A great many plays were produced by co–writing, sometimes involving several dramatists. Writing partnerships were fluid, and playwrights tended to participate in a range of co-operative endeavours with various combinations of other writers. Among the leading playwrights of the time, Beaumont and Fletcher's long-standing partnership stands out as an example, but John Webster's co-writers included Drayton, Munday, Middleton, Dekker, Chettle, Heywood, Wentworth Smith and Rowley. Dekker wrote with Drayton, Wilson, Chettle, Munday, Jonson, Day, Haughton, Middleton, Hathway, Webster, Hayward, Ford and Massinger.[17] Even Shakespeare collaborated with Middleton, Fletcher and possibly Rowley, and Jonson with Dekker, Chapman, Marston (and probably, if he had a hand in *Sir Thomas More*, with Munday and Chettle as well).[18] They are just a few of the numerous partnerships which together constitute a fairly tightly knit culture of theatre writing in the period.

These collaborations provided channels of influence connecting men of widely varying educational backgrounds and contributing to the establishment of particular formulae of writing, something which is only too evident from a survey of plays of the period.

Many collaborative relationships involved graduates, or at least men who had attended the universities and Inns of Court, working with ones who had not. Middleton, a member of Gray's Inn who included masques for the Inns of Court among his projects, worked in the course of his commercial career with both the Oxford graduate Philip Massinger, and several writers who had attended neither the universities nor the Inns, such as Dekker, Munday, Rowley, Drayton and Webster. John Marston, an Oxford graduate, collaborated with Webster and Jonson as well as with Chapman, of whose education nothing is known. Massinger, another Oxford man, worked with the Cambridge graduate, Robert Daborne, as well as the non-university men Nathan Field, Tourneur, Dekker and Fletcher. What emerges is a picture of a writing culture that had a significant input of men who had been through the academic mills of the universities and the Inns of Court. Even in the case of the major non-graduate playwrights, Shakespeare's and Jonson's work shows a considerable embrace of academic learning, in Jonson's case frequently self-consciously so.[19] It suggests a ready acceptance of the idea of the playwright as a learned man, at least by the playwrights themselves (the reservations about the business of playwriting expressed by dramatists such as Jonson and Greene notwithstanding). The profession of playwright could even perhaps make possible the blurring of the educational background of its members, as is suggested by the fact that Francis Meres describes William Rowley as 'a scholar of Pembroke Hall, Cambridge', whereas the records of the college indicate that this was not possible, and Rowley actually started his career as an actor (*DNB* Vol. 17, 363).

The academy had some influence in the matter of source material for the drama, and an important feature of the vernacular Inns of Court plays is their use of both classical and foreign models. Gascoigne and Kinwelmershe's *Jocasta* was translated from *Giocasta*, by Lodovico Dolce, itself a translation of Euripides's *Phoenissae*; Gascoigne's *Supposes* was a translation of Ariosto's *Gli Suppositi*, and *Gismond of Salerne* by Wilmot and others was based on material from Bocaccio. These plays were both the natural products of the tradition of Latin (and Greek) drama in the universities and Inns, and the interest of Innsmen in foreign writing. Though this was unequivocally 'academic' drama, it did help to establish the use of classical and foreign sources for the drama of commercial contexts as well. One of the most direct ways in which the academic institutions were able to influence the nature of writing for the commercial stage, was as auspices for the humanist importation of foreign and classical models. The Inns of Court were especially instrumental in making available foreign material, as several translators of Seneca were Innsmen including Arthur Golding, John Studley and Thomas Newton.[20] If the humanist revolution in education was responsible for the introduction of classical and foreign narratives, what followed was the proliferation of these in popular translations. It was on these that the stage chiefly drew, and Stephen Gosson complains in 1582, in his *Plays Confuted in Five Actions* that: 'I may boldely say it, because I haue seene it, the Palace of pleasure, the Golden Asse, the Aethiopian historie, Amadis of Fraunce, the Rounde table, baudie Comedies, in Latine, French, Italian and Spanish haue beene thoroughly ransackt, to furnish the Playe houses in London' (D5^v). Despite the insinuations of low-life associations in Gosson's Puritan outburst, paradoxically the use of such texts might be seen ultimately to proceed from academic and elite sectors of the culture. In fact, their popularization was a large part of the problem. Narratives whose salacious aspects might have been less problematic had they been contained within circumscribed academic contexts, become subversive once loosed into an uncontrolled public realm.[21]

If the proliferation of foreign and classical narratives on the early modern stage can be seen as relating ultimately to the products of academic culture, so too can the stage's interest in history and politics. The interlude plays of the earlier sixteenth century frequently included political content precisely because they were produced for audiences in the Court or the noble households that were the legitimate sites for the consideration and debate of matters of state, being the sector of the population possessed of the greatest political power or influence.[22] The institutions of higher learning were also natural centres of political discourse, whether deemed to be so, or simply by their very nature. The universities always had close connections with the Court and state administration, particularly after their effective nationalization by Henry VIII, but perhaps the most significant academic forums of political debate in the period were the Inns of Court, which is unsurprising given their position in English public life. They were in the business of training politicians and, during the time of his chancellorship, enjoyed Burghley's benevolent patronage. Drama constituted part of the cultural life of Inns, and was almost inevitably a medium for political debate and discourse. The political nature of the Inns drama derived particularly from the connections between the institution and the Court. Marie Axton has argued that most of the plays which originated in the Inns in the mid- to late century concerned the question of the succession (1977, 38–87). Several writers of the *Mirror for Magistrates*, Thomas Norton, Thomas Sackville, George Ferrers and William Baldwin, were also involved in dramatic activity or writing, and the *Mirror* furnished the material for a number of Elizabethan dramatic tragedies (Campbell, 1938, 3). The sophistication of their audiences was taken for granted, not only in the matter of rhetoric and argument, but in their engagement with issues of political philosophy. It is thus understandable that, in *Gorboduc*, it was at the Inns that the first vernacular classical tragedy or history play (depending on how it is viewed) should have been produced. What *Gorboduc* did was to establish the engagement of drama with English history as humanist example, following Elyot's precept in *The Governor* that the purpose of history is to teach by examples so that an individual might 'aprehende that which is commodious'. The humanist project envisaged a whole range of dramatic and other literature as relevant experience. *Gorboduc* (and the other Inns plays dating from the middle of the sixteenth century) also set up a neoclassical, secular mode in which the drama could articulate political ideas. While not abandoning the allegorical entirely, it substituted for the theological basis of authority on which the interlude drama was based, the whole body of narrative and chronicle literature. English history became, of course, a recurrent topic on the commercial stage, but the educational nature of this type of drama was never entirely lost sight of. It was one of the justifications for the stage cited by Thomas Heywood in the *Apology for Actors*:

> playes haue made the ignorant more apprehensiue, taught the vnlearned the knowledge of many famous histories, instructed such as cannot reade in the discouery of all our *English* Chronicles: & what man haue you now of that weake capacity, that cannot discourse of any notable thing recorded euen from *William* the *Conqueror*, nay from the landings of *Brute*, vntill this day, beeing possest of their true vse. For, or because Playes are writ with this ayme, and carryed with this methode, to teach the subiects obedience to their King, to shew the people the vntimely ends of such as haue moued tumults, commotions, and insurrections, to present them with the flourishing estate of such as liue in obedience, exhorting them to allegyeaunce, dehorting them from all trayterous and felonious stratagems.
> (1612, F3^{r-v})

The academic dimension of the practice of writing is also highly relevant to the complicated status of playwriting in the period.[23] Francis Meres in his *Palladis Tamia* of 1598 subtly intertwines ideas of pre–eminence in writing skills with attitudes to social and academic status. The entry on tragedy runs as follows:

> As these Tragicke Poets flourished in Greece, *Aeschylus, Euripedes, Sophocles, Alexander Aetolus, Achaeus Erithnaeus, Astydamas Atheniensis, Apollodorus Tarsensis, Nicomachus Phrygius, Thespis Atticus*, and *Timon Apolloniates*; and those among the Latines, *Accius, M. Attilius, Pomponius Secundus* and *Seneca*; so these are our best for tragedy, the Lorde *Buckhurst*, Doctor *Leg* of Cambridge, Doctor *Edes* of Oxforde, maister *Edward Ferris*, the Authour of the *Mirrour for*

Magistrates, Marlow, Peele, Watson, Kid, Shakespeare, Drayton, Chapman, Decker and *Beniamin Iohnson.*
(283^r/Oo3^r)

The entry for comedy follows a similar pattern:

> The best Poets for Comedy among the Greekes are these, *Menander, Aristophanes, Eopolis Atheniensis, Alexis Terius, Nicostratus, Amipsias, Atheniensis, Anaxandrides Rhodius, Aristonymus, Archippus Atheniensis* and *Callias Atheniensis*; and among the Latines *Plautus, Terence, Naenius, Sext. Turpilius, Lucinius Imbrex,* and *Virgilius Romanus*; so the best for comedy amongst vs bee, *Edward* Earle of Oxforde, Doctor *Gager* of Oxforde, Maister *Rowley* once a rare Scholler of Learned Pembrooke Hall in Cambridge, Maister *Edwardes* one of her Maiesties Chappell, eloquent and wittie *Iohn Lilly, Lodge, Gascoyne, Greene, Shakespeare, Thomas Nash, Thomas Heywood, Anthony Mundye* our best plotter, *Chapman, Pater, Wilson, Hathway,* and *Henry Chettle.*
> (283^r/Oo3^r–283^v/ Oo3^v)

Meres is clearly an advocate of the acceptance of the cultural value of even the commercial drama, and in the way he presents his playwrights he makes skilful use of contemporary social attitudes. Firstly he prefaces his listing of English playwrights with classical ones, thus implying an elevated cultural tradition of which the current playwrights are a part, and placing English writing for the stage in a context of classical learning. He then starts his English list in each case with an aristocrat – Lords Buckhurst and Oxford respectively, and follows them with academic playwrights, giving Legge, Gager, and Edes their academic titles. George Ferrers (called by Meres 'Edward Ferris'), Edwardes and Rowley are also accorded their academic titles of 'Master' although they were not all academic playwrights. Possibly because of the attitudes to comedy, Meres takes care to stress the academic or social credentials of some comic writers: Rowley's scholarship at Pembroke Hall and Edwardes's position at Court.[24] The other playwrights are listed with the graduates first. Meres is quite obviously conscious of both the importance of stressing the participation in the business of dramatic writing of those whose gentle status is beyond question, and then underscoring the academic qualification of others.

What is most pertinent to social ideologies which inform modes of representation in the drama, is how this academic sophistication is translated into constructions of social identity. If the basis of the academic drama was strongly classical, this impulse informed the development of the commercial drama as well. The strongly classical training of the graduate playwrights meant that their influence would have added to the classical grounding that most non-graduate writers would have received as part of their school education. As a mode of discourse and representation, classicism is not innocent of ideological and social implications. The cultural conditions of the period place the classical firmly in the elite camp. This association is ascribable most particularly to the ways in which the elite were becoming defined by their education and that a classical education was advocated by humanist theorists to be an appropriate preparation for the governing class. An opposing view is presented by the Puritan Lawrence Humphrey who, in his tract *The Nobles*, is critical of aristocratic display and is also inclined to turn to the Bible rather than the classics for models of what constitutes gentle behaviour. Humphrey is critical of Virgil and Homer precisely because they present too well the values of traditional aristocratic culture (Kearney, 1970, 43). The humanist theorists may have conceived their views for social improvement as being of benefit to society as a whole, but they had clear opinions about which section of society should have the benefit of classical learning. The humanist influences in education had, within the first few decades of the century, effected the introduction of Latin and other texts as a staple of elite education (Esler, 1966, 4). The realities of the access to education were no less disposed to reinforce the connection between elite status and classical training. These were areas to which access was restricted (apart from the fortunate and gifted few among the 'meaner sort') to those for whose education sufficient funds could be found. If classicism has a particular social dimension, it therefore has more than anything to do with the ways in which educational institutions were shaping cultural assumptions in the period. A sensibility that made a connection between social superiority and sophistication of learning would flow naturally from conditions such as these.

The classical provided the means by which elite culture could celebrate and define itself. Certainly the Jacobean Court's theatricalization of itself in mythical, classical terms in the masques of Jonson and Jones, of Daniel and others might be compared to the presentation of themselves to the court by the universities in the mounting of classical plays. The motivation is somewhat different however; the Court is reinventing itself in terms of a classical frame of reference, while the universities are demonstrating their mastery of classical culture and learning. The reinvention of royalty in classical terms is found, too, of civic pageantry such as Royal Entries in which classical imagery, mythology and literary reference is something of a staple.[25] The open availability of this pageantry to the masses (as opposed to the private performance of masques) could even make the erudition of classicism seem problematic. In the preface to his 1604 account of the 'Magnificent Entertainment Given to King James in 1603' (describing the 'Device') Dekker comments: 'The multitude is now to be our Audience, whose heads would miserably runne a wooll-gathering, if we doo but offer to break them with hard words' (Bowers, 1955, Vol 2, 255). In the case of the drama itself, aside from the universities and Inns of Court, it was in the fare provided for the Court that the classical first became established as a mode. G. K. Hunter has observed that: 'Lyly's court comedies are the earliest domestications into English of the stylistic control, conceptual sophistication and inner coherence of classical and Italian comedy' (1997, 70).

The authority inherent in the classical is readily accommodated in contexts such as academic or state ceremonial. In the commercial theatre, the situation is rather more complicated. Because it is placed alongside other modes of representation one might be tempted to read it as being in equal competition with them, as Michael Bristol has done in the following description of the theatre as:

> a cultural activity mandated by a 'dialogic' imperative rather than any prior allocation and structuring of authority. Poetic language, rhetorical ornament, and classical learning are compelled to share communicative space with vernacular speech and with vernacular misinterpretations of high culture. This is a virtual and immediate form of heteroglossia, not simply a literary production within a text, and it corresponds to Stubbes's conception of the 'scurrilitie' of playing.
> (1985, 122–3)

This, however, does not take account of the status accorded to the classical as opposed to demotic forms of utterance. The (often comic) ignorance or crudity of low-life figures is important not only to justify their demeaned status in the social hierarchy, but also to define by contrast the elevated status of the elite in cultural terms.[26]

If there was a hierarchy in forms of literary production, the classical was thus at its head. The classical authors were read precisely because they provided models of elegant and accomplished rhetoric which was a central aim of a humanist education (Kristeller, 1961, 13). Terence's *Andria* was published in 1520 in an English translation *Terence in English* to help give polish to the English language, as yet considered crude and uncultivated. Classical learning was seen as a matter of advancing the general level of civilization. Of the classical scholar, Thomas Lupset, the Oxford university authorities wrote to Thomas Linacre in 1521: 'so plentifully does he bedew us with the figures of rhetoric and so eloquently does he daily strive to cultivate our taste, that, the dregs of barbarism having been removed, we trust that the very form of eloquence may soon live again' (Gee, 1928, 45). If, as Ascham, Elyot and others argued, the study of rhetoric through the classics was essential to the young who were destined to constitute the governing class, in dramatic representations of that class the classical therefore provided an appropriate mode. In some ways Sidney's objection to the departure from strict classical models by the drama of his period can be seen as motivated by a sense of a social betrayal – at the violation of the terms which privileged access to education had set up for the discourse of the elite. The convention of 'decorum' in dramatic representation was connected to classicism, and germane to this was the role of classical education in the refinement of behaviour and taste. In Cicero's *De Officiis* (translated in 1543 by Robert Whytinton as *The Three Books of Tully's Offices*) two divergent types of 'jesting' are identified. The plays of Plautus belong to the more elevated sort:

> There is vtterly but two maner of iestynges, that one carterly, scoldyng, vycious, and abhomynable. The other clenly, manerly, wysely, and with mery borde. In the whiche maner not onely Plautus our countreyman and the olde comedy of Athenes, but also the bokes of philosophers that folowed Socrates be replenysshed. And many wordes of dyvers manerly spoken, as those whiche were gathered of Cato in his olde age, whiche he called I[n] greke Apothegmata. Therefore it is an esy distinctyon of a gentyll bourde & of a carterly iestyng. The one if it be done in tyme and with a mery stomake, becometh a gentyll man. The other vnfytting for a gentyll man, if so be that vyle termes be ioyned to the leude ded of the thynges.
> (F7^{r-v})

In the emergence of 'historical' characters on the stage, as opposed to the allegorical figures of the morality drama, classical models had a part to play particularly in respect of the ways in which dramatic characters were socially defined. These figures were as much determined by the modes of writing that constructed them as the narratives which they populated.[27] While decorum had formerly been based simply on the notion that there was a qualitative difference between social ranks and that literary propriety demanded that this difference be reflected in generic and modal contrasts, the changing social role of education provides, in the course of the century, a material context for this convention which invests it with a more immediate relevance. If a classical education in the real world was what made a gentleman (or at least helped to confer on him the mystique of superiority), the classical dimension to the convention of decorum was an appropriate corollary in the contexts of dramatic representation. It was not simply that certain modes of drama were deemed suitable for the representation of certain social levels, but also that classical education was available only to those who were, or were on their way to becoming the elite. The changed social realities of the sixteenth century thus gave a renewed meaning to the decorum that determined dramatic representations of social types, and this was informed by classicism.[28] The convention carried with it 'natural' associations of elite identity, so that these did not need to be spelled out. The classical involved behaviour informed by a particular moral code based on notions of honour which were perhaps equivalent to, and a replacement of the medieval chivalric codes. It is perhaps something of an irony that at a time when these chivalric elements were becoming redundant to the elite class, they were forming the material for romantic popular drama.[29]

In a drama which was responding to commercial imperatives, the question of adherence to a set of what were essentially literary conventions is rather more complex than any formal critical prescription. It was considered in the period that the classic rules of decorum were being flouted on the commercial stage and there was clearly some pressure on dramatists to provide what their audiences demanded. However, there was a contrary impulse, which kept the early modern drama considerably more socially conservative than it might otherwise have been. First of all there was no absolute abandonment of principles of decorum, even where they appear to have been violated. In a study of Shakespeare's approach to decorum, Thomas Macalindon has concluded that Shakespeare did, by and large, abide by its rules, and where he departed from them it was for particular reasons (1973). However, even if it is recognized that early modern dramatists were given to a somewhat fluid approach to decorum, a clear demarcation might nonetheless be observed between the broad social categories of 'gentle' and 'non-gentle' which is reflected in the structures and representational conventions of plays. In some cases, the actual divergence from what was understood to be the appropriate style was the means by which literary effects were achieved. Hence the portrayal of the curate Dr Rat in William Stevenson's early academic comedy, *Gammer Gurton's Needle* (written for presentation at Christ's College Cambridge in the 1560s or 1570s) is farcical and coarse. The satire, probably on rustic clergy, is based precisely on an implicit understanding of the inappropriateness of Dr Rat's behaviour as an educated man, and mediated through the incongruity of the style of writing which constructs the character. In later drama, and particularly in the Caroline period, the relationship between social standing and education would be more complicated, too overt an embrace of academic modes of speech often becoming a way of satirically representing clumsy attempts at social mobility.

Playwrights who went through the university system were among those graduates who ended up working for their living.[30] They were given, often solely by virtue of their education, a claim to gentle status, though they did not have the independent financial means to sustain it. They were also working in a profession that involved learning and literary skill, but on the other hand the demeaned cultural position of the commercial drama compromised any social status which this might confer. That the drama of the academic institutions, both in the classical languages and the vernacular, retained a status sufficient to guarantee its prominent place in any public definitions of corporate identity by these organizations (such as at times of royal visits), could only have added to the ambiguity. A number of vernacular academic plays which focus specifically on the question of the relationship between learning and elite status are useful source of information on attitudes within these institutions, and arguably of the educated class on these issues.

One such play is *Club Law*, presented at Clare Hall, Cambridge in about 1599–1600. This is an example of the use of drama by a privileged – or at least aspirant – group to exercise their anxieties about their status, particularly in conflict with another status group, the town authorities.[31] The immediate context of the play was a long running dispute between the university and the town, in which the central government and members of the royal family were called in as arbitrators from time to time. There is therefore a specific political agenda, and this finds expression in certain of the characterizations which involve references to actual townsmen prominent in the disputes, and to some actual events. However, there is also an anterior social agenda that informs the political conflict but in some senses also stands aside from it. The political confrontation has to do with supply of goods, control of prices, monopolies, and local rights and privileges. The social agenda has much more to do with anxieties about social ascendancy and incursions upon the privileges of rank, especially as conferred or confirmed by education. Although their victory in the play is brought about by a combination of clever strategic tactics and *force majeure*, a more fundamental support is given to the claims of the university men by reference to their 'natural' superiority which proceeds from their status as educated gentlemen. Early in the play the two academics, Philenius and Musonius, discuss the crudeness of the townsmen of Cambridge and Philenius observes: 'I durst have sworne that this place where the muses be so conversant and the good Arts so nourished could not have byn so voyd of humanitie (i.e. civility and refined manners) I thought it unpossible that ignorance should have nestled where knowledg is so powerfull' (189–93). He goes on to complain of the townsmen: 'in stead of our servants they seeme to be our masters, their power is too absolute, they muddy slaves (thinke them selves) to good to be our servants' (201–3).

This position is supported in the representation itself. While these two academics (who represent the university in the play) are accorded classical names, the townsmen are given names like Mallice, Halfecake, Oliver Goosturd, Asselye, Alderman Tongue It, Mr Slugg and Goodman Ketlebasen. Some of these are likely to have made oblique reference to specific individuals, but the overall effect is to construct the townsmen in terms of farce and to contain them within a defined comic space. The contrast between the elevated classical sphere of which the academics are part and the somewhat homespun English world of the townsmen, is consistently re-emphasized by the repeated reference to the academics as 'gentle Athenians' and the townsmen as 'hoydens'. The townsmen are also called 'mechanicks' and reference is repeatedly made to their trade activities, in a way which undermines the ceremonial aspects of their roles as governors of the city.

In an early play already discussed above (see pp. 59–61), Medwall's *Fulgens and Lucres*, arguably the first English secular play, at least among those extant, the figures are placed in a classical context that is not an insignificant part of the delineation of their status. The elite protagonists are all given classical names, while the servants either have no names at all (A and B) or, in the case of the maid, is given an English name: Joan. This is a tendency to be found in many plays, to the extent that it becomes something of a convention, albeit never universally applied. Classicism is naturally associated with education, and education here is seen in terms of a natural right to social precedence. The classical in drama is far less about recalling or alluding to historical antecedents than setting up a frame of reference which has to do with social exclusivity.

In *Club Law*, the differences between the university men and the townsmen go beyond the matter of dignity of demeanour and gravity of comportment, however. The lack of learning of the townsmen is presented as invalidating their claims to authority:

> *Musonius*: Why Philenius theise are fitter to move pittie
> then procure patience, to see a heard of Asses thinking
> themselves a troupe of sages, I would never wish a
> better object to my sences than theise.
> *Philenius*: why, but canst thou be well pleased to see
> such sepulchers the Image of divine authoritie, and
> them governe others which can scarcely mannage their
> owne affaires?
> (177–84)

This view of the townsmen is supported by a number of illustrations in the text, perhaps most notably when Mistress Colby, the wife of a member of the Corporation, in bemoaning the attitude of her husband and his fellows towards the university men, betrays a combination of superstition and ignorance about the nature of learning (in a view of academics which the playwright is possibly implying to have derived from the popular theatre – a performance of a play such as *Doctor Faustus*, or Greene's *Friar Bacon and Friar Bungay*): 'Jesus blesse me, what doe our men / meane to abuse such proper Gentlemen, such learned / men, that conjure the devill into a Circle and put him / againe in hell, and doe such strang things as they be?' (813–16).

There is also a moral dimension to the notion of gentility implicit in the play. The 'gentle Athenians' are exposed to the lascivious attentions of the townsmen's wives, whom they befriend in order to gain some intelligence of their adversaries' tactics. They easily resist the sexual blandishments, Musonius declaring: 'I hope my thoughts are of a higher pitch than to enter into such kennell thoughts'. This contrasts with the antics of the newly elected mayor, Nicholas Niphle, who though conscious that it is in conflict with his office, has one of his sergeants procure a girl for him, and is caught by the university men in ignominious circumstances with her.

Another aspect of the (fairly conventional) association between gentle behaviour and morality is in the comparison made by the young student, Nicholas Cricket, between himself and Tavie: 'Ile warrent you, the villaine hath byn in as many Clerigalls (stocks) in his life as I have gathered phrases'. The term refers to the gathering of fine phrases from good authors which was part of the task of students of rhetoric. The contrast is then between the process of verbal and behavioural refinement through which Cricket's gentility is being constructed, and the moral disorder that defines Tavie. These are very much the terms in which the differentiation between the representations of the townsmen and the university men is made in the play.

The play ends with the rout of the townsmen. In Niphle's speech of submission, the social agenda is made fairly explicit. Addressing the university men he says:

> But you are
> termed gentle, therefore doe but consider, that it was
> but superioritie, for which wee doe contend, the desire
> whereof yee knowe (that be schollers) to be common
> to all beasts, which seeing it is so, wee hope, that it is pardonable.
> (2715–20)

The establishment of proper hierarchical relations is signified also by the fact that Tavie, a sergeant in attendance upon the Burgomaster and a prominent agent on the townsmen's side, is promised the lowly job of under-skinker in a university buttery and is pleased to accept it.

In *Club Law* the battle about economic rights and privileges is ultimately recast into an argument that power is a right belonging naturally to those in possession of gentle status. Gentility is represented as a superiority of manners and morals that is conferred by education. The play goes beyond the quarrel with the townsmen to become a re-enactment of academic claims to class status. The drama is a vehicle of discourse that is made available to the university men through their education, and it is used to celebrate the power and status identity that education confers or strengthens. It is an interesting illustration of the way in which the drama as a form is appropriated by a particular elite group.

The discontent of intellectuals at the difficulty of reconciling their status as educated men with poverty and a need to sell themselves and their services where they could, is acutely expressed in the trilogy of university plays produced between 1589/9 and 1602/3 at St John's College, Cambridge entitled *The Pilgrimage to Parnassus, The First Part of the Return from Parnassus* and

The Second Part of the Return from Parnassus. These plays articulate anxieties about the position of the intellectual in society, particularly about status and access to wealth. The pilgrimage in the first play (*Pilgrimage to Parnassus*) is presented as a process of gaining a social identity through learning. A student Studioso remarks:

> Our youth by trauellinge to Hellicon
> Must gett prouision for our latter years
> (*Pilg.* 449–50)

>   . . .

> Catullus, Ouid, wantome Martiall:
> heare them whilest a lasciuious tale they tell,
> Theile make thee fitt in Shorditche for to dwell
> (*Pilg.* 515–17)

His brother and fellow student Philomusus disputes this, but the principle remains of an acquaintance with poetic writers having a moral dimension.

There is repeated reference in the play to the poverty of scholars. This is in one instance presented as a virtue, the father of the students Consiliodorus observing: 'Thoughe I foreknewe that gold runns to the boore / Ile be a scholler though I liue but poore' (*Pilg.* 63–4). However, it is clearly based on an anxiety that relates to comparative social positions; Consiliodorus goes on to say:

> Let schollers be as thriftie as they maye,
> They will be poore ere theire last dyinge day
> Learninge and pouertie will euer kiss:
> Each carter caries fortune by his side,
> But fortune will with scholler nere abide
> (*Pilg.* 74–8)[32]

Philomusus complains in the *First Part of the Return from Parnassus* that: 'The partiall heauens do fauoure eche rude boore, / Mackes drouiers riche, and makes each scholler poore' (*1st Ret.* 100–1). The professions open to those who graduate from the university are poor ones:

> *Ingenioso*: hee met coming downe from the hill a companie of ragged vicars and forlorne schoolemaisters, who as the[y] walked scrached there vnthriftie elbowes, and often putt there handes into there vnpeopled pocketes, that had not beene possessed with faces this manie a day. There one stoode digginge for golde in a standishe (inkwell); another looking for a cockpence in the bottom of a pue: the third towling for silver in a belfree: but they were neuer so happie as Esopes cocke to finde a precious stone: nay they could scarce get enough to apparell there heade

in an vnlined hatt, there bodie in a frize Ierkin, and there feet in a clouted
paire of shoes.
(*Pilg*. 581–91)[33]

The anxiety becomes one which relates to social competition and concerns
about rank in a situation of social mobility, when traditionally 'base' types are
referred to as acquiring wealth and status (and even a false pretension to
refinement):

> *Ingenioso*: tapsters, ostlers, carters and coblers haue a fominge pauch (*sic*
> – either 'paunch' or 'pouch'), a belchinge bagg that serues for a cheare of
> est[ate] for *regina pecunia*? Seest thou not my hoste Iohns of the Crowne,
> who latelie liued like a moule .6. yeare vnder the grounde in a cellar, and
> cried anon, anon Sr, now is mounted vpon a horse of twentie marke, and
> thinkes the earth too base to bear the waighte of his refined bodie? . . .
> Why, Newman the cobler will leaue large legacies to his haires, while the
> posteritie of *humanissimi auditores* and *esse posse videatur* must be faine
> to be kept by the parishe.
> (*Pilg*. 622–34)

The question of status reveals itself in these plays as perhaps an even
more acute problem to scholars than that of poverty, to which it is closely
related. Their lack of a defined position in the social hierarchy is illustrated by
the rude treatment received by the young scholar Ingenioso at the hands of a
servingman in the house of a man whose patronage he is soliciting. Ingenioso's
reply to the man poignantly makes reference to the only source of social power
at his disposal:

> I would thy father had brought the vp to learninge, then woulde I make
> the mendes for my knockinge with an hundred latin sentences, which
> thou migh[t]est make vse of in the eleuation of the seruing mans black
> Iacke, or the confusion of a mes of brewes. But frend, for thy better
> instruction, answerr not a man so churleshlye againe while thou liuest.
> Why man, I am able to make a pamphlet of thy blew coate and the button
> in thy capp, to rime thy bearde of thy face, to make thee a ridiculous blew
> seeud creature, while thou liuest. I haue immortalitie in my pen, and
> bestowe it on whome I will.
> (*1st Ret.*, 243–53)

The confusion about status proceeding from the poverty of the scholars is
expressed in the comment by a tailor who remarks of them: 'The[y] came to
mee, & it were as curteous as passeth – I doe not like the[y] shoulde put of
theire hattes so much to mee – well, they needes vpon ould aquaintance woulde
borowe 40s fo three dayes' (*1st Ret.*, 484–8) .

The question of status also affects the work of the scholars. Studioso's description in *The First Part of the Return from Parnassus* of his conditions of employment as a tutor in an elite household contains repeated reference to his status and comparisons with baser people in the household. He has to wait at meals and work in the fields at harvest time, and would get as part of his wages some cast off suits of the master 'that his ploughman would scarse accept of' (649–50). He calls his employer an 'old churle' and ultimately loses his job because he will not agree to having one of the blue coats (servants) sitting above him at table. Philomusus, suffers the same fate because he refuses to take on tasks that he considers to be beneath him.

The sharp sense of competition with other classes emerges at several points. The scholar Academico, commenting on the non-gentle figures Stercutio and Immerito (the latter being the clownish son of a rich countryman), remarks bitterly: 'the time hath beene when such a fellowe medled with nothing but his plowshare, his spade, and his hob-nayles, and so to a peece of bread and cheese, and went his way: but now these (scuruy) fellowes are growne the onely factors for preferment' (*2nd Ret.*, 656–60). Another illustration of this is the preference shown by Amoretto, the son of an ignorant country squire, for Immerito over Academico. Immerito can provide material bribes in his pursuit of the living that Sir Raderick, Amoretto's father, has in his gift. Amoretto drives Academico away with hunting talk, which becomes here a language of exclusion since this is a pursuit of which Academico has no experience. This incident recalls the criticism by humanists, such as Elyot, of tendencies among certain members of the landed classes to put greater value on the acquisition of hunting skills than on formal education for their children (see p. 4 above).

Consiliodorus bewails the fate of his sons, decrying the values of the age which favour the non-gentle pursuits with material reward, whereas those activities which contribute to the store of civilized life go unrewarded: 'Mechanicke artes may smile, there followers laughe, / But liberall artes bewaile there destinie. / Since noe Mæcenas in this niggard age / Guerdons they sonns of Muses and of skill' (*1st Ret.*, 1070–73). It is indeed the intellectual and social refinement of scholars which marks them off and gives them the right to an elevated position in society. The employers or professional superiors of all the scholars are, in fact, churls or fools. In the *Second Return*, Ingenioso describes the lifestyle of Sir Raderick, the coarse squire, in terms which emphasize the inappropriateness of his gentle status:

> he that loues to liue in an od corner here in London, and affect an odde
> wench in a nooke; one that loues to liue in a narrow roome, that he may
> with more facility in the darke light vpon his wifes waiting maide; one
> that loues alife a short sermon and a long play; one that goes to a play, to

a whore, to his bedde in [a] Circle; good for nothing in the world but to sweate nightcaps & foule faire lawne shirtes, feede a few foggy seruing men, and pre-ferre dunces to liuings.
(1326–34)[34]

One focus of the question of gentility and refinement is centred on the 'false wit' figure of a foolish courtier called Gullio. He has aspirations to refinement and expresses his determination 'to proue a complet gentleman', but is described by Ingenioso as a 'base carle clothed in a sattin sute' (*1st Ret.*, 1445). This is something of a variation on the tirades against excessive dress in the period, not being predicated on the idea of dressing beyond one's rank so much as on a distinction between inner qualities of gentility (acquired through learning) and the mere outer trappings of rank. The plays reveal some ambivalence and discomfort even about this, and there is a clear satirical edge to the observation of the Recorder of Cambridge on the social mobility of humble scholars in the *Second Part of the Return from Parnassus*:

> Why ist not strange to see a ragged clarke,
> Some stamell weauer or some butchers sonne,
> That scrubd a late within a sleeueles gowne,
> When the Commencement, like a morice dance,
> Hath put a bell or two about his legges,
> Created him a sweet cleane gentleman:
> How then he gins to follow fashions?
> He whose thin sire dwell[s] in a smoky roufe,
> Must take Tobacco and must weare a locke.
> His thirsty Dad drinkes in a wooden bowle,
> But his sweet selfe is seru'd in siluer plate.
> (1160–70)

He goes on to say a little later:

> But had the world no wiser men then I,
> Weede pen the prating parates in a cage:
> A chayre, a candle and a Tinderbox,
> A thacked chamber and a ragged gowne
> Should be their landes and whole possessions;
> Knights, Lord, & lawyers should be log'd and dwel
> Within those ouer stately heapes of stone
> Which doting syres in old age did erect.
> (1177–84)

Gullio's pretensions to gentility are manifest in his aspiration, among other things, to a shallow refinement of behaviour which includes verbal accomplishment. Responding to Ingenioso's remarking on his quoting poetry, he says: 'As I am a gentleman and a scholler, it was but a suddaine flash of my Inuention. It is my custome in my comon talke to make vse of my readinge in the Greeke, Latin, French, Italian, Spanishe poetts, and to adorne my oratorye with some prettie choise extraordinarie sayinges' (*1st Ret.*, 1133–7).

Gullio, in fact, uses plays in his acquisition of verbal style and wit. Ingenioso observes of his speech: 'We shall haue nothinge but pure Shakespeare, and shreds of poetrie that he hath gathered at the theators' (*1st Ret.*, 986–7). Later rounding on him he exclaims: 'What youe whorsonne tintunabulum, thou that art the scorne of all good wittes, the ague of all souldiers, that neuer spokest wittie thinge but out of a play' (*1st Ret.*, 1441–3).[35] Gullio, in fact, expresses an admiration for Shakespeare: 'O sweet Mr Shakspeare, Ile haue his picture in my study at the courte' (*1st Ret.*, 1032–3). The academic attitudes towards the public drama which are revealed here are part of an anxiety about intrusions on modes of discourse that were perceived in these contexts to be properly the reserve of the elite.[36] Ingenioso in *The Second Part of the Return from Parnassus* also attacks John Bodenham, the anthologizer, for his popularizing work in collecting and publishing literary fragments:[37]

> Who blurres fayer paper with foule bastard rimes,
> Shall liue full many an age in after times:
> Who makes a ballet for an ale-house doore,
> shal liue in future times for euer more.
> Then, Bodenhame, thy muse shall liue so long
> As drafty ballets to thy praise are song.
> (184–9)

Later, musing on Bodenham's coat of arms, Ingenioso continues: 'his deuise might / haue bene better, a foole going into the market place to be / seene, with this motto, *scribimus indocti*, or a poore beggar / gleaning of eares in the end of haruest, with this word, *sua / cuique gloria*' (192–6).

The contemptuous representation in the play of Gullio's admiration for Shakespeare is informed by the implicit recognition that the public drama was instrumental in making available in a broad social arena precisely the sort of literate *savoir faire* which was both the stock-in-trade and the social capital of students aspiring to rise through their acquisition of a superior education. The complication here was that playwrights were, in one way or another, intellectuals themselves, while their work and livelihood involved peddling the fruits of their learning to a socially broad audience. The dismay of the scholars in the Parnassus plays about this sort of free distribution of esoteric knowledge might even be seen as in some ways comparable to the ecclesiastical and scholastic opposition to the translation of the scriptures in an earlier period, informed by the same awareness of the potential for undermining of authority.

The social implications of the translation of humanist texts in the early seventeenth century is made the subject of speculation in a play by Thomas Tomkis first published in 1607, *Lingua, or The Combat of the Tongue and the Five Senses for Superiority*. The 'trial' is mock-formal and the tone here is comic, but it does raise an issue which is the subject of serious discussion elsewhere.[38] The figure of Lingua is on trial, and is accused by Memoria as follows: '*Inprimis* we accuse *Lingua* of high Treason and sacrilege, against the most Honourable Common-wealth of Letters, for vnder pretence of profiting the people with Translations, she hath most vily prostituted the hard mysteries of vnknowne Languages to the prophane eares of the vulgar.' Another figure, Phantastes, adds: 'This is as much as to make a new hel in the vpper world, for in hel they say *Alexander* is no better then a Cobler, & now by these Translations euery Cobler is as familiar with *Alexander*, as he that wrote his life' (E2^v).

The very process of the (elite and academic) consumption of drama is part of the means of defining social sophistication. *The First Part of the Return from Parnassus* opens with an induction, in which the stage keeper dismisses the Prologue with the words: 'Sirra be gone, you play noe prologue here, / call noe rude hearer *gentle*, debonaire. / Wele spende no flatteringe in this carpinge croude, / Nor with gold tearmes make each rude dullard proude' (74–77). The irony here is that the play is being directed at a university audience, and so the comments about rude hearers and dullards are ironical in a self-celebratory way which proceeds from an implicit awareness of the practice in the public theatre of inappropriately flattering addresses to the base members of theatre audiences.

In *The Second Part of the Return from Parnassus*, the representation in the narrative of actual figures from the commercial theatre introduces some implicit comparisons between the academic and commercial stage. The figures of 'Kempe' and 'Burbage' both criticize the acting style and dramatic writing of scholars. 'Burbage' remarks patronizingly: 'A little teaching will mend these faults, and it may / bee besides they will be able to pen a play' (1764–5). The irony of this rather superior attitude on the part of non-academics is underlined by 'Kempe's' analysis of the academic drama a little further on:

> Few of the vniuersity [men] pen plaies well, they smell too much of that writer *Ouid*, and that writer *Meta-morphoses*, and talke too much of *Proserpina* & *Iuppiter*. Why heres our fellow *Shakespeare* puts them all downe, I and *Ben Ionson* too. O that *Ben Ionson* is a pestilent fellow, he brought vp *Horace* giuing Poets a pill, but our fellow *Shakespeare* hath giuen him a purge that made him beray his credit.
> (1766–7)

The satirical comedy in this passage is based on 'Kempe's' ignorance and misunderstanding of the classics, while Shakespeare and Jonson, not university educated and writers for the despised public stage, are implicitly included in the satire by his promotion of them. However, the comic tone here masks a real concern, consistent with those in the rest of the play. Not only are Shakespeare and Jonson materially successful but they (and especially Jonson) appear to have a command of the classical culture which is properly the realm of scholars. What is more, they put this to commercial use and thereby facilitate the success of just such men as Will Kempe. This gives expression to an anxiety that emerges in the play about need forcing some scholars to use their learning in writing for public players; Philomusus complains: 'And must the basest trade yeeld vs reliefe? / Must we be practis'd to those leaden spouts, / Than nought doe vent but what they do receiue?' (*2nd Ret.*, 1846–8). A little later Studioso echoes these sentiments:

> But ist not strange these mimick apes should prize
> Vnhappy Schollers at a hireling rate?
> Vile world, that lifts them vp to hye degree,
> And treads vs downe in groueling misery.
> *England* affordes those glorious vagabonds,
> That carried earst their fardels on their backes,
> Coursers to ride on through the gazing streetes,
> Sooping it in their glaring Satten sutes,
> And Pages to attend their maisterships;
> With mouthing words that better wits haue framed
> They purchase lands, and now Esquiers are namde.
> (*2nd Ret.*, 1918–28)

Here it is not only the matter of the prostitution of learning that is at issue, but more directly the question of social competition. The problem is the perceived injustice of the acquisition of gentle status by actors, while the scholars whose intellectual capacity, education and work gave them the real qualifications for this status are professionally subordinated to them. This is a sentiment aired elsewhere too, as in Samuel Rowlands's *The Letting of Humour's Blood in the Head Vein* published in 1600, in which he asks of 'poets': 'Will you stand spending your inuentions treasure, To teach Stage parrats speake for pennie pleasure, / While you your selues like musicke sounding Lutes / Fretted and strunge, gaine them their silken sutes' (A3^r).

There is an implicit recognition in these plays of the powerful cultural and social position of the commercial theatre in a variety of ways. It involves an awareness that writing for the theatre is an activity that extensively overlaps with the sort of cultural productivity in which the scholars themselves are engaged, to the extent that it becomes a necessary avenue of work for a few of their number. It is also instrumental in popularizing areas of discourse, and in making broadly available modes of mental and verbal accomplishment that are deemed to be properly the province of the educated elite, and to be significant in defining their elite status. Conversely, the scholars see themselves as forced into roles which are inappropriate for their status, so that the world is turned upside down. Not only do Philomusus and Studiosus at one point become actors themselves, but when they are at another stage forced, in order to gain a living, into posing as a French physician and his man, they view this in terms of dramatic roles:

> *Studiosus*: More must we act in this liues Tragedy.
> *Philomusus*: Sad is the plott, sad the Catastrophe.
> *Studiosus*: Sighs are the Chorus in our Tragedy.
> *Philomusus*: And rented thoughts continuall actors bee.
> *Studiosus*: Woe is the subiect:
> *Philomusus*: Earth the loathed stage,
> Whereon we act this fained personage.
> *Studiosus*: Mossy barbarians the spectators be,
> That sit and laugh at our calamity.
> (*2nd Ret.*, 561–6)

The collaboration in 1561 between Thomas Sackville (son of Sir Richard Sackville the first cousin of Anne Boleyn) and Thomas Norton (the son of a grocer, albeit wealthy), which produced *Gorboduc*, gives some indication of a tendency for the new elite to define itself in terms of a shared culture derived from education. A partnership cutting so sharply across the class barriers was extremely unusual, but it is significant that where it did occur it was in a context like the Inns of Court. In the world of the commercial theatre there was also a social mix in respect of the origins of playwrights. Whereas some were from solidly gentle backgrounds, such as Beaumont (son of a judge), Fletcher (son of a bishop), Marston (son of a gentleman and poet) and Middleton (son of a gentleman), others were of more humble provenance, such as Webster (son of a tailor), Munday (son of a draper) and Chettle (son of a dyer). In the collaboration of William Cavendish and James Shirley on *The Country Captain*, a 1639/40 King's Company play at the Blackfriars, there is another instance of the bridging of a wide social gulf. Cavendish was the Earl of Newcastle (later Duke), while Shirley had started off his career as a schoolmaster. If the range of collaborations cited above helped to form a culture of writing for the theatre that was social as well as professional, the playwrights which composed this group could only have based their sense of social identity on their position as intellectuals.

An acute sensitivity to the intellectual basis of his social identity is what informs Robert Greene's famous 1592 outburst in *A Groatsworth of Wit* against the theatre business in general, and Shakespeare in particular. Though often cited, it is worth quoting here in full, because of the range of relevant social attitudes which are implicit in it. Addressing certain colleagues, he remarks:

> Base minded men all three of you, if by my misery yee bee not warned: for vnto none of you (like mee) sought those burs to cleaue: those Puppits (I meane) that speake from our mouths, those Anticks garnisht in our colours. Is it not strange that I, to whome they all haue bin beholding: is it not like that you, to whom they all haue bin beholding, shall (were yee in that case that I am now) be both of them at once forsaken? Yes trust them not: for there is an vpstart Crow, beautified with our feathers, that with his *Tygres heart, wrapt in a Players hyde*, supposes hee is as well able to bombast out a Blanke–verse as the best of you: and beeing an absolute *Iohannes fac totum*, is in his owne conceyt the onely Shake-scene in a Countrey. Oh that I might intreat your rare wittes to bee imployed in more profitable courses: and let these Apes imitate your past Excellence, and neuer more acquaynt them with your admyred Inuentions. I knowe the best Husband of you all will neuer proue an Vsurer, and the kindest of them all will neuer prooue a kinde nurse; yet whilst you may seeke you better Maisters; for it is pitty men of such rare wits, should bee subiect to the pleasure of such rude groomes.
> (F3^{r-v})

Greene's tirade is revealing for the way in which gentility is inextricably linked to, and based on, formal education. While the writers are referred to in terms of 'rare wits' and 'admired inventions,' the actors come in for the traditional abuse: 'apes', 'puppets', and 'anticks' – all names which refer to the mechanical rather than intellectual nature of their occupation. Greene ends by stressing the class dimension with 'rude groomes' and later in the text he calls them 'buckram gentlemen'. The vituperation of the 'upstart' Shakespeare proceeds from the idea that he is really one of these actors, rather than properly a writer, and his art is imitative of that of the conventionally educated men – he is 'beautified in our feathers' – and his lack of specialization (Iohannes fac totum) further invalidates his claim to be taken as a literary artist.

A converse view is taken several years later by Jonson, in his commendatory poem on the publication of Brome's *The Northern Lass* in 1632 when he implies an approval for his Caroline 'son's' learning through apprenticeship rather than formal education, in a favourable comparison with the courtier playwrights:

> By observation of those Comick Lawes
> Which I, your Master, did first teach the Age
> You learn'd it well, and for it serv'd your time,
> A Prentice-ship; which few do now adays:

Now each Court Hobby-horse will wince in rime;
Both learned and unlearned all write Playes.
It was not so of old: men took up trades
Than knew the Crafts they had been bred in right
(*Works*, Vol. 3, ix)

Jonson had, of course, good reason to promote the idea of the craft of writing as itself a means of acquiring learning. He might, had Greene lived, equally have become the target of his vitriol.

Greene's sense of an incursion on the terrain which properly belongs to the formally educated, echoes the complaints of the students in the Parnassus plays. His insistence on the poetic in playwriting, in his reference to blank verse, seeks to emphasize the social elevation and exclusivity of the area on which Shakespeare is intruding with his 'bombast.' [39] The reference to usury is a reminder of the economic aspects of the business, something which was as much a source of challenge to the pretensions to gentility of playwrights, as the perceived inequalities of reward between playwrights and actors was to their sense of justice.

If envy might be regarded as motivating Greene's outburst, it is a topic which is often to be found in the plays of the period, as in the portrait of the discontented scholar, Macilente, in Jonson's *Every Man out of his Humour*, who is described in the *dramatis personae* as: 'A Man well parted, a sufficient Scholler, and trauail'd; who (wanting that place in the worlds account, which he thinks his merit capable of) falls into such an enuious apoplexie, with which is iudgement is so dazeled, and distasted, that he growes violently impatient of any opposite happinesse in another.' It can also be seen to inform many of the pronouncements of playwrights in other contexts. It is perhaps understandably a product especially of an age of intense competition, in which personal advancement was increasingly seen as possible and to be sought after.

Playwrights in especially the seventeenth century were working in the changing contexts of an emerging capitalist culture that involved the necessary recognition of new economic realities. The rise to power and prominence of Henslowe and the Burbages were part of this, as was the rise to sustained pre-eminence by the most successful of the playing companies, the King's Men, with their gifted non-graduate in-house playwright, Shakespeare. The fact of company's economic success, coupled with continued royal patronage, gave it a supremacy in the field of dramatic entertainment which it maintained right up to the closure of the theatres. This prominence in turn, together with the strong royal interest in theatre in Charles's reign, paved the way for the domination of the company by courtier-poets in the Caroline period (Gurr, 1996, 377–86). The perceived opportunities for advancement available to others were particularly a problem for learned men who were aware that learning was often a means to economic and social promotion, but yet far from automatically being so. This is poignantly expressed in Thomas Nashe's 1592 tract, *Pierce Penniless*:

> I cald to mind a Cobler, that was worth fiue hundred pound, an Hostler that had built a goodly Inne, & might dispende fortie pound yerely by his Land; a Carre-man in a lether pilche, that had whipt out a thousand pound out of his horse tayle: and haue I more wit than all these (thought I to my selfe)? am I better borne? am I better brought vp? yea and better fauored? and yet am I a begger? What is the cause? how am I crost: or whence is this curse?
> (McKerrow, 1904, I, 158)

With particular reference to playwrights, Dekker complains in a letter to the Queen's Men prefacing his 1612 play, *If It Be Not Good The Devil Is In It*: '*Knowledge* and *Reward* dwell far a-sunder. *Greatnes* lay once betweene them. But (in his stead) *Couetousnes* now. An ill neighbour, a bad *Benefactor*, no paymaister to *Poets*. By *This Hard-Houskeeping* (or, rather, *Shutting* vp of *Liberalities Doores*,) *Merit* goes a *Begging & Learning* starues.'[40]

The situation of playwrights is particularly complex in relation to social competition and intellectual accomplishment. Many of them, including Greene, owe their position entirely to their learning.[41] As educated men within the social hierarchy they must have shared the concern about the effects of the popularization of learning, and yet their claim to social authority resided expressly in parading their own accomplishments in the public sphere in which their work was displayed. The sensitivity about particularly the social rights which learning ought to confer is most clearly illustrated in Ben Jonson. His personality aside, it is not improbable that this was part of what motivated Jonson's frequent outbursts, and his acute awareness of the distinctions between the refinements of gentility and the coarseness of the 'base' sort.[42] His own early life particularly is likely to have left lasting scars. He claimed descent from a prominent Borders family, the Johnstones. His father (according to Jonson himself) became a minister when he lost his estate and on his death Jonson's mother, to his perpetual embarrassment, married a bricklayer (Miles, 1986, 1–8; Riggs, 1989, 17–19). Even as a successful playwright, his detractors never allowed Jonson to forget this humble association. Despite his abundant talents, the lack of influential friends meant that he did not win a scholarship to Oxford or Cambridge (Miles, 1986, 13). He felt the lack of a formal higher education deeply, and much appreciated the honorary degree which was conferred upon him by Oxford in 1619. He was always very keen to display his learning, but since it had not been acquired at a university, it did not bring with it the automatic claim to gentle status that a degree would have. Although he sometimes shows ambivalent attitudes towards the privileges conferred by formal education, his work is replete with comments about the value of learning, and in the prologue to *Sejanus*, he betrays a touching reliance on learning used as a protection against censure:

> The next is, least in some nice nostril, the *Quotations* might sauour affected, I doe let you know, that I abhor nothing more; and haue onely done it to shew my integrity in the *Story*, and saue my selfe in those common Torturers, that bring all wit to the Rack: whose Noses are euer like Swine spoyling, and rooting up the *Muses* Gardens, and their whole Bodies, like Moles, as blindly working vnder Earth to cast any, the least, hilles vpon *Vertue*.
> (ll.26–33)

Relevant to the playwrights' view of themselves as artists, and their social standing within their society, is the *poetomachia* or 'war of the theatres' which started in 1598 and involved Jonson, Marston, Dekker, Munday and possibly Shakespeare. This essentially was conflict conducted through dramatic and poetic satire, and focused on writing styles and the status of the playwrights as literary writers. In his *Scourge of Villainy*, Marston attacked the 'new minted epithets' in Jonson's plays; in *Every Man out of his Humour*, Jonson introduces the characters Clove and Orange to talk 'fustian' and ridicule the language used by Marston; in Dekker's *Patient Grissil* the character Emulo with his 'gallimaufry of language' is thought to be a caricature of Jonson; in *The Poetaster* there is a disgorging of words by Crispinus (Marston) after he is given an emetic pill (Penniman, 1897, 11, 31, 68, 117).[43] Underlying this battle was the understanding that writing for the theatre *was* an enterprise of cultural value, and the *poetomachia* might be seen in similar terms to other literary battles of the period (such as that between Gabriel Harvey and Thomas Nashe referred to in Chapter 1 above) in being about contestation for primacy of position in the production of cultural discourse. The value and status of playwrights in the terms of this battle ultimately reposes on their skill, their ability to produce high art, and their learning, though the early unease expressed by Sidney about the marriage of the high art of poetry with the low art of theatre never entirely disappears in the period:

> I have lauished out too many wordes of this play matter. I doe it, because as they are excelling parts of Poesie, so is there none so much vsed in England, & none can be more pittifully abused. Which like an vnmannerly Daughter, shewing a bad education, causeth her mother Poesies honesty to bee called in question.
> (1595, K3^v)

The conventions of drama in the early modern period were a result not just of a requirement to produce a saleable product in the marketplace – as we do not have a fully-fledged capitalist system to deal with here – but also of the values of the writing culture from which the drama emerged. This culture was significantly determined by not only the education of writers, but what that education meant socially in the hierarchical structure of early modern society. The situation was made more complex, and the importance of formal education as a point of reference the greater, by the ambiguities surrounding the status of both playwrights and playwriting in the period. The emergence of the courtier playwrights in the 1630s may have helped the status of the drama, but it did not ultimately resolve these ambiguities. That the drive towards education, for both the acquisition of skills for public office and the refinement of behaviour, was assailing the traditional sources of elite identity and power, lends even more weight to the issue. However, this needs to be further explored with reference to audiences who were not only an influence in shaping the nature of commercial drama, but were themselves subject to the social changes which the spread of education was bringing about.

CHAPTER FIVE

'A thousand men in judgement sit': education and the audience

> It may be for all we know true that the basic mentality of the Elizabethan and early Stuart audiences is not essentially different from that of the majority audiences of today, and that in consequence we do not need to look very deeply into their composition. It is the knowing even that much which is difficult. Of course the returns on the labour of summarising and generalising about such intangibles are likely to be small. There was on average over that seventy years or so of London commercial theatre as many as a million visits to the playhouse a year. Any generalisation covering that number would have to be stretched thinly.[1]

Andrew Gurr's caveat about discussing the early modern theatre audience points to an essential difficulty, the very ephemeral nature of the beast and the consequent lack of detailed and informative records relating to it. Apart from this, it is self-evident that the actual requirements and responses of individual audience members would have varied widely, and the tastes and demands of audiences in general would have differed perhaps from theatre to theatre over the seventy years or so of the pre-Civil War commercial theatre.[2] Contemporary comments on audience reactions frequently refer to the responses of different sections of audiences to the same plays. This multiplicity of responses is implied by the actor Andrew Cane in the *Stage-Players Complaint* of 1641 in which he lists the various purposes of plays:

> we are very necessary and commodious to all people: First for strangers, who can desire no better recreation, then to come and see a Play: then for Citizens, to feast their wits: then for Gallants, who otherwise perhaps would spend their money in drunkennesse, and lasciviousnesse, doe find a great delight and delectation to see a Play: then for the Learned, it does increase, and add wit, constructively to wit: then to Gentlewomen, it teacheth them how to deceive idlenesse: then for the ignorant, it does augment their knowledge.
> (4)

It might be noted here that, though there are different things for different people, the instructive element is strongly emphasized throughout and for all levels of the audience. This is, after all, written as a defence of the stage.

A distinction is, however, persistently made in the period between serious audience members, and those who are seen as the massed rabble, and related to supposed ways in which plays are appreciated and consumed. This notion is at the heart of Hamlet's observation that groundlings 'for the most part, are capable of nothing but inexplicable dumb shows and noise' and says that overdone performance, 'though it make the unskilful laugh, cannot but make the judicious grieve; the censure of which one must, in your allowance, o'erweigh a whole theatre of others' (3.2.25–8). The idea that the judgement of a single informed spectator is of more value than that of all the uneducated commonality suggests a great deal about the social attitudes implicit here and throughout much of the drama of the period. Lawrence Stone has described the 'harmonization of axes,' the association of moral and intellectual qualities with rank in the early modern period, as a phenomenon which was part of an idealized picture of a 'fully integrated society in which stratification by title, power, wealth, talent, and culture are all in absolute harmony' (1965, 36). The repeated (though not consistently accepted) connection between superior understanding and superior rank in the period, is relevant to the idea of the 'judicious' spectator. It is true, as Gurr has pointed out, that the plays which survive in written form cannot give a full and accurate picture of the totality of the contemporary theatrical output (1996, 26–7). This might result in a distorted picture of dramatic representations of gentility. However, the clearly popular plays that are extant do little or nothing to challenge the implicit values present in the broad range of the extant dramatic material (see Ch 7 below).

The social dimension in contemporary references to audiences is invariably made very clear. This is perhaps the consequence of the coming together in close proximity of large numbers of people of different ranks – perhaps the only place in early modern society outside churches where this was the case. It is interesting to note the frequency with which the lower ranks are referred to as 'stinkards', their physical presence thus emphasized in the most negative of ways. Apart from the question of sheer proximity of different ranks in the playhouse, a source of disquiet in a society of such defined hierarchies may also have been the participation of a wide social spectrum in a common cultural event on an apparently equal basis. From the perspective of the playwright, Dekker, in *The Gull's Horn Book*, complains of the theatre:

> the place is so free in entertainment, allowing a stoole as well to the farmers sonne as to your Templer: that your Stinkard has the selfe same libertie to be there in his Tobacco-fumes, which your sweet Courtier hath: and that your Car-man and Tinker claime as strong a voice in the suffrage, and sit to giue iudgement on the plaies life and death, as well as the prowdest *Momus* among the tribe of *Critick*.
> (28)

In this situation it was perhaps necessary from an elite perspective to emphasize the difference in the nature of the experience of consuming theatre to different ranks, and the matter of social rank is almost never absent from observations about what audiences appreciate and respond to in the commercial theatre.[3] Though there was a social mix within the public playhouses, the seating arrangements themselves reflected the distinctions within the society very effectively, so that the theatre in its physical arrangement of audience space became a physical metaphor of social hierarchy.[4] References to the wide-ranging tastes in the socially diverse audiences of the public playhouse are invariably tied to issue of social rank. In a remark appreciating the exclusivity of his elite Court audience by comparison with the diversity found elsewhere, Jonson observes in *The Masque of Queens* that: 'a *Writer* should always trust somewhat to the capacity of the *Spectator*, especially at these *Spectacles*; Where Men, beside inquiring eyes, are vnderstood to bring quick eares, and not those sluggish ones of Porters, and Mechanicks, that must be bor'd through, at euery act, wth narrations' (105–10).

The assumption of the divergence of tastes according to rank is apparently so widespread (or at least so much an accepted formula) that Jonson is able to turn it round in an ironical way in his satirical portrait of Marston (here Antony Balladino) in *The Case is Altered* (1597):

> *Antony Balladino*: Why looke you sir, I write so plaine, and keepe that old *Decorum*, that you must of necessitie like it; mary, you shall haue some now (as for example, in plaies) that will haue euery day new trickes, and write you nothing but humours: indeede this pleases the Gentlemen: but the common sort they care not for't, they know not what to make on't, they looke for good matter, they, and are not edified with such toyes.
> (1.1.58–65)

Even in the private playhouse described in Richard Lovelace's epilogue to his lost play *The Scholars*, published in 1649, there is a notion of contrasting audiences in different parts of the theatre:

> His *Schollars* school'd, sayd if he had been wise
> He should have wove in one two Comedies;
> The first for th'Gallery, in which the Throne
> To their amazement should descend alone,
> The rosin-lightning flash and Monster spire
> Squibs, and words hotter then his fire.
> Th'other for the Gentlemen oth' Pit
> Like to themselves, all Spirit, Fancy, Wit.
> (*Poems*, 59–60)[5]

There was obviously an element of formal flattery directed at the elite in the various statements made in prologues, epilogues and other instances where audience are addressed or referred to in plays. However, it is repeated with sufficient frequency as to be almost a commonplace.[6]

This flattery, alongside the willingness to insult non-gentle members of the audience, implies an acute awareness on the part of playwrights of who constituted their regular (and therefore target) audience, particularly in the private playhouses. It is unlikely that the disparaging comments made about the lower ranked members of the audience would have been forthcoming if they had been perceived as more than occasional visitors to the theatre. When considering the early modern audience as a factor determining the social values and perceptions present in the drama, it is arguable that the playwrights' perceptions about who they were writing for is of overriding importance. The references to differences in the responses and tastes of sections of the audience is also fairly routinely related to education and understanding. Andrew Gurr has suggested that: 'There is rather more evidence for divisions between audiences in their social and cultural character than in their learning or intellect' (1988, 102). However, the two are so frequently connected that it is difficult to make a clear distinction between them. An instance of the association of social elevation with intellectual superiority is made in the prologue to the Court performance of Jonson's *The Staple of News* (thus, admittedly, involving a strong element of conventional flattery):

> Wee bring; and hope it may produce delight:
> The rather, being offered, as a *Rite*,
> To *Schollers*, that can iudge, and faire report
> The sense they heare, aboue the vulgar sort
> Of Nut-crackers, that onely come for sight.
> (5–8)

This was a play produced for the Blackfriars stage, but there is a clear sense here of a particular group – courtiers – for whom it is most appropriate. However, though the prologue written for the commercial stage makes no such distinctions, the play is the same product when performed on that stage and it remains primarily a 'rite to schollers'. As ever, the implicit social distinctions are cast in terms of educated taste and 'wit'. What is involved here is the notion of a target or primary audience, to which the drama is essentially addressed, whose values and cultural experiences it validates and whose world-view (or view of itself) it articulates even while incorporating conflict and dissension. This notion does not necessarily refuse the presence of a non-target or secondary audience. The secondary audience may suffer little or no tangible exclusion from the material circumstances and spaces of representation, and their presence may even be necessary to the economic viability of plays as commodities in the marketplace. However, the values and preoccupations of the secondary audience become at best subsidiary, or are represented in terms of contrast, 'otherness' or some other specific dramatic purpose.[7]

The association between a lack of understanding and 'stinkards' (who are always the lower orders) becomes commonplace, as in the 'dull Audience of Stinkards sitting in the Penny Galleries of a Theater, and yawning upon the Players' referred to in Middleton's *Father Hubburd's Tales* of 1604 (B4^r). Several years later, in 1632, Jonson made a similar association with those 'mechanicals' whose physical work has hardened their hands, in his Blackfriars play *The Magnetic Lady*:

> *Damplay*: Who should teach us the right at a *Play*?
> *Boy*: If your own science cannot doe it, or the love of Modesty and Truth; all other intreaties, or attempts – are vaine. You are fitter *Spectators* for the *Beares*, then us, or the Puppets. This is a popular ignorance indeed, somewhat better appareld in you, then the People; but a hard-handed, and stiffe ignorance, worthy a Trewel, or hammer-man; and not onely fit to be scorn'd, but they be triumph'd ore.
> (Chorus after act 2, 68–76)

In the deep contempt which is to be found in the comments on the less educated elements of the audience, it is difficult not to discern a sense of resentment on the part of playwrights at having to cater to such people. This is directly stated in Beaumont's verses on Fletcher's 1608 Blackfriars play, *The Faithful Shepherdess*:

> Why should the man, whose wit nere had a staine,
> Vpon the publike stage present his vaine,
> And make a thousand men in iudgement sit,
> To call in question his vndoubted wit,
> Scarce two of which can vnderstand the lawes
> Which they should iudge by, nor the parties cause
> (11–16)

In the trenchantly cynical prologue to Dekker's *If It be Not Good the Devil is In It* (1612) a connection between low social status and poverty of aesthetic judgement is made in a way which makes reference to all the dimensions of the playwright's problem in having to cater for a broad audience for financial reasons, while his art requires an address to more educated tastes. Understanding is, by strong implication, a function of elite status here:

> A play whose *Rudenes*, *Indians* would abhorre,
> Ift fill a house with Fishwiues, *Rare*, *They all Roare*.
> It is not Praise is sought for (Now) but *Pence*,
> Tho dropd, from Greasie-apron *Audience*.
> Clapd may he bee with *Thunder*, that plucks *Bayes*,

With such *Foule Hands*, & with *Squint–Eyes* does gaze
On *Pallas Shield*; not caring (so hee *Gaines*,
A Cramd *Third-Day*, what *Filth* drops fro[m] his *Braines*.
Let *Those* that loue *Pans pipe*, daunce still to *Pan*,
They shall but get *long Eares* by it: Giue me *That Man*,
Who when the *Plague* of an Impostumd *Braynes*
(*Breaking* out) infects a *Theater*, and hotly raignes,
Killing the *Hearers* hearts, that the vast roomes
Stand empty, like so many Dead-mens toombes,
Can call the *Banishd* Auditor home, And tye
His Eare with *Adamantine Pen*, (euen creatures
Forg'de out of th'*Hammer*, on tiptoe, to *Reach* vp
And (from *Rare silence*) clap their *Brawny hands*,
T'*Applaud*, what their *charmd* soule scarce vnderstands.

Of course it was highly possible that the playwrights had some cause to make
these distinctions between the behaviour of the artisan class and other non-
gentle members of their audiences, and that of the more refined sectors.
However, the vehemence of their observations and the regularity with which
they are made suggest the likelihood that other factors were also operating, that
had much more to do with the ambiguities of their own position in the social
hierarchy. The emphasis on lower class ignorance – such as Webster's
reference to the public theatre audience as 'ignorant asses' – is more than
simply a concern about possible incomprehension of the refinements of the
plays on offer.[8] It is to do with the unnatural situation of men – even the
humblest of writers – whose education and profession gave them some claim
(or at least aspiration) to gentle status, having to cater to sections of their
clientele perceived as socially beneath them. There is also something obviously
strategic in the playwrights' presenting what they see as an appropriate
understanding of the complexities and artistic qualities of their work, as
essentially something that defines the socially superior elements in the
audience. Foregrounding learning and aesthetic judgement as the *sine qua non*
of gentle status by implication assures the right of the playwrights themselves –
as masters of the cultural medium and the educational accomplishment
required for its production – to a claim on esteem as members of the cultural
elite. The position of the playwright can be compared to that of the pedant in
Bourdieu's analysis:

> The fact remains that the 'pedant's' situation is never entirely
> comfortable. Against the 'populace' and with *mondain* aristocracy – who
> have every reason also to accept it, since they have an interest in
> birthrights – he is inclined to accept the ideology of innate tastes, since it
> is the only absolute guarantee of his election; but against the *mondain* he

is forced to assert the value of his acquirements, and, indeed, the value of the work of acquisition.
(1984, 74)

However, the existence of some (though fewer) satiric comments and representations on the ill-informed consumption of drama and behaviour at the theatre by certain members of the elite, appears to challenge the neat formulation which paired social status with levels of judgement. In *The First Part of the Return from Parnassus,* the foolish gallant, Gullio, has sufficient social status to use this as a pretext to refuse to fight a duel with the scholar, Ingenioso, saying: 'Fare well base peasante, and thanke god thy fathers were noe gentlemen, els thou shouldest not liue an howre longer. Base, base, base, peasant, peasant' (1450–52). Yet the picture painted of him in the play does not suggest someone capable of sophisticated aesthetic judgements. The behaviour of gallants – who are socially privileged young men – in the theatre is often the subject of satiric comment, as in the portrait of the stage-struck gallant in Marston's *Scourge of Villainy,* Satire 10, or the description of the gallant on the stage in Dekker's *Gull's Horn Book.*[9] In *The Case is Altered* (Act 2, Scene 7) Jonson has a character describe '*Caprichious* gallants' who 'haue taken such a habit of dislike in all things, that they will approue nothing, be it neuer so conceited or elaborate, but sit disperst, making faces, and spitting, wagging their vpright eares, and cry filthy, filthy.' Other comments which Jonson lets slip also indicate his view that the wealth and social status of audience members does not necessarily translate into educated ears in the theatre. In *Discoveries* (1641) he says:

> *Indeed,* the multitude commend Writers, as they doe Fencers, or Wrastlers; who if they come in robustiously, and put for it, with a deale of violence, are received for the *braver-fellowes*: when many times their own rudenesse is a cause of their disgrace; and a slight touch of their Adversary, gives all that boisterous force the foyle. but in these things, the unskilfull are naturally deceiv'd, and judging wholly by the bulke, thinke rude things greater then polish'd; and scatter'd more numerous, then compos'd: Nor thinke this only to be true in the sordid multitude, but the neater sort of our *Gallants*; for all are the multitude; only they differ in cloaths, not in judgement or understanding.
> (634–46)

In the induction to *The Magnetic Lady,* the two gentlemen Probee and Damplay solicit a play for a socially superior clientele:

> *Probee*: ... Not the *Faeces*, or grounds of your people, that sit in the oblique caves and wedges of your house, your sinfull six-penny Mechanics –

Damplay: But the better, and braver sort of your people! Plush and Velvet-outsides! that stick around your house like so many eminences.

The boy replies, 'Of clothes, not understandings?' (31–7) [10]

These observations suggest that the association of gentility with an educated response to the theatre has more to do with being a convenient strategic formulation than anything else. Approval of plays can be construed as a consequence of the proper understanding both of what the writers were seeking to communicate, and of the rules of the medium. But the matter goes beyond eliciting audience approval and the desire for professional success, and has a more profound social dimension. Ideally, this understanding should be natural to the gentle, but alien to the uncomprehending commonality.[11] If playwrights find that economic necessity forces them to write also to entertain those whom they deem to be their social inferiors, their situation is made even more unsatisfactory by negative responses on the part of those members of the audience who belong to the social group with whom the playwrights are seeking to associate themselves. Further in the same play, Probee goes on to remark:

> It is the solemne vice of interpretation, that deformes the figure of many a faire *Scene*, be drawing it awry; and indeed is the civill murder of most good *Playes*: If I see a thing vively presented on the *Stage*, that the Glasse of custome (which is *Comedy*) is so held up to me, by the Poet, as I can therein view the daily examples of mens lives, and images of Truth, in their manners, so drawne for my delight, or profit, as I may (either way) use them: and will I, rather (then make that true use) hunt out the *Persons* to defame, by my malice of misapplying? and imperill the innocence, and candor of the *Author*, by his calumnie? It is an unjust becomming a *Gentleman* to appeare malignantly witty in anothers *Worke*.
> (Chorus after Act 2, 34–47)

By implication, in this view, gallants who damn plays and thus show (in the eyes of the playwrights) a lack of proper comprehension of the laws and aesthetics of the form, signally fail to carry the same currency on which the playwrights base their own claims to social esteem and position: intellectual superiority and refinement of aesthetic response. Through this rather circular argument, they are placed in the same category as the commonality to whom playwrights are also forced to cater. Richard Brome, in the prologue to his play, *The Novella* (acted at the Blackfriars in 1632) says: 'Hee'll 'bide his triall, and submits his cause / To you, the Jury, so you'l judge by Lawes. / If Pride or Ignorance should rule, he feares / An unfaire tryall, 'cause not try'd by's Peeres' (H5ʳ). The resentment expressed is the same as that which informs the comment by Ingenioso in the *Second Return from Parnassus*: 'Pity it is that gentler witts should breed / Where thick-skin chuffes laugh at a schollers neede' (225–6). Commenting on the complex status relationship between artists and the public who consume their work, Kenneth Burke remarks:

> Thus, as regards monetary tests, the artist who relies upon smartness as a mark of 'urbanity' may be 'socially inferior' to the 'ideal public' he is courting. Yet he is 'professionally superior,' and courts as an 'ideal public' many persons whom he would unquestionably despise in the particular. Yet again, as soon as you thus set him up, you must recall (as with the Arabian Nights relation) that the artist-entertainer is the servant of the very despot-audience he seeks to fascinate (as the spellbinder can tyrannize over his audience only by letting the audience tyrannize over him, in rigidly circumscribing the range and nature of his remarks).
> (1962, 809–10)

The playwrights often go further than a passive criticism of audiences in their response to plays. The implication that the true quality of gentility resides precisely in the ability to make the 'right' sort of aesthetic judgements is a logical extension of the perceptions that fine clothing and wealth do not in themselves ensure gentility. Dekker's ironical advice to an aspirant courtier in *The Gull's Horn Book* suggests a hierarchy of imitation in the reception of plays:

> It shall crowne you with rich commendation to laugh alowd in the middest of the most serious and saddest scene of the terriblest Tragedy: and to let that clapper (your tongue) be tost so high that all the house may ring of it: your Lords vse it; your Knights are Apes to the Lords, and do so too: your Inne-a-court-man is Zany to the Knights, and (many very scuruily) comes likewise limping after it: bee thou a beagle to them all, and neuer lin snuffing till you haue sented them: for by talking and laughing (like a Plough-man in a Morris) you may heape *Pelion* vpon *Ossa*, glory vpon glory.
> (30)[12]

Dekker goes on to say (with a clear ironical edge) that bad behaviour in the playhouse is a way in which the new courtier might indicate his idle gentlemanly status, since it suggests that he does not devour the play hungrily, because he is an *habitué* of the theatre. The disjunction between the appearance of gentility striven for, and the truly educated response which should characterize it, is attacked by Jonson in the induction to *Cynthia's Revels* (1600):

> As some one ciuet-wit among you, that knowes no other learning, then the price of satten and vellets; nor other perfection, then the wearing of a neat sute; and yet will censure as desperately as the most profess'd

critique in the house: presume, his clothes should beare him out in't. Another (whom it hath pleas'd nature to furnish with more beard then braine) prunes his mustaccio, lisps, and (with some score of affected othes) sweares downe all that sit about him; *That the old Hieronimo*, (as it was first acted) *was the onely best, and iudiciously pend play of Europe*. A third great-bellied juggler talkes of twentie yeeres since, and when MONSIEUR was heere, and would enforce all wits to bee of that fashion, because his doublet is still so. A fourth miscals all by the name of fustian, that his grounded capacitie cannot aspire to. A fift, only shakes his bottle–head, and out of his corkie braine, squeezeth out a pitiful-learned face, and is silent.
(ll. 201–17)

Though the quality of judgements of the drama on the part of the more well-heeled members of the audiences is at issue in these satirical portraits, what is perhaps most significant is the fact of the use of the consumption of theatre as a cultural form as a means of judging the 'authenticity' of elite identity. This is, of course, presented entirely from the partial and self-interested perspective of the playwrights themselves, but must have been based on some observation of social behaviour. However, though theatre is here being used to promote its own status as a cultural form, the fact that it constituted a public forum, with an inevitable input into the process of social opinion making, gives some weight to the position being advanced.

As they possessed an ideal combination of assured social status and education, the Inns of Court men are likely to have been foremost among those spectators deemed 'judicious' by the playwrights. Their impact would have been increased both by the fact of their being members, in effect, of a cultural and educational community of considerable importance, and principally by their reputation as having a strong penchant for theatre. Even after the main period of dramatic activity in the Inns of Court, their members continued to be major consumers and patrons of the arts, and playgoing was high among their favourite occupations (Prest, 1972, 157–9).[13] Remarks on the Innsmen's predelictions for the theatre occur throughout the period. In his *Pierce Penniless* of 1592, Thomas Nashe identifies the idle men-about-town who have the leisure to give themselves over to pleasures including the theatre as 'Gentlemen of the Court, the Innes of the Courte, and the number of Captaines and Souldiours about *London*' (McKerrow, 1904, I, 212). Another contemporary commentator John Earle, in his *Microcosmography* of 1629 remarked of the actor that: 'Your Innes of Court men were undone but for him, hee is their chiefe guest and imployment, and the sole business that makes them Afternoones men' (H3[r]). Francis Lenton's satirical poem, *The Young Gallant's Whirligig* published in the same year, furnishes a portrait of an Innsman and says:

Your Theaters he daily doth frequent
(Except the intermitted time of Lent)
Treasuring vp within his memory
The amorous toyes of euery Comedy
With deep delight.
(7)

He goes on to suggest their presence in both private and public theatres, according to their means. On succeeding to his father's fortune, his Innsman moves upmarket, but his habits of conspicuous consumption (tied up closely with theatre visiting) leads to his ruin:

The Cockpit heretofore would serue his wit,
But now vpon the Fryers stage hee'll sit,
It must be so, though this expensiue foole
Should pay an angell for a paltry stool
(13)

. . .

His silken garments, and his sattin robe
That hath so often visited the Globe,
And all his spangled rare perfum'd attires,
Which once so glistred in the Torchy Fryers,
Must to the Broakers to compound his debt,
Or else be pawned to procure him meate.
(16)

That the public drama even went so far as to play a part in the social apprenticeship of the men of the Inns of Court is an idea satirically mentioned in Thomas Nabbes's commercial theatre play *Tottenham Court* (c. 1634) in which a young Innsman says: 'Hang Cases and Bookes that are spoil'd with them: Give me *Johnson* and *Shakespear*; there's Learning for a Gentleman. I tell thee *Sam*, were it not for the Dancing-School and Play-Houses, I would not stay in the Inns of Court for the hopes of a chiefe Justice-ship' (3.1.B 4^r/p. 31). In the case of Francis Lenton's reprobate Innsman this also extends to playtexts: 'Instead of *Perkins* pedlers French, he sayes / He better loues *Ben: Iohnsons* booke of Playes, / But that therein of wit he findes such plenty, / That he scarce vnderstands a Iest of twenty' (4). In an anecdote entitled *A Poeticall Revenge*, found in a seventeenth-century commonplace book, a young scholar is scorned because of his threadbare coat by a gallant from the Inns of Court, a playgoer 'rauish'd with a Cocke-pit play'. The scholar curses him, and wishes that the gallant's father might catch him in study 'at Shakespeare's Plays instead of the Ld Cooke' (Osborn, 1937, 228). The sophistication of the Innsmen's attitudes to the theatre may even be what is being alluded to in a comment in Shirley's 1632 play, *The Ball*, in which a character called Freshwater who is comparing the French theatre with the English, remarks: 'But there are no comedies as we have here; yet the women are the best actors, they play their own parts, a thing much desired in England by some ladies, inns o' court gentlemen, and others' (5.1.p. 79).

Although primarily law schools, the Inns provided a broadly based humanist education and considerable emphasis was laid on courtly accomplishment. There is some evidence that attendance at the annual revels was compulsory as a necessary part of their education. Students had considerable leisure time too, in which they were expected to pursue a liberal education. Thus, as well as providing professional training, the Inns of Court functioned as a finishing school for acquisition of social skills and accomplishments. Sir John Fortescue had, in the fifteenth century, observed:

> In these greater inns, indeed, and also in the lesser, there is, besides a school of law, a kind of academy of all the manners that the nobles learn. There they learn to sing and to exercise themselves in every kind of harmonics. They are also taught there to practise dancing and all games proper for nobles, as those brought up in the king's household are accustomed to practise. In the vacations most of them apply themselves to the study of legal science, and at festivals to the reading, after the divine services, of Holy Scripture and of chronicles.
> (Chrimes, 1942, 119)

The residential arrangements of the Inns were collegiate, members living and dining together, something that encouraged and resulted in strong bonds of friendship between Innsmen (Parmiter, 1976, 7, Conley, 1927, 23–33). The impact of the Inns on the drama of London would have been enhanced by the fact of this residential dimension, so that Innsmen were not just individual theatre-goers, but formed part of a relatively close-knit community and were perceived as such.[14] In the self-deprecating preface to his translation of *Thyestes* in 1560, John Heywood mentions several writers at the Inns and stresses that they form a community of writers:

> But if thy will be rather bent
> a yong mans witt to proue,
> And thinkst that elder lerned men
> perhaps it shall behoue
> In woorke of waight to spend theyr tyme,
> goe where Mineruaes men,
> And finest witts doe swarme: whome she
> hath taught to passe with pen.
> In Lyncolnes Inne and Temples twayne,
> Grayes Inne and other mo,
> Thou shalt them fynde whose paynfull pen

thy verse shal florishe so,
That Melpomen thou wouldst well weene
had taught them for to wright,
And all their woorks with stately style
and goodly grace t'endight.
(7^{r-v})

The combination of cohesion and privilege was to give the Inns a central position in not only the political life of the realm but also in the cultural activity of the capital and the nation, and they can be regarded as providing an interesting nexus in English political, social and cultural life in the period. A combination of factors contributed to favour them uniquely in this respect. They brought together a body of privileged young men, the overwhelming majority of whom had already been through the universities. While the structure of the Inns bore some comparison with the collegiate organization of the universities, they were different in lacking endowments for the maintenance of poor scholars, which tended to reinforce their exclusivity and elitism (Charlton, 1965, 171–2). As the Inns were concerned with the law, a discipline seen as most essential for government and administration, they were brought close to the sources of power in the state and this was reinforced in Elizabeth's reign by the patronage of Lord Burghley. Another notable factor in the dominant position of the Inns was their geographical location: being in the capital was becoming an increasingly important advantage in a period in which English cultural and economic life was being centralized there to an ever greater degree.

This community had strong links with theatre-making at various levels and in a number of ways. Throughout the period works from the public stage were presented at the Inns of Court, ranging from *The Yorkshire Tragedy* (c.1605) to the plays of Shakespeare and Caroline drama. Several members of the Inns wrote for the public stage during the same period, including Ford, Middleton, Lodge, Beaumont, Marston, Shirley and possibly Webster.[15] George Ferrers of Lincoln's Inn and William Baldwin of the Middle Temple were providers of entertainment at the Court of Edward VI, and Richard Edwardes of Lincoln's Inn wrote *Damon and Pithias* for the Children of the Chapel Royal. Early in the sixteenth century John Rastell of the Middle Temple became the first publisher of drama.

An interest in the theatre was naturally encouraged by the activities and cultural orientation of the institutions in which they found themselves. The Inns revels played a role in the fostering of community cohesion similar to other comparable communal quasi-theatrical proceedings in analogous social contexts, both academic and otherwise.[16] Gerard Legh in his *Accedens of Armory* gives a fuller description of the same revels and in this the ceremonies are described in a very solemn light (1562, Dd5^{r}–Ee3^{r}/212^{r}/218^{r}). The

Christmas revels were the most important of the annual celebrations, and they usually lasted about a month from the middle of December to the middle of January. It is not certain whether these were held each year, but they do seem to have taken a similar form in all four Inns and to have remained similar in format over the years. They consisted of a number of ceremonies and feasts, masques, processions, plays and dances. A 'prince' was elected on each occasion, who held rule for the duration of the revels, called in Grays Inn the Prince of Purpoole, in Lincoln's Inn the Prince de la Grange, in the Inner Temple the Prince of Sophie, and in the Middle Temple the Prince d'Amour. This obviously recalls the practice of electing a lord of misrule or *rex fabarum*; in the early sixteenth century in Lincoln's Inn, the Christmas Prince was called the King of Cocknies and he had a foil, or anti-king called Jack Straw, a practice which seems to have been forbidden from 1519.[17]

It is worth examining at this point in some detail an example of the revels of one of the Inns, the *Gesta Grayorum* of 1594 a description of which is fortunately extant.[18] In presenting a theatricalization of the community life of the Inns, the revels yield a useful insight into the preoccupations of the Innsmen, the ways in which they conceived of themselves, and the role of theatre in the community culture. However, in the particular manner in which they reconstitute the identity of the Inns communities in terms of state power, the revels suggest comparisons particularly with Royal Entries and court masques. The *Gesta* start with the enthronement of the Prince of the state of 'Graya', the reception of an 'ambassador' from the Temple (called the neighbouring state of Templaria – other Inns are given names like Bernardia and Stapulia, being Barnard's Inn and Staple's Inn respectively), the appointment of court officers, the issue of a general pardon (for all the misdemeanours committed against the 'Prince'), the list of exceptions to which constitute a promulgation of the laws of the 'state'. This is followed by the trial and imprisonment of a 'criminal' for witchcraft and causing disorder, the conferring of knighthoods, a procession of the 'Prince' to dine with the Lord Mayor, another barge procession of the 'Prince' from Greenwich, supposedly returning from a journey to Russia, a play and two masques.

Though misrule elements are present, the highly ceremonial nature of the proceedings tends to emphasize order rather than disorder. The proceedings of the constituted 'state' of Graya blend with the normal ceremonial of the Inn, which includes the designation of ranks, oration, declamation and debate, ceremonial feasting, and dancing. In reconstructing the institution theatrically in terms of a fictional state the *Gesta* succeed in affirming its autonomy, order, and ultimate authority, as well as defining the Inn's relations with the other Inns and with the Court. During these revels, not only is the ambassador from Templaria a guest, but at one point so is the Queen herself.

Fig. 3: The Hall at Gray's Inn
By permission of The Honourable Society of Gray's Inn

Perhaps an even more important function of the revels is in the training of the members for offices of state. There is evidence that participation in the revels was regarded as an integral part of legal training. The writers of Henry VIII's Royal Commission report on the Inns of Court (produced between 1534 and 1547), Nicholas Bacon, Thomas Denton and Robert Carey considered that the social training students acquired at the Inns equipped them for state service such as the diplomatic, and they pointed specifically to the revels:

> The Readers and Benchers at a Parliament or Pension held before *Christmas*, if it seeme unto them that there be no dangerous time of sickness, neither dearth of victuals, and that they are furnished of such a Company, as bothe for their number and appertaines are meet to keep a solemn *Christmas*, then doe they appoint and chose certain of the house to be Officers, and bear certain rules in the house during the said time, which Officers for the most part are such, as are in the King's Highness house, and other Noble men, and this done onely to the intent, that they should in time come to know how to use themselves. In this *Christmas* time, they have all manner of pastimes, as singing and dancing; and in some of the houses ordinarily they have some interlude or Tragedy played by the Gentlemen of the same house, the ground, and manner whereof, is devised by some of the Gentlemen of the house.
>
> (Bland, 1969, 188)

However, the revels are not all as solemn as this might imply. Besides the elements of physical disorder which are present during the period, much of the ceremony and many of the processes and speeches are parodic. The reading of the law is a comic parody of legal language especially in its absurdly detailed qualifications. The investiture of the 'knights' is also done in a mock-solemn way, as is the trial for witchcraft. However, almost always present is the display of accomplishment. This is true of the comic speeches and ceremonies, but particularly so in the exercise of rhetoric in the speeches of six counsellors to the Prince on various issues of government and state, speeches that in the *Gesta* were all written by Francis Bacon. The same is true of the masque held before the Queen towards the end of the revels. The display of self is very much in keeping with an institution of which the *raison d'être* is the inculcation of public skills of rhetoric and disputation, and it is easy to see the contribution which dramatic activity made to this. A testimony to the striving for rhetorical expertise by the Innsmen is an instructive manual, *Directions for Speech and Style* written between 1598 and 1603 by John Hoskyns, a member of the Middle Temple (in Osborne, 1937, 103–66). Hoskyns wrote a speech for the *Prince D'Amour* Christmas Revels of 1597–8, ridiculing aureate language ('Tuftaffeta Speech', Osborne, 1937, 98–102).

Another notable feature of the revels is the repeated collapse of the barriers between reality and representation. This is perhaps already apparent from the account so far, and it is clearly consistent with a form of dramatic fictionalization which is so reflexive and self-conscious. However, it is notable that the relationship between reality and representation is constantly being redefined in various ways. The parodic issue of laws, for example – which is largely a series of sexual jokes and double entendres – finishes with a reference to participation in the revels itself, both drawing attention to the fictiveness of the declaration and referring to genuine rules about attendance at revels. A mock-solemn exclusion from the pardon is made for those students who have absented themselves: 'All Fugitives, Failers and Flinchers that, with Shame and Discredit are fled and vanished out of the Prince's Dominions of Purpoole, and especially from his court at Graya, this time of Christmas, to withdraw themselves from His Honour's Service and Attendance, contrary to their Duty and Allegiance' (p. 27, 19–24). A further instance is a disturbance which leads to the abandonment of the entertainments on one of the Grand Nights and the Templarian ambassador's departure. This is followed subsequently by the 'trial' of a criminal accused of causing the disturbance by witchcraft. However, it is probable that the disorder was staged as part of the misrule, because after order had eventually been restored, Shakespeare's *Comedy of Errors* was staged and the evening was subsequently called the 'Night of Errors'. The rift with the ambassador also gave rise to a subsequent masque of amity to restore relations. Other manifestations of the confusion between representation and reality include the public progress to the Lord Mayor's house, when the people in the streets are reported to have thought that a great prince 'in very deed' was passing (p. 57, 23–9).[19] This blurring of the distinction between fiction and reality draws attention to the degree to which public and social life involved forms of theatrical self-display, and gives some indication that the training of men for public life inculcated an awareness of this.

Despite their sometimes riotous character, the *Gesta Grayorum* are thus based on some very sophisticated dramatic principles. Though the Inns of Court can thus be considered to have provided a training which, as an important (albeit unintended) by–product, developed a capacity in its students for a highly cultivated and informed understanding of theatre, it is possible to cite this only as a circumstantial factor in a discussion of the early modern audience. It arguably helped to make the Innsmen the most theatrically literate single sector of the London audience in the early modern period capable, for instance, of a ready apprehension of not only complex rhetoric but sophisticated theatrical principles such as reflexivity. They fulfilled the ideal of combining social ascendancy with a 'judicious' appreciation of the theatre, as such encouraging the prediliction of playwrights to make distinctions between an educated response associated with a social elite, and the supposition of a demand for crude 'shows' on the part of the rest.[20] In the induction to Jonson's *Every Man out of His Humour* (1598), the character Asper says of the few 'attentiue auditors' who 'come to feed their vnderstanding parts' that he will write for them:

> For these, Ile prodigally spend my selfe,
> Coine new conceits, and hang my richest words,
> And speake away my spirit into ayre;
> For these, Ile melt my braine into inuention,
> As polisht jewels in their bounteous eares.
> (204–8)

Jonson had great respect for the Inns and the following year he dedicated *Every Man out of his Humour* to them, describing them as 'robust nurseries of humanity and liberty'. He was also on terms of friendship with some Innsmen.[21] In 1638, Thomas Nabbes dedicated his play *The Bride* to the gentlemen of the Inns of Court too.

The importance of the Innsmen as audience members is hard to quantify in terms of numbers, since it is impossible to know what proportion of the private theatre audiences they composed, and to what extent they ventured to the public theatre. As a group they were numerically limited in terms of the general population.[22] However, the importance of their impact is related to the general weight of the elite sectors of the audience, of which (at least by reputation) they were a significant component. Anne Jennalie Cook has argued that the elite were much more dominant a sector of the audience than was supposed by Harbage and other commentators on the early modern audience (1981).[23] It is true that the private theatres accommodated hundreds rather than the thousands in the public theatres, and the elite would always have composed a small minority of the public theatre audiences. However, it is logical to assume that the relative regularity of their attendance – quite aside from their higher entry payments – would have made them a force which was disproportionately strong in terms of influence.[24] Plays were generally put on in the afternoon and if Innsmen could, in Earle's words, be 'afternoones men' this scheduling meant that most working people were unable to attend on a regular basis. Conversely, the presence of apprentices which is often commented upon in the period (and is perhaps a factor in emphasizing the popular dimension or the social diversity of the early modern audience) might not have been as influential as their numbers in the playhouse at any one time may suggest. Thomas Nashe in *Pierce Penniless* rebuts the notion that the plays routinely draw apprentices from their work:

> Whereas some Pettioners of the Counsaile against them obiect, they corrupt the youth of the Cittie, and withdrawe Prentises from theyr

worke; they heartily wishe they might bee troubled with none of their
youthe nor their prentises; for some of them (I meane the ruder
handicraftes seruants) neuer come abroade, but they are in danger of
vndoing.
(McKerrow, 1904, I, 213–14).

Contemporary perceptions by playwrights about 'judicious' spectators may
not have had a great impact on the nature of the theatrical fare, which would
logically have been governed far more by commercial considerations.
However, the combination of intellectual sophistication and social privilege
represented by the Innsmen would have helped to emphasize and reinforce
social distinctions as a matter, not just of material privilege, but of essential
quality. As such it would have stood against any potential that might have
emerged in the drama to challenge the values of deference and hierarchy in the
society which it served. It can, and has been argued, that the advent of the
commercial stage in the last quarter of the century altered the circumstances of
consumption of the theatre in a way that facilitated the emergence of a popular
theatre. This is by virtue of the fact that the drama on the public stage was
produced for open and universal consumption and made available to all who
could pay. However, it is not simply a matter of the straightforward production
and sale of a commodity. Paul Sweezy has argued for an intermediate period
after the fall of feudalism and before the emergence of fully-fledged capitalism,
of what he has termed 'pre-capitalist commodity production' (1978, 49). In its
continued – if largely symbolic – attachment to elite patronage arrangements,
and its awareness of a 'superior' sector of its clientele, the commercial drama
of the late sixteenth century might be seen in these terms. Though certainly
available to a broad range of the population, the theatre can nevertheless be
argued to have operated in ways which reflected the strongly socially
hierarchical society. Jean-Christophe Agnew has observed of the public theatre
that: 'From its pit to its heavenly canopy, the design of the London playhouse
reproduced the *structure* of rank to which men, in Hobbes's view, had freely
submitted themselves' (1986, 102).
      Society (as represented in the playhouse audiences) did not have a
specific and unified perspective, and so it was possible for the elite segment of
that audience to continue to have a strongly influential presence as a focus of
address, either as private theatre audiences, or as those components of
audiences of the public theatres perceived to be the more regular and valued
clientele. Andrew Gurr has pointed out that the playing companies switched
easily between the amphitheatre and the private theatres and the social
distinctions between the two types of theatre were not clearly matched by
distinctions in repertories. When, under Charles, the repertories did begin to
divide socially it coincided with a general upward social movement (1996,

149–51).[25] A reference to one instance of the shift of contexts (and transfer of audience) is Shirley's address to the gentle members of the public playhouse in his prologue to his play, *The Doubtful Heir*, first performed in Dublin, later put on at the Globe (in 1640) but 'which should have been presented at the Black-Friers':

> *Gentlemen*, I am onely sent to say
> Our Author did not calculate his Play,
> For this Meridian; The Bank-side he knowes
> Is far more skilful at the ebbes and flowes
> Of water then of Wit.
> (1646, 154)

He goes on to talk dismissively of the fare that might be considered more appropriate for the Globe and concludes by telling them that the play was 'meant for your persons, not the place'.[26] Given that the bulk of the Globe audience would *not* have been made up of those who were normally attenders of the Blackfriars, it indicates the playwright's willingness to dismiss a substantial swathe of those who had paid to see his play. In a situation in which the drama does not readily divide into discrete repertories serving different social constituencies, the potential impact of a favoured sector of the audience becomes that much greater.

A number of plays from the period represent audiences in the process of attending plays, and yield useful perspectives on playwrights' attitudes to the audience. One of the most interesting to theatre historians is Francis Beaumont's play, *The Knight of the Burning Pestle* of 1607, which was presented at the private Blackfriars theatre by a boys' company. Discussions of this play frequently focus on what it reveals about citizen taste in theatre, or on the reasons for its failure in its reception. However, though the satire on citizen taste is relevant here, what is perhaps more interesting for the present discussion is the attitude it reveals to the relationship between social rank and the right to judgement in the theatre. The social attitudes in *The Knight of the Burning Pestle* are apparent even in the title of the play, with its comically incongruous juxtaposition of the concept of chivalry with a tool of the grocer's trade. The central figures in the play, the grocer and his wife, are represented as fundamentally unsophisticated yet demanding audience members who sit on the stage and interfere with the action. The coarseness and vulgarity of this couple are apparent every time they open their mouths, and Beaumont draws much of the comic effect from the contrast between the dominant position which the grocer and his wife claim (by virtue of their trade-generated wealth) in the elite context of the private Blackfriars theatre in which the play was both presented and set, and their lack of 'natural' qualities of social pre-eminence.

The wife insists on sitting on the stage alongside her husband, despite the fact that it would have been considered somewhat inappropriate behaviour for a woman. She also admits that she is not a regular theatregoer:

> I'm a stranger here; I was ne'er at one of these plays, as they say, before; but I should have seen *Jane Shore* once, and my husband hath promised many time this twelvemonth to carry me to *The Bold Beauchamps*; but in truth he did not. (Induction, 50–53)

The grocer and his wife represent the nightmare (to the established elite) of a thrusting and financially empowered middle class who are able to intrude upon the contexts of cultural activity in which the more abstract qualities that were deemed to inform a superior social identity – knowledge, judgement, taste and understanding – are supposed to operate. Pierre Bourdieu's observation on taste is relevant here:

> Taste is a practical mastery of distributions which makes it possible to sense or intuit what is likely (or unlikely) to befall – and therefore to befit – an individual occupying a given position in social space. It functions as a sort of social orientation, a 'sense of one's place' guiding the occupants of a given social space towards the social position adjusted to their properties, and towards the practices and goods which befit the occupants of that position. It implies a practical anticipation of what the social meaning and value of a chosen practice or thing will probably be, given their distribution in social space and the practical knowledge the other agents have of the correspondence between goods and groups.
> (1984, 466–7)

In the play, the sense of an invasion is palpable and is visually underlined by the seating position of the couple in the theatre. However, the comic thrust of the piece resides in the exposure of the extent to which the couple spectacularly fail to exhibit knowledge, judgement, taste or understanding. Their preference for romance drama and prose narratives was regarded in the period as typical of citizen taste, and they also reveal a familiarity with puppet shows. What would have been considered equally characteristic is their desire for the spectacular – scenes of fighting, a physical freak, and an interest in other visual aspects of theatre such as 'reparel' – as well as their interest in the 'huffing' part they desire for their boy, Rafe. On the other hand, they fail utterly to understand classical references and they manifest a profound lack of understanding of the whole process of dramatic representation.[27] The wife in particular lacks any comprehension of the nature of drama in her interaction with the actors, in which she persistently and comically confuses representation and reality. The incapacity of either the wife or her husband to understand the nature of narrative structure is summarily displayed in his dismissive 'plot me no plots' (2.266). They also ride roughshod over the dramaturgical judgements of the players in insisting on having Rafe take the part of which the Prologue states: 'we never have a boy play him' (Induction, 57). The satire of the grocer and his wife is confined to what their crudity and artlessness in their consumption of theatre reveals about their cultural identities. Otherwise, they are not negative figures and are presented in a fairly engaging light; even their terms of endearment for each other, though somewhat ridiculous, suggest a warmth of affection.[28] The satire is nonetheless an uncompromising picture of cultural deficiency, and its implications for social identity.[29]

The Knight of the Burning Pestle is a useful example of the ways in which the aesthetic / intellectual and the social were intertwined in the representations of the early modern theatre, but also the way in which the reflexivity of the drama is employed to promote the cultural merits of the medium itself. If there is a tendency in the statements by playwrights about audiences to connect refinement of judgement in the theatre with social superiority (at least as an ideal), here a sophisticated understanding of the theatre is by implication given a prominent role in defining what is 'gentle'. The mercantile values displayed by the grocer and his wife in 'purchasing' sequences and changes of direction in the play, or in inserting their boy as a central player, are in direct conflict with the tacit understanding of the aesthetic values involved in being an appropriately sophisticated audience member. In the travesty of their effectively taking over and replacing the playwright, the normal practice of playwriting is by contrast implicitly elevated to a learned art, the violation of which is ascribable to not only intellectual but social barbarism.

The Præludium to another private theatre play, *The Careless Shepherdess* by Thomas Goffe written in the late 1630s – though the play itself dates from 1619 – dramatizes an exchange involving four men who find themselves seated alongside each other in a private theatre, the Salisbury Court. These are a courtier, Spruce, an Inns of Court man, Sparke, a country gentleman, Landlord, and a citizen, Thrift. On his arrival in the theatre, Sparke says to Spruce: 'since 'tis my fortune / To sit neer you: If the Play should prove dull / Your company will satisfie my ears.' When Landlord enters, he begs leave to sit next to them, so that he may judge the play. He is welcomed by Thrift, but Sparke rounds on him:

> Dare you presume to censure Poetry?
> Tis the Prerogative of the wits in Town,
> 'Cause you have read perhaps a Statute–Book,
> And been High-Constable, do y' think you know
> The Laws of Comedy and Tragedy?
> Prethee, what kinde of beast is *Helicon*?
> You may have skill in Horse and Sheep, and yet

Know neither *Pegasus*, nor *Pastorals*.
Alas you're ignorant of any stile
But what stands on a hedge; you never heard
Of more then the four humours of the body;
Nor did you ever understand a Plot
Unlesse that grand one of the *Powder–Treason*.
You've worn perchance a pair of Spatterdashers,
But scarce e're saw a Buskin; and my Nose,
Tells me your feet never yet wear Socks.
(B2^{r-v}/3–4)

He is joined by Spruce who weighs in against Thrift:

And you too would usurp *Apollo's* Chair,
As if th'Exchange did ever breed a wit.
Though you can give words soft and smooth, as is
Your Sattin Ribbon, yet your speech is harsh
To the round language of the Theater.
'Cause you sell *Phansies*, and can cast account,
Do y' think your brain conceives Poetique Numbers?
You cannot tell, if you were ask'd the question,
Whether a *Metaphor* be flesh or fish;
You may perchance have judgement to discerne
What Puppet dances well, or understand
Which Juglers mouth is best at the Bay leafe,
But who deserves the Lawrell wreath, you know
No more, then you do know which Land i' th' field
Bears Barley, and which Wheat, which Rye, which Oats.
(B2^{v}/4)

The countryman and the citizen then go on to justify the prejudices of Spruce and Sparke by revealing a very crude and uninformed response to the theatre. When Thrift suggests that the idleness of theatre may be appropriate to courtiers, but that Innsmen might be diverted from their serious pursuits by it, Sparke vigorously defends their interest in it as an essential part of their recreational culture:

When we are tir'd with reading *Littleton*,
Penning a Scene does more refresh our brain
Then Sack, or *Hide-Park* ayr, Poetry is
The sawce that makes severer meats digest,
And turns rude Barbarism into delight.
(B4^{v}/ 7)

If Beaumont and Goffe were seeking to flatter the elite sections of their audience through a contrast with the ignorance of the non-gentle in matters theatrical, Shakespeare in an earlier play which represents an audience – *A Midsummer Night's Dream* (c. 1595) – effects the same sort of flattery in a slightly less direct way. Though very probably part of wedding celebrations, the play is not so much about romantic love as about the process of theatrical representation itself and its consumption. The way in which it celebrates its elite audience is through its recognition of their *savoir faire* as spectators, and thereby their qualities as an elite group. Certainly, the plot is ostensibly about romantic intrigue and its resolution. However, if understood as straightforwardly a treatment of romantic love, the play presents considerable problems. The use of the potion by Puck to make Titania dote on Bottom turns the emotion of love into something grotesque, and in the case of the four young Athenians, the device is used to create a situation of crossed and thwarted affections and then to resolve it in a way that is both extremely artificially patterned and profoundly self-conscious as a formula. The very notion of a love potion in itself undermines any conception of love as a natural and sacred human emotion. Yet each of these situations is framed with conventional romantic elements. Oberon introduces the trick on Titania with sublime romantic verse: 'I know a bank where the wild thyme blows', and the Athenians fall into their situation as a result of going into the woods for the 'observance of the morn of May'. If *A Midsummer Night's Dream* was written for aristocratic nuptial celebrations, this treatment of romantic love as something arbitrary, swiftly changeable and even whimsical would hardly have been appropriate if the play were to be taken simply as a romantic comedy. Given the assumption of an exclusive and cultivated context for its initial performance, the piece is much more likely to have been presented as a knowing, reflexive and playful exercise in the sophisticated understanding of theatre. What the play foregrounds – and subverts – are the conventions of theatre itself. *A Midsummer Night's Dream* actually makes fun of the formulaic elements of romantic comedy, arguably as part of a process of flattering the capacity of its elite audience fully to comprehend and enjoy its playing around with theatrical convention.

The theatrical self-consciousness of the piece is underlined by the artisans' play-within-a-play. Though this is apparently a small sub-plot strand of narrative, it is introduced early in the play (in Act 1, Scene 2) and comes to fruition at a climactic point near the end, making regular appearances throughout. Far from being a subordinate element, it is central to the play's theatricalist reflexivity and to its handling of the issue of representation and the reception of drama. As in *The Knight of the Burning Pestle*, the comedy in these sequences arises precisely from the artisans' lack of understanding of the process of theatrical representation. And as in that play, this lack of comprehension of the conventions and processes of theatre is something which also helps to define their social identity as low-life figures. The same sort of ignorance of representational convention which informs Quince's assumption that the roaring of Bottom's 'lion' on stage – 'And you should do it too terribly, you would fright the Duchess and her ladies, that they would shriek and that were enough to hang us all' (1.2.70–73) – is illustrated by the fright of the wife in Beaumont's play: 'By the faith o' my body, 'a has put me into such a fright that I tremble, as they say, as 'twere an aspen leaf. Look o' my little finger, George, how it shakes. Now, i'truth, every member of my body is the worse for't' (3.130–34).

The yawning social gulf between the main plot figures and the artisans of the sub-plot is essentially conceived of in terms of intellect and understanding, and it constitutes the major part of the comic force of the play. It is not just the ignorance of the artisans about the making of theatre which is a source of amusement, but the incongruities arising from the juxtaposition of this ignorance with the sophistication of their audience. Even at the most basic level, the contrast in social identities is implicitly presented in terms of differences in educational frames of reference and specifically in the naming of characters in the practice – by now something of a dramatic convention – of assigning classical names and identities to the socially elevated figures and English ones to the low-life figures in the play (and, incidentally, a distinction is also made in these terms between Oberon, Titania and the lower ranked fairies). As has already been discussed, this refers implicitly to the distinction between the classical education that embellished, or was part of the definition of gentility, and the more rudimentary education which was available to those of lower status. The neoclassical world of the play–within–a–play is thus fundamentally unfamiliar cultural territory to the artisans, let alone the skills involved in playmaking. If this is represented here in intellectual / cultural terms, it is nevertheless squarely social in its implications.

The qualities of the noble audience in the play are, by contrast, signalled by their profound familiarity with the principles of theatre and a capacity to bring a refined judgement to bear on the theatrical fare presented to them (in the exercise of which they implicitly represent the audience of *A Midsummer Night's Dream*). Theseus's comment on lovers and poets at the beginning of Act 5, Scene 1 is interesting in this respect and worth quoting. Referring to the story of their forest adventure related by the young Athenians, he remarks:

> More strange than true. I never may believe
> These antique fables, nor these fairy toys.
> Lovers and madmen have such seething brains,
> Such shaping fantasies, that apprehend
> More than cool reason ever comprehends.
> The lunatic, the lover, and the poet,
> Are of imagination all compact.

One sees more devils than vast hell can hold;
That is the madman. The lover, all as frantic,
Sees Helen's beauty in a brow of Egypt.
The poet's eye, in a fine frenzy rolling,
Doth glance from heaven to earth, from earth to heaven;
And as imagination bodies forth
The forms of things unknown, the poet's pen
Turns them to shapes, and gives to airy nothing
A local habitation and a name.
(2–17).

In making a comparison between lovers and poets, he both recognizes the fictiveness of the representation of which he is a part, and prepares for the commentary which he and others will deliver on the artisans' play. What is noteworthy is that a running commentary is kept up throughout the short performance, so that the audience within the play remains a central point of focus. And if there is a distinction between the noble audience and the artisans in respect of a comprehension of the principles of representation, there is even a hierarchy of critical judgement among the nobles. First of all, only the most socially elevated among the women, Hippolita, comments. She, Lysander, and Demetrius are all accorded a critical view, characterized by Hippolita's comment that 'This is the silliest stuff I ever heard', but it is left to Theseus – socially the most senior – to offer the most complex and informed perspective. It is he who is able to stand back and see the process from a detached point of view: 'The best in this kind are but shadows; and the worst are no worse, if imagination amend them'. This is not just an interesting bit of metatheatrical observation; it actually places Theseus in complicity with the audience watching the play in which he is a character, and thereby also with the playwright. In allowing no stone of theatrical self-awareness to remain unturned, Shakespeare celebrates his audience's knowingness and capacity to understand the representational formula as just that.

Another play to represent an elite audience is Marston's Middle Temple play *Histrio-mastix, Or The Player Whipped*. This was probably written in 1598 and published in 1601 (therefore slightly later than *A Midsummer Night's Dream*) and is the piece which started the polemic known as the *poetomachia*, several of the characters being probable allusions to actual figures of the period. The play is principally a satire on players, particularly in respect of their arrogance and greed, but it offers several perspectives on the matter of audience. Here again, the actors are artisans, with the quasi-comic English names of Belch, Gulch, Clout, Gut and Incle. The nobles who make up their audience are given, by contrast, either classical or Italian names. The expectation of a superior level of intellectual life for those of an elevated social

position is unequivocally stated early in the play in a speech by the figure of
Peace, who says:

> O pittied state! most weake, where nobles want
> The love and knowledge of the liberall Arts;
> Are you the men (for birth and place) admir'd?
> By whose great motions, lesser wheeles turne round?
> And shall your mindes affect so dull a course?
> As if your sence were most irrationall?
> What is a man superiour to a beast
> But for his mind?
> (1.1.p. 248)

An aristocratic Italian, Landulpho calls the play offered by the artisan players:
'Most ugly lines and base-browne-paper-stuffe / Thus to abuse our heavenlie
poesie, / That sacred off-spring from the braine of Jove.' His English
companion, Mavortius, replies: 'I see (my Lord) this home-spun country stuffe,
/ Brings little liking to your curious eare, / Be patient for perhaps the play will
mend' (both 2.1.p. 264).

The nobles disagree about the play. Landulpho despises it and in this
gains the support of Mavortius while another noble, Philarchus, likes the piece
and considers the Italian affected. However, the arbiter of taste in the play – a
character called Chrisoganus who is thought to have been based on Jonson – is
scathing about the offerings of the troupe in general (performing under the
name, Sir Oliver Owlet's Men). In the speech castigating them he delivers
perspectives on both audiences and the matter of stage fare:

> Write on, crie on, yawle to the common sort
> Of thickskin auditours: such rotten stuffs
> More fit to fill the paunch of Esquiline,
> Then feed the hearings of judiciall eares,
> Yee shades tryumphe, while foggy Ignorance
> Clouds bright *Apollos* beauty: Time will cleere
> The misty dullness of Spectators Eeys,
> Then wofull hisses to your fopperies
> (3.1.pp. 273–4)

In the usual association of the 'common sort' with crude tastes which are
inappropriate for 'judiciall eares,' the passage gives expression to one of the
repeatedly stated concerns about the theatre: that it is a vehicle for the
debasement of elite culture and that the intellectual dimension of high art is
obscured by a (commercially-driven) provision for uncultivated tastes.
Conversely however, there is also a suggestion that audiences in general are
educable and will in time come to discernment, the implication thus being that

the theatre itself is an instrument for the promotion of refinement of taste and judgement.

A later entertainment which shows some elements of similarity to both *A Midsummer Night's Dream* and *Histrio-mastix* is James Shirley's private masque *The Triumph of Beauty*, published in 1646 (performance date unknown). This involves the same juxtaposition between a classical elite level and low-life figures (here shepherds) whose names are not only English, but comically rustic: Bottle, Crab, Clout, Toad-Stoole, Shrub, Scrip, and Hobbinoll. The prince, Paris (of classical legend), is in a fit of melancholy and the shepherds decide 'to make him merry with some rare and pleasant device' (3). After rejecting the idea of a presentation on water, and one representing animals, they consider mounting the story of Jason and the Golden Fleece. The discussions between the shepherds are almost farcical in the disjunction between their rustic simplicity and the task which they seek to undertake, the irony of which would no doubt have been played up to its full extent by the 'young Gentlemen' for which the piece was written.[30] At one point, one of the shepherds – Bottle – admits that 'all the Shepheards wit is not a wool-gathering' (9). The good-natured enthusiasm of the shepherds contrasts with Paris's world-weariness and the prince complains: 'This busie shepheard will afflict me stil with his unseasonable mirth.' The shepherds end up performing a dance for Paris which does, in fact, succeed in cheering him up. After this, the god Mercury descends to summon him to judge the contest of the three goddesses. The rustics episode acts as a sort of antemasque to this main sequence of the entertainment. In very much the same way as *A Midsummer Night's Dream*, the entertainment presents the process of theatrical consumption as a naturally elite cultural activity precisely by representing the understanding of the medium by the non-elite as comically inadequate.

Another play in which the occurrence of a play-within-a-play offers some perspectives on the question of rank, learning and the reception of drama – and which dates from broadly the same period as *A Midsummer Night's Dream* – is *Sir Thomas More* written as a collaborative venture between writers who included Munday, Chettle and possibly Shakespeare. Sir Thomas More in the play, as a host and patron, feels free to comment on the play during its progress (rather like Theseus and his family) indicating a commanding and involved rather than a passive role as principal audience member. When one of the actors is found to be absent, having been delayed while collecting a beard from a prop-maker, More steps in to take the part. Though this may reflect a recorded predilection of the real More for theatrical performance, it also implies a natural sympathy between the educated nobility and the art of playmaking.[31] Later, one of the players comments on More's performance: 'Doo ye heare, fellowes? would not my lord make a rare player? oh, he would vpholde a companie beyond all hoe, better than Mason among the kings players! did ye marke how extemprically he fell to the matter, and spake Lugginsses parte almoste as it is in the very booke set downe?' (67).

The play is interrupted for dinner, but the players are later informed that the play cannot, after all, be resumed. One of the players regrets the delay caused by his colleague's absence: 'For otherwies the playe had bin all seene, / Wher now some curius cittisin disgraiste itt, / And discommendinge ytt, all is dismiste' (68). The reason for the non-resumption is actually that More is later called away on state business, but it is revealing that it is gratuitously ascribed to the disapproval of a 'citizen'. It underlines by contrast the more sympathetic relationship between playmakers and the noble elite which the play suggests. So too does the generous payment More gives to the players; like Theseus, More manifests a profoundly sympathetic and accommodating attitude to the company. When, as host and patron, he has chosen a play from the repertory offered by the troupe, he announces: 'They say it is *The Marriage of Wit and Wisedome*, / A theame of some importe, how ere it prooue; / But, if arte faile, weele inche it out with looue' (58). As with Theseus, More's nobility of spirit is represented in terms of his treatment of the actors. When his steward tries to cheat the company out of some of their reward, More intervenes personally, dismissing the steward. The positive picture presented of More is contributed to strongly by the representation of his relationship with the players, an episode which has otherwise little narrative function in the play. More's nobility also encompasses his being an educated man, and one player comments: 'God blesse him! I wold ther weare more of his minde! a loues our qualletie; and yet hees a larnid man, and knows what the world is' (70).

The drama is represented in these plays as situated most appropriately within the cultural experience of the elite precisely by virtue of its being informed by the learning and intellectual frame of reference which is depicted as their natural milieu. They range in date from the late sixteenth century to the Caroline period and are mostly addressed to the elite, being conceived for coterie theatres or other private performance. It is true that this fact would encourage flattery, but the terms in which it is presented are significant. The flattery of the elite in each case is offered in terms of an even greater understanding of the medium of theatre than even the players themselves, whether they be inept artisans or not. The refinement of response to plays is equivalent to, or an aspect of the refinement of behaviour, so that an audience's capacity for sophisticated response defines it socially. It is the faculty of urbane and polished discrimination that is at issue here and though the plays make no special claims for the *moral* superiority of rank, they clearly advance the notion of a hierarchy of cultural discernment. It is in these ways that they might be seen to celebrate and culturally construct the elite among their audiences, or at least participate in their construction of themselves.

These representations of noble audiences as endowed with a particular sympathy for and fine judgement of the drama, along with the flattery of the gentle sections of audiences in which playwrights of the period regularly and ritually indulge, has its basis in both social ideology and the material realities of the theatre business. One major aspect of the latter factor was undoubtedly the substantial presence of men from the Inns of Court in the London audience, men perceived as both learned and discerning in their judgements, and known to be of unquestionably elite status. However, what informs perceptions about the audience more broadly are the processes of educational change and growth that gathered pace early in the sixteenth century, and which had profound consequences for the way in which the elite was defined and demarcated itself. The association of 'understanding' and social status also places the playwrights – through a common comprehension of the mysteries of their art – in the same social category as their more elevated clients, a position emphasized by the distance put between this category and the 'base' sort. Leo Salingar has argued that when Hamlet used the term 'judicious' in 1600 (3.2.25–7) the term was still new in the language, and that between 1599 and 1613 there was a large growth in plays which contain an appeal to the audience's judgement, a phenomenon which he links with both the increased literary pretensions of playwrights and a stronger gentry presence within the playhouses (1991, 209–34). The stage was even seen as itself instrumental in developing educated judgement. In the prologue to his play of 1638 for the King's Men, *The Unfortunate Lovers*, William Davenant ascribes to this the critical sophistication of his elite Caroline audience, casting a nostalgic though patronizing look back at Jacobean and Elizabethan audiences:

> you are grown excessive proud;
> Since ten times more of Wit then was allow'd
> Your silly Ancestors in twenty year,
> You think in two short hours to swallow here.
> For they to Theaters were pleas'd to come,
> E're they had din'd, to take up the best Room.

> . . .

> Good easie judging Souls, with what delight
> They would expect a Jigg or Target-Fight,
> A furious Tale of *Troy*, which they ne'r though
> Was weakly Writ, if it were strongly Fought:
> Laught at a Clinch, the shadow of a Jest,
> And cry'd, *A passing good one I protest!*
> Such dull and humble-witted People were
> Even your Forefathers, whom we govern'd here:
> And such had you been too . . . had not

The Poets taught you how to unweave a Plot,
To trace the winding-Scenes, and to admit
What was true Sense, not what did sound like Wit.
They arm'd you thus, against themselves to fight.
(Gibbs, 1972, 141–2)

In promoting the notion of the true quality of gentility as being reflected in superior aesthetic and intellectual judgement, and imbuing both their plays and their pronouncements with this idea, the dramatists of the period were contributing in a significant way to the development of a class consciousness based on the refinement or otherwise of manners and behaviour. As such they were participating in a process of change in cultural attitudes which was being promoted by the changes in and expansion of educational provision and its uptake. These attitudes do not tell us so much about the *actual* nature of the audiences as about the playwrights' preferred perceptions of them, and they indicate far more about the theatre audience as a concept within the context of social transformation in the period. It is the very recognition of, and unease with the social comprehensiveness of real audiences that animate the recurrent distinctions between the 'judicious' elite and the others. In the face of economic encroachments of the non-gentle on the domain of the traditional elite, a quality of 'inner' exclusiveness (on which it was arguably more difficult to make onslaughts) was necessary if their superior social position was to continue to be justified. If the peculiar nature of the drama as at once a commercial enterprise marketed to all, and a cultural activity with pretensions to high culture, provided the basis on which these social perceptions were developed, the fact of the theatre's powerful position as a public discursive medium in the capital in the late sixteenth and early seventeenth centuries would have ensured the greatest impact for their promulgation.

CHAPTER SIX

'Morrals teaching education':
the issue of education in the sixteenth-
century interlude

> Those men which most excell in learning & eloquence, ought most to be
> renowned, praised, and preferred.
> (Nicholas Ling *Politeuphuia: Wit's Commonwealth*, 46ᵛ)

> I was a country Author, passing at a Morrall, for twas I that pende the
> Morrall of mans witte, the Dialogue of Diues, and for seuen yéers space
> was absolute Interpreter to the puppets. But now my Almanacke is out of
> date:
>> The people make no estimation
>> Of Morrals teaching education
> (Greene, *A Groatsworth of Wit*, C1ʳ)

The issue of education became increasingly important in the elite social
discourse of the sixteenth century. Old ideas of chivalric accomplishment as
the hallmarks of nobility and gentility were being challenged by a combination
of the need for the acquisition of more directly utilitarian skills on the one
hand, and the refinement of behaviour as an ever more important signifier of
elite social identity on the other. The ideas underlying this change were
encapsulated in a letter to Colet early in the century from Richard Pace, a
diplomat and later Dean of St Paul's (prefixed to Pace's *De Fructu* of 1502):

> When, two years ago, more or less, I had returned to my native land from
> the city of Rome, I was present at a certain feast, a stranger to many;
> where, when enough had been drunk, one or other of the guests – no fool,
> as one might infer from his words and countenance – began to talk of
> educating his children well. And, first of all, he thought that he must
> search out a good teacher for them, and that they should at any rate attend
> school. There happened to be present one of these whom we call
> gentlemen (*generosus*), and who always carry some horn hanging at their
> backs, as though they would hunt during dinner. He, hearing letters
> praised, roused with sudden anger, burst out furiously with these words.
> 'Why do you talk nonsense, friend?' he said; 'A curse on those stupid
> letters! all learned men are beggars: even Erasmus, the most learned of
> all, is a beggar (as I hear), and in a certain letter of his calls την καταρατ
> ον πενιαν (that is, execrable poverty) his wife, and vehemently
> complains that he cannot shake her off his shoulders right into βαθυκητε

α ποντον that is, into the deep sea. I swear by God's body I'd rather that
my son should hang than study letters. For it becomes the sons of
gentlemen to blow the horn nicely (*apte*), to hunt skilfully, and elegantly
arry and train a hawk. But the study of letters should be left to the sons of
rustics.' At this point I could not restrain myself from answering
something to this most talkative man, in defence of good letters. 'You do
not seem to me, good man,' I said, 'to think rightly. For if any foreigner
were to come to the king, such as the ambassadors (*oratores*) of princes
are, and an answer had to be given to him, your son, if he were educated
as you wish, could only blow his horn, and the learned sons of rustics
would be called to answer, and would be far preferred to your hunter or
fowler son; and they, enjoying their learned liberty, would say to your
face, 'We prefer to be learned, and, thanks to our learning, no fools, than
boast of your fool-like nobility.'[1]

By the end of the sixteenth century, Jonson was happy to ridicule the attitudes
being attacked here by making the foolish gull, Stephano, in the quarto version
of *Every Man in his Humour* (acted in 1598), express a similar point of view:

and a man haue not skill in hawking and hunting now a daies, ile not giue
a rush for him; hee is for no gentlemans company, and (by Gods will) I
scorne it I, so I doe, to be a consort for euerie *hum-drum*; hang them
scroiles, ther's nothing in them in the world, what doe you talke on it? a
gentleman must shew himselfe like a gentleman.
(1.1.38–43)

The bringing up of youth is a recurrent theme of the sixteenth-century interlude
literature and, given the exhortations of humanist philosophers to the nobility
and gentry about the necessity of education, this may be considered to proceed
directly from the elite auspices of this form of drama and the concerns of the
audiences which it primarily addressed. It is of relevance that it was in the
context of an argument about education that Thomas Elyot mounted a strong
advocacy of the interlude:

First comedies whiche they suppose to be a doctrinall of rybaudrie, they
be vndoutedly a picture or as it were a mirrour of mans life, wherin iuell
is nat taught but discouered; to the intent that men beholdynge the
promptnes of youth vnto vice: the snares of harlottes & baudes laide for
yonge myndes: the disceipte of seruantes: the chaunces of fortune
contrary to mennes expectation: they beinge therof warned: may prepare
them selfe to resist or preuente occasion. Semblably remembering the
wisedomes: aduertisementes, counsailes: dissuasion from vice, & other
profitable sentences, most eloquently & familiarely shewed in those
comedies: Vndoubtedly there shall be no litle frute out of them gathered:
And if the vices in them expressed shulde be cause that myndes of the
reders shulde be corrupted: than by the same argumente nat onely

entreludes in englisshe, but also sermones, wherin some vice is declared, shulde be to the beholders and herers like occasion to encreace sinners. (1531, 50^{r-v}/G2^{r-v})

An important development in sixteenth-century drama was the historicization of the central figure in interludes. The universality of reference of the allegorized humanity figure was inevitably circumscribed by the development towards a more psychological conception of dramatic character. Once these figures became thus individualized, they also gained a specific social identity. The early presence of quasi-historical figures within a basic morality structure, and the move towards (at least a metaphorical) specificity of social focus, is illustrated in two early plays, *Nature* by Henry Medwall, dating from the 1490s, and *The World and the Child* (*Mundus et Infans*), printed in 1522 but dating probably from the first decade of the century. Both are 'ages of man' plays, particularly the latter, though in both the bulk of the action is concerned with the youthful life of the central figure. In *Nature* conventional morality elements are strongly present – including the seven deadly sins and their corresponding virtues or 'remedia' – and there is much in the construction of the mankind figure which defines him in formal allegorical terms too. However, the process of historicization puts an emphasis on social trappings and, though the central figure is still just called 'Man', he is fixed in an elite position with all its obligations and privileges. He quickly becomes located in terms of status as a person of 'hygh honour and of great dygnyte' (I. 413). The dress he acquires, his behaviour and the many references to his rank designate his social status clearly and his vices stem from the opportunities offered by these circumstances. He is flattered by the World into accepting servants 'accordyng to a man of your degre' (I. 526). Later, one of these servants, Worldly Affection, undertakes to survey all of Man's lands (I. 695).

In *The World and the Child*, though the generalized allegorical 'ages of man' structure is even more evident, certain indicators point to a distinctive social position for the central figure. He is dubbed a knight, a fact which is insisted upon at several points. This is, of course, a metaphorical way of indicating his induction into worldliness, but a particular frame of social reference is established. A suggestion of *noblesse oblige* is introduced when Conscience tells him that it is his duty as a knight to defend holy church (p. 259). He claims to be 'as gentle as a jay on a tree' (p. 254) and he follows a fairly classic upper class educational and life trajectory, first being apprenticed for seven years in the household of the World at the age of seven, and later accepting into his own service the vice Folly (pp. 247, 263). Manhood addresses Folly on first meeting clearly as a social inferior: 'hark, fellow, art thou any craftsman' (p. 262) and later Folly asks only 'for meat and drink' as

Fig. 4: Sir Thomas Elyot, by Hans Holbein the Younger (1497/8–1543)
The Royal Collection © 1999, Her Majesty Queen Elizabeth II

Manhood's servant, putting himself effectively in the position of a servingman (p. 264). The satire in the play is also specifically targeted at members of elite groups, courtiers and bankers (pp. 262, 265–6). In these two plays, dramatic moral metaphors are cast in social terms; worldly power is seen in terms of aspiration to social position and display. What is important here is that this fixes the focus on elite social ranks, however problematically.

Since the interludes constituted a discourse situated within an intensely hierarchical deference society, this must be considered an important factor in the drama's engagement with social issues. The didactic agenda of the plays promoted the construction of central figures who were elevated in social status. This privileged social position parallelled humanity's primacy within Creation, a position which was too easily abused by a tendency towards a fall into sin, and it also helped in the development of the recurrent theme of pride as a source of humanity's downfall. The access to material means, which social privilege invariably involved, also facilitated the dramatization of profligacy and made possible striking contrasts between material well-being and the decline into misery as a consequence of depravity. However, if this was a convenient metaphor for moral teaching, it also became a dramatic convention which was highly significant for the social focus of the drama. This was not simply a matter of theatrical and didactic convenience, however, as arguably the focus on gentle and noble protagonists was also a product of the drama's orientation towards the elites that provided its patronage and constituted its primary audiences. Anne Barton has argued that when the sixteenth-century play moved into the banqueting hall its universality was lost and we have, instead of a sense of 'everywhere and nowhere', repeated references to specific time and place; she goes on to observe that: 'Their central characters, occupying a definite place in society, possessing certain attributes and weaknesses, are well on their way to being individuals rather than symbols' (1962, 31–2).[2] The limitation of focus also brought with it a concentration on issues that were most particular to the concerns of the elite primary audience. The issue of education receives much less of an airing in the drama of the seventeenth century, by which time the patterns of noble and gentry exploitation of the structures of state educational provision had been firmly established.[3]

In the interlude drama, the anxieties about inheritance and the maintenance of family wealth are indicated by the extent to which the irresponsible spending of reckless young heirs is repeatedly at issue throughout the century. This is most obvious in what could be called the 'profligate youth' plays: *Youth* (c. 1520), *Lusty Juventus* (c. 1550), *Nice Wanton* (1550), Thomas Englelond's *The Disobedient Child* (c. 1560), *The Trial of Treasure* (c. 1565), William Wager's *The Longer Thou Livest the More Fool Thou Art* (c. 1566), *Liberality and Prodigality* (c. 1567), *Jacob and Esau* (1568), Ulpian Fulwell's

Like Will to Like (c. 1568), *Misogonus* (1571), and George Gascoigne's *The Glass of Government* (1575 – probably a closet drama). Other plays with a youth interest include *The World and The Child* (c. 1507–8), *Hick Scorner* (c.1514), *The Play of Wit and Science* by John Redford (existing in two versions, one dating from 1539, and a later one published in 1570 as *The Marriage of Wit and Science*), and Francis Merbury's *The Marriage of Wit and Wisdom* (c. 1575, based on the Redford play).

Taken as a whole, this group includes classical plays, allegorical plays, semi-allegorical interludes, an early domestic tragedy, and even a play loosely based on scriptural narrative. Certain of these plays, such as *Nice Wanton*, *Lusty Juventus*, *The Disobedient Child*, *Misogonus*, *Jacob and Esau* and *The Glass of Government*, have been linked to the Continental, and more particularly Dutch Prodigal Son dramatic trope of the 1520s and 1530s, which was part of the Christian Terence tradition.[4] There certainly was an awareness of this tradition, as indicated by the fact that in 1540 John Palsgrave made an English translation (or, more accurately, an ekphrasis) of the Dutch Latinist Gnaphaeus's *Acolastus* (1529). However, the problem with too great an insistence on the connections with the Dutch plays is that it tends to focus critical attention largely on the formal, neoclassical aspects of this drama, and to view its existence in terms of a response to Continental influence rather than taking account of domestic social referents. Another problem is that the English plays far from uniformly adhere to the neoclassical format of the Christian Terence drama. Moreover, they do not follow a consistent narrative pattern; in fact only one of those mentioned above, *Misogonus*, has the full 'fall and reconciliation' structure of the Prodigal Son story, along with a lost English play of probably the 1570s or 1580s, that survives in a German translation and is entitled *The Comedy of the Prodigal Son*. Finally, and most importantly, an insistence on a formal Prodigal Son tradition obscures the fact that these plays form part of a broad range of English plays on the question of youth, education and delinquency. At one extreme of this range are plays that follow the lines of allegorical religious drama (for example *The Play of Wit and Science*), and at the other those which are highly neoclassical in conception and structure (for example. *Lusty Juventus*). In between are plays that are biblical, or have a mixture of allegorical and historical figures, with varying degrees of formality of act and scene division (for example. *Jacob and Esau, The Disobedient Child, Misogonus*).

The interlude drama engages several aspects of the upbringing of youth, but most recurrently the problem of profligacy and the influence of bad companions (including the dangers of bad marriage) or bad servants. The approach to all of these matters is ostensibly from a moral point of view, but all have a decidedly socio-economic dimension. Also significant in the plays is the issue of formal education itself, and its attendant difficulties, including the

questions surrounding the disciplining of children. That the problem of the
dissolute heir crops up in very different plays, in various forms, and repeatedly
across several decades gives some indication of the persistence of the anxieties
surrounding this issue in the period.

In the interlude of *Youth*, dating from the first decades of the century,
the definition of the self in socially localized terms is important for the play's
articulation of concerns specific to an elite audience: the question of rank and
its obligations, and the tensions surrounding the notion of social mobility.
While the play is broadly constructed around the usual formulae of morality
drama, its central issue is the problem of the control of that class of youth on
whom little material constraint is placed because of their prospects for
inherited wealth. Very early in the play a reference is made to Youth's being
the heir to all his father's lands (l. 56) and soon after, in l.71, there is a
reference to his wealth. The play abounds in other markers of his social rank as
well, and there are also several references to extravagant dress. Later when he
engages one of the vices, Riot, as a servant, it is done with an eye to his own
social position:

> I am heyre of my fathers land,
> And nowe they be come to my hand
> Me thynke it were best therfore
> That I had one man more
> To wayte me upon.
> (307–11)

He says to Riot: 'And thou wylt my servaunt be / I shall geve the golde and
fee.' This could either mean a fixed wage or land 'held on condition of homage
and service to a superior lord, by whom it is granted and in whom the
ownership remains' (note on l. 330). Youth sets great store by both his elite
ancestry and his access to the means to display his wealth and position, an
attitude in which he is encouraged by his companion, the Vice Pride, who
promises him 'hye degre' (l. 336). He aspires to royal rank and claims
ascendancy over duke, baron and knight (ll. 583–5). The extravagance of
Youth's claims are a matter of theatrical intensification, but fundamentally the
point is his preoccupation with the trappings of his position, with no regard to
those qualities which humanists were arguing constituted the essential nature of
nobility. Pride exhorts him to:

> Considre ye have good ynowe,
> And think ye come of noble kinde,
> Above all men exalte thy minde,
> Put downe the poore, and set nought bi them.
> Be in company with gentlemen.

Iette up and downe in the waye,
And your clothes loke they be gaye.
The pretye wenches wyll saye than,
Yonder goeth a gentelman;
And pore felowe that goeth you by
Will do of his cap and make you curteisie.
(340–50)

The ease of access afforded by wealth to the material benefits of an elevated position constitutes a danger to young heirs, in that it does not encourage rigour in the acquisition of qualities of mind and manners that the elite were increasingly coming to believe (or at least were being told) defined them. Though the question of formal education is not directly explored in the play, Youth's rejection of it is suggested by his mocking response to Charity's aureate and Latin-interspersed speech early in the plot:

What, me thynke ye be clerkyshe,
For ye speake good gibbryshe.
Syr, I pray you, and you have any store,
Soyle me a question or ye cast out any more,
Least whan your connynge is all done
My question have no solucyon.
Syr, and it please you, thys:
Why do men eate mustarde with saltfysshe?
Sir, I pray you, soile me thys question,
That I have put to your discrecyon.
(112–21) [5]

The exhortations to the nobility to be aware of education grew out of a humanist endeavour to encourage the perception of nobility as a quality of mind, as part of a project for the reformation of the realm. The sort of attitude exhibited by Richard Pace's fellow dinner guest is bemoaned by Thomas Starkey, the chaplain to Henry VIII, in his *Dialogue between Cardinal Pole and Thomas Lupset* of 1533–6:

Fyrst and most pryncipal of al yl custumys vsyd in our cuntre commynly, aftur my jugement, ys that whych touchyth the education of the nobylyte, whome we see custummabyly brought vp in huntyng and haukyng, dysyng and cardyng, etyng and drynkyng, and, in conclusyon, in al vayn plesure, pastyme, and vanyte. And that only ys thought to perteyne to a gentylman, euen as hys propur fayte, offyce, and duty, as though they were borne therto, and no thyng els in thys world of nature brought forth.
(Cowper, 1927, 129) [6]

This attitude (also complained of by Elyot, Ascham, Latimer and others) is at the heart of the problem in *Misogonus*. The Father, Philogonus, bewailing his misguided rearing of his son, reveals:

> An vnwise man I was, for thus then I thoughte
> what nede he tuters or masters to haue
> for larning[e] & discipline he shall not care oughte
> he shall learne to looke bigge stand stoute & go braue.
> What should I doe wth my landes and possessions
> I am able to kepe him gentleman wise.
> I esteme not gramer and thes latine lessones
> let them studye such which of meaner sort rise
> And as for his conditions I am sure they will be
> both honest and gentle, as all his kinne were
> the like bredes the like (eche man sayd) to me.
> his nature to be good, you nede not to feare.
> (1.1.69–80)

The irony in the final lines of this passage is a direct challenge to both the notion of nobility as conferred by birth, and the idea contained in Richard Mulcaster's assertion that children of noble parents inherited an inclination to virtue (1581, 198–201). The opposing side of the debate, made up of arguments about the acquirability of noble qualities, advance a rather different view of nobility. In the middle of the century, these arguments inform the perspectives on childrearing found in *The Institution of a Gentleman* (1555):

> Of this chaunge and degeneracyon whereby a manne dooeth not appere lyke vnto hys gentle auncitours, the fault is oft times found in the parentes, or other his kindred to whose tuicion suche one is in his youthe committed, vnder them nurished and brought vp from hys infancye: which father mother or others do not thincke good to chastice the faultes of theyr children, no not so much as to correcte them in wordes which manye fonde mothers doo cal snepping of a childe, dyscoraginge his boldnes, and so by this mean they graft in theyr children suche a lybertye to doo theyr willes, that in processe of yeres it groweth to an impudency, called in our language an vnshamefastenes: then such one by continuaunce of yeres comming to the age of man hauing grafted in his harte this slyp of lybertye, loueth better the secte of a Royster then the state of quiet gentlemanne, and so alwayes after he becommeth vngentle. (C2[r]–C3[r])

Towards the end of the century they are summed up in *The Mirror of Policy*, a 1598 translation of La Perrière's *Le miroir politique*:

> The stocke and linage maketh not a man noble or ignoble, but vse, education, instruction, and bringing vp, maketh him so: for when a man

from infancie is instructed in good manners, all the rest of his life hee
shall bee inclined vnto acts of Nobility and Vertue. And on the contrary,
if he be euilly instructed in hi yong yeares, he will haue as long as hee
liueth such manners as are barbarous, strange, and full of all villany.
(Hh3ʳ)

Frank Whigham has remarked: 'Movement across the gap between ruling and
subject classes was becoming increasingly possible, and elite identity had
begun to be a function of actions rather than of birth – to be achieved rather
than ascribed' (1984, 5).

A concern with the role of upbringing and education in the acquiring
true nobility is repeatedly a feature of interludes. The idea of nobility as
residing in appropriate forms of behaviour complicates the relationship
between social status and wealth. In *Youth* the exhortations on Charity's side
are made in the name of virtue, whereas the Vice's claims are made in the
name of rank. The Vice also leads Youth into a profligate life style that
compromises the position to which his status as an heir entitles him. Both the
promises of the Vice about enhancing his social status and the manifest decline
of Youth articulate an anxiety about the need for the inculcation of values in
the young gentleman appropriate to his rank. In the later (1570) version of *The
Marriage of Wit and Science* the parental figure of Nature recognizes the
potential in the gentle youth that can only be exploited through education:

If therunto (i.e. education) thy self thou wilt encline
The massy golde, the connyng hand makes fyne:
Good groundes are tilde, as well as are the worste
The rankest flower will aske a springing tyme,
So is mans wit vnperfit at the first
(113–17)

It was learning which could enable the noble youth to hold his own in his
social rank in terms of knowledge and manners. The son in the 1530 fragment
The Prodigal Son is represented as not only having to do demeaning work, but
being humbled by his everyday ignorance as well. A servant comes in speaking
a strange tongue, at which the son says: 'I crye you mercy mayster I stande in
your waye / I praye you pardon me I wote not what ye saye / I can vnderstande
no laten, I was neuer at Oxynby / No, nor yet in Cambrydge nor other
insteuynste.' His ignominy is emphasized when the servant has to correct him:
'Syr ye sholde say vniuersyte, not insteuynste' (p. 29, ll. 55–9). In other
instances of poorly educated heirs engaging in behaviour inappropriate to their
class, the wastrel son in *Misogonus* is given to the physical abuse of those
about him and in *The Disobedient Child* a servant provides a description of the
gross behaviour of his master's dissolute son at at his own wedding.

Wealth as an actual obstacle to the acquisition of the refined manners and learning which should accompany it, is repeatedly referred to. In *The Trial of Treasure*, the figure of Just complains:

> Thus fewe men a friendly monition will beare,
> But stoutly persiste and mainteine their ill;
> And in noblemen's houses truly I do feere,
> There are to many haue suche froward will.
> (p. 7)
>
> . . .
>
> Where moste wealth is, and most dilectation
> There Luste is commonly of moste estimation.
> (p. 8)

He also warns the youthful protagonist Lust that: 'There not a few, euen of thy propertie / Untill you be put into pouerties scholes, / Ye will not forsake this folishe insolency' (p. 7). In *Liberality and Prodigality*, the very dangers of wealth to the education of young nobility are expressed in Virtue's response to Prodigality's lavish spending:

> O wretched worldlings, subiect to all misery,
> When fortune is the proppe of your prosperitie!
> Can you so soone forget, that you haue learn'd of yore,
> The graue diuine precepts, the sacred wholsome lore
> That wise Philosophers, with painefull industry
> Had written and pronounst, for mans felicitie?
> (110–15)

The youth figure in *Misogonus* also implies a sort of inimical opposition between wealth and moral education:

> O all ye youthfull race of gentle bloude take heed by this my fall
> trust not to much to your heritadge & fortunes vayne alurements
> take heed of ill company, flye cardes & dice, & pleasures bestial.
> eschewe a hore as ye woud a scorpion & beware of hir intisments
> Children obay your parents wth dwe reverence & feare
> care not for your vaine pastymes for they be but momentary
> schollers your maisters good lessones often read & heare
> besides godliness & learninge all thinges in this world are but
> transitory
> (4.4.33–40)

If the problem was presented in certain interludes as principally one of moral and social behaviour, it did also have a more directly economic aspect which constituted the subtext of many of the plays. Alan Macfarlane has asserted that children in the early modern period provided parents with no economic, social or political benefits, but were simply loved for the pleasure they brought (1986, 57–90). Though it may have been broadly true that in a post-feudal society children had no direct economic role, it was also true that the status of an ever larger percentage of families came to depend on the economic performance of their members, and it was increasingly perceived that the proper equipping of children for future office was the key to the maintenance or enhancement of that status. The relationship between individual and family fortunes was crucially important, and the ascent or descent of individuals had implications for their whole families. This is particularly a feature of the system of primogeniture that was prevalent in England at the time, an inheritance system to which the rapid growth and independence of the English gentry in the period has been in part ascribed (Brodrick, 1881, 99). It was especially important in a deference society undergoing substantial social change and widespread manifestations of social aspiration. The idea is summed up in an observation in Pettie's 1581 translation of Guazzo's *Civil Conversation*: 'First I giue the father to vnderstand, that there is nothing in this worlde wherein there ought more care and diligence to be bestowed, then in the nurture and education of children, for thereof proceedeth for the most part, the maintenance or the decay of houses' (Third book, 35^r). In the first quarter of the following century, John Brinsley wrote urging parents to be sure to educate their children: 'And that hereby they may adorne your houses, increase their own honour in euerie kinde, to become principall lights, and pillars of their countrey, and not to liue to the ouerthrow, or the dishonour of your houses' (1622, C2^v/12).

William Harrison, giving an account in his *Description of England* (dating from the latter half of the sixteenth century) of the ascent of yeoman families, recognizes education (alongside the acquisition of land) as a significant route to social mobility and competition:

> they are able and daily doe buy the landes of unthriftie gentlemen, and after setting their sonnes to the schooles, to the Universities, to the lawe of the Realme, or otherwise leaving them sufficient landes whereon they may live without labour, doe make their saide sonnes by those meanes gentlemen.
> (1577/87, 133)

If there is implicit in this a concern about the ways in which the non-gentle classes are gaining in the competition for social ascendancy, it is echoed in the middle of the next century by James Howell (a writer and pamphleteer, later appointed historiographer to Charles II) who disapproved of the proliferation of schools and who in 1646 noted in a letter to the Earl of Dorset:

> *Learning* is a Thing that hath been much cried up and coveted in all Ages,
> especially in this last Century of Years, by the People of all Sorts, tho'
> never so mean and mechanical: every Man strains his Fortunes to keep
> his Children at School; The Cobler will clout it till Midnight, the Porter
> will carry Burdens till his Bones crack again, the Plough-man will pinch
> both Back and Belly to give his Son *Learning*; and I find that this
> Ambition reigns nowhere so much as in this Island.
> (*Familiar Letters*, pp. 523–4)

The need to acquire both marketable skills and social refinement was perhaps
most necessary for the emergent middle class with aspirations to economic and
social improvement through office. However, the importance of acquiring the
means of maintaining their ascendancy was repeatedly being urged on the
existing elite by humanist writers. In the period, the connection between
learning and the acquisition of wealth was a relatively new phenomenon. The
idea (held by Richard Pace's fellow dinner guest) that there was an inverse
relationship between wealth and learning was still not uncommon, and Ascham
complained in *The Schoolmaster*: 'I heare saie, some yong Ientlemen of oures,
count it their shame to be counted learned' (G1^v/17^v). The expansion of the
civil service under Henry VII and his successors, and the opportunities which
that opened up for the rise of families into and within the elite through the
holding of political and administrative office, gave rise to many exhortations to
the sons of the nobility to recognize their responsibilities and equip themselves
for the position of leadership in which their birth had placed them. Elyot,
Latimer, Ascham and others castigated nobles who failed to get an education
and thus put themselves in danger of losing out in the competition for public
office to the children of families lower down the social scale. Early in the
century Edmund Dudley (in his 1509 tract, *The Tree of Commonwealth*)
remarked:

> I feare me, the gentlemen of England be the worst brought vp for the
> most parte of any realme of christendom, And therfore the children of
> poore men and meane folke are promotyd to the promocyon and auctorite
> þ^t thee childeren of noble Blood should haue yf thei were mete therfore.
> (45)

Later Ascham complained in *The Schoolmaster*: 'The fault is in your selues, ye
noble men sonnes, and therfore ye deserue the greater blame, that commonlie,
the meaner mens children, cum to be, the wisest councellours, and greatest
doers, in the weightie affaires of this Realme' (F1^v/13^v).

These are instances of the repeated occurrence of this issue in the
hortatory tracts directed at the elite, or in texts which sought to codify and
define social structures and trends in the century. It is unsurprising, therefore,

that this was also one of the recurring themes of the interlude drama, particularly as this drama was intensely responsive to the social and political concerns of the day. Furthermore, since some of it was associated with educational contexts, or played by boys, the matter of education and the upbringing of youth would have appeared to be a natural topic for representation. The critical literature has more often than not considered these plays in terms of the *speculum principis* or 'advice to princes' trope, or the confrontation of specific political problems. However, the frequency with which the question of youth, its upbringing and education crop up in the drama suggests that, specific political referents notwithstanding, the plays were also articulating a persistent social concern. It is clear that the 'advice to princes' formula is just a formula, and that the plays are actually addressed to a broader range of the elite.[7] Conversely, where the citizen class is apparently the subject of the drama – as is the case most clearly in *Nice Wanton* – it is likely that this is also metaphorical and it may simply be that the consequences of downward social mobility can most easily be illustrated in this social group, providing a convenient theatrical means of representing connections between learning and economic progress.[8]

While the young heir in *Youth* is shown to be aware of issues such as social mobility and social competition, he signally fails to acquire the appropriate skills to manage this, and his financial recklessness is encouraged by the fact of his inheritance:

> By the masse I recke not a chery
> What so ever I do.
> I am the heyre of my fathers lande:
> And it is come into my hande,
> I care for no more.
> (54–8)

The material decline of Youth is marked visually; he clearly possesses fine clothes at the beginning of the play, but a fall from his erstwhile splendour of attire is suggested in Pride's later admonition of Charity for accosting him: 'Who learned the, thou mistaught man, / To speake so to a gentylman? / Thoughe his clothes be never so thinne / Yet he is come of noble kinne' (477–80).

Despite the moral rhetoric of the play, the economic dimension is powerfully present, as it is in other interludes of the period. Prodigality in *Liberality and Prodigality* is the same sort of free spending gallant who falls into poverty and, in the *Comedy of the Prodigal Son*, the father ruefully points out to the son demanding his patrimony that some go into the world without taking their family's wealth. While some sons take vast sums and dissipate them, these instead learn the liberal sciences and virtue. The uncertainty of financial well-being is a principal idea in another allegorical play, *The Trial of Treasure*, where the figure of Time comes to carry off Treasure.

The importance to the maintenance of family status and wealth of the system of primogeniture that had become prevalent in England by the sixteenth century, is illustrated in a contemporary tract, *A Health to the Gentlemanly Profession of Servingmen*:

> the good Gentleman, meditating in his minde, sayes with him selfe: If I leaue my Land and liuing, my Kine and Coyne, equally deuided amongst my children, imparcially proporcioning to euery one his part, the youngest to the heire and eldest, no way inferiour for worldly fortune: then shall the dignitie of my degree, the hope of my house, & the mayntenance of these before mentioned members, be quite (as Issue extinct) buried in the bottomles pit of obliuion . . . Thou, my eldest Sonne that shall suruiue thy dying father, holde heere wholly my Land I leaue thee, that my name may remayne registered in thy posteritie, thy byrthright by holy writ doth challenge it.
> (Hazlitt, 1868, 108–9)

As a result of this system, and especially in a period of social mobility and competitiveness, the reliability of the heir becomes paramount, and therefore a source of anxiety for both established and rising elite families. The problem of individual profligacy on the part of the heir is frequently connected to the question of family wealth and well-being. In *The Disobedient Child* a father disinherits his son as unworthy to succeed to the family fortune:

> That now agaynst me thou doest rebell,
> And for thyne owne furtherance wylt not agree.
> Wherfore of my goodes thou gettest not a peny,
> Nor any succoure els at my handes,
> For such a childe is most unworthy
> To have any parte of his fathers landes.
> (14)

The son in this play has, in fact, been reduced to menial work through a combination of a poor marriage and financial recklessness.

The problem of the passing of the family fortune to a profligate also occupies the father in *Misogonus* who believes that his dissolute son is his only heir, until a virtuous twin who had been sent away secretly at birth turns up. The first reaction of the father, Philogonus, on hearing about this son is to assert that: 'he as by righte shall haue my goodes & landes' (3.1.275). The freedom to disinherit the natural heir was a feature of primogeniture. In *Jacob and Esau* the biblical narrative is the basis for a comparison between the legitimate but reprobate heir, and the responsible younger brother who has no automatic right to the family inheritance. Despite his being a scriptural figure, the character of Esau is constructed as a dissolute son of a landowning family in almost entirely contemporary terms. Given the repeated complaints by humanists that the nobility placed more emphasis on training their children in country sports than in giving them a formal education, it is significant perhaps that Esau's dissoluteness is most clearly expressed in the play in terms of his passion for hunting.

Related to the problem of profligacy are the dangers to the property-owning elite of usury and corruption in law. Usury was frequently represented as posing a threat to the wealth of established families through the profligacy of young heirs who borrowed on their prospects of inheritance in order to maintain a life of extravagance, more often than not represented in terms of elaborate dress. Heirs were also seen as prey to unscrupulous lawyers. This is a recurrent topic in plays that frequently occasions a shift from the allegory to direct satirical reference to the courts and lawyers of London (a target of satirical attack which persisted well into the following century). In *The World and the Child*, Folly identifies himself:

> Syr, in Holborne I was forthe brought;
> And with the courtyers I am betaught;
> To Westmynster I vsed to wend.
>
> . . .
>
> For I am a seruaunt of the lawe;
> Couetous is myne owne felow.
> (572–4, 576–7)

The Vice Imagination in *Hick Scorner* claims: '. . . into lordes favours I can get me soone / And be of theyr prevy counseyll' (229–30), and he makes plain his skill in separating them from their property by legal means:

> In Westminister Hall every terme I am;
> To me is kynne many a grete gentyll–man;
> I am knowen in every countre.
> And I were deed, the lawyers' thryfte were lost,
> For this wyll I do yf men wolde do cost:
> Prove ryght wronge, and all by reason,
> And make men lese both hous and londe.
> (217–23)

Though presented in moral terms, as the result of a process of corruption, the 'fall' of young heirs in the interludes is thus persistently economic. The more broadly and theologically based ideas of 'virtue' and 'vice' which inform the psychomachic structures of earlier moralities, although paid lip-service to in these interludes, actually gives way to values which have much more to do with social competition.

The issues of competition, social mobility and the erosion of class and rank privilege are important dimensions of the economically driven anxieties about the education and social induction of youth exercised in the interludes. In *Liberality and Prodigality* Fortune initially gives her son, Money, as a companion to the young gently–born roister Prodigality, but because of Prodigality's profligate behaviour, Money is later reassigned (albeit temporarily) to Tenacity, a peasant farmer. More often, however, it is in the efforts of lower ranked servingmen to bear 'high sail' that the problem is articulated. In *The Glass of Government* the vicious figures plot to entice gentlemen into vice for the sake of 'lyberall gyfts' (Act 1, Scene 5) and at one point the roister Dick Droom, remarking on the ease of trapping young gentlemen, notes that they are 'caught without a net' (Act 3, Scene 1). In the *Comedy of the Prodigal Son*, the process of fleecing the heir is fully represented as he is both cheated in gambling and has money stolen from him by an unscrupulous innkeeper and his family. He then falls into beggary. In a fragment of an interlude called *Love Feigned and Unfeigned* (dating from between 1540 and 1560) the vice Falsehood declares that one can by trickery deceive an heir out of his lands.

The question of the appropriate company for heirs is almost endemic in the structure of corruption of youth interludes. This is a issue raised by Sir Thomas Elyot in his 1535 treatise, *The Education or Bringing Up of Children*, in which he remarks: 'Dissemblers of friendshyppe is an vnhappy kynde of people, absteynynge from all lybertie of speche, onely flatterynge the great men, and skornynge the poure men, also prepared to disceyve yonge men' (F3ʳ). In sixteenth-century plays the issue is presented both in terms of educating heirs to the wiles of those who would lead them to economic ruin, and in terms of the bad social education which is to be got from disreputable associates (generally of a socially inferior sort). The Vice figures of the early moralities (in those plays components of the moral psyche of the humanity figure) become bad companions, most particularly in the role of servants. Repetitively in the interludes, the corruption of the central humanity figures is effected through the agency of servants who insinuate themselves into their service. This may owe its origins partly to a recurrent feature of the *speculum principis* trope (mostly in non-dramatic literature) in which the ruler is led astray by flatterers, and partly to the natural subordination in terms of dramatic presence of the allegorical moral qualities to the central figure in the moralities. The role of the Vices as servant figures develops in the course of the century and the master-servingman relationship evolves as part of the increasing historicization of the central humanity figure, often taking on specifically economic dimensions. Both in pamphlets addressed to the elite and in the drama servingmen are frequently seen as problematic, and a distinction needs to be made between these men – who occupied a position between senior servants and professional companions – and servants employed to do the heavy work of households. In *A Health to the Gentlemanly Profession of Servingmen* the duties of servingmen are defined as follows:

> their Soueraignes, Lordes, and Maisters serious business, waightie affayres, and worldly wealth, was for the most part committed to their custodie and care: whose vigilant eye, willing minde, and faythfull forecast diligently to discharge that duetie, was thought so necessarie, as choyce they were of them they admitted to this calling.
> (Hazlitt, 1868, 106)

Servingmen were often kept to enhance the prestige of their masters, rather than for the utility of their services, as it was sometimes regarded as a mark of a gentleman that he should have a number of idle servants in his employment, essential not to their master's livelihood, but only to his status (Youings, 1984, 116). The problem was that, while being seen as necessary to the definition of status, they could be potentially damaging the economic well-being of their employers and were often represented as an overly expensive luxury. William Cecil, Lord Burghley, in his *Certain Precepts for the Well Ordering of a Man's Life* (c. 1584) addressed to his son Robert, warns him against servingmen of sufficient status to be companions: 'Let thy servants be such as thou mayest command, and entertain none about thee but yeomen to whom thou givest wages, for those that will serve thee without thy hire will cost thee treble as much as they that know their fare' (Wright, 1962, 28).

This problem also impinged on the question of social competition. In the *Description of England* William Harrison, describing how the yeomanry of the late sixteenth century progress economically and thereby raise the status of their families, comments: 'keeping of seruants (not ydle seruaunts as the gentlemen doo, but such as get their owne and part of their maisters liuing), by these means do come to great wealth' (1577/87, 133). The idle servingmen of the gentry and nobility, by contrast, are ruinous to their employers:

> diuerse of them also, coueting to beare an high saile, doo insinuate themselues with young gentlemen and noble men newlie come to their lands, the case is too much apparant, whereby the good natures of the parties are not onelie a little impaired, but also their liuelihoods and reuenues so wasted and consumed, that if at all, yet not in manie yeares, they shall be able to recouer themselues.
> (1577/87, 135)

The aims of the servingmen–Vices in the interludes are often made explicit as the economic ruin of their victims. The figure of Cloaked Collusion in Skelton's *Magnificence* (1520–22) has a name which more fully expresses his treachery as an historical servingman character than it does his qualities as an allegorized vice. He confesses:

> Cumberance and trouble in England first I began.
> From that lord to lord I rode and ran,
> And flattered them with fables fair before their face
> And told all the mischief I could behind their back
> (715–18)
>
> . . .
>
> I am never glad but when I may do ill,
> And never sorry but when I see
> I cannot mine appetite accomplish and fulfil
> In hinderance of wealth and prosperity.
> (731–4)

In *Impatient Poverty* (1560), the Vice Envy vows to ruin the central figure, Prosperity, and does so by persuading him to engage in his service Misrule, renamed Mirth. 'Mirth' claims to be 'beloued with lordes & ladyes of byrthe' (p. 22). He reveals his intentions towards Prosperity: 'I wyll brynge hym to classhe, cardes and dyse / And to proper trulles that be wanton and nyse / whych wyll not be kept wyth a small pryce' (p. 22). The figure of Money in Thomas Lupton's *All for Money* (1578) puts servingmen among other categories of person injurious to wealth: 'But the Seruing man, the spender, the vsurer and the lender / Doe sende me abroade day and night' (Aiv^v).

A good example of an heir of noble kin who makes the wrong choice of companions is the eponymous central figure of *Youth* (1513–29). His corrupt servingman, Riot, leads him to a tavern where he can be parted from his money (426–68). A similar figure in *Like Will to Like* (c. 1568), Rafe Roister, boasts:

> I intice yong gentlemen all vertue to eschewe,
> And give them to riotousnes, this is true.
> Serving men by me are also seduced,
> That all in bravery their mindes are confused;
> Then, if they have not themselves to maintaine,
> To pick and steale they must be fain.
> (421–6)

The economic aspect is perhaps uppermost in *Wealth and Health* (1553–7), a play which argues for the importance of wealth to the well-being of the commonwealth at large, and advocates its proper management. Wealth and Health are two noble friends who entrust their households respectively to Ill-Will and Shrewd-Wit, two untrustworthy servants. As a result of the activities of these two, the noblemen suffer a decline in fortunes, and Health reports: 'As for welth is fallen in decay and necessitie / By wast & war, thorow yll wyll and shrewdwit / And lybertie is kept in duraunce and captiuitie / God helpe vs all, and sende vs good remedy for it' (807–10).

There is frequently a conspiracy among the low life vice figures in these plays to ensnare the nobly born youth figures. In *The Trial of Treasure* a young nobleman, Lust, is brought to grief by a conspiracy of Vices, including a figure called Greedy Gut whose appearance and speech define him as a provincial peasant. The corruption of the central figures by characters who enter their service is thus something of an allegorical convention in interludes, but given the frequency of complaints in other contexts about the ruinous economic effects and bad moral influences of dissolute servingmen, this is arguably more than simply a narrative convenience and emerges more as reflecting a source of social disquiet.

The problem surrounding the choice of appropriate company for heirs is complicated by the fact that servingmen were often people of some rank themselves, with similar educational backgrounds, so that it is not simply a matter of contaminating contact with members of the lower orders. Taking a diametrically opposite position to that of Burghley's advice to his son, *A Health to the Gentlemanly Profession of Servingmen* describes the ideal choice of servingmen in terms of rank:

> amongst what sort of people should this Servingman be sought for? Even the Dukes sonne preferred Page to the Prince, the Earles second sonne attendant upon the Duke, the Knights seconde sonne the Earles Seruant, the Esquirees sonne to weare the Knightes, and the Gentlemans sonne the Esquiers Seruingman.
> (Hazlitt, 1866, 107)

Those aspiring to positions as servingmen in the plays often make claims for their own elevated provenance. In *Lusty Juventus*, the Vice Hypocrisy, seeking to enter Juventus's service, declares: 'Although I be simple and rude of fashion / Yet by linage and generacion / I am nie kin to your mastershyp' (577–9). In *Nature* Pride, who is later inducted into Man's service by Sensuality, enters claiming: 'Wote ye not how great a lord I am, / Of how noble progeny I cam? – / My fader a knyght, my moder callyd madame, / Myne aunceters great estatys?' (I. 731–4). He then goes on to enquire of Sensuality about Man:

> Syr, I understand this gentylman is borne to great fortunes and intendeth to inhabyt here in the contray. And I am a gentylman that alway hat be

brought up wyth great estatys and affeed wyth them, and yf I myght be in
lyke favour wyth this gentylmean, I wold be glad therof and do you a
pleasure.
(l.834+)

The servingman Crafty Conveyance in Skelton's *Magnificence* complains
about the manner in which he is addressed and claims gentle status: 'God's
foot, I warrant you I am a gentleman born; / And thus to be faced I think it
great scorn.' His fellow Vice, Counterfeit Countenance, expresses his doubts
about this: 'I cannot well tell of your dispositions. / And ye be a gentleman, ye
have knave's conditions.' On his first entry, Freewill in *Hick Scorner* asks the
audience to make room for a 'gentleman' and utters a French greeting to
corroborate his claim, though later his pretension is cast in ironic terms: 'I am
come of good kynne, I tell the: / My moder was a lady of the stewes blode
borne, / And, knyght of the halter, my fader ware an horne' (704–6). In *Wealth
and Health* the Vices make false pretension to social status, but Shrewd-Wit
admits to the nobleman, Remedy, that his companion Ill-Will is 'a scant
gentylman borne' (630) and Remedy replies: 'For somwhat in his face I loke /
In dede his mastership standes a crooke / For false shrewes both of you I tooke
/ And chyldren that be past grace' (632–5). Remedy later complains: 'I am
halfe ashamed, that long it hath ben sayd / That noble men by such wretches
hath ben deceiued' (896–7).

It was not just the economic dimension of the social associations of the
young that was of concern in the period, but a question also of the effect on
manners and behaviour. The issue of companions of youthful heirs of noble
and gentle families featured prominently in writing on education. Ascham's
anecdote in *The Schoolmaster* is a good illustration of this:

This last somer, I was in a Ientlemans house: where a yong childe,
somwhat past fower yeare olde, cold in no wise frame his tonge, to saie, a
litle shorte grace: and yet he could roundlie rap out, so manie vgle othes,
and those of the newest facion, as som good man on fourescore yeare
olde had neuer hard named before: and that which was most detestable of
all, his father and mother wold laughe at it. I moche doubte, what
comforte, an other daie, this childe shall bring vnto them. This Child,
vsing moche the companie of seruing men, and geuing good eare to their
taulke, did easilie learne, which he shall hardlie forget, all daies of his life
hereafter: So likewise, in the Courte, if a yong Ientleman will ventur him
self into the companie of Ruffians, it is ouer great a ieoperdie, lest, their
facions, maners, thoughtes, taulke, and deedes will verie sone, be euer
like. The confounding of companies, breedeth confusion of good maners
in the Courte and euerie where else.
(F4ᵛ/16ᵛ)

The anxiety here is based precisely on the notion that the issue of manners was an increasingly important aspect of elite identity. The fact of the social mixing of ranks with a consequent 'infection' of manners, made a discrete social identity for the gentle classes more difficult to achieve.

In Rastell's *Four Elements* (printed 1520) the Vice Sensuall Appetyte, whose role and general demeanour identify him as a servingman, inducts the 'gentylman' Humanity into profligate pursuits of drinking and dining. In *Lusty Juventus* (c. 1550) the Vice Hypocrisy is a butcher and is clearly coarse mannered; the central protagonist's language later becomes coarse under the influence of the Vices. The foolishness of the central figure, Moros (a gentleman's son, whose bad upbringing and education leads him to become a bad ruler), in William Wager's *The Longer Thou Livest* (1560–68) is signalled by his embracing of popular pursuits, and especially songs which were taught to him by a servant: 'I haue Twentie mo songs yet / A fond woman to my Mother / As I war wont in her lappe to sit, / She taught me these and many other' (A3^v). In Fulwell's *Like Will to Like*, a play which takes as its main theme the desirability of finding suitable company, the point is made that: 'A gentleman never seeketh the company of a lout; / And roisters and ruffians do sober company eschue' (307–8). This implicitly connects gentility with a particular form of behaviour and advocates exclusiveness of social association. A contrast to the unsatisfactoriness of relationships between people of differing ranks in the interludes comes in the eulogy of friendship in Richard Edwardes's *Damon and Pithias*. Here the intense and noble friendship of two young men of equal rank is contrasted with the perfidy and untrustworthiness of low-life friendships found in the sub-plot (though it is also true that they contrast with the false friendship of a pair of courtiers as well, one of whom is corrupt).

The concerns relating to the induction of youth into economic and social life might be seen in terms of an informal, social education, but there is also in the plays a repeated anxiety in respect of the failure of youth figures to gain an appropriate formal education, and their consequent unfitness for lucrative office. The point is made in the prologue of *The Disobedient Child* which talks of the rich father in the play:

> Who lovynge his sonne most tenderlye,
> Moved hym earnestly, now and than,
> That he would gyve his mynde to studye,
> Sayinge that by knowledge, scyence and learnynge,
> Is at last gotten a pleasaunt life,
> But throughe the want and lacke of this thynge,
> Is purchased povertie, sorowe, and stryfe.
> (pp. 3–4)

The gaining of education is a matter of becoming equipped for power and rule. Within the play, the Father exhorts the Son: 'And if thou woldest folowe the booke and learnynge, / And with thyselfe, also, take a wyse waye, / Then thou mayst get a gentleman's lyvynge, / And with many other beare a great swaye' (p. 13). In the 1530 *Prodigal Son* fragment (otherwise *Pater, Filius et Uxor*), the son (who, like the son in *The Disobedient Child*, is reduced to selling faggots to earn a living) laments: 'I wolde the erth had me swallowed / My fathers wyll when I not followed / He wolde haue had me a clarke' (p. 28, ll. 34–6). [9] Tom Tosspot in *Like Will to Like* similarly complains:

> But all licenciously was my up bringing.
> Wherfore learn by me your faults to amend.
> But neither in vertue, learning, nor yet in honest trade
> Was I bred up my living for to get:
> Therfore in misery my life away must fade.
> (1015–19)

Gascoigne's *The Glass of Government* makes the point clearly in that the two studious but less intelligent younger sons gain prestigious positions in the Church and the civil service, while the more intelligent elder brothers who neglected their studies fall into crime. The figure of Liberality in *Liberality and Prodigality*, who is steward to Virtue (a prince-like figure) is approached by a courtier who asks to be preferred to an office which has fallen vacant. Liberality replies that this must be earned by merit. Interestingly, an argument for the necessity of education as a means of economic advancement for those less well placed in society is made in the earlier version of *The Play of Wit and Science* by the mother (Nature) in a statement about why the accomplishments of the mind should be acquired rather than inborn. She points out that, if these qualities were inborn:

> The great estate that haue of me the fortune what they wil
> Shold haue no nede to loke to those, whose heads are fraght w^t skil
> The meaner sorte that nowe excells in vertues of the minde,
> Should not be once accepted there wher now they succor find
> For great men should be spedde of al & wold haue nede of none
> And he that were not borne to land should lacke to liue vpon
> (138–43)

Another topic which has a bearing on the discussion of the education of heirs in the period is the question of marriage. Despite the prominence of the theme of the upbringing of children, the sixteenth-century interludes are, remarkably, relatively silent on the issue of marriage. The relative absence of women as characters in these interludes is notable and revealing in itself. Marriage is thus rarely a focal concern, but its treatment in the plays generally yields interesting perspectives on social assumptions relating to status, power, gender and the nexus between affective and economic life. In this, the drama again reveals its engagement with essentially elite concerns. Particularly among the upper classes, marriage was a major economic matter as marriage settlements on women by their families became ever more significant during the course of the sixteenth and seventeenth centuries. The practice was to pay the settlement from the father of the bride directly to the father of the groom, who was then free to dispose it as he wished and such payments were often used, in turn, to finance dowry settlements on daughters (Stone, 1965, 176–8).[10] In the drama, social status is connected to marriage, especially in plays such as *Fulgens and Lucres*, the two *Wit and Science* plays and *The Marriage of Wit and Wisdom*. Though these plays are not primarily about marriage, the morality structure uses the marriage quest as a metaphor for moral contention or progress. In each case the reward for the male questors is not simply the bride, but the raising of their own status and material position.

Marriage signals the end of the process of upbringing and formal education, and the type of marriage made by an heir defines the success or otherwise of these. In the interludes which are constructed around marriage allegory, *The Marriage of Wit and Wisdom* and *Wit and Science* plays, the frame of reference is on the one hand moral (or even metaphysical) and on the other social and material. In both interludes the central figures and the matches between them are allegorical; the plays represent a pilgrimage of moral improvement on the part of the prospective grooms, the reward for which is the attainment of the brides. However, the social and economic dimension cannot be ignored. The fathers of both brides are men of wealth and social position; Reason, the father in *The Play of Wit and Science*, even feels the need to explain why he 'woolde bestowe my dowghter thus baselye' (13). The notion of a materially advantageous match as a reward for studious self-improvement is clearly present, as it is in the case of the 'new man' Gaius in Medwall's *Fulgens and Lucres*. Wit in *The Play of Wit and Science* at one point strays from the path of self-perfection and, thinking that he has destroyed his chance of winning his bride, reflects on his supposed loss in squarely social and material terms:

> Alas from Reson had I not varyd
> Ladye Science or this I had maryd.
> And those fower gyftes which the World gave her
> I had woon, to, had I kept her favor;
> Wher now in sted of that lady bryght
> Wyth all those gallantes seene in my syght –

Favor, Ryches, ye, Worship and Fame –
I have woone Hatred, Beggry, and Open Shame.
(835–42)

The marriages attained by the male protagonists bestow on them a rise in social and economic status, matches for which they make themselves eligible through a process of educational self-fashioning. Education is thus represented as a preparation for the more elevated social identity that is then formally conferred by these marriages. A parallel but converse process takes place in the plays about reprobate heirs. In *Misogonus* the heir marries a whore against his father's wishes and in *The Disobedient Child* the son, also in the face of parental disapproval, marries a woman who turns out to be a shrew who afterwards beats him and makes his life a misery. The marriage in this case signifies in a dramatic way his loss of personal power, just as his resultant poverty ensures his decline in social position: 'Although that I be a gentleman borne, / And come by my auncetours of a good blood, / Yet am I lyke to weare a cote torne, / And hither and thither go carye wood' (p. 44).

Failure to pursue an appropriate education is a significant contributing factor to the personal disasters into which the youthful figures in the plays fall. In *Nice Wanton* the son and daughter are hanged for theft and die from venereal disease respectively. The two reprobate sons in *The Glass of Government* are whipped and exiled, and executed respectively. In *Liberality and Prodigality* the gallant is sentenced to death. Allowance must be made for dramatic exaggeration, but the harshness of these outcomes do suggest something of the intensity of the concerns which the plays articulate.

The plays also raise certain issues and problems connected with formal education, exercising anxieties which might perhaps be seen to emerge from the growing use by the elite of the public educational system. One of these is the conflict between tender feelings towards children, and a perceived need for the imposition of discipline. There are many non-dramatic texts which advocate the rigorous disciplining of children. In Alexander Barclay's *The Ship of Fools* (a 1508 translation of Sebastian Brant's *Narrenschiff*) the contention is made that, children being pliant and impressionable, licence leads to misrule (xxiv). Barclay goes on to say:

Say folysshe fader haddst thou leuer se
Thy sonnes necke unwrested wyth a rope.
Than with a rod his skyn shulde brokyn be.
And oft thou trustest: and halt a stedfast hope
To se thy son promoted nere as hye as is the Pope
But yet perchaunce mourne thou shalt ful sore.
For his shameful ende: fortuned for lacke of lore.
(xxv/D5^r)

He then argues that parental example alone is insufficient to pass on the quality of gentility:

> Why art thou proude thou foul of that nobles
> Whyche is nat gotten by thyne owne vertue.
> By thy goode maners / wyt nor worthynes:
> But this forsothe oft tymes fynde I true
> That of a goode beste / yl whelpes may weshewe
> In lyke wyse of a Moder that is bothe chast and goode.
> Often is brought forth a ful vngracious Brode.
> (xxvi/D6^r)

It is possible that the repeatedly stated idea of excessive parental indulgence towards their children may be simply a matter of rhetorical convention on the part of the writers of humanist tracts on education. Some historians consider that early modern parents regarded their children as simply small adults, an attitude reflected in John Earle's statement that a child is 'a Man in smal Letter' (1633, B1^r), or lacked warmth towards them (Stone, 1977, 166–173; De Mause, 1976, 246–7, 252, 312, 319). However, more recent studies have questioned this and argued that diary and other evidence from the period does, in fact, indicate a considerable degree of tender feelings on the part of parents (see Collinson, 1988, 78–81; Pollock, 1983, 144–51). Certainly there is discernible, in both the non-dramatic literature on the subject and in the plays, a recurrently stated concern for the correct upbringing of children which involves parental strictness and rigour. The image that is often used is of a tender young plant which can be bent correctly while pliant, but is capable of distortion without proper care. The value of a proper upbringing and education seems especially prevalent in interludes that are strongly Protestant in character. Although the young are frequently addressed in these plays, the emphasis is placed heavily on parents to make sure their children get an education and in *Like Will to Like* the negligent rearing of children is even raised to the status of a mortal sin:

> Oh all ye parents, to you I doo say,
> Have respect to your children and for their education,
> Least you answere therfor at the latter day,
> And your need shall be eternall damnation.
> If my parents had brought me up in vertue and learning
> I should not have had this shamefull end.
> (1009–13)

William Wager's *The Longer Thou Livest, the More Fool Thou Art* goes further, suggesting consequences for the state and commonwealth:

By this faith *Valerius* he doth admonish,
That rich men sonnes be from euell manners refrained
Least that with profuse fondnes we do them norish,
Vertue of them euer after be disdained:
So that when authoritie, they haue obtained,
They them selues being giuen to inconuenience,
Oppresse their subiects under their obedience,
Oh how noble a thing is good education,
For all estates profitable: but for them chiefely
Whiche by birth are like to haue gubernation,
In publikque weales, that they may rule euer iustly.
(Prologue, A2^r)

Though there is obvious exaggeration here, these plays are among several which exhort parents to strictness and even harshness in the rearing of their children. The prologue to *Lusty Juventus*, argues that: 'man is naturally prone / To euil from hys youth' (1–2), and goes on to urge parents: 'Giue him no libertie in youth, nor hys folly excuse, / Bowe downe his necke, and kepe him in good awe, / Leaste he be stubburne' (8–10). Wager's play concerns itself with the issue of parental leniency, dramatizing its disastrous consequences. In *The Longer Thou Livest* the figure of Discipline states:

Two thinges destroye youth at this day,
Indulgentia parentium, the fondnes of parents
Which will not currect there noughty way,
But rather enbolden them in there entente,
Idlenesse alas Idlenesse is an other.
(D3^v)

In a slightly earlier play by another Wager (Lewis), *The Life and Repentance of Mary Magdalene* (c. 1550) the central figure – who is a rare example of a female profligate heir – has her prodigal ways ascribed to a negligent upbringing. Here it is not that the parents lacked virtue themselves or that they did not provide guidance, but that they did not follow it up with proper chastisement and spoiled their child. Mary relates:

Certainly my parents brought me vp in chyldhod
In vertuous qualities, and godly literature,
And also they bestowed vpon me muche good
To haue me nourtred in noble ornature.
But euermore they were vnto me very tender,

XXIIII

¶ Of the erudicion of neglygent faders anenst theyr chyldren.
¶ That fole that suffreth his Chylde for to offende
Wythout rebukynge / blame / and correccion.
And hym nat exhorteth / hymselfe to amende.
Of suche fawtes as by hym ar done.
Shal it sore repent: god wote howe sone
For oft the faders folp / fauour / and neglygence
Causeth the Chylde for to fall to great offence

De eruditiōe
puerorum.

Qui parcit vir
gæ odit filium
suum qui aūt
diligit illū in=
stanter erudit
Noli subtra=
here a puero
disciplinā. Si
eni pcusseris
eū virga: non
morietur. Tų
virga percu=
tis eū & aiam
eius ab infer=
no liberabis.

Prouer.xiii.
Eccle.xxx
lib.dis.cũ.bea.

A Myserable Fole euermore shal he be.
A wretche vnaupsed / and a Captyf blynde.
Whiche his chyldren fawtes forseth nat to see
Hauynge no care for to induce theyr mynde
To godly vertue: and byce to leue behynde.
For whyle they ar yonge fereful and tender of age.
Theyre byce and foly is easy to asswage.

¶ Two dyuers sortes of these foles may we fynde.
By whome theyr chyldren ar brouht to confusion.
The one is neglygent. the other is starke blynde.
Nat wyllynge to beholde his chiloes pl condicion.
Whyle he is in youthe: But for a conclusion
He is a Fole that wyl nat se theyr byce.
And he that seyth: and wyl it nat chastyce.

Fig. 5: Misbehaving children and blindfolded parent, from Sebastian Brant's *Shyp of Folys*,
translated by Alexander Barclay (British Library: Shelfmark G11593, fol. 24ʳ)
By permission of the British Library

They would not suffer the wynde on me to blowe,
My requests they would always to me render,
Wherby I knew the good will that to me they did owe.
At their departing, their goodes they distributed
Among vs their children, whom they did well loue.
But me as their dearlyng, they most reputed,
And gaue me the greatest part, as it did behoue.

To this the Vice Infidelitie replies: 'Of parentes the tender and carnall sufferance, / Is to yong maidens a very pestilence, / It is a prouocation and a furtherance. / Unto all lust and fleshly concupiscence' (248–64). In *The Marriage of Wit and Wisdom* the remark is made that: 'Such pampring motheres doe more harme / then ere thay can doe good' (99–100) and in *Jacob and Esau* a neighbour, Zethar, explains Esau's reprobate behaviour in terms of the absence of parental discipline (159–68). The father in *Misogonus* shows indulgence towards his son in not making him jump through educational hoops. He blames himself in the end for his child's errant ways: 'I cockered and dandled him a great while the lenger, / Whereof, like a fool, too late I repent' (1.1.63–7). The father in *The Disobedient Child*, who has been equally remiss in compelling his son to persist with his education, is also moved to complain:

But alas! now a dayes (the more is the pyté),
Science and learnynge is so lytell regarded,
That none of us doth muse or studye
To see our chyldren well taught and instructed.
We decke them, we trym them with gorgeous araye,
We pampre and fede them, and kepe them so gaye,
That in the ende of all this they be our foes.
(p. 15)

However, the fullest treatment of the disastrous effects of indulgent parenthood is shown in *Nice Wanton*, a mid-century play that focuses principally on this issue. Here it is a mother who manifests what turns out to be a misplaced concern for the fatiguing effects of education on her children. As in practically every one of the youth plays, here only a single parent is present, something which possibly indicates that the writers are less concerned with the dynamics of family life than the presentation of a somewhat abstracted image of parenthood. The mother, Xantippe, is a classic example of an indulgent parent, refusing against the advice of her virtuous son, Barnabas, and her neighbour, Eulalia, to chastise her two spoiled children, Ismael and Dalila.[11] Through association with ill company, the wayward children fall into sin and then crime. The blame is laid squarely at their mother's feet, the figure of Worldly Shame declaring: 'It   must   nedes   greue   you   wonderous   sore   /   That

Fig. 6: A Tudor schoolmaster with pupils, from Stanbridge's *Paruulorum Institutio* (British Library Shelfmark C.135.E.11)
By permission of the British Library

they died so shamefully, both two. / Men wyll taunt you and mock you, for they say now / The cause of their death was euen verye you' (467–70). The play's principal message is stated explicitly at the end: 'Therfore exhort I al parentes to be diligent / In bringing vp their children, yea to be circumspect; / Least they fall to euill, be not necligent, / But chastice them before they be sore infect' (531–4).

If parental laxity was seen as a problem by those advocating the value of education, a converse source of perennial concern was the harshness of schoolmasters. Ascham remarks in *The Schoolmaster*:

> For commonlie, many Schoolmasters, some, as I haue seen, moe, as I haue heard tell, be of so crooked a nature as, when they meete with a hard witted scholler, they rather breake him, than bowe him, rather marre him than mend him. For whan the Schoolmaster is angrie with some matter, then will he sonest faul to beate his scholer: and though he him selfe should be punished for his folie, yet must he beate some scholer for his pleasure: though there be no cause for him to do so, nor yet fault in the scholer to deserue so.
> (C3^{r-v}/4^{r-v})

He continues: 'For in verie deede fond Schoolmasters, by feare, do beate into them the hatred of learning, and wise riders, by ientle allurementes, do breed vp in them, the loue of riding' (E2^r/10^r). Complaints about the brutality of schoolmasters were frequent, and the problem was partly that the schoolmaster's office was freehold, making it difficult to get rid of him (Lawson and Silver, 1973, 118–19). Elyot says in *The Governor* that: 'by a cruell and irous maister the wittes of children be dulled' (D4^r/28^r), sentiments which are echoed later in the century by Nicholas Ling in *Politeuphuia: Wit's Commonwealth*: 'Tyranny is vilde in a Schoole-maister, for youth shoulde rather be trained with curtesie then compulsion' (54^v). Early in the next century the argument is pursued by John Brinsley: 'Let euery mans experience teach whether extreamity or excesse of feare (which must needes follow vpon such cruell and continuall beating and dulling) doth not depriue and robbe the minde of all the helpes which reason offers' (1612, 277–8/Nn3^{r-v}). This is a view which he restated in another publication ten years later:

> Moreouer how must this needs trouble vs, when manie shall crie out of our seueritie: some shal wish, I would my child had neuer knowne him. If he had not dealt so cruelly with my child, he had bene a scholar, whereas now he is vndone. Or when our scholars coming to mans estate, shal curse vs, for that by our blowes they were made dunses or deafe (though this oftentimes vniustly) or to hate all learning.
> (1622, G2r/43)[12]

The harshness of life as a pupil is also illustrated by an anecdote in Thomas Middleton's *Father Hubburd's Tales* of 1604:

> and yet I was the valiant Captaine of a Grammer Schoole before I went (to the university), endurde the assault and battery of many vncleane lashes, and all the battailes I was in stood vppon points much; which once letdowne, the Enemy the Schoolemaister would come rereward & do such an exployt tis a shame to be talkt of.
> (F1 ^{r–v})

Though the plays are all about advocating the submission of children to education, inclining to urge severity in the upbringing of youth, some do make glancing references at the problem. As these dramatic texts are aimed against the leniency of parents, they are unlikely to foreground this problem and it may be a measure of how deeply contemporary concern ran that some mention it at all. The rigours of education are suggested allegorically in *The Play of Wit and Science* where Wit is assailed by the giant Tediousness in the course of his studies, to be revived by the figure of Recreation. In *The Marriage of Wit and Wisdom*, Wit is knocked down by the giant Irksomeness, but is revived by the Lady Wisdom. In *Nice Wanton* the mother refers to the harshness of the discipline in school: 'Alas! poore soules, they sit a' scoole all day / In feare of a churle; *and* yf a lytle they play, / He beateth them lyke a deuyl' (109–11). In *July and Julian*, an anonymous mid-century play, one scene – gratuitous to the plot – is given over to a boy's complaints about his masters' harshness, and their subsequent demonstration of it in their own behaviour. It is, however, in *The Disobedient Child* that the actual terrors of a schoolchild's life are given the greatest airing. The Son argues: 'Their tender bodyes both nyght and daye / Are whypped and scourged, and beate lyke a stone, / That from toppe to toe the skyn is awaye' (p. 7). When the Father points out that this is in the interests of moral correction and that this sort of treatment would not be meted out to obedient pupils, the Son replies: 'Of trouth, with these maisters is no dyfference, / For alyke towardes all is their wrathe and violence' (p. 8). He then goes on to add some graphic detail:

> Diseases amonge them do growe apase;
> For out of their backe and syde doth floe
> Of verye goore bloode merveylous abundance.
> (p. 8)

> . . .

> Men saye that of this man, his bloudy mayster,
> Who lyke a lyon most commonly frowned,
> Beynge hanged up by the heeles togyther,

Was bealy and buttocke grevouslye whipped;
And last of all (whiche to speake I trembled),
That his head to the wall he had often crushed.
(p. 9)

The ways in which the matters of education and the raising of youth are dealt with in the interludes articulates fairly faithfully the attitudes to education that were current in the humanist texts of the period.[13] The extent to which the arguments of these texts reflected the realities of education in the period is more difficult to determine, but they do show a considerable degree of consistency amongst themselves in their warnings about the pampering of children.

Apart from revealing a contemporary social concern, the issue of education in the sixteenth-century interlude is of some theatre-historical interest as well, in respect of the way in which moral ideas in the plays are recast in social terms. One manifestation of this is that the conspiratorial and morally undermining role of the Vices in the psycho-moral representations of earlier morality drama takes on a socio-economic dimension in the course of development of the interlude. Though these figures ostensibly remain metaphors for moral processes, they are conceived within a specific social frame of reference, in which the anxieties of a particular class are exercised. As a consequence, moral status is replaced by, or at least implicitly determined by social status. The recurrent articulation of elite fears about onslaughts on their wealth and position is presented in moral terms and solidifies into a conventional demonization of lower ranks in a constant interchange between moral and social metaphors. However, as this is also part of a process which involves a shift from a focus on the moral, in a broad theological sense, to the socially strategic, the role of education becomes central in this. If the interludes remain didactic, they are teaching no longer the salvation of the soul, but the means by which social and economic competition might be most successfully pursued. The economic implications are never far from the surface, but the moral gloss is retained not only by continued direct recourse to traditional theological frames of reference, but also increasingly by a stress on manners. The refinement of manners acquires a moral dimension, which conveniently supports another aspect of the ideologies of hierarchy. The drama was complicit in the process of social transformation which saw a complete *volte face* in attitudes to education. Whereas noble opinion had earlier been inclined to see it as a debasement of aristocratic identity, learning came to be embraced as an accomplishment that could even be considered a defining part of that identity.

However, the relationship of learning, rank and representation remains complex and fraught with paradox. The advocacy in the drama of learning as a route to advancement – or at least the avoidance of social decline – might be considered to pierce any mystique about the nature of rank. It does, after all, establish a connection between acquirable skills and the successful achievement or maintenance of social position. On the other hand, conventions of representation which recast moral worth in terms of superiority of manners necessarily involved reference to education. Behaviour was important in signifying distinctions of rank on the stage – at least idealized conceptions of it – and refinement through appropriate learning was part of this. Then again, superior education was never a necessary dimension of elevated rank or even the quality of gentility. If this was true in the interlude drama, it was even more so in the rather more complex relationships between education and social identity to be found in the drama of the commercial stage of the last quarter of the century and the seventeenth century, which will be considered in the following chapter.

CHAPTER SEVEN

'Philosophers and queint Logicians': plebeian wits, gentlemen and scholars on the London commercial stage

In the period of dramatic production from the establishment of the commercial theatre in the last quarter of the sixteenth century to the closure in 1642, a very large range of issues came into vogue as a subject of dramatic representation. Changing fashions and national preoccupations gave rise to a variety of not only new ideas on the stage, but developing styles of representation. In the light of this, it is all the more remarkable that the issue of wit and learning remained a perennial topic throughout the period, and that only in certain respects were there changes in the ways it was represented. It crops up in a wide range of plays, a number of playwrights showing a persistent interest in the issue and several others giving it an airing in one or more of their plays. Aside from Ben Jonson, those showing most interest included George Chapman in the late sixteenth and early seventeenth centuries, and later Richard Brome and James Shirley. It is worth noting that the sort of exhortations to education which were present in Tudor interludes are not to be found significantly in the drama of the commercial stage. Neither is profligacy on the part of heirs particularly related specifically to educational delinquency. Though this may have something to do with changes in the patterns of take-up of educational provision, it is much more likely to reflect the greater social range of commercial theatre audiences. The representation in the London theatres of the relationship between education and social rank took a number of forms and shows some variation both across the period, and in different theatrical contexts. However, a persistent ideal remains of a natural association between educated understanding and superior rank. Even the apparent divergences from this idea, for instance in the representation of lower class intelligence, or in satirical treatments of elite folly or inappropriate pretension to wit, are in some measure predicated on this ideal. The various representational conventions by means of which the commercial stage accommodates the ideal yield some interesting perspectives on the ways that perceptions of rank are inflected in the period.

Secular Wits

Thomas Nashe, in his letter to the 'Gentleman Students of Both Universities' prefacing Greene's *Menaphon* of 1589, remarks: 'Oft haue I obserued what I now set downe: a secular (i.e. uneducated) wit that hath liued all dayes of his life by What doe you lacke? to be more iudiciall in matters of conceit, then our quadrant crepundios, that spit *ergo* in the mouth of euery one they meete' (McKerrow, 1904, III, 314). The intelligence of low-born figures is a recurrent motif in both Elizabethan and Jacobean drama, serving a variety of purposes including the exposure of foolishness in those whose education or social position arouse the expectation of more commanding understanding. The intelligence of these plebeian characters is manifest both in their management of intrigues in which their betters are frequently duped, and in their role as commentators on the actions of those in command. Sometimes these functions are combined. The intelligence of the low-born 'secular wits' is essentially pragmatic, and even at times (especially where intrigue is involved) cunning. A dialogue by Nicholas Gent dating from 1618, *The Court and The Country*, has a countryman (contrasting himself with courtiers) saying, 'Now for my learning, I hold it better to spell and put together, then to spoile and put asunder: but there are some that in their Child-hood are so long in their horne–booke, that doe what they can, they will smell of the Baby till they cannot see to read' (Hazlitt, 1868, 188). In Lyly's 1584 Court play, *Sapho and Phao*, the page Criticus celebrates the skill of servants in a favourable comparison with the more educated: 'Then is it time lost to be a scholler. We pages are Politians: for looke what we heare our maisters talke of, we determine of: were we suspect, we vndermine: and where we mislike for some perticular grudge, there we pick quarrels for a general griefe' (1.3.24–8). The skill of servant figures in conducting intrigues is not only a feature inherited from classical drama, but clearly remains something which is driven by contemporary dramaturgical demands. As such it has limited implication for social attitudes in the drama. However, there are implications in the fact that the exercise of plebeian intelligence is most often governed by need – or the spirit of 'What doe you lacke?' – and this affects not only the skill with which they manage intrigues, but also their more philosophical observations. At other times these figures are used for displays of 'native wit' in some ways analagous to singing and dancing blacks in early American films.

John of Bordeaux (dating from the early 1590s, and possibly performed by Strange's Men at the Rose) gives a prominent role to the scholarly character of Friar Bacon and was probably written as sequel to *Friar Bacon and Friar Bungay* (c. 1590), possibly by Greene. Pierce is a witty servant to Friar Bacon who manages to trick two scholars out of their book, and then proceeds to instruct them in how to obtain meals in inns by deception. The play comically delineates the gulf between the detached and unworldly approach of the scholars and the sharper, more worldly-wise attitude of Pierce. Pierce's understanding of what wisdom and learning is, is illustrated in a scene in which the scholars ask him about what Bacon has taught him:

> *2nd Scholar*: But, Pierce, hath he taught (thee) to distinguish a noun adjective from a noun substantive?
> *Pierce*: Ay, that he hath, and this it is: a noun adjective is a barrel of strong beer, for if it be *ipse* – he – embarrelled or titled by the name of huff-cap, it will make a man not able to stand by himself but throw him for a noun adjetive quit[e] under the table.
> *1st Scholar*: Well said, Pierce. Now what's a noun substantive?
> *Pierce*: Oh my masters, 'war[e] of a noun substantive! It's a dangerous point of learning, for I knew a wench in Oxford deal so long with a noun substantive that first she cried out of a chopping boye and after was whipt up and down the toune for lechery.
> (2.1.27–39)

The figure of Will Summers in Samuel Rowley's *When You see Me You Know Me* (1604), performed by Prince Henry's Men at the Fortune, illustrates well the element of cunning which informs the pragmatic plebeian judgements. The jester intervenes at several points in the play in deliberations of state, and offers his comments to the King. When Henry is accorded the title of 'defender of the faith' by the papal legate, Campeius, Will sees through the ploy to get Henry's support for papal wars (C4^{r-v}). He also argues against a further pardon for a high-born murderer, reasoning that if the young man had not been pardoned at his first offence, his later victims would not have suffered (F2^r). He argues against Wolsey, and reveals the cardinal's wealth to the King (F2^v, K2^v). The King is presented as well meaning, but ultimately falling short of the cunning required for astute rule. Will also proves himself skilful at the wit combat of a rhyming challenge given him by the King, the visiting Emperor Charles V, and the Queen. This too is a display of quick native wit for amusement (L1^v). However, in another incident, when the young Prince Edward is being tested in logic, Will's interspersed comments, though pithy and amusing, contrast with the Prince's more academically weighty discourse and Edward is ultimately forced to dismiss him from his presence (G2^r–G4^v). Edward, who has been a truant from his studies, shows himself nevertheless able to perform successfully in the trial. A 'natural' competence in scholarship is here part of what informs his stature as a prince, and the contrast between his educated intelligence and Will's 'secular' comic wit helps to define this perspective.

The display of native wit for amusement is also a feature of several fool or clown figures, perhaps the best known being Shakespeare's: Feste in *Twelfth*

Night (1601), Lavatch in *All's Well that Ends Well* (1604) and the fools in *King Lear* (1605) and *Timon of Athens* (1605). Feste's displays of wit are extremely self-conscious, and his prominence in the play (appearing in all the acts) may owe something to its having been conceived for performance in the Middle Temple. From his invocation early in the play: 'Wit, and't be thy will, put me in good fooling!' (1.5.30) to Viola's observation: 'This fellow is wise enough to play the fool, and to do that well, craves a kind of wit' (3.1.61–2) and beyond, Feste's role and identity are narrowly constructed around his wit as performance. As is the case with the pedant figures which crop up in various plays, there is no sense of the wit and learning here being worn lightly as part of a larger social characterization; there is no *sprezzatura* here. It is what entirely makes up his dramatic character and function. In a similar, way Lear's Fool has no identity beyond his contorted aphoristic observations. Of course, such jester figures are a special case, as their role is clearly demarcated and there is no call to go beyond the fixed parameters of their dramatic functions. However, it is largely true of low-born wit figures generally that where they are endowed with analytical skills, these qualities have a very specific dramatic use within the plays rather than being part of a representation of character for its own sake. They also exemplify perceptions of 'What doe you lacke' practicality about loss and gain. It is in these terms that the fool baits Lear, and in *All's Well that Ends Well*, Lavatch states, 'I am driven on by the flesh, and he must needs go that the devil drives' (1.3.26–8).

A representation of plebeian wit that involves both cunning and elements of formal learning is to be found in Lyly's *Mother Bombie* (1589–90), an unusual play in the Lyly *oeuvre* and probably the only one not to have had a Court performance, though this fact has little bearing on the material. What possibly does have some relevance is the fact that this was a private theatre play, performed by the boys at St Paul's. Directed squarely at the elite, with an educational dimension to its context of performance, the play does appear to offer a satirical view of elite society in terms of questions of intelligence and understanding. Here the sharp and insightful servants run rings around their rather foolish and slow-witted masters. In a play so close to classical convention, this role of the servants (clearly the slaves, of Roman comedy despite the fact that the play is set in Kent) cannot be regarded in itself as carrying much social reflection; they are there largely to serve the ends of an intrigue comedy constructed with a highly symmetrically patterned plot. The plot, involves two wealthy men each trying to marry off their dim-witted offspring to what they mistakenly see as the more gifted child of the other, and two poorer men attempting to marry their genuinely more accomplished children to those of the richer men. However, in a piece that focuses on the question of rank, education and intelligence, it is curious that Lyly chooses to go beyond constructing the servant figures simply as skilfully plotting factotums, not only by giving them reflective intelligence but also by endowing their speech liberally with Latin quotations, something which is pointedly not done with the elite figures in the play. The only other character to demonstrate a facility with Latin is Candius, the scholarly son of the poor father. The characterization of the servants might be considered to point up satirically the gulf between the expectations of intellectual and educational accomplishment implicitly associated with rank, and a reality which falls short of this.

A rather different use of plebeian commentator figures is to be found in Robert Wilson's (possibly Court) play, *The Cobbler's Prophecy* (1590–4), and more famously in the gardener scene in *Richard II* (1595). In the Wilson play the plebeian commentator is Ralph, a cobbler endowed with the gift of prophecy. He is placed in the context of an array of figures from different estates, each making claims for their merits: a Courtier, Country Gentleman, Soldier and Scholar. Ralph addresses the scholar in derisive tones, dismissing his learning as insufficient to protect the realm and even predicting that learning will decline:

> Nay and you speake Latin, reach me my laste.
> Harke ye mas Scholler, harke ye.
> The time shall come not long before the doome,
> That in despite of Roome,
> Latin shall lacke,
> And Greeke shal beg with a wallet at his backe.
> For all are not sober that goes in blacke.
> Goe too scholler, theres a learning for your knacke.
> (307–14)

He takes over the Scholar's role, warning against danger to the commonwealth and exposing the Courtier's plot to kill the Duke. However, at the end of the play, the Cobbler returns to his trade, while the Duke honours the Soldier and Scholar. In Shakespeare's play, the gardener scene (3.4.24–107) is, on one level, simply a way of inserting a relatively commonplace garden allegory of the state into the play.[1] Nevertheless, the scene illustrates the operation of a 'secular wit' in that the gardener's observations on the state proceed directly from insights gained through the necessities of his humble occupation. The Queen's objection to the gardener's knowledge is delivered with specific reference to his lowly station: his 'harsh rude tongue' (74) and that he is a 'little better thing than earth' (78).

The use of low-born 'secular wits' is one of those aspects of wit and learning on the early modern stage that exhibit some change over the course of the period. Margot Heinemann has rightly pointed out that:

The parody of serious matters by the wise clown or sceptical commoner indeed tends to disappear in a later drama increasingly directed towards a gentle audience. The common soldiers and rebels in Beaumont and Fletcher (*Philaster*, *Bonduca*) or Ford (*Perkin Warbeck*) are merely contemptible or ridiculous.
(1990, 193)

It is arguable, though, that the wit of low-born figures had never very much to do with a reflection on this level of society anyway, but acted rather more as an admonition to those of more elevated rank who fell short of the intellectual performance which their roles and social positions demanded of them.

Another aspect of the representation of wit was to undergo some change in the period, also involving the display of intelligence in the low-born or at least materially dispossessed. The poverty of scholars is sometimes treated comically, as in the remarks of the servant Dromio's to Candius (the learned son of a poor father) in *Mother Bombie*:

Give me leave to pose you, though you bee a graduate; for I tell you we in Rochester spurre so many hackneys that we must needs spurre schollers, for wee take them for hackneys.
Livia: Why so, sir boy?
Dromio: Because I knew two hired for ten grotes apece to saie service on Sunday, and that's no more than a post horse from hence to Canterbury.
(4.1.1357–64)

There is a similarly comic representation in the episode of the two scholars in *John of Bordeaux*, and a sympathetic treatment in Act 3, Scene 2 of Greene's *Friar Bacon and Friar Bungay* in which Friar Bacon gives poor fare to the King and the German Emperor on visit to Oxford, in order to demonstrate how badly scholars eat. Rather more bitter is the attitude of the poor scholar, Macilente, in Jonson's *Every Man out of his Humour* (1599).[2] Speaking of a wealthy citizen, Deliro, he says:

I see no reason, why that dog (call'd *Chance*)
Should fawne vpon this fellow, more then me:
I am a man, and I haue limmes, flesh, bloud,
Bones, sinewes, and a soule, as well as he:
My parts are euery way as good as his,
If I said better? why, I did not lie.
Nath'lesse, his wealth (but nodding on my wants)
Must make me bow, and crie: (I thanke you, sir)
(2.4.9–16)

Campeius, a scholar in Dekker's *The Whore of Babylon* (1606), complains that the cultural refinements which scholars provide to enrich the lives of others, do not materially benefit the scholars themselves:

> In disputation
> I dare for latine, hebrew, and the greeke,
> Challenge an vniuersitie; yet, (O euill hap!)
> Three learned languages cannot set a nap
> Vpon this thred-bare gowne: how is Arte curs'd?
> Shee ha's the sweetest lymbes, and goeth the worst:
> Like common Fidlers, drawing down others meate
> With lickorish tunes, whilst they on scraps do eate.
> (2.2.130–37)

In Chapman's *The Memorable Masque* presented in 1613 by the men of the Middle Temple and Lincoln's Inn before the King, the scholar Capriccio discusses the poverty of learned men with Plutus, the God of Riches. He complains:

> How hard this world is to a man of wit? hee must eate through maine Rockes for his food, or fast; a restles and tormenting stone, his wit is to him: the very stone of *Sisyphus* in hell; nay, the Philosophers stone, makes not a man more wretched: A man must be a second *Proteus*, and turne himselfe into all shapes (like *Vlisses*) to winde throught the straites of this pinching vaile of miserie.
> (20–25)

Plutus employs him to put on an antemasque, afterwards dismissing him without reward, saying: 'I haue imployd you, and the grace of that, is reward enough' (170–71).

In Robert Wild's *The Benefice* (date uncertain, but earlier than 1639), the impassioned complaint of a learned young divine, Bookworm, directly connects poverty with learning:

> The Ominous Night-Crow, envying my Light,
> Would try to scare me from my *Aristotle*,
> Beating her self against my Window Bars,
> Whilst I within have learn'd upon this Elbow
> Searching *Philosophy*, as dark as Night,
> And conning *Plato*, as Boys do their *Grammars*;
> Brooding each Line, and sitting on each Verse,
> As close as Moth or Canker, till mine Eyes
> With so much Labour, oft would sweat a Tear
> Upon my knotty Task.

> . . .

But – now I see I studied Poverty,
And purchas'd Beggary at too dear a rate.
(3.1.p. 28)

Bookworm later becomes an almanac seller, and has some comments to make on other openings available to those with an education and but no power:

> I had rather confute *Bellamire*, or turn *Aquinas* into English Verse. Yet this (i.e. almanac selling) is better than the Mill of School, where they grind Grammar Toll-free; and the poor Master turns round in's *Accidence* till his Eyes drop out. Nay, faith, it's better than a Parlour Lecture, tho not so sweet and gainful; where the Men with their smooth Chin, and Velvet Caps, stand damning the Tongues.
> (4.1. p. 37)

The most interesting dramatic study of the relationship of power and education in a low-born man is also among the earliest, Marlowe's *Doctor Faustus*, dating from 1588. Faustus, like Baldock in *Edward II* who says of himself that: 'I fetched my gentry from Oxford, not from heraldry' (and also like the dramatist himself, whose Cambridge degree conferred gentle status upon him), was 'borne, of parents base of stocke' and is socially constructed by his education. Leaving aside the religious dimensions, Faustus's crisis is one of dealing with the problem of the limitations of his power. The issue is one which emerges precisely from the social mobility made available by education. If Faustus is able to move up the social ranks by virtue of his own developed intellectual powers, in what is otherwise a society relatively hostile to such mobility and which tends to place limits on it, he has thereby already undermined and overcome the constraints imposed by its hierarchical structure. His bid for power on a more cosmic level is simply an extension of his basing his own identity, not on the limiting referents of the hierarchical world in which he finds himself, but on his own developed powers to which he has not yet been able to determine any limitations. Faustus links power directly to study: 'O what a world of profite and delight, / Of power, of honour, and omnipotence, / Is promised to the Studious Artizan?' (1.1.80–83). Despite his early rhetoric on the matter, and for all the potential he has for worldly power, Faustus ultimately seeks not to rule, but continues to occupy the role of scholar; it is his scholarly prowess and knowledge that are demonstrated by his spectacles late in the play for the Emperor of Germany. His education does not so much translate into political dominion as an attempt to undermine authority through knowledge. It is not hard to see Marlowe's social and religious iconoclasm as proceeding fairly directly from the insights afforded him by a similar combination of his own developed critical intelligence, and the experience of the crossing of barriers of rank made possible by his education.

In several plays, scholars are represented as turning to intrigue and being adept at it precisely because of their learning. Such figures include Priscian in Middleton and Rowley's *Wit at Several Weapons* (1613), Lugier in Fletcher's *The Wild Goose Chase* (1621) and Compass in Jonson's *The Magnetic Lady* (1632). In *Wit at Several Weapons*, Witty-pate, the son of Sir Credulous Old-craft, ('a shallow-brain'd scholar') teams up with a poor scholar Priscian to gull his father and Sir Gregory Fop, an elite fool. Act 1, Scene 2 has Sir Credulous testing Priscian's Latin, somewhat discomfiting Sir Gregory, who is unable to understand it. Then Witty-pate steps in, purportedly to test Priscian's 'Hebrew, Greek and Syrian', and engaging in nonsense talk with the scholar which succeeds in duping and impressing the foolish older men. In *The Wild Goose Chase* the gentleman-intriguer De Gard seeks to set up a plot to trap the anti-marriage Mirabell into marriage with the heroine Oriana. He enlists the help of a tutor called Lugier in this project, saying: 'I know ye are a Scholar, and can do wonders'. To this Lugier replies: 'There's no great Scholarship belongs to this Sir' (3.1.1–2), but he nevertheless devises the intrigue successfully. Jonson's Compass is also a scholar, a mathematician, whose skills of social manipulation have been developed by his education: 'This is a piece / Of *Oxford* Science, staies with me ere since / I left that place' (1.1.72–4). He is able to understand and analyse other characters, and see through their pretensions. His talents are ultimately rewarded in that he manages to marry an heiress in the end, thereby gaining a fortune.

Another, rather darker theme was that of the discontent of intellectuals without status, deriving from their material deprivation and disempowerment. The dangers arising from the combination of discontent of scholars and the possibilities afforded by their acute intelligence or learning, are recurrent ideas on the Elizabethan and Jacobean stage. The scholarly intriguer has a threatening representation in the learned malcontent who turns his skills to dubious and self-seeking purposes.[3] An early example of such a type is to be found in Robert Greene's *The Scottish History of James IV* which probably dates from around 1590, in which the poor scholar Ateukin creeps into the service of the King. His assistant, Slipper, is under no illusions about the effects of necessity on the scholar: 'Because, sir, liuing by your wit as you doo, shifting (trickery) is your letters patent' (2.1.776–7). Ateukin, who as a scholar claims gentle status, is angered by this comment: 'If I liue, knaue, I will bee reuenged. What gentleman would entertaine a rascall thus to derogate from his honour? (beats him)' (2.1.782–3). Slipper's observations prove to be accurate, however, as Ateukin uses his skills (albeit unsuccessfully) to engineer a plot on behalf of the King to have the Queen murdered. His poverty is referred to repeatedly early in the play, and his scholarly identity is also constantly kept before the audience. A fairly gratuitous reference late in the intrigue helps to cement the connection between Ateukin's deviousness and his learning; when he asks his servant, Andrew, about some lost papers on which he had been working, the servant enquires: 'Which sir? your annotations upon Machiavel?' (3.1.1228).

Later plays also portray scholars turned villains through necessity. One such figure is Cockledemoy in Marston's *Dutch Courtesan* (1604), a debauched scholar who prefers conycatching to the liberal sciences. He has confidence in his knavish abilities precisely because he is 'a scholler, and hast read *Tullies Offices*' (1.2.59). Another is George Pye-Boord in *The Puritan*, an anonymous private theatre play of 1606, who confesses that he was sent down from university for stealing cheese (through poverty) and thereafter he uses his wits to become a schemer and plotter, again driven by economic necessity. Probably the most famous of the scholars in the drama of the period to fall into criminal ways through discontent at the failure legitimately to derive material benefit from his education is, however, Flamineo in Webster's *White Devil* (1612):

> For want of meanes, the University judge me,
> I have bene faine to heele my Tutors stockings
> At least seven yeares: Conspiring with a beard
> Made me a Graduate – then to this Dukes service –
> I visited the Court, whence I return'd
> More courteous, more letcherous by farre,
> But not a suite the richer
> (1.2.314–20)

These discontented intriguer figures do perhaps give some expression to the social tensions produced by the relative dearth of employment for the glut of educated men in the early seventeenth century.[4] However, they are also part of a dramatic formula which is varied later in the period. As with the plebeian commentator figures, these types are not to be found in the later drama, giving way instead to gayer gentleman intriguers who, though making their appearance as early as the work of Chapman and Jonson, come into their own in the Caroline theatre, particularly of Shirley, with no discernible scholarly dimension.

Wit and Gentility

In both popular and elite drama in the period, there is considerable evidence of the ideology described by Lawrence Stone's as 'harmonization of axes,' (the association of moral and intellectual qualities with social status – see above p. 104) underlying the representation of rank. This informs the idealizing description by a courtier of Court life in Nicholas Gent's 1618 dialogue, *The Court and the Country*, in which the luxurious circumstances and recreational pursuits of the elite are seamlessly interwoven with superiority of taste and intellectual judgement:

> the witty, learned, noble and pleasant discourses all day, the variety of wits, with the depth of iudgments, the dainty fare, sweetly dressed and neatly serued, the delicate wines and rare fruites, with excellent Musique and admirable Voyces, Maskes and Playes, Dauncing and Riding; deuersity of Games, delightfull to the Gamsters purposes; and Riddles, Questions and Answers; Poems, Histories, and strange inuentions of Witt, to startle the Braine of a good vnderstanding.
> (Hazlitt, 1866, 178)

On the other hand, the satirical impulse of some playwrights seems to cut right across and to challenge this ideal. This impulse, particularly in the more elite plays of the private theatres, produces the representation of foolish gentlemen in which there is a comic disjunction between social position or wealth on the one hand, and limited intellectual capacity and cultivation on the other. Such figures abound in the plays of practically every writer who wrote comedy.[5] In *Epicoene or The Silent Woman* (1609) Jonson's witty hero, Truewit, is scathing about the 'Collegiates', a group of fashionable elite women with pretensions to educated judgement, and also about Sir John Daw, whom he describes as: 'a fellow that pretends onely to learning, buyes titles, and nothing else of bookes in him' (1.2.76–7). The folly of such figures involves a range of qualities including affectation of manners, ignorance, pretension, scorn for more genuinely learned men, and a susceptibility to gulling. They occur in pretty well similar form from the Elizabethan to the Caroline stage, showing a stronger tendency towards courtly affectation in the Caroline drama, with its greater orientation towards elite audiences and its preoccupation with sophistication of manners. Particularly in view of this, it becomes clear that, far from challenging the ideology of rank that Stone describes, the satire involved in the occurrence of these well-born fools on the stage is actually based squarely on the assumption of that ideal (of which the elite fools fall short). It also informs more positive images of elite urbanity in the drama, something which was to characterize particularly the drama of Shirley later in the period.

An early gesture towards the ideal of the association of rank with intellectual ability is to be found in *Mother Bombie*. Lyly, despite his use of clever and educated servant figures, uses the romance device of children substitued at birth to restore something of the idea of inherent intellectual qualities of rank. Ultimately the foolish children of the elite parents are revealed to be the son and daughter of the nurse, who exchanged them at birth, while the elite-born children, who have been raised as poor, demonstrate natural qualities of superiority. Though this early example of essentialism is rarely carried into later dramatic representations, Shirley's much later play *The Gentleman of Venice* (1639) is another 'blood will out' changeling story. While Thomazo, the supposed son of the Duke, is a coarse and cowardly reprobate, the virtuous Giovanni, growing up as the Duke's gardener's son, has a strong and inexplicable drive towards learning and refinement. In the end it revealed that Giovanni is actually the Duke's son while Thomazo is the gardener's, prompting one courtier to remark to the Duke:

> I shall believe your nobleness liv'd there
> In Giovanni, not suppress'd in poverty;
> And their rude coarse condition, notwithstanding
> The helps of education (which seldom
> Do correct nature) in Thomazo's low
> And abject spirit.
> (5.4.p. 84)

Interestingly, the idealized connection between rank and intellectual superiority is not especially a product of elite-orientated drama. This romanticized view of nobility as manifested in a 'natural' refinement of behaviour is also found in a range of (usually popular) plays about noblemen displaced into plebeian contexts where they live incognito among rougher people from whom they naturally stand out.[6] More often, however, the relationship between the cultivated mind and rank is rather less absolute than this. There are various facets to the ways in which the educated mind is represented in the gentle figures in the drama and, depending on the role and function of the figures, one or other tends to be emphasized. The aspect which most closely resembles that of the 'secular wits' is the *savoir faire* born of a developed intelligence, involving a practical capacity to plot and manipulate, and to understand social politics. However, in the elite intriguers, this forms part of an urbane and commanding social identity; knowingness is represented as an appropriate quality of the gentle town wit. The aspect that most narrowly relates to formal education is what might be called 'deep learning' and is associated with those who actively profess to be scholars. It is sometimes associated with the quality of 'melancholy' and in the case of elite figures (though not in the case of the low-born), involves a detachment from the practicalities of life. The third aspect is courtly accomplishment, a command over the sort of acquired proficiencies forming part of the make-up of the cultivated courtier that are discussed by Castiglione at some length. These include dancing, musical, rhetorical and literary skills. These are sometimes demonstrated, and frequently alluded to in plays.

A relatively early writer in whose work all of these dimensions of intellectual engagement are explored is George Chapman. Chapman's view of education combines a secular humanist approach, similar to Mulcaster's advocacy of the control of the body by the mind as a principle of elite identity, and the more strictly religious view advocating scriptural knowledge as proposed by Laurence Humphrey in *The Nobles*. One of the clearest statements of Chapman's view of education comes in his philosophical poem, *Euthymiae Raptus or The Tears of Peace* (1609):

> But this is Learning; to haue skill to throwe
> Reignes on your bodies powres, that nothing knowe;
> And fill the soules powres, so with act, and art,
> That she can curbe the bodies angrie part;
> All perturbations; all affects that stray
> From their one obiect; which is to obay
> Her Souerayne Empire; as her selfe should force
> Their functions onely, to serue her discourse;
> And, that; to beat the streight path of one ende
> Which is, to make her substance still contend,
> To be God's image.
> (*Poems* p. 184, ll. 504–14)

This quasi-religious view of education is most evident in Chapman's tragedies, where there is a strong connection between virtue and learning.[7] In *The Revenge of Bussy D'Ambois* (Whitefriars?, c. 1610) the scholarly figure of Clermont declares that 'wits sharpnesse' should be employed and that: 'In noblest knowledge, wee should neuer waste / In vile and vulgar admirations' (3.2.20–22). In the comedies the social dimensions are clearer to see, and true learning for Chapman is not mere academic study, but the embrace of a higher state of social and moral being.

The gentleman scholar crops up a few times in Chapman's plays. In *A Humourous Day's Mirth* (1598), one of the few plays he wrote for the public theatre, he inserts the figure of Dowsecer, a melancholic who has shut himself away from the world. Dowsecer is inessential to the plot, only appearing in the scene in which he is the centre of focus (Act 2, Scene 2), and at the end. The scholar is here presented as a curiosity: he is supposed to be in a 'frenzy' but the King then pronounces this to be a 'holy fury', still a mystification, but one which is validated for the audience. His scholarly identity is firmly established, and this is a reason for his success at the end of the play. The connection between learning and melancholy is also suggested in Ford's play of 1621, *The Lover's Melancholy* (which draws on Burton's *Anatomy of Melancholy*). Corax, the physician of the melancholic Prince Palador, exclaims when the prince enters reading a book:

> A book! Is this the early exercise
> I did prescribe? Instead of following health,

Which all men covet, you purchase disease.
Where's your great horse, your hounds, your set at tennis,
Your balloon ball, the practice of your dancing,
Your casting of the sledge, or learning how
To toss a pike? All changed into a sonnet?
(2.2.49–55)

Clarence in Chapman's *Sir Giles Goosecap* (Blackfriars, 1602) is another such unworldly scholarly figure. He enjoys the protection of his patron, Momford, who appreciates his learning and promotes Clarence's suit to his widowed niece, Eugenia, who is herself no mean scholar (Chapman was a supporter of education for women). Eugenia is reluctant, reasoning that because of Clarence's poverty and relatively lower social position: 'my honour and good name, two essentiall parts of mee, woulde bee lesse, and lost' (2.1.175–6). Momford argues that Clarence is 'welthilie furnished with true knowledge' (2.1.191) and Eugenia later in the play comes around to accepting his suit. Both these figures exhibit a detachment from the social maelstrom, but they have an intellectual authority which gives them weight, and they triumph through this. A similar case is to be found in the anonymous *Wily Beguiled* of 1602 (probably private a theatre play) in the form of a poor scholar, Sophos, who is a suitor to Lelia, the daughter of a rich usurer who despises the scholar's poverty and wants to marry her off to a wealthy farmer's son. Learning in the play is uncomplicatedly associated with moral and social worth, and the scholar gets his bride in the end. The plot consists of intrigue and counter-intrigue involving a devious lawyer, Churms, but Sophos is carefully kept clear of any of it.

Scholarly detachment finds another form in Chapman's gentle intriguers; though this time it is not disengagement from the world. Rather, these figures pursue their activities with a degree of intellectual disinterest. Rinaldo in *All Fools* (Blackfriars, 1601) is a scholar at Padua who engages in an intrigue 'to varie / The pleasures of our wits' (2.1. 213–14). The scholar Lodovico in *May Day* (Blackfriars, 1602) becomes an intriguer and justifies his actions as an attempt to eschew idleness. He has a very applied and practical notion of learning, and he construes (wrongly) the romantic frenzy of another scholar, Aurelio, as drunkenness:

> Is it not a pitty to see a man of good hope, a toward Scholler, writes a theame well, scannes a verse very well, and likely in time to make a proper man, a good legge, specially in a boote, valiant, well spoken, and in a word, what not? and yet all this ouerthrowne as you see, drownd, quite drownd in a quarte pott.
> (1.1.172–6)

While Aurelio's frenzy is related to the disengagement of the melancholic intellectual from the everyday world, Lodovico's view represents a willingness to uses his skills in a social game which must be played successfully as an exercise in *savoir faire*, rather than being driven by need. A similar degree of personal disinterest is demonstrated in a gently-born and scholarly intriguer in a different genre of play, Marston's *Antonio's Revenge* (Paul's, 1600–1601). Antonio is unusual in the revenge genre in being a revenger who survives. This is a result perhaps of his detachment and avoidance of ambition, something which is affirmed by his refusal to accept the political power which is offered him at the end of the play. He chooses rather to retire from the everyday world to a higher plane of philosophical thought. In the Caroline drama, the inheritors of this playful intrigue as a display of social skill are the socially elite manipulators in Shirley's private theatre plays, whose actions are driven by the desire to display their wit as urbane gallants. However, with all these intrigue figures, as in the case of the ingenuity of low-born schemers, the possible implications about social attitudes underlying the construction of these figures cannot be pursued too far, as they are too narrowly involved in serving the demands of plot and narrative development, in what was often highly formulaic drama.

Learning as a validation of social ascendancy, with implications of moral superiority, is present in a number of plays. In Massinger and Fletcher's *The Elder Brother* (Blackfriars, 1624/5), the plot turns around two brothers. The elder, Charles, is a scholar and the younger, Eustace, is a courtier and each is highly reputed by their rival followings for their success in their respective capacities. The hard headed heiress, Angellina (the daughter of a lord), who is the centre of their rivalry in love, says that neither would make an adequate husband for her without an estate, scholarly or courtly accomplishments on their own being insufficient. Their father, Brisac, seeks to settle the estate on the younger son as the better marriage prospect, as the elder is too detached from the world in his learning, so much so that he forgets to eat and sleep (2.4.1–13). This results in a marriage agreement between the younger son and Angellina. Brisac is concerned that Charles's learning does not equip him practically to run the estate, and proposes to get him to sign away his birthright (2.1.89–98). He is opposed in this by the boys' uncle, his brother Miramont who, though not himself a scholar, puts a value on 'deep learning' and champions Charles's cause. Miramont becomes the chief mouthpiece for the play's promotion of the value of scholarship. Charles himself is uninterested in wealth and shows an inclination to do what his father is suggesting, but when he sees the beautiful Angellina he is jolted out of this attitude and refuses to sign. He then seeks her hand himself, and she quickly accepts him, arguing that her contract with Eustace depended on his getting the estate. A conflict between the two brothers ensues, but the play comes down on the side of scholarship over courtly accomplishment, not only in the way the two young men are represented, but in according Charles the prize in the end. It is not simply through his right as elder brother that he merits the estate and marriage, but in being possessed of greater substance and moral depth gained through learning. A similar outcome is found in Shirley's entertainment entitled *A Contention for Honour and Riches* (privately performed, 1631) which places Ingenuity, a scholar, in competition for the hand of Lady Honour with a soldier and a courtier, both unnamed. Honour chooses the scholar. This formed the basis of his later strongly allegorical closet play, *Honoria and Mammon* (1658), in which the scholar Alworth is again in contention with Conquest, a soldier, and Alamode, a courtier, for the hand of Lady Honoria. Alworth wins easily, a victory that is signalled by Honoria's crowning him with a wreath.

A recurrent issue, particularly later in the period, was the contrast or contention between book learning and 'natural' witty sophistication. The central problem was that this distinction was hard to make, and it was an area where Castiglione's notion of *sprezzatura*, involved downright deception. At least in dramatic representations, this consisted of a command over literary and other aspects of culture which was only acquirable through formal education, and the lack of it could attract charges of shallowness and insubstantiality. In Chapman's *All Fools*, Gostanzo, the father of one of the young gallants complains:

> I did not as you barraine Gallants doe,
> Fill my discourses vp drinking *Tobacco*;
> But on the present furnisht euer more
> With tales and practisde speeches . . .
> I could haue written as good Prose and Verse,
> As the most beggerlie Poet of em all,
> Either *Accrostique*, *Exordion*,
> *Epithalamions*, *Satyres*, *Epigrams*,
> *Sonnets* in Doozens, or your *Quatorzaines*,
> In any Rime *Masculine*, *Feminine*,
> Or *Sdruciolla*, or *cooplets*, *Blancke Verse*:
> Y'are but bench–whistlers now a dayes to them
> That were in our times.
> (2.1.162–78)

If the gallants being castigated here by Gostanzo are neglectful of acquired accomplishments, Jonson presents a converse figure in his town gull, Matthew, in the folio version of *Every Man in his Humour* (1616). He attempts to 'creepe, and wriggle into acquaintance with all the braue gallants about the towne' (1.4.69) and is a figure who bases his social aspirations on the idea of academically acquired accomplishments. The son of a fishmonger, his attempts at social climbing are represented particularly by the fact that he attempts to embrace literary culture in affecting to be a poet, and his failure by the fact that he resorts to plagiarism. The true wit (and better born) Edward Knowell says of him: 'Well, Ile haue him free of the wit-brokers, for hee vtters nothing, but stolne remnants' (4.2.56–7). The implications are that he is trying to adopt a discourse that is not legitimately his, for reasons of class as well as personal ability; his incompetence represents a failure which is at once intellectual and social. He does not have the acumen or education to discern how foolish his attempts are, and he is attempting to steal a social identity which is not properly his own.

Sophisticated social behaviour and discourse, aside even from the classic courtly accomplishments, is consistently represented as involving a cultivated intelligence which assumes a sound basis of formal education, at least in the rhetorical arts. This occurs in plays spanning the Elizabethan to the Caroline periods, and the public and private theatres. The conversations of witty lovers such as Beatrice and Benedick in *Much Ado about Nothing* (Curtain?, 1598), or Carol and Fairfield in Shirley's *Hyde Park* (Cockpit, 1632) are examples of this, substantially separated in time. In such cases the idea of making an issue of learning is a negation of *sprezzatura* and as such can be regarded as inappropriate for a gentleman, and certainly for a courtier. This idea informs the satirical barb in Carol's question to Fairfield in Act 3, Scene 2: '(Have) you no prompter, to insinuate / The first word of your studied oration?' and she goes on to parody the sort of address which might have been expected from him (p. 502).

The difficulty of making distinctions between formal learning and courtly sophistication did not prevent the repeated occurrence of the issue in plays. The difficulty was even likely to be one reason why it continued to provide material for debate in drama from the Elizabethan to the Caroline periods and became, if anything, more marked in the Caroline comedy of wit. In Lyly's *Sapho and Phao* (Blackfriars, 1584) the courtier Trachinus says to the scholar Pandion: 'In vniuersities vertues and vices are but shadowed in colours, white and blacke, in courtes shewed to life, good and bad' (1.2.12–14) and he goes on to ask: 'What hath a scholler found out by study, that a courtier hath not found out by practise' (1.2.21–2). Pandion, though, rejects the falseness of court life:

> *Trachinus*: Cease then to lead thy life in a study pinned with a fewe boardes, and endeuor to be a courtier to liue in emboste rouffes.
> *Pandion*: A labour intollerable for Pandion.
> *Trachinus*: Why?
> *Pandion*: Because it is harder to shape a life to dissemble, then to goe forward with the libertie of trueth.
> (1.2.27–33)

In his 1605 Blackfriars play, Chapman gives the foolish Monsieur D'Olive a defence of the Court over the academy as a source of education:

Paris, or *Padua*, or the famous Schoole of England called *Winchester*, famous (I meane) for the Goose, Where Schollers weare Petticoates so long, till their Penn and Inckhorns knocke against their knees: All these I say, are but Belfries to the Bodie or Schoole of the Court: Hee that would haue his Sonne proceed Doctor in three dayes, let him sende them thither; there's the Forge to fashion all the parts of them: There they shall learne the true vse of their good Partes indeed.

(*Monsieur D'Olive* 4.2.22–8)

Farneze in Dekker's *Patient Grissil* (Fortune, 1600), on the other hand, presents the case unironically from the scholarly side when he talks disparagingly of:

one of those changeable Silke gallants, who in a verie scuruie pride, scorne al schollers, and reade no bookes but a looking glasse, and speake no language but sweet Lady, and sweet *Signior* and chew between there teeth terrible words, as though they would coniure, as complement and Proiects, and Fastidious, and Caprichious, and Misprizion, and the Sintheresis, of the soule, and such like raise veluet tearmes.

(2.1.54–60)

This position is supported in the ironical statement of Carlo Buffone who, in *Every Man Out of His Humour* (1599) says of the fool, Fastidius Briske:

I am perswading this gentleman to turne courtier. He is a man of faire revenue, and his Estate will beare the charge well. Besides, for his other gifts of the minde, or so, why they are as nature lent him 'hem, pure, simple, without any artificiall drug or misture of these two thred-bare beggarly qualities, learning, and knowledge, and therefore the more accommodate, and genuine.

(4, 8, 8–15)

In *Cynthia's Revels* (Blackfriars, 1600), Jonson's scholar Crites is aware of being scorned by gallants. He is described by Hedon as a 'whore-sonne booke worme, a candle waster' (3.2.2–3) while Anaides says of him:

Death, what talke you of his learning? he vnderstands no more than a schoole-boy; I haue put him downe my selfe a thousand times (by this aire) and yet I neuer talkt with him by twice, in my life: you neuer saw his like. I could neuer get him to argue with me, but once, and then, because I could not construe an Author I quoted at first sight, hee went away, and laught at me.

(4.5.40–46)

He rejects their criticism describing them (Hedon and Anaides) as: 'The one, a light voluptuous reueller, / The other a strange arrogating puffe, / Both impudent, and ignorant inough' (3.3.25–7). This is Jonson's spleen but may express, albeit exaggeratedly, the distance between the scholar and the courtier from the point of view of the scholar. This play is not thought to have been well received by the Court, and if so, this may be the reason. Jonson's plays abound with satirical jibes against ignorance in those who enjoy the advantages of a socially and economically privileged position.

Anti-academic attitudes on the part of fashionable society are repeatedly found on the Caroline stage, something which often comes in for satirical treatment.[8] The 'schools' in Brome's and Shirley's plays (*The New Academy* and *Love Tricks or the School of Compliment*) are schools of compliment and gesture, rather than anything involving an academic discipline. Shirley's satire, when not directed at the moral failings of the elite, is aimed at these preoccupations. In *The Lady of Pleasure* (Cockpit, 1635) Sir Thomas Bornwell lays out to his nephew the ideal of the educated gentleman: 'Learning is an addition beyond / Nobilitie of birth; honour of bloud / Without the ornament of knowledge is / A glorious ignorance' (2.1.28–31). Sir Thomas's affected wife, Lady Aretina, a country gentlewoman who is intent on pursuing the sophisticated pleasures of the town, is however appalled by her nephew Frederick's academic appearance. He is at university, but Aretina feels that he would have been better served if he had been sent to France to learn courtly manners instead. She complains: 'I feare hee's spoild for ever, he did name / Logicke, and may for ought I know be gone / So farre to vnderstand it. I did always / Suspect they would corrupt him in the Colledge' (2.1.79–82). In Act 3, Scene 2 Aretina displays her social skills in a wit-combat exchange of compliments in French with her social rival, Celestina Bellamour, and when Frederick addresses Celestina in Latin, his aunt exclaims in horror: 'O most unpardonable! Get him off' (3.2.138). [9]

Frederick himself is at once defiant and increasingly uncomfortable about his learning, as he becomes sucked into the social milieu of his aunt's affected world:

> . . . Who laughes at me?
> Go, I will root here, if I list, and talke
> Of Rhetoricke, Logicke, Latine, Greeke, or any thing,
> And understand 'em too, who says the contrary?
> Yet in a faire way I contemn all learning,
> And will be as ignorant as he, or he
> Or any taffata, satten, scarlet, plush
> Tissue or cloath, a bodkin gentleman,
> Whose manners are most gloriously infected.
> (3.2.162–70)

He is later dressed according to fashion (4.2) and coached on how to wear his clothes. Later, drunkenly, he attempts to show off his newly learned skill in compliments (5.2). Though Shirley does not especially come down on the side of either scholarship or courtly accomplishment, Frederick's drunken and ungainly courtly manners contrast unfavourably with his identity as a scholar, and this complements the play's satirical representation of his aunt's excessive affectations.

In those of Shirley's characters who manifest a fashionable distaste for the academic, this attitude is frequently satirically represented as proceeding from shallow values and affectation. It also becomes a comment on the misalignment of material wealth and intellectual substance. In *A Contention for Honour and Riches*, the Lady Riches says of Ingenuity, the scholar: 'How rank he smells / Of Aristotle, and the musty tribe / Or worm–eaten philosophers. Get him from me!' (Scene 1, p. 292). She is a woman who has to choose between a citizen, Gettings, and a countryman, Clod, as suitors. In the later *Honoria and Mammon*, the Lady Mammon is in a similar mould, and her gentleman usher, Phantasm, declares:

> My lady keeps no library, no food
> For book-worms (sir,) I can assure you that.
> Learning is dangerous in our family;
> She will not keep a secretary, for fear
> Of the infection.
> (1.1.p. 6)

In both the positive and negative representations of scholars and scholarship within the drama, we are faced with largely conventional sets of attitudes. Scholars are to a considerable extent stock types, often occupying defined social roles which may have little to do with what might actually be expected from such figures, and frequently much more to do with the narrative and often comic requirements of the pieces in which they are represented. Hence, for instance, Peter Hausted's *The Rival Friends* (acted in 1631) features a variety of scholar figures in minor roles, including Nodle Emptie, an ignorant Inns of Court man. In Fletcher's *The Pilgrim* (Blackfriars, 1621) a scholar is among a group of madmen who are identified by either nationality or profession. There is no attempt here to endow him with appropriate defining characteristics. A high value placed on scholarship is often most clearly seen in those plays in which the scholar figure plays a central or dominant role, and where the playwright is seeking to make a point. Where they occupy minor roles, they are more usually cast simply as a social category or 'estate', frequently in contrast with other such categories. Unsurprisingly, a common juxtaposition is scholar-courtier, as in Thomas Goffe's university play *The Courageous Turk* (1619), and several of the plays referred to or discussed above. In Middleton and

Rowley's masque, *The World Tossed at Tennis* (1620), a soldier and a scholar are in competitive juxtaposition and, though here there is some interest in the characteristics which attach to these roles, they are largely simply representative social types. The juxtapositions in the plays do, however, involve social definition by contrast, often with a satirical purpose. In an increasingly style-conscious theatre, rhetorical and linguistic modes are, not unnaturally, an important part of this. The eponymous central figure in Thomas Randolph's *Aristippus* (a dialogue, rather than a full length play, from 1626), says of a scholar's conversation: 'If you discourse but a little while with a Courtier, you presently betray your learned Ignorance, answering him he concludes not Syllogistically, and asking him in what Moode and figure he speakes in, as if Learning were not as much out of fashion at Court, as Cloathes at *Cambridge*' (p. 12).

A frequent source of dramatic comedy is the ludicrous incongruity of those who have laboriously acquired learning, and are unable either to use it within measure, or to confine it to appropriate contexts. The satire here is not on education itself, but rather its social misuse by those who are propelled, through their own eccentricity or the uncertainty of their social background, into an overly zealous embrace of it. An early instance of the oblique mockery of academic pomposity is to be found in the 'fustian' that Clove and Orange speak in Act 3, Scene 4 of *Every Man out of his Humour* in trying to pass themselves off as scholars. The satire of academic language is often targeted not only on intellectual pretension but also social aspiration in relation to learning. These involve both the low-born who seek to use learning as a means both of acquiring material gain and gentle status, and those who are already possessed of an elite position and social identity, but aspire to a higher level of self-definition through the acquisition and display of learning and refinement.[10] Shakespeare provides one of the earliest and most important examples of both types of aspiration in *Love's Labours Lost*, probably written for first performance in a private and elite context as early as 1593, and later (in 1604) staged privately in the home of the Earl of Southampton as an entertainment for James I. This elite connection, along with fact that the play was also publicly acted both in the private theatre of Blackfriars and the public Globe theatre (as the first Quarto title page informs us), perhaps accounts for the fact that the satire of noble aspiration to model their behaviour on learning receives a much milder satirical treatment than the low-born social aspiration through education.

The sharpest satirical barbs in the play are reserved for the two foolish characters in the subplot, Holofernes and Don Armado, the latter a man with aspirations to being a courtier. He is referred to as 'Monarcho', an allusion to an actual crazy hanger on at Court in the period.[11] Holofernes is a man whose social ambitions are founded on scholarship, and the character is likely to have been based on Gabriel Harvey. Though there are echoes in the play of the pamphlet war between Thomas Nashe and Harvey, Shakespeare does not engage with the issues of that polemic, and confines himself to using perceptions about its protagonists to construct his sub-plot figures. In *Have with you to Saffron Walden*, Nashe describes Harvey – who was the son of a ropemaker from Saffron Walden, and who acquired his education through being a sizar at Cambridge – particularly in terms of his social climbing:[12] 'There did this our *Talatamtana*, or Doctour *Hum* thrust himselfe into thickest rankes of the Noblemen and Gallants, and whatsoeuer they were arguing of, he would not misse to catch hold of, or strike in at the one end, and take the theame out of their mouths, or it should goe hard' (McKerrow, 1904, III, 75). A little further on he describes a university play of 1581 which evidently satirized Harvey, also representing him as a schoolmaster:[13]

> What will you giue mee when I bring him vppon the Stage in one of the principallest Colledges in *Cambridge*? Lay anie wager with me, and I will; or if you laye no wager at all, Ile fetch him aloft in *Pedantius*, that exquisite Comedie in *Trinitie Colledge*; where, vnder the cheife part, from which it tooke his name, as namely the concise and firking finicaldo fine School-master, hee was fully drawn & delineated from the soale of the foote to the crowne of his head. The iust manner of his phrase in his Orations and Disputations they stufft his mouth with, & no Buffianisme throughout his whole bookes, but they bolsterd out his part with. (McKerrow, 1904, III, 80)[14]

The use of Harvey as a model is significant, as Shakespeare could not but have been aware of the vitriolic satire on the man's social ambitions based on his education, something that strongly emerged in the pamphlet war. Armado, Holofernes and Nathaniel base their pretensions on what they see as refinement of language. They manifest an anxiety to distinguish themselves from the ignorant rabble, to establish their identities through learning. It is precisely through the exclusiveness which learned forms of speech afford, that an elevated social identity can be achieved. This is implicit in the exchange between Moth and Armado in Act 1, Scene 2:

> *Moth*: Then I am sure you know how much the gross sum of deuce-ace amounts to.
> *Armado*: It doth amount to one more than two.
> *Moth*: Which the base vulgar call three.
> (42–5)

Armado says to Holofernes: 'Arts-man (scholar), preambulate: we will be singled from the barbarous.' Later he refers to 'the posteriors of this day, which the rude multitude call the afternoon.'[15] It is almost in the same breath that he claims, 'Sir, the king is a noble gentleman, and my familiar, I do assure ye, very good friend.'[16] An associate of Holofernes, Sir Nathaniel the curate, makes a comparison between education and food which implicitly calls upon the idea that the refined food eaten by the nobility nourishes those superior qualities which constitute elite status, in a comparison which also links status (or the right to it) naturally with learning. Talking about the constable, Dull, he says:

> Sir, he hath never fed of the dainties that are bred in a book.
> He hath not eat paper, as it were; he hath not drunk ink: his intellect is not
> replenished; he is only an animal, only sensible in the duller parts;
> And such barren plants are set before us, that we thankful should be,
> Which we of taste and feeling are, for those parts that do fructify in us
> more than he;
> (4.2.23–7)

The self-conscious display of learning on the part of these comic figures is also, somewhat paradoxically, a product of their lack of self-awareness. This is illustrated in the monstrously pedantic Holofernes's criticism of Armado's mode of speech: 'He draweth out the thread of his verbosity finer than the staple of his argument. I abhor such fanatical phantasimes, such insociable and point-devise companions' (5.1.16–19). Their overt awareness of, and comic obsession with, language means that they continually betray a preoccupation with what they perceive as the technical means of constructing an elite identity, in a manner which is diametrically opposite to *sprezzatura*, and in fact makes their aspirations to this utterly preposterous.[17] By contrast the sophisticated nobleman, Berowne, is able and resolved to forswear formulaic expression (here also implicitly speaking for his noble companions as well):

> O! never will I trust to speeches penn'd
> Nor to the motion of a school-boy's tongue,
> Nor never come in visor to my friend,
> Nor woo in rhyme, like a blind harper's song,
> Taffeta phrases, silken terms precise,
> Three-pil'd hyperboles, spruce affection,
> Figures pedantical
> (5.2.402–8)

Holofernes and Armado could never do this without abandoning their social ambition; they cannot naturally occupy this space and have only the formula available to them, which they grossly misapprehend.

The contrast of actual literary competence and exercise of 'wit' between the King and courtiers on the one hand and Armado and Holofernes on the other, is another way in which broader social contexts in the play help to contain and draw the sting of any satirical edge to the treatment of the noble companions. Rosaline describes Berowne in the following terms:

> His eye begets occasion for his wit;
> For every object that the one doth catch
> The other turns to a mirth-moving jest,
> Which his fair tongue (conceit's expositor)
> Delivers in such apt and gracious words
> That aged ears play truant at his tales,
> And younger hearings are quite ravished'
> So sweet and voluble is his discourse.
> (2.1.69–76)

The sonnets composed by the young men testify to their literary competence – no matter that the circumstances of their delivery are a source of embarrassment to them – and provide a corrective contrast to their later lamentable performance as disguised Muscovites. Holofernes and Armado, by comparison, invite ridicule with every statement they utter, while apparently being immune to embarrassment. The contrast between the two social levels is most pointed in the two love letters: Armado's read in the sophisticated company of the Princess and her courtiers in Act 4, Scene 1, and Berowne's in the very next scene, read by Sir Nathaniel to Holofernes and his associates. The reading is preceded by a preposterous verse written by Holofernes. While the linguistic accomplishment of the courtiers is never in question, the affectations of these men are precisely what illustrates Berowne's warning about 'taffeta phrases' and 'three pil'd hyperboles'. The King views Armado's self-conscious cultivation of verbal sophistication with a detached amusement, describing him as: 'A man in all the world's new fashion planted, / That hath a mint of phrases in his brain; / One who the music of his own vain tongue / Doth ravish like enchanting harmony' (1.1.161–6). He ends up saying: 'But I protest I love to hear him lie, / And I will use him for my minstrelsy', to which and Longaville adds: 'Costard, the swain, and he, shall be our sport.' In the presentation of the Worthies in Act 5 by Armado, Holofernes, Sir Nathaniel and Moth, sport is precisely what the courtiers engage in. Their treatment here recalls the comment made in Nicholas Ling's 1597 tract, Wit's Commonwealth: 'The ignorant are . . . the play of great Lords' (57[r]). The Princess, whose cultural sophistication is strongly established right from the outset, recognizes the comic qualities of their pretensions too in her observation:

> That sport best pleases that doth least know how,
> Where zeal strives to content, and the contents
> Dies in the zeal of that which it presents;
> Their form confounded makes most form in mirth,
> When great things labouring perish in their birth
> (5.2.512–16)

In response to this the astute Berowne, referring to the courtiers' own earlier abortive disguising as Muscovites, ruefully observes to the King: 'A right description of our sport, my lord (5.2.517). The Worthies episode consists largely in the mockery of the presentations, something which helps, by means of contrast and despite Berowne's parallel, to redeem the status of the young courtiers who have themselves been embarrassed by the response of the women to their own efforts. Berowne astutely recognizes that: ''tis some policy / To have one show worse than the king's and his company'. The entry of these socially inferior figures into what is seen as the natural preserve of the noble elite makes them fair game, particularly in view of the way in which their pretensions to higher culture have been repeatedly emphasized earlier in the play. The episode also allows the courtiers re-establish their cultural hegemony by becoming critics of cultural performance, rather than targets of criticism for their own performance.

In a play in which the idea of social performance and its refinement is so significant, a reflexive perspective on theatre inevitably emerges, and Berowne remarks: 'Our wooing doth not end like an old play; / Jack hath not Jill: these ladies' courtesy / Might well have made our sport a comedy' (5.2.866–8). When the King says: 'Come, sir, it wants a twelvemonth and a day / And then 'twill end', Berowne replies: 'That's too long for a play' (868–70). Theatrical performance as a source of social education is also suggested when Moth tells Armado how to carry off his courtship successfully:

> . . . to jig off a tune at the tongue's end, canary to it with your feet, humour it with turning up your eyelids, sigh a note and sing a note, sometime through the throat as if you swallowed love with singing love, sometime through the nose, as if you snuffed up love by smelling love, with your hat penthouse-like o'er the shop of your eyes; with your arms crossed on your thin-belly doublet like a rabbit on a spit; or your hands in your pocket, like a man after the old painting; and keep not too long in one tune, but a snip and away. These are complements, these are humours, these betray nice wenches, that would be betrayed without these; and make them men of note (do you note, men?) that are most affected to these.
> (3.1.9–23)

What he is describing is essentially the art of acting. When Armado asks him: 'How hast thou purchased this experience?', he replies, 'By my penny of observation', very likely referring to attendance at a theatre. This would have been made more pointed by the fact that the actor playing Moth is delivering this speech in a theatre, and at one point (the words in parenthesis within the quotation above) addresses the audience directly.

The attempt of the King of Navarre to get his court to seclude themselves in three years of learning goes against the ways in which a nobleman should carry his education. The important thing is that he should have it, but that he should carry it with apparent insouciance. When Berowne remarks in Act 4, Scene 3, 'Learning is but an adjunct to ourself' (310), he is not devaluing formal learning so much as recognizing that, far from being an end in itself, it should compose a natural rather than self-conscious part of a gentleman's social identity. Implicitly, the idea is that the behaviour of the King and courtiers should be governed by *sprezzatura*. Both Castiglione's idea and the satire at the two social levels in the play have at their base an understanding of the relationship between between class and 'natural' cultural competence also formulated in Pierre Bourdieu's analysis of this relationship in his discussion of taste:

> The ideology of natural taste contrasts two modalities of cultural competence and its use, and, behind them, two modes of acquisition of culture. Total, early, imperceptible learning, performed within the family from the earliest days of life and extended by scholastic learning which presupposes and completes it, differs from belated, methodical learning not so much in the depth and durability of its effects – as the ideology of cultural 'veneer' would have it – as in the modality of the relationship to language and culture which it simultaneously tends to inculcate. It confers the self-certainty which accompanies the certainty of possessing cultural legitimacy.
> (1984, 66)

> . . .

> The ideology of natural taste owes its plausibility and its efficacy to the fact that, like the ideological strategies generated in the everyday class struggle, it *naturalizes* real differences, converting differences in the mode of acquisition into differences of nature; it only recognizes as legitimate the relation to culture (or language) which least bears the visible marks of its genesis, which has nothing 'academic,' 'scholastic,' 'bookish,' 'affected' or 'studied' about it, but manifests by its ease and naturalness that true culture is nature – a new mystery of immaculate conception.
> (ibid., 68)

Especially in the context of a society which discouraged illegitimate ambition, the pursuit of social distinction by Holofernes and Armado constitutes a desire to rise inappropriately above their station, and is thus a legitimate target of ridicule at the very least.[18]

A contrasting relationship between social aspiration and learning is to be found in Chapman's *The Gentleman Usher* (Blackfriars, 1601). Here the pretender is someone who illegitimately occupies an elite position at Court while patently lacking learning, a fact which arouses suspicion as to his true identity. The treatment is characteristic of Chapman's profound respect for learning, and the representation draws implicitly on the ideal of an association between intellectual competence and rank.[19] Medice (who later turns out to be called Mendice) is described as: 'That fustian Lord, who in his buckram face / Bewraies . . . a map of basenesse' (1.1.105–6), and the Duke's son, Vincentio says of him: 'Faith I would faine disgrace him by all meanes, / As enemy to his base-bred ignorance, / That being a great Lord, cannot write nor reade' (1.1.122–4). For his part, Medice says of courtiers who are scornful of him: 'They stand vpon their wits and paper-learning: / Giue me a fellow with a naturall wit, / That can make wit of no wit; and wade through / Great things with nothing, when their wits sticke fast' (2.1.58–61). At one point, Sarpego, a pedant who possesses learning without any pretension to social rank, is allowed to display his rhetorical skills to a favourable reception by the courtiers and thus provide a specifically positive contrast to Medice's ignorance (Act 1, Scene 1). Though the Medice/Mendice story is a nominally a sub-plot element, it becomes very significant narrative strand in the structure of the play.

If Medice aspires socially while neglecting scholarship, another Chapman character exhibits both social and intellectual pretensions. In *Monsieur D'Olive* the eponymous central figure is a ridiculous country gentleman with aspirations to greater things, especially based on his view of himself as an intellectual. He says:

> I will haue my chamber the Rende-vous of all good wittes, the shoppe of good wordes, the Minte of good iestes, and Ordinary of fine discours; Critickes, Essayists, Linguists, Poets, and other professors of that facultie of witte, shall at certaine houres ith day resort thither, it shall bee a second *Sorbonne*, where all doubts or differences of Learning, Honour, Duellisme, Criticisms, and Poetrie, shall bee disputed.
> (1.2.110–16)

His foolishness and excessive ambition are demonstrated when he is appointed an ambassador, with satirically comic consequences when his desire for self-display are shown to be in inverse proportion to his abilities.

An example of the representation of an aspirant to social advancement through education in non-courtly contexts is Tim Yellowhammer in

Middleton's *Chaste Maid in Cheapside* (Swan, 1613), a foolish character who, along with his equally ridiculous tutor, shows a complete lack of natural sense or social competence. Tim's self-consciousness in the role of scholar – exemplified most markedly in his excessive use of Latin – is what constitutes his foolishness and is the absolute antithesis of *sprezzatura*. It represents a satirical portrait of inappropriate middle class pretension as his being at university is the result of the aspirations of his ambitious citizen parents. His father describes him as: 'an Universitie Man, / Proceeds next Lent to a Batchelor of Art / He will be call'd *Sir Yellowhammer* then / Over all Cambridge, and that's halfe a Knight' (1.1.163–6). If he is keenly aware of its social implications, the father is elsewhere less taken with his son's learning itself, complaining when he cannot understand a letter written by his son in Latin that: 'He's growne too verball, this Learning is a great Witch' (1.1.65). Tim's being tricked into marriage with a whore at the end of the play is not only an implicit comment on his incompetence, but represents also the punishment of his parents for their social ambitions.

The changed priorities of the Caroline comedy of wit, produced by writers who had their focus firmly on the private theatre audience, resulted in shifts in the ways in which scholarliness was represented on stage. As with their lack of interest in the representation of low-born 'secular wits' the Caroline writers seem to have concerned themselves relatively less with the question of social and material ambition through education, and preferred to focus on the possibilities for the satire of manners. The scholar Geron in the sub-plot of Richard Brome's *The Love-sick Court* (1639) might just serve as a minor example of plebeian social aspiration through learning, especially in the attitudes he reveals when he warns the woman he is wooing against talking to Tersulus, a tailor and Varillus, a barber:

> . . . *Doris*, take heed
> Be wary in your conversation
> (As *Whilom Tully* warnd his tender son)
> With such *Plebeians*, least their vulgar breeding
> Corrupt your education.
> (4.1.p. 137)

However, here and elsewhere on the Caroline stage, the satire of scholarly pretension is more dominant motif and object of satire than straightforward social aspiration. In this play, Geron, the son of Garula the court midwife, is a figure who is locked into his academic world and is unable to tailor his speech and behaviour appropriately to social situations. His wooing (aided by his mother and her friend Thymilis) of the bemused maidservant, Doris, is highly comic in the incongruity of his language:

Thymilis: ... he loves you, *Doris*
Doris: That's more then I ere knew, or read, by al
He speaks or writes to me. He cloaths his words
In furres and hoods, so, that I cannot find
The naked meaning of his business, Madam
Thymilis: Speak plainly to her, *Geron*.
Garula: To her Son.
Geron: My business is the same, that *Whilome* drew *Demosthenes* to
Corinth, some repentance, so I pay not too dear.
Doris: Lo you there, Madam
Garula: You must speak plainer, Son.
Thymilis: And you be kinder, *Doris*.

. . .

Geron: O forfeit not the praise
That *Whilome Aristotle* gave your Sex,
To be inrich'd with piety and pitty.
Doris: I know not what to pitty, but your want
Of utterance. It is some horrid thing
That you desire, and are asham'd to speak it.
(3.1.p. 123–4)

Thymilis continues later: '*Geron*, you speak too learnedly, as if / You woo'd a Muse: and *Doris* understands not, / But by your posture what you'ld have' (3.1.p. 124).

Geron's foolishness proceeds largely from his inability to understand that his acquired mode of speech, which he perceives has endowed him with the social power that his birth has denied him, is simply failing to be effective in this context.[20] He becomes an example of what the Inns of Court man, Exhibition, in Edward Sharpham's *Cupid's Whirligig* of 1607 had described as: 'your punies lately come from the Vniuersitie, such as take so much on them by the reading of *Aristotles problemes*, as they thinke they could teach their owne Fathers to make Children' (4.1.p. 57: 24–7). The point is comically driven home by the barber, Varillus, who warns Doris about Geron's likely performance as a husband: 'Take heed *Doris* / How you become his wife: for he will love you / So by the book, as he will never lie with you / Without an Author for it' (4.1.p. 137). Another such example, again a minor part in a play, is the bashful scholar Kataplectus who retreats into talking Latin when he is bidden to address a lady in Scene 2 of Randolph's *The Muses Looking Glass* (Salisbury Court, 1630). These figures illustrate the point made by Shirley's Lady Aretina Bornwell about her nephew's classical education: 'Will your Greeke sawes and sentences discharge / The Mercer, or is Latin a fit language / To court a mistresse in?' (*The Lady of Pleasure*, 2.1.79–85).

The detachment and unworldliness of scholars is the basis of a charge levelled at a scholar named Algebra by another character, Master Caution, in the anonymous *Wit's Triumvirate* (c. 1635): 'O, you scholars will be wise men in time! You dream of an utopia, a philosophical world that never was, is, or shall be. And so long as you rule yourselves to that mystical world, you cannot be wise in this wicked one' (2.1.226–30). However, unusually and despite the conventional attitude expressed here, Algebra, who plays a major role in the action of the play, actually avoids being gulled by tricksters (unlike several others in the play) and his understanding of human psychology is imputed to his study of nature.

Though there was a dramatic conventionality about the representation of scholars as comically inept, this attitude is to be found in arguably more authoritative contexts as well. Burton's *Anatomy of Melancholy* has this to say about the matter (Burton himself having spent most of his life in an academic environment):

> Because they cannot ride an horse; which every Clowne can doe; salute and court a Gentlewoman, carve at table, cringe and make congies, which every common swasher can doe, *hos populus ridet &c.* they are laughed to scorne, and accompted silly fooles by our Gallants. Yea, many times, such is their misery, the deserve it: a meere Scholler, a meere Asse.
> (1.2.3.15, p. 305)

He goes on to lay part of the blame for this one the scholars themselves:

> Your greatest students are commonly no better, silly soft fellowes in their outward behaviour, absurd, ridiculous to others, and no whit experienced in worldly businesse; they can measure the heavens, range over the world, teach others wisdome, yet in bargaines and contracts they are circumvented by every base Tradesman.
> (1.2.3.15, p. 306)

In the drama the satire of excessive scholarly language was also part of the implicit way in which the urbanity of true wits was represented. In Shirley's *The Sisters* (Blackfriars, 1642) there is the brief appearance of a scholar who, as a wooer, presents one of the sisters with a piece of paper containing a lover's eulogy of her. She responds by saying: 'I pity men of your high fancy should / Dishonour their own names, by forming such / Prodigious shapes of beauty in our sex' (4.2.pp. 399–400). She then proceeds to satirize the elaborate metaphorical excesses of formal, courtly language, thereby demonstrating an urbane superiority to the scholar in not only having a command of his rhetoric, but being able to criticize it. Shirley had earlier exploited the comic potential of this sort of high-flown language in *Love Tricks, or The School of Compliment*

(Cockpit, 1625). Ingeniolo, a yeoman's son who is a pupil at Gasparo's school
of courtly manners, delivers a wooing speech he has learned (which he intends
to address to a farmer's daughter), a speech that is ridiculous for both its
rhetorical excess and its incongruity:

> Thou art some Goddess, that to amaze the earth
> With thy celestial presence, hast put on
> The habit of a mortal, gods sometimes
> Would visit country houses, and gild o'er
> A sublunary habitation
> With glory of their presence, and make heav'n
> Descend into a hermitage: Sure thy father
> Was Maia's son, disguis'd in shepherd's weeds,
> And thou dost come from Jove; no marvel then
> We swains do wonder at thee, and adore,
> Venus herself the queen of Cytheron,
> When she is riding through the milky way,
> Drawn with white doves, is but a blowze, and must,
> When thou appearest, leave her bird-drawn coach,
> And give the reins to thee, and trudge afoot
> Along the heavenly plains, paved with stars,
> In duty of the thy excellence, while the gods
> Looking amazed from their crystal windows,
> Wonder what new–come deity doth call
> Them to thy adoration.
> (3.5.pp. 48–9)

However, a more trenchantly satiric treatment of the gratuitous verbosity of
affected academic language is found in Wild's *The Benefice* in the form of a
letter from Fantastes, 'a meer Scholar, newly come from the University'
addressed to Marchurch, the potential dispenser of a living:

Most Propitious Patron
As I was equitating in these Rural Dimensions, the intelligence of the
Vacuity of your Worship's Ecclesiastical Donation, did dexterously occur
and perforate my Auricles; And forthwith, gratifying my Beast with a
measure of Pinguifying Provender, I did approperate to your resplendent
Habitation, to impenetrate the Beneficial *Presentation* to me, A profound
Aristotelian. – Sir *Fortune* hath not Beatify'd me with Mundane
Promotions, neither have I conglomerated any Terrestrial Substance; but
if you please, with your perspicuous Luminaries to contemplate and
perscrutate these Testifications, you shall be animadverted of my
Deportment in the *Oxfordian* Society, in my modification for Literature.
Here is moreover in this Membrane with the cerous Assignments, the
Episcopal Assign to gratify your Supplicant, (ponderating the Premises)
you shall vivificate the mortiferous Essence of my Intellectuals and
invocate this Domical one that will not contaminate your Family; but

perprecate the Deities for the longitude of their Benediction upon your
Propagation: and remain
Your Incarcerated Creature,
Fantastes
(4.1. p. 37)

The pretentiousness of scholarly speech is not always simply a matter of
making the speaker of it ridiculous. In Henry Glapthorne's *Wit in a Constable*
(Cockpit, 1639) the satire is directed at a citizen who is uncritically dazzled by
this sort of language. A young gallant named Thoroughgood wishes to court
Clare, the niece of the social-climbing Alderman Covet. In order to do this, and
with his collusion, he impersonates his reputedly scholarly cousin Jeremy, the
son of Sir Geoffrey Hold-fast. When asked his name, he affects an exaggerated
style of academic language: 'My *appellation* or *pronomen*, as / (It is tearm'd by
the *Latins*) is *hight Ieremie*, / But my Cognomen, as the English gather, / is
called *Holdfast*.' He continues in the same vein when further questioned about
his kinship: 'The Nominalls, the Thomists, all the sects / Of old and moderne
Schoole-men, doe oblige me, / To pay to that Sir *Geffrey* fillial duty' (1.1.C4^r).
Even when engaged in the wooing of Clare herself he does not change his
tone:

> If you will love me Lady, Ile approach your eares
> Not in a garbe Domesticke or termes vulgar,
> But hourely change my language, court you now,
> In the *Chaldean*, or *Arabicke* tongues,
> Expound the *Talmud* to you, and the *Rabbines*
> Then read the Dialect of the *Alanits*,
> Or *Ezion Gebor*, which the people use
> Five leagues beyond the Sun-rising, in stead
> Of pages to attend you, I will bring
> Sects of Philosophers and queint Logicians,
> Weel Procreat by learned art, and *I*
> Will generate new broods of Schollers on you,
> Which shall defend opinions far more various
> Then all the Sectaries of Amsterdam
> Have ever vented.
> (2.1.C4^v–D1^r)

This speech, followed by others of a similar nature, has the effect not only of
convincing the Alderman, but sending him into transports of delight, and he
exclaims, 'Heare him but speake, and he will put you downe / Ten Universities,
and Innes of Court, / In twentie sillables' (2.1.C4^v) .

Though the topic of scholars and the learning was never a dominant a
preoccupation on the early modern stage it did crop up regularly, albeit
variously inflected according to the preoccupations and constituencies of

playwrights, and to the shifts of emphasis in changing styles of plays on the stage over the course of the period. The great majority of the plays that engage the topic are private theatre plays, which is hardly surprising since the issue is largely of elite interest. Nonetheless, the values that inform these plays are not substantially challenged in the surviving popular material. As education was an issue that was rarely represented without some reference to social politics, it is able to provide some perspectives on certain of the sources of social tension in the period. Much of this derives from the somewhat uncomfortable and even contradictory roles that education played in the ways in which early modern society represented itself on the stage. For those lower down the social scale, while it nominally provided the basis for advancement, it frequently failed to provide the material means. For those of the elite with aspirations to courtliness, while it was a necessary commodity it could not be too overtly displayed without some compromising of gentlemanly sophistication, and it had the further taint of being able to be turned to material gain. Satire of the scholarly in Jacobean and especially Caroline drama sat alongside satire of courtly pretension which involved a rejection of the overtly scholarly. However, while the drama never did present a single viewpoint, the greater interest of Caroline dramatists to cater to the elite audiences of the private playhouses was partly responsible for a clear shift towards favouring the courtly over the academic (Shirley's positive scholar figures notwithstanding). Another factor was probably an evolving class consciousness in sections of the elite, a direction that reached its high point in the period after the Interregnum, illustrated in Dryden's comment on Jonson's *The Silent Woman* in his *Defence of the Epilogue*:

> That the wit of this Age is much more Courtly, may easily be prov'd by viewing the Characters of Gentlemen which were written in the last. First, for *Jonson*, *True–Wit* in the *Silent Woman*, was his Master-piece, and *True–wit* was a Scholar–like kind of man, a Gentleman with an allay of Pedantry: a man who seems mortifi'd to the world, by much reading. The best of his discourse is drawn, not from the knowledge of the Town, but Books, and, in short, he would be a fine Gentleman, in an University. (1672, 215)

CHAPTER EIGHT

Conclusion

Despite the early links between the drama and both the processes of learning and the institutions of secondary and higher education, it is clear that drama in the public domain became clearly separated from these connections, particularly with the advent of the commercial theatre. The formal advances in drama which emerged in educational contexts, particularly the Inns of Court, would probably have been more directly influential if the sort of relative continuity between academic and non-academic drama that is to be found in the pre-commercial interlude drama of the sixteenth century had persisted. As it was, the coming of the commercial stage put a sharp social barrier between the two forms of activity. Whatever influence the higher educational institutions continued to have over this important area of cultural production had to be effected in other, more indirect ways. One of these was the fact of the substantial percentage of playwrights who were trained in these institutions and enjoyed the sort of classical education they provided. Though academic drama cannot be claimed in itself to be a strong influence on the public product, insofar as it constituted a significant dimension of the exercise of neoclassical culture in the universities and the Inns of Court it did constitute part of the early formative cultural milieu of those playwrights who did go to university.

Education as a topic continued to enjoy a representation in plays throughout the period, though certainly the drama's perspectives on it altered over the course of the sixteenth and seventeenth centuries, and was affected by changing conditions of production and reception. These changes included the substantial developments in the nature of the theatrical product itself, in the considerable distance travelled from the Tudor interlude to the Caroline drama. The extent to which in certain respects the theatre (or certain types of theatre) continued to be viewed and view itself as an instructive medium, however problematically for some, was also germane to the medium's relation to the processes of education. In the interlude drama of the sixteenth century there is a continuity of purpose observable between drama as pedagogical exercise, and drama which is overtly didactic in respect of religion or some aspect of social morality. This is probably most true of plays in emanating from educational auspices. It is possible to see, for instance, Edwardes's *Damon and Pithias* both as an exercise in the interests of developing 'audacitye' in the scholars who performed it, and as a play about honourable behaviour and friendship. Equally, *Gorboduc*, though an Inns of Court play with a clear purpose of political education and persuasion, is not unconnected with the rhetorical exercises practised in the sort of institution that produced it. However, there is little to distinguish these plays, in terms of didactic impulse, from the general run of interludes in the period. Teaching, in whatever form, is their primary purpose. One of the significant changes which accompanied the coming of the commercial stage involved the drama's taking on a far more discursive or polemical role rather than continuing to be so clearly an instructive medium as the sixteenth century interlude was. Of course polemic is also persuasion, and a form of teaching. Nevertheless, in a product on offer in the public theatre with a clearer connection between its appeal to the audience and its profitability than had ever been the case with the earlier interludes, there was certainly less scope for overt didacticism. There were also other factors aside from commercialization that contributed to the change, such as the diversity of religious opinion, the secularization of the medium, and effect of the drama itself in producing an increasingly sophisticated audience. In the face of all this, it is interesting to note a persistence in the didactic impulse of the commercial drama, albeit cast in social and political rather than religious or moral terms. This, more than anything, is what constituted any claim the drama had to seriousness as a cultural form. As such, it was able to be conceived as a source of social authority by playwrights whose position in both the society and cultural production was uncertain, and who were certainly sensitive to this fact.

However, it is less drama *as* education than the treatment in the drama of the issue of education and social behaviour that yields the most useful perspectives on the social impact of education in the period. The unequivocal advocacy of education in Tudor interludes can be contrasted with the rather more complicated and ambivalent attitudes shown in the later drama to the value of scholarship. But, whereas a relationship is discernible between the burgeoning elite interest in education in the sixteenth century and the treatment of the issue in the interlude, the drama can be only a very crude marker of this social phenomenon. The difference in the treatment of the issue in the commercial drama up to the Caroline period is also only a very imprecise reflection on the refinement of manners and its implications for elite identity. Over the whole period, the treatment of the issue is affected and often obscured by other frequently more overt agendas in the drama. It is not very surprising that the subject of education should keep cropping up in plays, albeit often obliquely or peripherally, as it was an issue that would persist in having a strong social dimension and occupying a contentious place in cultural change; it continued to make available social mobility, but there was never a consensus about its value. It is therefore far more in the ways in which the topic is handled that reflections emerge on the social attitudes implicit in much of the drama on offer in both public and private playhouses.

Recognition of the possibilities offered by education makes available a radical interrogation of the very basis of the notions of social superiority on which the mental structures of the deference culture reposed. This potential was present in the very fact of the acquirability of education and the awareness of the changes which it wrought, recognized in the provision that a university degree automatically conferred gentility. Secondly, where it came to a capacity for benefiting from education, there was an awareness (evident in the writings of theorists such as Elyot, Ascham and Mulcaster) of a spread of ability across the population. Despite the notion of the 'person of quality', this left little room for the idea of an elite intrinsically possessed of superior qualities. This potential challenge does not, however, get much of a showing in the drama. In both the sixteenth century interlude and, in a somewhat less clearcut way, on the London commercial stage there is certainly a consciousness of the importance of education in social competition. Furthermore, in the commercial drama both upper-class ignorance and stupidity are the targets of frequently stinging satire. However, none of this is in the interests of any egalitarian project. The objects of satire are shown to fall short of an ideal of elite behaviour, but this does not amount to questioning substantially social hierarchies of rank and the ideas of distinctions of 'quality' between people which accompany them. Neither does the representation of the lower-class 'native wits' ever bring this sort of question into debate. As Margot Heinemann has pointed out, the wisdom of yokels was presented as part of a fairytale 'world turned upside down' conception of society, and popular discontent was represented in terms of very traditionalist views of society (1992, 152–3).

If the issue of education was not exploited to any significant extent by dramatists in order to present a thoroughgoing interrogation of the status quo, questions about the definition of the quality of gentility or nobility were present in a variety of forms on the early modern stage, and the ideal of the educated gentleman was used to exercise uncertainties about what exactly constituted elite identity. Chapman's scholarly heroes represent probably the most straightforward example of the ideal of the moral benefits of scholarship as a natural component of, or at least complement to, elite status. In the work of other playwrights can be found the articulation of anxieties about elite behaviour, presented in terms of its relationship to learning. Jonson's satire of foolish aspirants to cultural sophistication, whether in poetic accomplishment or critical judgement, proceeds ultimately from the notion of an ideal of social superiority married to intellectual accomplishment. His satirical targets are shown to fail in their aspiration to real elite sophistication in the measure that they fail intellectually. A variation on this position (and a complication of it) is present in Shirley's comic figure of Aretina Bornwell who exemplifies the distinction between laboured scholarship and the *ésprit* of witty elite sophistication which relates to to Castiglione's notion of *sprezzatura*, but at the same time is made a target of satire for shallowness and affectation. Implicit in all this is the idea that successful elite social identity is essentially performative, involving a display of superiority as a justification for privileged status. This is not primarily a moral ascendancy – particularly as it involves deception to a certain extent – but may include giving the appearance of it. What it does require is a command over those accomplishments that are the products of study, but which are skilfully managed to avoid self-consciousness. This permits both the impression of intellectual superiority and the sense of *naturally* inhabiting the world of high culture. Satirical portraits of clumsy, pedantic scholars constitute an effective foil to this. Not only are their efforts self-conscious and apparent, but they depend on their accomplishments for gain, frequently with pathetically little success.

The representation of scholars, and the issue of the educational accomplishment or otherwise of protagonists, is thus a sufficiently recurrent idea in a wide variety of the plays of the commercial stage to contribute significantly to producing insights into the social attitudes implicit in this drama, or at least the drama which is extant.[1] This is particularly the case when what we can gauge about the playwrights' attitudes both to their audiences and to their own position as writers is taken into account. What emerges is a fairly consistently elite perspective on the social hierarchy and on social behaviour, which even at times overrides (or at least circumvents) conventional moral evaluations. This becomes part of an implicit process inherent in representational conventions, which Kathleen McLuskie has called: 'the narrative, poetic and theatrical strategies which position the audience to understand their events from a particular point of view' (1985, 92). These can also be seen in terms of a formulation by Raymond Williams:

> There are often in fact close connections between the formal and conscious beliefs of a class or other group and the cultural production associated with it: sometimes direct connections with the beliefs, in included manifest content; often traceable connections to the relations, perspectives and values which the beliefs legitimize or normalize, as in characteristic selections (emphases and omissions) of subject; often again, analysable connections between belief–systems and artistic forms, or between both and an essentially underlying 'position and positioning' in the world.
> (1981, 27)[2]

This has implications for debates about the stage's role in the subversion of the values supporting the social hierarchy, or its containment of opposition to these values. In the introduction to this study I cited Theodore Leinwand's challenge to the binary oppositions which constitute the contesting positions in this debate. I would argue here that not only the social impact of education but the treatment of the issue of learning in the plays supports Leinwand's view of the complexities of the matter of the drama's attitudes to the social status quo. The wider spread of education in the period, along with regular exposure to the theatre, clearly led to the development of audiences who were not only more critical, but politically aware. This tended to sharpen the political challenges that had been present in theatre since the Tudor interlude drama. However, the very fact of an educated and critical audience in many ways only served to underline the social polarities. The complexities thrown up by relationship of education to the drama allow for some discriminations to be made within the broad dichotomy of 'oppositionality' and 'containment', between different ways in which the theatre could be at once challenging and accommodating to the status quo. Some distinction might be made here between, on the one hand *state* politics (encompassing political factions, religious conflict, issues surrounding kingship, national agrarian and economic changes, war and foreign affairs) and on the other *social* politics (which involve such matters as recognition of rank and patterns of deference, class conflict and contestation between elite groups, the position of women, and personal preferment and advancement). Of course, there was considerable overlap between these two categories, but political orthodoxy need not automatically be seen as existing on a continuum with what might be termed social orthodoxy. This complicates the notion of oppositionality and dissidence since it was perfectly possible for dissension from, say, state policies on religion or foreign affairs to go together with complete orthodoxy in the matter of rank and deference. If the emphasis in this study has been on the factors which dispose the drama to a more conservative stance, it is because it has been concerned particularly with the relationship between education and conceptions of social identity. In many ways, political contention in the drama was itself an indicator of a degree of social exclusivity in contexts of performance and reception. Martin Butler has, for instance, argued that the private theatres, especially in the Caroline period, functioned as political debating chambers for the gentry (1984, 135–40). Furthermore, it needs also to be remembered that the elite was increasingly not a homogeneous body anyway, and conflicts of interests were endemic in its composition (Sinfield, 1985, 259–77).

The position of the writers of the plays is also a factor this. On the one hand, the role of playwrights as intellectuals (and often self-consciously so) disposed them to engagement in political polemic and to social satire. Their frequently demonstrated willingness and capacity to pierce any mystification attaching to notions of gentility and nobility was considerably enhanced by their situation of being either formally educated men, or men working and moving in an educated milieu, but whose own status in their society remained uncertain. Jonson's cynical view of courtiers (and later courtier dramatists) is a case in point. On the other hand, the fact of their access to gentle status made

available by education, inclined the dramatists towards allying themselves with
the values and social perceptions of the elite.[3] The drama's claims to dignity
and seriousness as a medium generally involved an emphasis on its appeal to
'superior' judgements. The fact that it involved a literary dimension was part of
this, and the very sensitivities which led to this disquiet about the public theatre
were a force to ensure a continued emphasis on this dimension. This is
exemplified by the prefatory letter to the second issue of *Troilus and Cressida*
in 1609 ('A neuer writer, to an euer reader. Newes'):

> Eternall reader, you haue heere a new play, neuer stal'd with the Stage,
> neuer clapper-clawd with the palmes of the vulger, and yet passing full of
> the palme comicall; for it is a birthe of your braine, that neuer vnder-
> tooke any thing commicall, vainely: And were but the vaine names of
> commedies changde for the titles of Commodities, or of Playes for Pleas;
> you should see all those grand censors, that now stile them such vanities,
> flock to them for the maine grace of their grauities: especially this authors
> Commedies, that are so fram'd to the life, that they serue for the most
> common Commentaries, of all the actions of our liues, shewing such a
> dexteritie, and power of witte, that the most displeased with Playes, are
> pleasd with his Commedies.

This is, of course, the presentation by a publisher of a play as literary writing,
specifically excluding dramatic performance, and his claim for its seriousness
as such resides partly in putting a distance between the piece as written and the
more dubious medium of the public stage. However, the language of
contamination is striking, particularly in the alliance between informed
judgement and social status. He makes the point that this play has not had
exposure to the commonality, but in fact the same principle is used for the
commendation of all of Shakespeare's comedies – including those which have,
in fact, been 'stal'd with the Stage' and 'clapper-clawd with the palmes of the
vulger'. These plays are praised for the high cultural values which they exhibit,
the 'main grace of their grauities' and their 'power of witte'. They are thus
being promoted by a publisher conscious of the self–perception of the section
of the reading public that he is addressing, as being appropriate for reception
by the elite precisely because of their appeal to superior intellects and more
informed judgements.

The tendency towards social conservatism encouraged by the impact of
education on the drama is not just a question of writing for a particular
audience. In making a distinction between the official and learned 'great
tradition' of culture and the 'little tradition' of the uneducated, Peter Burke
cites the emergence of private theatres: 'By the early seventeenth century, the
public theatres, where Shakespeare had been played to noblemen and
apprentices alike, were no longer good enough for the upper classes, and

private theatres were established where a seat cost sixpence' (1978, 277). There are, though, problems in basing a distinction between elite and popular culture on the supposed differences between the public and private theatres. It is true that the private theatres may certainly be seen as symptomatic of the elite's desire for exclusive locations, and in many ways the theatrical experience would have been a different one from that in the public theatres. The smaller, enclosed space and the more exclusive audience would have ensured this. However, in broader cultural terms – and particularly in respect of the drama which was presented in them – it is more difficult to make such a clear-cut distinction between the private theatres and the public. The fact of the traffic of plays between them is one factor, and the fact that the elite attended both private and public theatres is another. In certain respects it is possible to regard the commercial theatre as a whole in terms of Burke's 'great tradition', despite its availability to the masses. The repeatedly stated anxieties about its pernicious effects on the culture and values of the nation in the period may be considered to stem from the fact that, though essentially an elite form which continued to make reference to an elite educational and cultural frame of reference, it was placed apparently so indiscriminately and unexclusively in the public domain.

Even the fact of the existence of a popular end to the spectrum of theatrical entertainment does not of itself necessarily give the theatre subversive or challenging role with respect to the values of the social hierarchy. Alexander Leggatt has suggested that the diminution in opposition to the drama from civic authorities after the accession of James may have been partly due to their realization that, 'in some playhouses at least citizen values and citizen interests were being promoted' (1992, 29). It is certainly true that there was popular fare on the stage, and plays which presented positive images of citizens. However, these and others in that range of drama from the Elizabethan to the Caroline periods that was orientated towards the lower end of the social spectrum, were by and large traditionalist in their view of society and did little to challenge the social conceptions which underpinned deference and hierarchy.[4] The 'popular' commercial drama differs in at least one significant respect from community festivals of the sixteenth century as popular culture. It is drama that, though popular in consumption, was made and handed down by educated men whose position in society gave them cause to be acutely conscious of the relationship between learning and status. The distinction between 'popular' and 'aesthetic' drama which Leggatt makes (in a formulation that accurately reflects the values of the period) points to the nub of the issue. It can be pointed out that 'popular' is actually a social designation, while 'aesthetic' involves questions of intellect and cultivated taste. The implicit idea that the 'aesthetic' has a social dimension feeds into a linkage between intellectual quality and rank that lies at the very heart of class distinction.

A public medium as broad in its address as the drama in the early modern period was likely to be fraught with stresses and ideological contradictions, and it is clear that contributing significantly to these were the tensions surrounding the relationship of rank, social behaviour and education. This effect was made more acute by the fact that it involved the drama's being, in important ways, persistently informed by the values of a particular and relatively circumscribed social group, while at the same time operating in circumstances of consumption which challenged those values. In a society whose notions of rank were evolving in a way that tended to favour social performance and display, the drama's potential to be centrally complicit in the construction of ideologies of class was all the greater. The complexities surrounding the social position of playwrights, and the fact that they perceived it as being in their own interests to promote the truest and most legitimate manifestations of their art as being most appropriate to a target audience defined in terms of both educational and social superiority, only contributed further to this. Thus the conflicts and tensions present in the theatre's view of itself may be regarded as not just a reflection of the stresses within the society, but endemic in the cultural position of the drama itself in society. There is, however, a certain circularity of implication here, because the position of the drama is in itself a product of the social, economic and cultural circumstances which the changes in the period had brought about and continued to affect. The position which theatrical activity occupied within the culture, makes any study of this form of public art a study of the varying *mentalités* of the society itself.

Notes

1. Introduction

[1] This is taken from *Pierce's Supererogation,* (B3^v–C1^r), a text which formed part of Harvey's pamphlet war with Thomas Nashe.

[2] See Clay, 1984; Hill, 1955, and Stone, 1965 for accounts of the broader socio-economic landscape.

[3] The attitudes that resulted from these developments are partly what inform the complaint of Orlando, the brother of Jaques, in the opening speech of *As You Like It*:

> My brother Jaques he keeps at school, and report speaks goldenly of his profit. For my part, he keeps me rustically at home – or, to speak more properly, stays me here at home unkept; for call you that keeping for a gentleman of my birth, that differs not from the stalling of an ox? His horses are bred better, for besides that they are fair with their feeding, they are taught their manège, and to that end riders dearly hired. But I, his brother, gain nothing under him but growth, for the which his animals on his dunghills are as much bound to him as I. Besides this nothing that he so plentifully gives me, the something that nature gave me his countenance seems to take from me. He lets me feed with his hinds, bars me the place of a brother, and as much as in him lies, mines my gentility with his education
> (1.1.4–17).

However, although he focuses here on the refinement of behaviour as a means of defining his gentle status, as a younger brother Orlando would also have been acutely aware of the importance of education for the pursuit of a career.

[4] For a discussion of self-fashioning in the early modern period, see Stephen Greenblatt's classic study, 1980, especially 1–9.

[5] The swelling stream of manuals on behaviour and accomplishments appropriate to gentlemen and nobility is listed by Ruth Kelso as: 'Institutions, Moral Methods, Courtiers, Governors, Complete Gentlemen, Schoolmasters, Quintessences of Wit, Blazons of Gentry, Books of Honour and Arms, Horsemanship, Hunting and Hawking' (1929, 14). These texts are a testimony to the perceived need to acquire the trappings of social status in the forms of appropriately fashioned behaviour. The role of these courtesy manuals and their significance for the role of drama is further discussed in Chapter 3 below.

[6] See also the letter by Richard Pace on pp. 134–5 below.

[7] For an account of the university arts curriculum, especially at Oxford, in the sixteenth and seventeenth centuries (from which this information has been drawn) see Fletcher, 1996, 157–99 (sixteenth century), and Feingold, 1997, 211–357 (seventeenth century). Feingold argues that: 'The anti-rhetorical stance of modern scholarship

makes it difficult to appreciate the centrality of eloquence to early modern culture and the vitality it once possessed' (246).

[8] For a useful setting-out of the terms of the debate, see Dollimore's essay 'Shakespeare, cultural materialism and the new historicism', in Dollimore and Sinfield, 1985, 2–17; Greenblatt's essay 'Invisible Bullets' is reprinted in the same volume, 18–47. See also Dollimore, 1984, 1–28.

[9] Discussing Dekker's *Match me in London* of 1623 she observes:
> The anti–Spanish attitudes which might be assumed from the play's setting in a corrupt Spanish court, are complicated by the king's integrity and his ultimate refusal to exercise his lustful power . . . However, this apparent commitment to the values of the public theatre is compromised by Dekker's dedication of the 1631 edition of the play to the courtier dramatist Lodowick Carlell. In a blatant request for courtly patronage, he writes 'Glad will you make mee, if by your Meanes, the King of Spaine speakes our Language in the Court of England.'
> (1994, 174–5)

[10] For an account of plebeian attendance at university, see Stone, 1974, Vol. 2, 18–21.

2. 'Ornaments to the City': the emergence of national institutions

[1] Stephen Orgel has remarked of the building of dedicated theatres in London:
> Before this moment, the concept of theatre had included no sense of *place*. A theatre was not a building, it was a group of actors and audience; the theatre was any place they chose to perform . . . [Once] embodied in architecture . . . theatre was an institution, a property, a corporation. For the first time in more than a thousand years it had the sort of reality that meant most to Renaissance society; it was *real* in the way that real estate is real; it was a location, a building, a possession – an established and visible part of society.
> (1975, 2)

[2] By comparison with other large European centres, London was very poorly served with educational resources by the late fifteenth century, but by the mid-seventeenth century it possessed probably the best schools in Europe in the period (Jordan, 1960, 219). In more general terms, David Cressy suggests that the migration of people to London may have involved the creaming off of talent, education and energy from the provinces (1980, 149).

[3] At another level in the sixteenth century, the drama furnished the means of connection between the elite schools in and around the capital and Court, and as such helped to define the privileged status of these schools. Udall brought his Eton boys to present a play before Cromwell in 1538, for which he was paid £5 (Brewer, 1895, 334). John Ritwise brought the boys of St Paul's to Court to act before Cardinal Wolsey, and before the King and visiting French ambassadors in 1527 (McDonnell,

1977, 18–19, Collier, 1831, 107–11). Under Richard Jones, they participated in pageants to celebrate the King's wedding to Anne Boleyn in 1533. Henry Machyn records a performance before Elizabeth in August 1559 at Nonsuch Palace (1563, 206). Under Elizabeth the children of St Paul's became the most regular dramatic company playing at Court (Hillebrand, 1964, 127). From the mid-1560s, Westminster children were also to be found acting at Court (Hillebrand, 1964, 127). The dominance of the boys' companies at Court is indicated by the fact that, between 1558 and 1576, of 78 rewards for Court performances, the Paul's boys received 21, other schoolboy companies 10, and the children of the royal chapels 15 while the adult companies had only 32 (Chambers, 1923, Vol. 2, 4). This situation only changed with the mid-1570s emergence of permanent adult company theatres and the resultant growth in that sector. Although the boys' companies performed conventional interludes, the classical basis of the educational role made neoclassical plays most predominant, and the most frequent references are to tragedies and comedies. Paul's boys performed many of Lyly's courtly pastorals in the years 1587–90 (Hillebrand, 1964, 137–43).

[4] The grammar was compiled by William Lily in 1540–1542 in two parts, Latin and English, and prescribed for use in schools throughout the realm. It continued to be prescribed in the Royal Injunctions of Edward VI (1547) and Elizabeth (1559), and the Ecclesiastical Canons of 1571 and 1604 (Charlton, 1965, 137).

[5] The decline of gilds both in economic terms and in terms of their role in urban social life, and the increase in government support of urban oligarchies tended to lead to urban authoritarianism (James, 1986, 41–4; Phythian-Adams, 1979, 269–74). Social polarization and the emergence of a class consciousness on the part of urban elites which transcended their local allegiances were significant aspects of the changing consciousness of the period (Clark and Slack, 1976, 106–9). All this contributed to the 'structural stress' in provincial towns identified by Phythian-Adams (1979, 250; also ibid., 249–90).

[6] On the state control of the theatre: see Dutton, 1991, esp. 17–40, 97–116; Clare, 1990; Gildersleeve, 1961, esp. 1–88.

[7] Instances of this include the statutes for the school at Bury which stipulate that poor men's children should be given preference for admission (though those who could not read and write were not to be admitted, thus excluding the very poor) and the provision for 100 'poor men's sons' to be admitted free (with 50 more at reduced fees) among 250 boys in all, at the foundation of the Merchant Taylors grammar school in 1561 (Page, 1907, 304; Anglin, 1985, 36). The statutes drawn up in 1580 by Sir Roger Manwood for the Free Grammar School at Sandwich state that scholars are to be admitted 'according to their well doinge to have the highest places with other preferments and priviledges of favor, and in no case aney respect therein shall be had of birth, welth, parentes, or any thing but profyting in learning' (Carlisle, 1818, Vol. 1, 606). This extended to university education too. The injunctions framed by Edward VI's Visitors at Cambridge declared: 'In the election of fellows and scholars, the sons of poor persons, being apt and of good abilities, are to be preferred to the sons of rich and more powerful persons' (Heywood, 1840, 34).

[8] In 1535 Elyot also published another text on education, *The Education or Bringing Up of Children, translated out of Plutarche.*

[9] *The Schoolmaster* was only published in 1570, after Ascham's death, though he had written it several years before he died.

[10] Mulcaster's two works on education, *Positions* and the *Elementary* appeared in 1581 and 1582 respectively.

[11] J. E. Neale has noted:

> Of the 420 members in the 1563 parliament, it has been calculated that about 67 went to Oxford or Cambridge and 108 to the Inns of Court. Since 36 of the latter prefaced their legal with a university education, the figures give us a total of 139 members with higher education. By 1584 the numbers had grown strikingly. The university figure is 145 and the Inns of Court 164, of whom 90 also went to university – a total of 219 of a House now numbering 460. In the 1593 parliament, 161 of the members had been to the university and 197 to the Inns of Court, with an overlap of 106 who attended both, giving us a total of 252, or appreciably more than half the House.
> (1949, 302–3)

[12] See Stone, 1965, 683–7. Stone observes of the period that: 'This was one of the really decisive movements in English history by which the propertied classes exploited and expanded the higher education resources of the country. By doing so they fitted themselves to rule in the new conditions of the modern state and they turned the intelligentsia from a branch of the clergy into a branch of the propertied class' (672).

[13] Christopher Hatton and Walter Raleigh were both examples of commoners whose entry into the Court was through the Inns. However, the exclusiveness of the Inns was ensured by the high cost of attendance, especially early in the period. In around 1470 Sir John Fortescue had described them as follows:

> In these greater inns, no student could be maintained on less expense than £13 6s 8d a year, and if he had servants to himself alone, as the majority have, then he will by so much more bear expenses. Because of this costliness, there are not many who learn the laws in the inns except the sons of nobles. For poor and common people cannot bear so much cost for the maintenance of their sons. And merchants rarely desire to reduce their stock by such annual burdens.
> (Chrimes, 1942, 117–19)

[14] See Curtis, 1962, 25–43 for an account of graduate discontent in the seventeenth century. The problem was not limited to graduates. In 1611 Francis Bacon wrote to the King advising him that there were too many grammar schools which drew potential servants and workmen from the countryside and resulted in 'there being more scholars bred than the state can prefer and employ, and the active part of that life not bearing a proportion to the preparative, it must needs fall out that many persons will be bred unfit for other vocations, and unprofitable for that in which they are brought up; which

fills the realm full of indigent, idle and wanton people, which are but *materia rerum novarum*' (Spedding et al., 1868, 252–3).

[15] 'The quest for patronage, education and marriage drew swarms of aspiring courtiers to London and Westminster; by 1560 half of England's peers owned London houses, many of them on the sites of pre-Reformation episcopal palaces along the Strand between the City and Westminster. Their presence transformed London into a centre of conspicuous consumption, an emporium for the specialized luxury goods imported by the city's merchants and manufactured by its craftsmen' (Manley, 1986, 7). For a further discussion of the centralization of elite culture in London in the early seventeenth century, see Smuts, 1987, 53–72.

[16] Thomas Nashe also argues for the dignity of the English theatre in *Pierce Penniless* (1592):

> Our Players are not as the players beyond sea, a sort of squirting baudie Comedians, that haue whores and common Curtizens to playe womens partes, and forbeare no immodest speech or vnchast action that may procure laughter; but our Sceane is more statelye furnisht than euer it was in the time of *Roscius*, our representation honourable, and full of gallant resolution, not consisting, like theirs of a Pantaloun, a Whore, and a Zanie, but of Emperours, Kings and Princes: whose true Tragedies (*Sophocles cothurno*) they do vaunt.
>
> (McKerrow, 1904, I, 215)

[17] Andrew Gurr finds that there is little direct evidence about the attitudes of patrons to their companies, but states that the Earl of Leicester saw his company as one of his political tools, and that his brother the Earl of Warwick considered the treatment of his company as a reflection on his own status (1996, 32–3). The fact that plays were frequently a vehicle for the expression of political ideas is perhaps one indication of their importance within the elite culture of the period. Right from the early fourteenth century and possibly before, companies of players had been retained by the royal household and other noblemen (Chambers, 1903, Vol. 2, 186–7, 240–58). In the sixteenth century, troupes were patronized by a large range of noblemen who had very different bases and degrees of power, but who relied on the exercise of political influence. These included, at the top end, men at the centre of power such as the courtiers the Duke of Suffolk, the Earl of Dorset and the Duke of Norfolk, as well as the politician Thomas Cromwell. Lower down there were men whose power was based in the shires, such as George Talbot, the Earl of Shrewsbury and John de Vere, the Earl of Oxford, and less politically important noblemen such as Lord Cobham, Lord Daubeney, and Lord Grey of Powis. Even non-noble courtiers and administrators such as Sir Edward Belknap and Sir Edward Guildford had troupes (Walker, 1991, 8)

[18] This is further confirmed by the routinely higher payments made to royally patronized companies by provincial urban authorities, as evidenced in the civic records printed in the *REED* volumes.

[19] For a discussion of the economics of the acting profession in the period, see Chambers, 1923, 348–88.

[20] The attitude of the soldier, Tucca, in Jonson's *Poetaster* is perhaps typical:

> A player? Call him, call the lowsie slaue hither: what, will he saile by, and not once strike, or vaile to a *Man of warre*? Ha? Doe you heare? You, player, rogue, stalker, come backe here: no respect to men of worship, you slaue? What, you are proud you rascall, are you proud? Ha? You grow rich doe you, and purchase, you two-penny teare-mouth? You haue *fortune*, and the good yeere on your side, you stinkard? You haue? You haue?
>
> (3.4.120–27)

[21] The City of York House Books for 1476 make the following stipulations for the selection of actors for the civic plays:

> Also it is ordeined and stablished by þe ful consent and auctoritee of þe Counsaile aforesaide þe day and yere within writen from þis day furth perpetually to be obserued and keped That is to saie þat yerely in þe tyme of lentyn there shal be called afore þe Maire for þe tyme being iiij of þe moste Connyng discrete and able playeres within þis Citie to serche here and examen all þe plaiers and plaies [and] pagentes thrughoute al þe artificeres belonging to corpus christi Plaie And all suche as þay shall fynde sufficiant in personne and Connyng to þe honour of þe Citie and Worship of þe said Craftes for to admitte and able and all oþer insufficiant personnes either in Connyng or personne to discharge ammove and avoide.
>
> (*REED: York*, 109)

[22] For a full account of the King's Men between 1594 and 1642, see Gurr, 1996, 278–305, 366–93.

[23] '*Hamlet*. My lord, you played once I'th'university, you say? / *Polonius*. That did I, my lord, and was accounted a good actor' (3.2. 97–100).

[24] In the 'contract' between the playwright and the audience found in the induction to *Bartholomew Fair*, Jonson treats more ironically the relationship between rank, or at least wealth, and judgement:

> It is further agreed that euery person here, haue his or their free-will of censure, to like or dislike at their owne charge, the *Author* hauing now departed with his right: it shall bee lawfull for any man to iudge his six pen'orth, his twelue pen'orth, so to his eighteene pence, 2 shillings, halfe a crowne, to the value of his place: Prouided alwaies his place get not aboue his wit. And if he pay for halfe a dozen, hee may censure for them too, so that he will vndertake that they shall bee silent. Hee shall put in for *Censures* here as they doe for *lots* at the *lottery*: mary if he drop but sixe pence at the doore, and will censure a crownes worth, it is thought there is no conscience, or iustice in that.
>
> (85–96).

For a full discussion of theatre and commerce, see Bruster, 1992, especially 1–11. Bruster, however, sees Jonson's view as less satirical than I do.

[25] In Marston's *Histrio-mastix* there is satirical reflection on players relating to the nature of their work:

> *Belch*: I pray sir, what titles have travailing *Players*?
> *Post-hast*: Why *proper-fellowes*, they play Lords and Kings
> (1.1.p. 250)

Later in the play, the artisans-turned-players have become extremely arrogant, which leads another character, Philarchus, to observe:

> How soon they can remember to forget
> Their undeserved Fortunes and esteeme:
> Blush not the peasants at their pedigree?
> (3.1.p. 276)

[26] G. E. Bentley has argued that the status of the theatrical profession improved between 1590 and 1642, but that it remained relatively low, and he cites the problem of the association of playwrights with 'trade' (1971, 38–61).

[27] See also Greene's outburst in his *Groatsworth of Wit* quoted on p. 98 below.

[28] Thomas Nashe, pointing out the readiness of actors to forget their humble beginnings, takes a sharply satirical view of their social ascendancy in his preface to Greene's *Menaphon*:

> Sundry other sweete Gentlemen I doe know, that haue vaunted their pennes in priuate deuices, and tricked vp a company of taffaty fooles with their feathers, whose beauty if our Poets had not peecte with the supply of their periwigs, they might haue antickt it vntill this time vp and downe the Countrey with the King of *Fairies*, and dined euery day at the pease porredge ordinary with *Delfrigus*. But *Tolossa* hath forgotten that it was sometime sacked, and beggars that euer they carried their fardels on footback: and in truth no maruaile, when as the deserued reputation of one *Roscius* is of force to enrich a rabble of counterfeits.
> (McKerrow, 1904, III, 323–4)

[29] Bentley connects the publication of Jonson's folio in 1616 to a rise in the status of actors in the early seventeenth century. Jonson put the names of players in his folio, under 'Tragœdians' or 'Comœdians' (1984, 8–11).

[30] For a fuller account of this, see Hosking, 1952, 159–66, 174–8.

[31] In many cases the members of the merchant classes, who were themselves the products of upward mobility through earned wealth, were a major source of donations for the building up of the educational resources of the realm. During the period 1480–1660 members of the London mercantile elite contributed huge amounts to the endowment of educational institutions, and donations for educational purposes were the biggest single item of charitable giving after poor relief. London merchants founded schools throughout the country (Jordan, 1960, 67–8, 206–8, 220–34).

[32] For an account of Alleyn as benefactor, see Wright, 1965, 155–60. Alleyn was also, in a modest way, a patron of the arts; see Hosking, 1952, 195–7.

3. 'Good behaviour and audacitye': drama, education and the quality of gentility

[1] Kenneth Burke poses the contrasting questions: 'docs the tribe give birth to its members (universal *ante rem*), or does the tribe exist in its members (universal *in re*) or is the tribe merely a name for the sum of its members (universal *post rem*)' (1962 (1945), 27). The first position, which he terms 'medieval realist', he sees as 'well attuned to feudal collectivism'. It is arguable that social developments in the sixteenth century progressively shifted cultural perceptions of group identity from the first to the second position.

[2] For a fuller examination of the Italian influence on English humanist ideas on nobility and education, see Charlton, 1965, 74–85; for a discussion of Renaissance notions of gentility and education, see Kelso, 1929, 111–29.

[3] Indeed, the Earl of Essex in a letter to the young Earl of Rutland in 1595, complained that 'the most of the noblemen and gentlemen of our time have no other use of their learning but table talk' (Devereux, 1853, I, 331). Students seemed very conscious of their gentle status and, as William Harrison observed in 1577, were all too prepared to trade on it:

> For standing vpon their reputation and libertie, they ruffe and roist it out, excéeding in apparell, and banting riotous companie (which draweth them from their bookes vnto an other trade). And for excuse when they are charged with breach of all good order, thinke it sufficient to saie, that they be gentlemen, which gréeueth manie not a little.
> (Holinshed, 1577, 252).

[4] For a discussion of these aspects, see James McConica's discussion of the sixteenth-century history of Oxford University (1986, 645–66). The effectiveness of social training was, however, compromised by recurrent problems with indiscipline and McConica remarks: 'the triumph of cultivated manners was as slow to reach the college as it was to reach the gentry household' (666).

[5] By the early seventeenth century this had extended to table manners, as illustrated by the anecdote of the Earl of Carlisle who reputedly dismissed a man because he took a knife out of his pocket to cut his meat, 'the cognisance of a clown' (Stone, 1965, 50–51). The courtesy text, *The Court of Civil Courtesy* (see below, p. 49) also devotes a section to table manners, as does *The School of Good Manners* (translated from the French by W. F. in 1595).

[6] Keith Wrightson, in a discussion of the shift in the period from the notion of 'estates' to that of class, concludes that: 'Gentility, then, was ultimately a matter of relative wealth and lifestyle' (1991, 38).

[7] Compare Pierre Bourdieu's remarks on the issue of manners in the definition of class:

> The differences in manner that indicate differences in modes of acquisition – i.e. in seniority of access to the dominant class – which are generally associated with differences in composition of capital, are

predisposed to mark differences within the dominant class, just as differences in cultural capital mark the differences between the classes. That is why manners, especially in the manner of relationship to the legitimate culture, are the stake in a permanent struggle. There can be no neutral statement in these matters: the terms designating the opposing dispositions can be taken as complimentary or pejorative depending on the point of view. It is no accident that the opposition between the 'scholastic' (or 'pedantic') and the *mondain*, the effortlessly elegant, is at the heart of debates over taste and culture in every age: behind two ways of producing or appreciating cultural works, it very clearly designates two contrasting modes of acquisition and, in the modern period at least, two different relationships to the educational system.
(1984, 68–9)

[8] See also Curtis, 1959, 261–81.

[9] Dilwyn Knox has argued that the humanist arguments for the refinement of comportment were effectively a continuation of the idea of 'disciplina corporis', the inculcation of moral rigour through physical discipline, in the clerical manuals on behaviour for the monastic orders (1991, 107–35).

[10] Compare the following description by Thomas Elyot of the quality and effects of 'majesty':

Maiestie: which is the holle proporcion and figure of noble astate, and is proprelie a beautie or comelynesse in his countenance, language, & gesture apt to his dignitie, and accommodate to time, place, & company: which like as the sonne doth his beames, so doth it caste on the beholders and herers a pleasaunt & terrible reverence ... yet is nat Maiestie alwaye in haulte or fierce countenaunce, not in speche outragious or arrogant: but in honorable and sobre demeanure, deliberate and graue pronunciation, wordes clene and facile, voide of rudenesse & dishonestie: without vayne or inordinate ianglinge, with suche an excellent temperance, that he amonge an infinite nombre of other persones by his maiestie may be espied for a gouernour.
(1531, 106^{r-v})

[11] Kenneth Burke has remarked that the 'conditions for mystery' are set up by any personal and social distinction (1950, 638–51).

[12] The issue of the refinement of the English language can also be related more broadly to developing ideas of nationhood in the period. For a discussion of this with particular reference to Thomas Wilson's *Art of Rhetoric* (1553) and other sixteenth century texts on language and literature, see Schmitt, 1997, 183–97.

[13] Lawson and Silver argue that the insistence on 'polite learning' reflected changes which were taking place in the social function of the universities, and the fact that students were increasingly being drawn from the gentry (1973, 99). In his *Advancement of Learning*, Bacon says: 'Then did *Car* of *Cambridge*, and *Ascham* with their Lectures and Writings, almost deifie *Cicero* and *Demosthenes*, and allure all

young men that were studious vnto that delicate and polished kinde of learning (Book 1, E3^v/17^v). Compare also the Earl of Clarendon's statement in his autobiography that his interests as a student at the Middle Temple early in the seventeenth century were principally 'polite learning and history' (1847, 917).

[14] Much the same point is made in the anonymous *Education of Children in Learning* of 1588 (possibly derived from Elyot's statement):

> the Parents first care is, assoone as his child beginneth to speake, to prouide that he vse none other companie, then such as are both honest and ciuill, aswell in behauiour, as in language. He shall therefore seclude from his Child barbarous nursses, clownish playing mates, and all rusticall persons: neither shall he himself speake in the hearing of his Child either wantonly, or otherwise, any rude or barbarous speach, much lesse shall he teach him any leawde or vnhonest talke, as many do, or suffer him to be in the companie of vnthriftie and vnhonest perssons.
> (E3^v–E4^r)

[15] This sort of handbook on social behaviour and accomplishment continued to be used in the next century, with a performative or theatrical dimension. Compare also Martin Butler's description of, and comments on, *The Academy of Compliments* (1640):

> an anonymous compilation of 'Complementall, Amorous, High expressions, and formes of speaking (t.p.)' the centre of this guide to proper deportment being eighty pages of dialogues to cover all likely social situations. Each dialogue is essentially a little playlet, as when a gallant is depicted planning to help a friend 'beat away the Vsurers daughter' (p. 96). Here society's forms are developing in a manner directly parasitic on theatrical prototypes.
> (1984, 111)

[16] Martin Esler states:

> by the 1520s and '30s, the work of the English humanists had borne fruit, and the pagan classics were winning a central place for themselves in the educational curriculum of the English ruling classes. The future governors of England were no longer trained exclusively in fighting, hunting, and other gentlemanly pastimes; now they were set to parsing their Latin and steeping themselves in the practical wisdom of the ancients.
> (1966, 4)

[17] As Stephen Greenblatt points out:

> The manuals of court behavior which became popular in the sixteenth century are essentially handbooks for actors, practical guides for a society whose members were nearly always on stage. These books are closely related to the rhetorical handbooks that were also in vogue – both essentially compilations of verbal strategies and both based on the principle of imitation. The former simply expound the scope of the latter, offering an integrated rhetoric of the self, a model for the formation of an artificial identity.
> (1980, 162).

[18] The relatively non-scenic nature of the London commercial stage is arguably a product of a dramatic tradition produced by the essentially educational and discursive role of the interlude drama in elite contexts. While it is true that the Court revels and masques are the most sophisticated examples of highly wrought scenic staging, the visual aspects of these owe more to foreign importation and to the visual arts than any native dramatic tradition. They are to be distinguished from the sort of popular scenic drama of the saint or urban plays. Most interludes are heavily dependent on dialogue rather than action, and several shade into being pure dialogue, with little or no concession towards dramatic gesture or action; such pieces include *Gentleness and Nobility* and some of Heywood's plays such as *The Pardoner and the Friar*, *The Four PP* and *A Play of Love*. This emphasis on words and argument made the interlude drama a suitable vehicle for Protestant ideas, as particularly illustrated by the plays of John Bale, Protestantism being in its very essence logocentric. It also made them an appropriate mode of humanist discourse, since dialogue was central to humanist literary expression (Wilson, 1985, 2).

[19] The text essentially consists of extracts from three plays by Terence, *Andria*, *Eunucho* and *Heautontimorum* with running English translations.

[20] In his treatise, *De Regno Christi* (1551), Bucer counters ecclesiastical anti-theatrical attitudes by arguing for the effectiveness of drama in inculcating piety especially in youth but, while advocating religious drama, he recognizes that it is actually 'the acumen and wit and pleasantness of speech which people admire in Aristophanes, Terence and Plautus, and in the tragedies the gravity, cleverness and elegance of dialogue of Sophocles, Euripides and Seneca' (Pauck, 1969, 352).

[21] Vives makes a distinction between Plautus and Terence:
> The works of Plautus are much less pure [than those of Terence] for he was an antiquarian, and allowed his slave-characters great licence, while he sought to gain the laughter and applause of the theatre by the frowardness of speech and by not too much purity in his ideas. I should like to see cut out of both of these writers those parts which could taint the minds of boys with vices, to which our natures approach by the encouragement, as it were, of a nod.
> (*On Education* [*De Tradendis Disciplinis*], 136)

[22] 'Three thinges chiefly, both in *Plautus* and *Terence*, are to be specially considered The matter, the vtterance, the words, the meter. the matter in both, is altogether within the compasse of the meanest mens maners, and doth not stretch to any thing of any great weight at all, but standeth chiefly in vtteryng the thoughtes and conditions of hard fathers, foolish mothers, vnthrifty yong men, craftie seruantes, sotle bawdes, and wilie harlots, and so, is moch spent in finding out fine fetches, and packing vp pelting matters, soch as in London commonlie cum to the hearing of the Masters of Bridewell. Here is base stuffe for that scholer, that should be cum hereafter, either a good minister of Religion, or Ciuill Ientleman in seruice of his Prince and contrie: except the preacher do know soch matters to confute them, whan ignorance surelie in soch thinges were better for a Ciuill Ientleman, than knowledge' (1570, 59[r]).

[23] Ascham remarks:

> And here, who soeuer hath bene diligent to read aduisedlie ouer, *Terence*, *Seneca*, *Virgil*, *Horace*, or els *Aristophanus*, *Sophocles*, *Homer*, and *Pindar*, and shall diligently make the difference the vse, in proprietie of wordes, in forme of sentence, in handlyng of their matter, he shall easilie perceiue, what is fitte and *decorum* in euerie one, to the trew vse of perfite Imitation.
> (1570, 57ʳ)
> . . .
> But surelie, if iudgement for the tong, and direction for the maners, be wisely ioyned with the diligent reading of *Plautus*, than trewlie *Plautus*, for that purenesse of the Latin tong in Rome, whan Rome did most florish in well doing, and so thereby in well speaking also, is soch a plentifull storehose, for commone eloquence, in meane matters, and all priuate mens affaires, as the Latin tong, for that respect, hath not the like agayne. Whan I remember the worthy tyme of Rome, wherein *Plautus* did liue, I must nedes honor the talke of that tyme, which we see *Plautus* doth vse.
> (58ᵛ)

Neither is this just a matter of competence in classical languages:

> And this not onelie to serue in the Latin or Greke tong, but also in our own English language. But yet, bicause the prouidence of God hath left vnto vs in no other tong, saue onelie in the Greke and Latin tong, the trew preceptes, and perfite examples of eloquence, therefore must we seeke in the Authors onelie of those two tonges, the trew paterne of Eloquence, if in any other mother tong we looke to attaine, either in perfit vtterance of it to our selues, or skilfull iudgement of it in others.
> (ibid., 56ᵛ)

[24] The plays listed by Bale were: *Patient Griselda, Melibeus, Titus and Gisippus, The Burning of Sodom, The Condemnation of John Huss, The Revolt of Jonah, Lazarus and Dives, The Courage of Judith, The Afflictions of Job* and *The Deliverance of Susannah* (*Scriptorum Illustrium*, 700).

[25] G. W. Fisher, *The Annals of Shrewsbury School* cited in Motter, 1929, 208–10.

[26] F. H. Motter even suggested that schools may have preferred dramatic directors for their headmasters (1929, 58)

[27] Queens College Codex Chadertonianus Bk 62, p. 43 (1546–7):

> And lest any youth [who is] a student of this college of a degree inferior to a master of arts [and is] not even a fellow should refuse to take part [in the comedy or tragedy], or to be absent when the comedy or tragedy is being put on publicly, or in some other way behave obstinately or perversely at a time when he seems to the president or his deputy [to be] suitable to undertake some duties in the comedy or tragedy, we order and decree by this present [statute] that the one or ones who have offended in any of these matters against the decision of the president or his deputy

shall be expelled from the college by authority of the president or his deputy.

(*REED: Cambridge*, 147, trans. 1117)

The statutes of 1559–60 for Trinity College impose an obligation on readers to mount plays:

> Nine domestic readers shall put on individual comedies and tragedies in pairs, so that the youth may spend the Christmas season with greater profit, except for the senior reader, whom we wish to show one comedy or tragedy on his own. And they shall be responsible for putting on all these comedies or tragedies in the hall privately or publicly during the aforesaid Twelve Days or a little afterwards at the will of the master and the eight senior [fellows]. But if they do not make themselves responsible, then for each comedy or tragedy omitted, each one of those through whose negligence it is shall be fined ten shillings.
>
> (*REED: Cambridge*, 209, trans. 1131)

[28] 'One Edward Watson, a Scholar of Grammar, who had studied Grammar four years, and had read and taught it most of his time, had his Grace granted to him for the Degree of Bachelaur conditionally that he compose an hundred verses in praise of the University, and also make a Comedy within one year after he had taken his degree' (Wood, 1796, II, 720).

[29] The connection between drama and the teaching of rhetoric was underlined by one of the two plays presented to the Queen on her second visit to Oxford, *Bellum Grammaticale* by Leonard Hutten (the other on this occasion being Gager's *Rivales*). Hutten's play was an allegory on the complexities of Latin grammar (see also the 1613 play in English, *Heteroclitanomalonomia* which also deals with matters of language and grammar). In his *Apology for Actors*, Thomas Heywood contended that the performance of drama at the universities:

> is held necessary for the emboldening of their *Iunior* schollers, to arme them with audacity, against they came to bee imployed in any publicke exercise, as in the reading of the Dialecticke, Rhetoricke, Ethicke, Mathematicke, the Physicke, or Metaphysicke Lectures, It teacheth audacity to the bashfull Grammarian, beeing newly admitted into the priuate Colledge, and after matriculated and entrid as a member of the Vniuersity, and makes him a bold Sophister, to argue *pro et contra*, to compose his Sillogismes, Cathegoricke, or Hypotheticke (simple or compound) to reason and frame a sufficient argument to proue his questions, or to defend any *axioma*, to distinguish any Dilemma, & be able to moderate in any Argumentation whatsoeuer.
>
> (C3^v)

[30] See also p. 83 below.

[31] For fuller recent discussions of early dramatic activity at the universities, see Nelson, 1994 (for Cambridge) and Elliott, 1995 and 1997 (for Oxford).

[32] In considering the question of the role of dramatic performance in the formation of social identity, it is worth noting Dugdale's observation (though it was made later than

our period): 'Besides these solemn Revells or measures aforesaid, they had wont to be entertained with Post Revells, performed *by the better sort* of the young Gentlemen of the Society' (1666, 205) (my emphasis). Whether Dugdale was referring to talent or social position is not clear, but the term was generally used to refer to rank.

[33] For a discussion of forms of academic rhetorical structure with particular relevance to the drama, see Altman, 1978, 31–106, and Elton, 2000.

[34] Relevant here is Ascham's observation: 'The whole doctrine of Comedies and Tragedies, is a perfite *imitation*, or faire liuelie painted picture of the life of euerie degree of man' (1570, 47^r). He goes on to assert: 'This foresaide order and doctrine of *Imitation*, would bring forth more learning, and breed vp trewer iudgement, than any other exercise that can be vsed' (ibid., 48^r). Ascham is referring narrowly to the learning of rhetoric, but this applies equally well to the drama's capacity to teach social skills. The principle of imitation he describes as 'a facultie to expresse liuelie and perfitlie that example: which ye go about to folow. And of it selfe it is large and wide: for all the workes of nature, in a maner be examples to folow' (O1^v). On the educational value of imitation, see also Ascham's letter of 1568 to Johann Sturm (Vos, 1989, 265-82).

[35] Indeed, the forms of conversation in the courtesy texts themselves provide models of courteous discourse, quite apart from the arguments they make. This may be one reason why they are routinely presented in this way. K. J. Wilson has suggested that the rise of published dialogues in the early modern period is a product of the broadening and secularization of education, and its extension to non-clerics (1985, 52–4). Some plays (such as *Gentleness and Nobility*, discussed below) are in the form of debates or have debates as their central focus (as in *Fulgens and Lucres*, also discussed below). This is a sort of bridge between the dialogues of courtesy and similar instructive literature, and plays proper, which have interactive behaviour, rather than mere statements of position. But even here, the protagonists function as people as well as articulations of an argument. As people, certain figures are granted a predominant right to theatrical space, which reinforces the right of their arguments to recognition.

[36] David Bevington discusses *Fulgens and Lucres* in terms of the political competition between the old aristocracy and the 'new men', but recognizes that the ending does not force a conclusion strongly on the audience (1968, 42–51). This tentativeness might be argued to be effectively a product of the play's subordination of the debate between competing elite groups to a celebration of the *de facto* position of material power, to which they are both able to lay claim.

[37] The scatological aspects of the 'fart-prick-in-cule' game are discussed in Meredith, 1984, 30–39.

[38] In *The Governor* (Book 2, xi and xii), Thomas Elyot delivers a lengthy discourse on friendship and especially the noble principles of honour on which it resides, making specific reference to the Damon and Pithias story (144^v–5^r).

[39] Jonas Barish points out that a fundamental source of Puritan objections to the theatre was its basis in mimicry, allowing people and things to be presented or become that which they were not (1981, 96). Puritan tolerance of drama in pedagogical contexts might thus possibly be explained by the fact that education was recognized as a legitimate process of changing youth, allowing them to become that which they were not. As such, the function of dramatic exercises in preparing scholars for roles that they would later occupy was allowable.

[40] For an account of certain aspects of the instructive dimension of Elizabethan drama – both interludes and the drama of the public stage – see Altman, 1978. Altman argues that the rhetorical structure of a large body of Elizabethan drama was shaped in such a way that the plays became forms of philosophical enquiry.

[41] Other writers who spoke approvingly of the pedagogical function of the stage include Julius Scaliger who, as early as 1561 remarks in his *Poetics*:

> The end is the giving of instruction in pleasurable form; for poetry teaches, and does not simply amuse, as some used to think ... because primitive poetry was sung its design seemed merely to please; yet underlying the music was that for the sake of which music was provided only as a sauce. In time this rude and pristine invention was enriched by philosophy, which made poetry the medium of its teaching. Now is there not one end, and only one, in philosophical exposition, in oratory, and in the drama? Assuredly such is the case. All have one and the same end – persuasion.
> (Padelford, 1905, 2)

Chapman's lines of 1606 on Jonson's *Sejanus* speak approvingly of this function of the drama:

> Thy *Poëme*, therefore, hath this due respect,
> That it lets passe nothing, without obseruing
> Worthy Instruction; or that might correct
> Rude manners, and renowme the well deseruing.
> (93–6)

Francis Bacon in Book II, Chapter 13 of his *De Dignitate et Augmentis Scientiarum* of 1623 (an expanded version of the *Advancement of Learning*) identifies the psychological dimensions of the process of education in the theatre:

> And though in modern states play-acting is esteemed but as a toy, except when it is too satirical and biting; yet among the ancients it was used as a means of educating men's minds to virtue. Nay it has been regarded by learned men and philosophers as a kind of musician's bow by which men's minds may be played upon. And certainly it is most true, and one of the great secrets of nature, that the minds of men are more open to impression and affections when many are gathered together.
> (Spedding et al., 1868, 440)

[42] Thomas Nashe, writing of poets in *Pierce Penilesse*, argues:

> First and formost, they haue cleansed our language from barbarisme, and made the vulgar sort here in *London* (which is the fountaine whose riuers flowe round about *England*, to aspire to a richer puritie of speach, than is

communicated with the Comminalitie of any Nation vnder heauen.
(McKerrow, 1904, I, 193)

[43] As to playwrights, Nashe probably had in mind Thomas Kyd. See below p. 78.

[44] Similarly Nashe, creating a satirical portrait of a gallant (in the context of a discussion of sloth in *Pierce Penniless*), remarks that, 'my vagrant Reueller haunts Plaies, & sharpens his wits with frequenting the company of Poets' (McKerrow, 1904, I, 210).

[45] On this point, see also the note on John Bodenham below (p. 229, n. 37).

[46] Compare also the remark made by Candius to Silena in Lyly's *Mother Bombie* (1590): 'Now I perceiue thy folly, who hath rakt together all the odde blinde phrases that helpe them that knowe not howe to discourse; but when they cannot aunswere wisely, eyther with gybyng couer theyr rudenesse, or by some newe coyned by-word bewraie theyr peeuishnesse' (2.3.68–72). Thomas Tomkis, in his 1614 university play *Albumazar* has a farmer, Trincalo, use the theatre to hone his verbal skills as a suitor to woo a maidservant: 'O. 'tis *Armellina*: now if she haue the wit to begin, as I meane she should, then will I confound her with complements drawn from the Plaies I see at the Fortune, and Red Bull, where I learne all the words I speake and vnderstand not' (C1ʳ). Henry Crosse comments in *Virtue's Commonwealth* (1603): 'Againe, if a man will learne to be proud, fantasticke, humorous, to make loue, sweare, swagger, and in a word closely to doo any villanie, for a two-penny almes hee may be thoroughly taught and make a perfect scholler' (P4ᵛ).

[47] Although issues of public order were ostensibly at stake, this attitude may have informed the 1574 Act of Common Council of London which, in reaction to 'sondrye greate disorders and incovenyences . . . found to ensewe to this Cittie by the inordynate hauntyinge of great multitudes of people, speciallye youthe, to playes, enterludes, and shewes', placed a restriction on all publicly performed plays which contained 'anie wourdes, examples, or doynges of anie vnchastitie, sedicion, nor suche lyke vnfytt and vncomelye matter'. The Act expressly did not extend to 'anie plaies, Enterludes, Comodies, Tragidies, or shewe to be played or shewed in the pryvate house, dwellinge, or lodginge of anie nobleman, Citizen, or gentleman, which shall or will then have the same thear so played or shewed in his presence for the festyvitie of anie marriage, Assemblye of ffrendes, or otherlyke cawse withowte publique or Commen Collection of money of the Auditorie or behoulders theareof' (printed in Chambers, 1923, Vol. 4, 275–6). This gave greater licence to drama mounted in exclusive and, by implication, thereby more legitimate contexts of performance. A similar attitude probably prevailed in the case of the Catholic priest, Father Leak imprisoned (laxly) in the Clink for his faith in 1618. The Archpriest of England prohibited him from attending the public playhouse but he was allowed to go to plays at the Inns of Court, the King's or Queen's Court, the universities, or performed in noblemen's and gentlemen's houses (Bradbrook, 1962, 94–5).

4. 'Poesies sacred garlands': education and the playwright

[1] On the large volume of printed material on the market in the early seventeenth century, see Bridenbaugh, 1968, 339–47.

[2] Not all gentry shared Bodley's view; others, like Sir John Harington, were happy to buy quartos of plays. Harington bought 90 of the approximately 110 plays in quarto that were printed between 1594 and 1610 (Gurr, 1996, 244).

[3] The implicit recognition of this is suggested by the fact that Charles I had no qualms about keeping a stock of plays in his library, and treating them as literature; see Gurr, 1996, 140.

[4] See Butler, 1990, 152. William Cartwright, another academic playwright from Oxford, had a brief semi–professional career (ibid., 150). Thomas Goffe, who wrote plays while at Oxford, also wrote for the professional theatre.

[5] Playing companies might occasionally perform at the universities, however. There was a performance of *Volpone* at Oxford and Cambridge in 1606 and 1607 respectively. This may have been an exceptional occurrence, hence perhaps Jonson's epistle to the two universities thanking them for the acceptance of his play. There is, though, also some evidence that *Hamlet* was acted at Oxford (Boas, 1923, 14–31).

[6] See also the chronological table of plays at Cambridge in Smith, 1923, 50–72.

[7] However, in 1622–3 a play was presented by scholars outside of college contexts. *Fucus Histriomastix* was acted before the King at Newmarket on 12 March 1623 by some of the scholars of Queen's College. 'On Fucus', a poem by Henry Moll relating the event compares college players favourably with London players (*REED Cambridge*, 878–80).

[8] The centrality of the academic stage in university life is suggested by the elaborateness of the demountable stages and other theatrical equipment which some colleges possessed (Nelson, 1994, 77–117). At the Inns of Court, the importance of the drama is suggested by the fact that Arthur Brooke, the writer of *Romeus and Juliet*, was admitted to the Inner Temple in recognition of the plays he produced at the Inns (Inderwick, 1896, 220).

[9] For an account of these and other Inns plays of the sixteenth and seventeenth centuries, see Wigfall Green, 1931, 142–57.

[10] Sidney *Apology for Poetry*:

> Our Tragedies, and Comedies, (not without cause cried out against,) obseruing rules, neyther of honest ciuilitie, nor of skilfull Poetrie, excepting *Gorboduck*, (againe, I say, of these I haue seene,) which notwithstanding, as it is full of stately speeches and well sounding Phrases, clyming to the height of *Seneca* his style, and as full of notable moralitie, which it doth most delightfully teach; and so obtayne the very

end of Poesie: yet in troth it is very defectious, in the circumstances; which greeueth mee, because it might not remaine as an exact model of all Tragedies. (J4^v–K1^r).

[11] Ramus (Pierre de la Ramée) was a French humanist educational reformer who lived between 1515 and 1572; for an account of his life and work see Graves, 1912; Ong, 1958; Howell, 1961, 146–281. For discussions of the relationship between humanist education and the arts, see Grafton and Jardine, 1986, 161–200; Bolgar, 1973, 8–21; Jardine, 1975, 16–31.

[12] Bruce Smith has pointed out that classical norms actually increased in influence from 1500 to 1700 in the drama (1988, 6). For a discussion of the classical background to Shakespeare, see Baldwin, 1944.

[13] It should be pointed out, however, that there is little demonstrable proof of the participation in any capacity whatsoever of graduate playwrights in university drama during their time as students. The converse may have been true in most cases, and this may have been a matter of the lack of leisure time. Johnstone Parr suggests that a possible reason for Robert Greene's apparent abstention from university theatricals at Cambridge during his time there was the fact that he was a sizar, and thus had little time for activities beyond his duties and studies (1962, 542).

[14] On the education of John Fletcher, see Taunton, 1994, 63–97.

[15] G. K. Hunter lists the following as the 'university wits': Lyly, Greene, Peele, Lodge, Marston and Nashe. He suggests 'associate membership' to Kyd and Shakespeare (1997, 22).

[16] The collaborative system also helped the induction of new playwrights into the profession. Neil Carson has pointed to the careers of John Day and Chettle as illustrations of this. Day was sent down from university for stealing a book. Both began by collaborating with other writers, Day initially being helped by Chettle (1988, 60–62).

[17] The information on both the education of playwrights and on writing collaborations is drawn from the relevant entries in the *Dictionary of National Biography*.

[18] For further discussion of joint authorship in the early modern theatre, see Bentley, 1971, 197–234.

[19] Classical teaching had so improved in grammar schools by the late sixteenth century that there was no longer a need for universities to provide any grammar training in Latin (Feingold, 1997, 243, 283). For a discussion of Shakespeare's learning, see Baldwin, 1944, and Rowse, 1981; for an account of Jonson's education see Miles, 1986, 11–18. Jonson's reputation for learning was such that he was granted in 1619 an honorary degree by Oxford as he was 'happily versed in all humane literature' (Riggs, 1989, 262).

[20] See Boas, 1914, 10–25 (*et seq*) for an account of the origins and later development of classical drama in the universities. Carey Conley records that of 54 known translators of the classics between 1558 and 1572, 23 or 25 were actually members of the Inns of Court while two and possibly four others had some status there (1927, 26). See also Bolgar, 1954, Appendix II, 512–15, 524–5, 534–7 for a catalogue of the translations of the classics into the vernacular.

[21] However, Ascham expresses similar disquiets about the emerging phenomenon of the foreign tour to complete the education of young men of rank and means. Discussing the practice of young gentlemen travelling and spending time in Italy, he expresses disapproval of Italy morally while recognizing the cultural value of Italian as a language, and he praises the Queen's learning in Latin, Italian, French and Spanish (1570, $H3^{r-v}/23^{r-v}$, $H1^{r}/21^{r}$). He also talks of the mischief of Italian books translated into English (ibid., $I2^{v}/27^{v}$).

[22] Greg Walker notes: 'of its very nature, the Interlude was an exclusively elite form of drama, written for members of the governing classes and performed in an environment formed by and saturated with their values and attitudes' (1991, 28). For the political content of Tudor interludes, see also Bevington, 1968.

[23] On the social status of playwrights, see Bentley, 1971, 43–61. Bentley comments that their status was raised in the period by 'greater financial success, increasing royal and aristocratic patronage, and the accumulation of printed texts' but that by 1640 after a half century of rising respectability, 'the playwright and his professional environment were less esteemed than most readers of Shakespeare, Jonson, Ford and Webster are likely to assume' (1971, 43).

[24] The fact that Pembroke Hall was Meres's own college may also have had something to do with its mention here.

[25] On royal and civic pageantry, see Bergeron, 1971, 1–8, 273–308, and Kipling, 1977, 37–56

[26] Ralph Berry has argued that in Shakespeare's drama, the forms of language and the structures of writing in which it is contained, confirm class identification of characters. Blank verse is generally a medium of the gentry, though the aristocracy may condescend to prose at times (1988, xv, xvi).

[27] The early aesthetic philosopher and poetic theorist, Julius Scaliger, in 1561 described literary decorum in relation to the ways in which superiority of rank was defined in terms of refinement of understanding and manners:

> The grand style is that which portrays eminent characters and notable events. The sentiments are correspondingly choice, and they are couched in choice and euphonious diction. These eminent characters are gods, heroes, kings, generals, and citizens. If inferior characters, such as sailors, merchants, tradesmen, and hostlers are introduced, it is because when men associate together they constitute a society which has, as it were, the character of an organism, the members of which, according to the nature and end of their functions, share in its nature and office. It is the nature of

the kingly office to be superior to others; its end is to govern. So the king's share will be preèminent strength and wisdom, and his office to apply his strength in affording protection, and his wisdom in governing. Notable events are wars in behalf of peace and concord, deliberative counsels, judicial decisions, the pursuit of heroic deeds, and whatever else is attendant upon these. Choice sentiments are those which abhor vulgarity; choice diction, that which is not trite; and pleasing language, that which marries sense and sound.
(Padelford, 1905, 71)

[28] It should be noted however that, as G. K. Hunter has pointed out, classicism was never completely dominant in the period, and was one strand among several (1997, 110).

[29] The citizen taste for chivalric romance is given a satiric treatment in Beaumont's *The Knight of the Burning Pestle*, rendered particularly trenchant by the incongruous juxtaposition of chivalry with the demeaned concerns of the mercantile class. For a fuller discussion of this play, see pp. 122–4 below.

[30] Bentley lists twenty-two playwrights who were known to have paid for their work between 1590 and 1642 (1971, 27). This list is likely to be incomplete (it does not include Massinger for instance), but of the playwrights listed on it, seven are known to have had a higher education, eight are known not to have done so, four are likely to have had, and three are likely not to have had.

[31] *Club Law* is likely to have been acted to a closed audience. Thomas Fuller's *History of the University of Cambridge* of 1655 relates an anecdote of the university men inviting the mayor and his colleagues to a performance of the play and placing them in a position in which not only could they be observed, but that they could not easily leave until the performance was over. This account goes on to say that the townsmen sought redress through the Privy Council but dropped the case when that body would only proceed if the play were performed again, with the townsmen present. The editor of the play, Moore Smith, doubts this pointing out both that the Privy Council records make no reference to this case, and that the epilogue to the play addresses itself entirely to a university audience (Introd. xxix–lv).

[32] Compare Nashe's complaint in *Pierce Penniless* (1592):
A worthlesse Wit, to traine me to this woe
Deceitfull Artes that nourish Discontent:
Ill thriue the Follie that bewitcht me so;
Vaine thoughts adieu, for now I will repent:
And yet my wants persuade me to proceede,
Since none takes pitie of a Scollers neede
(McKerrow, 1904, I, 157).

[33] An observation by Henry Peacham in *The Complete Gentleman* (1622) is relevant here: Is it not commonly seene, that the most Gentlemen will giue better wages, and deale more bountifully with a fellow who can but teach a Dogge, or reclaime an

Hawke, then vpon an honest, learned and well qualified man to bring vp their children?' (31–2/F2^{r-v}).

[34] The attitudes which inform this representation can also be seen in the bitter portrayal of the usurer Gorinus in Greene's *Groatsworth of Wit*. Having rejected his scholar son, Roberto, Gorinus boasts: 'How manye Schollers haue written rymes in *Gorinus* praise, and receiued (after long capping and reuerence) a sixpeny reward in signe of my superficial liberality' (B2^{r}).

[35] Compare the description of the gallant in the 'proemium' to Dekker's *Gulls Horn Book* (1609): 'haunting *Theaters*, he may sit there like a popiniay, onely to learne Play-speeches, which, afterward may furnish the necessity of his bare knowledge, to maintaine table talke' (3).

[36] In *Virtue's Commonwealth*, Henry Crosse, who is opposed in principle to the plays of his own period but not to ancient plays, compares the two on the basis of the multiplicity of the former and the paucity of the latter, complaining of the drama: 'for now nothing is made so vulgar and common' (P2^{r}–P4^{v}).

[37] Bodenham (1558/9–1610), the son of a wealthy London grocer, published anthologies of extracts including *Palladis Tamia* and *Wit's Theatre* (for which the material was collected by Nicholas Ling) both constituting parts of Meres's *Wit's Commonwealth*. He was also involved in the production of the anthologies, *England's Helicon*, and *Belvedere, or the Garden of the Muses* (*DNB*, Vol. 2, 753–4).

[38] See also pp. 67–9 above.

[39] A comparable accusation is levelled by Dekker at Jonson; in *Satiromastix* (1601) the poet Horace (who represents Jonson) is charged not to 'bumbast out a new Play, with the olde lynings of Iestes, stolne from the Temples Reuels' (5.2.295–6), and a speech in Marston's *Histrio-mastix* slightly earlier in 1598 there is another instance of the anxiety of playwrights about incursions into their profession by unlearned men, particularly for commercial gain. This echoes Nashe's reference to Kyd, cited above (p. 78):

> O age when every Scriveners boy shall dippe
> Prophaning quills into Thessaliaes Spring,
> When every artist practice that hath read
> The pleasant pantry of conceipts, shall dare
> To write as confident as *Hercules*.
> When every Ballad-monger boldly writes:
> And windy froth of bottle-ale doth fill
> Their purest organ of invention:
> Yet all applauded and puft up with pryde,
> Swell in conceit, and load the Stage with stuffe,
> Rakt from the rotten imbers of stall jests:
> Which basest lines best please the vulgar sence
> Make truest rapture lose preheminence.
> (3.1.p. 274)

[40] In a non-dramatic context – the prefatory 'Address to the Reader' of *The Wonderful Year* in 1603 – Dekker complains bitterly at the convention which obliges him to address his readers as '*Gentle Reader*, *Courteous Reader*, and *Learned Reader*, though he haue no more *Gentilitie* in him than *Adam* had (that was but a gardner) no more *Ciuilitie* than a *Tartar*, and no more *Learning* than the most errand *Stinkard*, that (except his owne name) could neuer finde any thing in the Horne-book' (A3ʳ).

[41] Greene acquired his education at Cambridge by working as a sizar (Mildenberger, 1951, 546–9).

[42] On Jonson's attitudes to his audiences, see Rowe, 1988, 38–67.

[43] For an account of the quarrel which differs in some details, particularly relating to the targets of the satire in the plays, see Small, 1899.

5. 'A thousand men in judgement sit': education and the audience

[1] Taken from Andrew Gurr, *The Shakespearean Stage* (1992), third edition, p. 212

[2] For more information on this, see Gurr, 1988, 105–90.

[3] This complicates Muriel Bradbrook's idea that each member of the common audience in the Elizabethan playhouse was a Chief Spectator. She does, however, modify this view in relation to the Jacobean theatre (1962, 100).

[4] In references to the audience, mention is often made of their position within the playhouse. The experience of being an audience member at the reconstructed Globe in London gives a clear indication of audience dynamics. As a 'groundling', aside from implications for the experience of relative status within the playhouse arising from the discomfort and lack of fixity involved in standing, the height of the stage elevates the actors above this section of the audience so that they do not relate on equal terms to it. The actors effectively talk over the heads of the groundlings, and there is no question of a parallel with the position of a present day stalls audience. For those seated in the galleries, however, there is a much more naturally direct line of sight and level of address. The sight lines make a direct connection between those audience members seated in the lower gallery, or place those higher up in a position where the actors have to talk up to them.

[5] Gurr sees this as suggesting that more of the non-gentle audience of the Globe might have been present in the Blackfriars than the hall playhouse's writers cared to admit (1988, 188). The presence of a broad social range in the private playhouse may also have been perceived by some as an advantage. The satirically drawn Count in Francis Beaumont's *The Woman Hater* (1607) uses the playhouse to display his own rank and it becomes a form of social theatre:

> or if I can find any companie, Ile after dinner to the Stage, too see a play;
> where, when I first enter, you shall haue a murmure in the house, euery
> one that does not knowe, cries, what Noble man is that; all the Gallants

on the Stage rise, vayle to me, kisse their hand, offer mee their places: then I picke out some one, whom I please to grace among the rest, take his seate, vse it, throw my cloake ouer my face, and laugh at him: the poore gentleman imagines himselfe most highly grac'd, thinkes all the Auditors esteeme him one of my bosome friendes, and in right special regard to me.
(B2^v–B3^r)

[6] These discriminations have their origins in the elite drama of the hall which predates the advent of the permanent theatres in London. In the conclusion of *Fulgens and Lucres* of 1497, Henry Medwall remarks:

all the substance of this play
Was done specially therfor
Not onely to make folke myrth and game,
But that suche as be gentilmen of name
May be somewhat mouyd
(889–93)

Compare also the prologue of *The Contention between Liberality and Prodigality* of (c. 1567, though Stafford's printing of 1602 refers to a performance in 1601):

No play, no part, can all alike content.
The graue Diuine calles for Diuinitie;
The Ciuell student, for Philosophie;
The Courtier craues some rare sound historie:
The baser sort, for knacks of pleasantrie
(7–11).

In this analysis, it is notable that the three elite categories are distinguished by particular interests, all of which are cerebral, while the 'baser sort' are lumped together in their debased tastes.

[7] Note, however, the following comment by Gurr:

The social and educational range creates an initial difficulty because almost all the evidence for audience reactions comes from the literate and usually from the most educated. The evidence itself is predisposed to favour the learned. In theatres where the spoken word and spectacle gave stage performances a special value for the illiterate, that is a limitation. (1993, 7)

[8] Webster's remark is in his preface to the published version of *The White Devil*. He goes on to describe them as people 'who visiting stationers' shops their use is not to enquire for good books, but new books'.

[9] Dekker charges: 'By sitting on the stage, you haue a signd pattent to engrosse the whole commodity of Censure; may lawfully presume to be a Girder: & stand at the helme to pierce the passage of Scænes yet no man shal once offer to hinder you from obtaining the title of an insolent ouer–weening Coxcombe' (28–9). For the Marston reference, see p. 68 above.

[10] In a non-dramatic context, Marston's *Scourge of Villainy* ('In Lectores prorsus indignos') makes the same point about well-heeled readers (including Innsmen):

> Fye Satyre fie, shall each mechanick slaue,
> Each dunghill pesant, free perusall haue
> Of thy well labor'd lines? Shal each sattin sute,
> Each quaint fashio[n]-monger, whose sole repute
> Rests in his trim gay clothes, lye slauering
> Taynting thy lines with his lewd censuring?
> Shale each odd puisne of the Lawyers Inne,
> Each barmy-froth, that last day did beginne
> To reade his little, or his *nere a whit*,
> (That neuer turned but browne Tobacco leaues
> Whose sences some damn'd *Occupant* bereaues)
> Lye gnawing on thy vacant times expence?
> Tearing thy rimes, quite altering the sence?
> (B1ʳ)

[11] The (fawning) prologue to Lyly's *Midas* suggests a connection between gentility, good judgement and favourable (or at least polite) reception of plays on the part of audience members: 'Wee are ielous of your iudgementes, because you are wise; of our owne performance, because we are vnperfect; of our Authors deuice, because he is idle. Onelie this doeth encourage vs, that presenting our studies before Gentlemen, thogh they receiue an inward mislike, wee shall not be hist with an open disgrace' (21–5). The play was a private theatre piece presented by Paul's boys in 1590.

[12] This notion of audience members 'learning' their aesthetic judgements by aping other members of the audience (that Jonson terms 'censure by contagion' in the induction to *Bartholemew Fair*) is also described in Beaumont's verses on Fletcher's *The Faithful Shepherdess*: 'Among the rout there is not one that hath / In his owne censure an explicite faith. / One company, knowing they iudgment lacke, / Ground their beliefe on the next man in blacke' (A3ᵛ).

[13] For instances of the playgoing of identified Innsmen, see Sturgess, 1987, 22–4.

[14] The community ethos of the Inns is illustrated by the number of collaborative writing projects that were undertaken by members, whether dramatic or not. William Baldwin in 1559 published *The Mirror for Magistrates* along with Thomas Sackville, George Ferrers, John Day and several others (though this was some time after they had ceased being students there). Robert Wilmot collaborated with up to four other contributors to write *Gismond of Salerne*. The 1588 play *The Misfortunes of Arthur* was authored by Thomas Hughes, with the help of Thomas Trotte, Francis Flower, Christopher Yelverton, John Lancaster and Francis Bacon.

[15] There is no absolute proof that Webster was at the Inns of Court, but see Eccles, 1977; Eccles cites a John Webster who entered the Middle Temple in 1598.

[16] On the Inns, their revels and their connection with other forms of dramatic entertainment, see Axton, 1977, and Finkelpearl, 1969, 32–61.

[17] Henry Machyn in his diary describes a procession which formed part of Inner Temple revels for 1561–62 and calls the Christmas Prince a 'lord of mysrull' (273–4).

[18] The edition of the Revels referred to in this discussion is that of Bland, 1968.

[19] When the Queen was present at Inns revels, the presence of the real Court complicated the fictional representations of a court. During the 1561/2 Inner Temple revels, when *Gorboduc* was presented to the Queen at Westminster Hall, it is likely that three 'courts' were present – the Queen's, the Christmas Prince's and Gorboduc's – at three different levels of display and of theatricalization. The customary practice of seating the sovereign in a prominent position to be seen by other spectators meant that her Court was as much a performative element in the procedures as the dramatized ones.

[20] The reality was probably more complicated. The capacity of people of all ranks to understand and appreciate complex verbal arguments is suggested by the popularity among a wide range of the population of John Donne's highly wrought sermons at Paul's Cross (Bald, 1970, 322). It is also an interesting irony that Jonson's greatest battles against the prevalence of spectacle over poetry occurred in his disagreements with Inigo Jones over the production of masques in the unquestionably elite contexts of the Court.

[21] The Earl of Clarendon's autobiography describes a set of friends he had made early in the seventeenth century while a student at the Middle Temple:
> Whilst he was only a student of the law, and stood at gaze, and irresolute what course of life to take, his chief acquaintance were Ben Johnson, John Selden, Charles Cotton, John Vaughan, Sir Kenelm Digby, Thomas Man, Thomas Carew, and some others of eminent faculties in their several ways. Ben Johnson's name can never be forgotten, having by his very good learning, and the severity of his nature and manners, very much reformed the stage and indeed English poetry itself.
> (1842, 923)

See also Riggs, 1989, 56.

[22] The population of London rose from about 120,000 in 1550 to around 200,000 by the beginning of the sixteenth century (Sharpe, 1987, 85). The men of the Inns of Court numbered just over 1000 at any one time, and 1700–1800 if the Inns of Chancery are taken into account (Finkelpearl, 1969, 5).

[23] Cook's conclusions have been challenged by Martin Butler (1984, 129–40, and especially 293–306).

[24] David Riggs has also argued that the spectators at the Blackfriars were not merely paying customers, but many were prospective patrons as well (1989, 69).

[25] Martin Butler has also pointed to the cross-fertilization between the private and public theatres in especially the Caroline period (1984, 131–2, 303). Keith Sturgess, however, makes a case for more of a distinction between the audiences of the public and private houses (1987, 11–26).

[26] Gurr has pointed out that the attitudes expressed in this passage this should be read in the context of the takeover in the mid-1630s of the King's Men by a group of

courtier poets who commandeered the company's repertory for the Globe summer seasons (1996, 10).

[27] Another play which uses, for satirical purposes, incomprehension on the part of certain audience members of the principles of stage representation is Thomas Randolph's *The Muses Looking Glass* of 1530. Here two Puritans, a feather-seller called Bird, and a pin-seller by the name of Mistress Flowerdew, find themselves in a theatre:

> *Bird*: Nay, and I have heard
>   That in a Tragedy I think they call it,
>   They make no more of killing one another
>   Then you sell pins.
> *Flowerdew*: Or you sell feathers brother,
>   But are they not hang'd for it?
> *Bird*: Law grows partiall,
>   And findes it but Chance-medly: and their Comedies
>   Will abuse you, or me, or any body;
>   We cannot put our monies to increase
>   By lawfull usury, nor break in quiet,
>   Nor put off our false wares, nor keep our wives
>   Finer then others, but our ghosts must walk
>   Upon their stages.
> *Flowerdew*: Is not this flat conjuring
>   To make our ghosts to walk ere we be dead?
>   (K3^v)

[28] Alfred Harbage considered that the play failed because its satire of the citizens was 'without animosity' (1952, 107).

[29] It is perhaps significant that the ignorance manifested by the citizens in this play is principally in respect of the comprehension of, and taste in the consumption of a particular cultural product. In terms of broader educational attainment, the London citizen elite (of which the citizen and his wife here are clearly representatives) presented a greater degree of rivalry to the gentry. They had, for instance, an almost complete command of literacy (Cressy, 1980, 134).

[30] The title page contains the information: 'As it was presented by some young Gentlemen for whom it was intended at a private recreation.'

[31] See William Roper's *Life of More*: 'thoughe he was younge of yeares, yeat wold he at Christmas tyde sodenly sometimes steppe in among the players, *and* neuer studyeng for the matter, make a parte of his owne there presently among them, which maed the lookers on more sporte then all the plaiers beside' (1626, 5).

6. 'Morrals teaching education': the issue of education in the sixteenth–century interlude

[1] Quoted in Furnivall 1868, xiii. The letter is in Latin and this is Furnivall's translation. Compare also the comment in Skelton's 'Colin Clout' of 1521–2: 'But noble men borne / To lerne they have scorne / But hunte and blowe an horne / Lepe over lakes and dykes, / Set nothing by polytykes. / Therefore ye kepe them base' (619–24

[2] Compare also the remarks of Greg Walker in a discussion of political plays of the sixteenth century: 'The very forms of the interlude, a play performed between or immediately after the courses at a banquet, made it an ideal vehicle for the dissemination of opinions, advice or information to an elite (and therefore influential) audience' (1991, 10–11). Glynne Wickham has also drawn a distinction in sixteenth century drama between that written for worship, appealing to a universal audience, and that of social recreation, appealing to a small sectional audience (1959, I, xliii).

[3] Where 'prodigal son' elements occur in late sixteenth- or seventeenth-century drama, as in Shakespeare's *1 Henry IV*, *2 Henry IV*, Jonson's *Every Man in his Humour*, *Cynthia's Revels*, and *The Staple of News*, Dekker's *If This Be Not Good, the Devil is in it*, or in an anonymous play entitled *The London Prodigal* of 1603, the issues are prodigality of behaviour rather than a stress on deficiencies in upbringing or education. A play in which the subject of education is raised in connection with the prodigal is Randolph's *The Drinking Academy* of c. 1623–4, but here the notion of education is entirely ironical. Where schoolmasters occur in the later drama, they are more figures of fun or satire than anything else, such as the social climbing pedant Sarpego in Brome's *The City Wit* of 1630. In 1622 Henry Peacham observed that the schoolmaster is made a comic figure in many contemporary plays (1622, 27/E4[r]).

[4] For an account of this tradition, see Young, 1979, 55–79 and Norland, 1995, 149–60.

[5] Compare the taunting of Mercy in similar circumstances by Mischief in the late fifteenth-century play *Mankind*:
> I beseche yow hertyly, leue your calcacyon.
> Leue yowr chaffe, leue yowr corn, leue yowr dalyacyon.
> Yowr wytt ys lyttyll, yowr hede ys mekyll, ye are full of predycacyon.
> But, ser, I prey this questyon to claryfye:
> Mysse-masche, dryff-draff,
> Sume was corn and some was chaffe,
> My dame seyde my name was Raffe;
> Onschett yowr lokke and take an halpenye.
> (45–52)

[6] Compare also Marston's comments much later in the century in *The Scourge of Villainy* (1598), Satire 10:
> In fayth I am sad, I am possest with ruth,
> To see the vainenes of fayre *Albions* youth;
> To see their richest time euen wholy spent

In that which is but Gentries ornament.
(H8^r)

. . .

To daunce & sing
To vault, to fence, & fairely trot a ring
With good grace, meanely done. O what repute
They doe beget, but beeing absolute,
It argues too much time, too much regard
Imploy'd in that which might be better spard,
Then substance should be lost.
(H8^{r-v})

[7] The title page of Wager's *The Longer thou Livest* announces that the comedy is 'specially for such as are like to come to dignitie and promotion'.

[8] A subplot sequence in *The Disobedient Child* may equally be taken in a metaphorical way. The banter among the servants preparing the son's wedding feast includes an exchange between the cook and the maid. The maid says: 'Thoughe nowe in the kytchyn I waste the daye, / Yet in tymes paste I went to schole, / And of my Laten prymer I tooke assaye' (p. 20). The male cook, addressing the audience, comments: 'Maysters, thys woman dyd take such assaye, / And then in those dayes so applyed her booke, / That one word therof she carryed not awaye, / But then of a scholer was made a cooke' (p. 20). Indeed, given the limitations on education for girls, especially among the non-elite, the passage can hardly be taken to have any direct social reference.

[9] This play (like, in all probability, *The Disobedient Child*) is based on Ravisius Textor's *Juvenis, Pater et Uxor* which contains complaints by the boy about excessive beating by his schoolmaster, a disastrous marriage, and the boy's having to sell faggots for a living.

[10] For a further account of marriage and the family economy in the period, see Amussen, 1988, 67–94.

[11] Anthony Fletcher points out that, in the material on the upbringing of children published between 1560 and 1634, none 'shows any sign at all of gender distinctions, and it is taken for granted that a mother's disciplinary powers are equal to those of the father, though he was normally expected to take the initiative' (1994, 329).

[12] In the same year Henry Peacham also suggested that many scholars developed a hatred of learning because of the severity of schoolmasters (1622, 25/E3^r).

[13] Neither is this only the case when their exhortations are aimed at the nobility. Early in the sixteenth century Edmund Dudley, in his *Tree of Commonwealth* (1509), addressed his comments to the mercantile elite:

> And ye honest marchauntes and other wealthie comyners be not shamid
> to gyve your childeren parte of theis paringes; lett not the (femynine)
> petie of your wyves distroie your childeren; pompe not them at home in
> furrid cotis and shertes to be Warmyd agenst ther vprising, and suffer not

them to lie in there beddes tyll tenne of the clock and then a Warme
brakefast or there handes be Washid. His nature is so tender he may
nether lerne nor labor; Master John he must be callid, and his father, Ser
marchant. Set ther bodies to some busynes and þ^t bytymes. Remember
your selfes how you wan your thriftes. Dandle them not to derely lest
folie fasten one them. For oftetymes all þ^t ye leave, although ye warr long
in getting therof with mutche penurie and pain, shortly thei will spend it
with vnthriftie maner [as] experience will shew more then all this.
(68)

7. 'Philosophers and queint Logicians:' plebeian wits, gentlemen and scholars on the London commercial stage

[1] For a list of other contemporary examples of this, see Peter Ure's Arden edition of
the play, note on 3.4.37–9.

[2] For another reference to Macilente, see p. 99 above. Compare also the character of
the scholar Poore in the fragmentary *Play of Poore* (c. 1617/8). Only the part of Poore
is extant, and this starts with the attempt of the scholar to kill himself out of
desperation born of his poverty.

[3] The susceptibility of poor learned men to corruption is summed up in a comment by
Dekker's machiavellian king in *The Whore of Babylon*: 'Learning's fort is strong, /
But poorely man'd, and cannot hold out long / When golden bullets batter' (2.2.27–9).

[4] See above pp. 212–3, n. 14.

[5] A few examples will suffice: Shakespeare's Thurio in *Two Gentlemen of Verona*
(1593), Rudesby, Foulweather, and Sir Giles in Chapman's *Sir Giles Goosecap*
(1602), Jonson's Sir Amorous La Foole in *Epicoene* of 1609 (especially Act 1, Scene
4), Middleton and Rowley's Sir Gregory Fop in *Wit at Several Weapons* (1613),
Lackwit in Marmion's *A Fine Companion* of 1623 (especially in Act 2, Scene 6); and
Depazzi, the foolish lord in Shirley's *The Humourous Courtier* (1631).

[6] G. K. Hunter has listed these (late sixteenth-century and early seventeenth-century)
plays as follows:
The Weakest Goeth to the Wall (Duke of Bullen)
Ist Part of the Blind Beggar of Bednall Green (Momford)
Royal King and Loyal Subject (Earl Marshall)
Look All About You (Earl of Gloucester)
Trial of Chivalry (Princes of France and Navarre)
A Shoemaker, A Gentleman (Crispin and Crispianus)
Nobody and Somebody (Elidure)
(1997, 365 n.)

[7] For a discussion of this see Rees, 1954, 2–28.

[8] Compare also Robert Burton's comment on the attitudes of wealthy heirs in *The Anatomy of Melancholy*: 'Because they are rich, and have other meanes to live, they thinke it concernes them not to knowe, or to trouble themselves with it; a fitter taske for younger brothers, or poore mens sonnes, to be pen and Inkhorne men, pedanticall slaves, & no whit beseeming the calling of a Gentleman, as *Frenchmen* & *Germans* commonly doe, neglect therefore all humane learning' (1.2.3.15.p. 318).

[9] The display of competence in foreign manners and a modern languages is, of course, at this point a matter of fashion, but it does have a basis in the strong educational interest in modern languages shown by the upper classes in the sixteenth and seventeenth centuries; see Feingold, 1997, 269.

[10] By contrast, in the school play *Apollo Shroving* composed by a schoolmaster, William Hawkins, for performance by his boys before the mayor and citizens of Hadley in Suffolk in 1626, the possibilities for advancement offered by education is (unsurprisingly) presented in an unequivocally positive light. The diligent scholar, Philoponus, declares: 'This education which he (his father) affoords me, I take for a more goodly and durable inheritance, then if he could haue left mee thousands of flockes and acres, without any bringing vp in qualitie other then the gentle vanities of the times. I enuy not our spruce gallant Gingle, that now forsooth scornes to be our schoole-fellow any longer' (1.4. pp.2–13). However Gingle's foolish and mother, Indulgence, betrays a particular brand of elitist snobbery in her attitudes: 'Doe they thinke my childe is so low–borne as to be made a nitty scholler? Shall such a keene refin'd wit be dul'd and imbased by plodding on a booke?' (4.3.p. 64).

[11] For an account of references to this figure in the period, see the Arden edition of *Love's Labours Lost* by R. W. David, 67 (note on 4.1.100).

[12] On sizars, see p. 26 above. For an account of Harvey's learning and aspiration to office, see Whigham, 1984, 22–3, and Stern, 1979, 31, 39, 50, 97, 158–9, 177.

[13] There have been other associations, particularly with schoolmasters of the period such as John Florio and Richard Lloyd (see Arden edition xxxiii–xxxiv). The fact of Holofernes's being a schoolmaster may something to do with a general perception about the pretensions of such men.

[14] There was apparently another university play satirizing Harvey as well. Nashe goes on to say, 'Let him denie that there was a Shewe made at *Clare-hall* of him and his two Brothers, called, *Tarrarantantara turbu tumultuosa Trigonum, Tri-Harueyorum, Tri-harmonia*' (McKerrow, 1904, III, 80).

[15] Two anecdotes from Nashe's *Have with you to Saffron Walden* illustrate Harvey's obsessions with language: 'A word it is that the Doctor lay a whole weeke and a day & a night entranced on his bed to bring forth, and on the Munday euening late, causd all the bels in the Parish where he then soiourned, to be rong forth, for ioy that he was deliuered of it' (Epistle dedicatory, in McKerrow, 1904, III, 15). The second is an account of Harvey's reception of a gentleman who had come to visit him out of curiosity:

with amplifications and complements hee belaboured him till his eares tingled and his feet ak'd againe. Neuer was man so surfetted and ouer-gorged with English, as hee cloyd him with his generous spirites, renumeration of gratuities, stopping the posternes of ingratitude, bearing the launcier too seuere into his imperfections, and trauersing the ample forrest of interlocutions.

(McKerrow, 1904, III, 92)

[16] Compare one of the many accounts Nashe gives at Harvey's excessive delight at being spoken to by the Queen (who took him for an Italian). This occurs in *Strange News* of 1592:

In which respect, of [the Queen's] owne vertue and not his desert, it pleased hir so to humble the height of hir iudgement, as to grace him a little whiles he was pronouncing, by these or like tearmes. *Tis a good pretie fellow, a lookes like an Italian*; and after hee had concluded, to call him to kisse her royal hand. Herevppon hee goes to his studie, all intraunced, and writes a whole volume of Verses; first *De vultu Itali*, of the countenance of the Italian; and then *De osculo manus*, of his kissing the Queenes hande.

(McKerrow, 1904, I, 277)

[17] The figure of Puffe in Marston's *Jack Drum's Entertainment* (1601) occupies much the same role as Holofernes and his companions. Puffe is a minor comic figure who acts as a foil to the hero, and is defined by the self-conscious use of elaborate language, as in this opening greeting: 'Sir, I enrowle you in the Legend of my (*Puffe*) intimates, I shall be infinitely proud if you will daigne to value me worthy the embracement of your (*Puffe*) better affection' (B4ᵛ). Compare also the comment of Fynes Moryson in his *Itinerary*: 'wee seldome commend or follow any man of meane sort, taking vpon him to bring in new words into our language, or new manners into practice, or clothes into wearing' (1617, 249).

[18] Thomas Lodge in *Wit's Misery* of 1596 gives a description of ambition: 'If hée arise from obscurity . . . hée laboureth tooth and naile to be skilfull in those things which are most plausible to the greater sort, and tollerable among the commons: his studie is for ostentation, not vertues sake: his bookes like *Mausolus* tombe, are comely without, but within nothing but rotten bones' (B3ᵛ/6). For a discussion of official attitudes to ambition in the period, see Esler, 1966, especially 24–50.

[19] Note, however an essay by J. W. Huntington arguing that Chapman's enthusiasm for William Jones's translation, *Nennio, or a treatise of Nobility* (1595) shows a deviation from the humanist tradition of linking 'true knowledge' and aristocracy (1996, 291–312).

[20] A scholar figure who does show some awareness of linguistic distinctions is Tulley in *Every Woman in her Humour* (1607/8 possibly by Lewis Machin) who, when asked to woo a woman on behalf of a friend, says of the language of courtship: 'All which to me are problematique mines, / Obscured enigmaes, and to my studies / Incognite language' (2.1.35-7).

8. Conclusion

[1] Andrew Gurr has warned about problems in separating the 'great' (or canonical) cultural tradition from the 'little' of populist culture because of the unevenness of the survival of plays into print, and the resulting paucity of evidence from the populist side (1996, 122 and see also 26–7).

[2] The development of a particular social world view or orientation implicit in the conventions of drama may also involve an element of self-generation. Stephen Greenblatt has remarked: 'Shakespeare's representational equipment included not only the ideological constraints within which the theater functioned as an institution but also a set of received stories and generic expectations including, as his career progressed, those established by his earlier plays' (1988, 16).

[3] Leinwand has remarked of Shakespeare: 'Yet it seems clear that he was in many ways an interhierarchical figure: capitalist and artist, bourgeois and artisan, shareholder and actor, urban and provincial. He is perhaps less this or that than a stage for contestation and intermixing' (1990, 487).

[4] A relatively early play that Leggatt correctly points to as celebrating 'hard work and middle-class ambition' is Dekker's *The Shoemaker's Holiday* of 1599. This presents a comic portrait of Simon Eyre, a madcap shoemaker of Cheapside who repeatedly calls himself a 'gentleman of the gentle craft' and who becomes Lord Mayor of London. It is true that the play does explicitly legitimize social mobility, but at the same time it implicitly preserves the validity of social distinctions. Early in the play Eyre declares: 'I am a man of the best presence, Ile speak to them and they were Popes: gentlemen, captaines, colonels, commanders: braue men, braue leaders, may it please you to giue me audience, I am *Simon Eyre*, the mad Shoomaker of Towerstreete' (1.1.124–7). He is a mouthpiece for satirical observations on the excesses of courtly manners: 'a courtier, wash, go by, stand not vppon pisherie pasherie: those silken fellowes are but painted Images, outsides, outsides *Rose*, their inner linings are torne' (3.3.40–42). However, in terms of class rhetoric, the ambiguities of his status are such that they can be accommodated only with difficulty in the play. The incumbent mayor, Sir Thomas Otley (whose daughter marries an earl) might also be a citizen, but he has acquired a knighthood and the rhetoric of the elite. In Eyre's case, his strong dramatic presence alongside the king is made possible only by turning him into a sort of court jester. The King declares, on hearing about him: 'I am with child til I behold this huffe cap / But all my doubt is, when we come in presence, / His madnesse wil be dasht cleane out of countenance' (5.3.10–12). Indeed, when Eyre meets the King, he says: 'I beseech your grace, pardon my rude behauiour, I am a handicrafts man, yet my heart is without craft, I would be sory at my soule, that my boldnesse should offend my king' (5.5.9–11). It is only when the King 'licenses' him by giving him express permission to pursue his madcap manner that he continues. Formal aspects of prosody, such as the distinction between the King's verse and Eyre's prose, help rhetorically to underscore the social distinctions. The play gives fairly explicit recognition to the possibilities of change in social status, but there is nonetheless a clear behavioural difference between those in command of the social and political rhetoric – acquired by breeding or social advancement through professional means – and the others.

Bibliography

Abbreviations

DNB   *Dictionary of National Biography*, ed. L. Stephen and S. Lee, London, Oxford
        University Press, 1917
EETS   *Early English Text Society*
ELR   *English Literary Renaissance*
MET   *Medieval English Theatre*
MLN   *Modern Language Notes*
MLR   *Modern Language Review*
P&P   *Past and Present*
PMLA *Proceedings of the Modern Language Association of America*
R&R   *Renaissance and Reformation*
REED *Records of Early English Drama*
RenD   *Renaissance Drama*
RES   *Review of English Studies*
TLS   *Times Literary Supplement*
TN   *Theatre Notebook*

Secondary and Non-Dramatic Primary Texts

For early works, titles are given in the original spelling, though they are cited in a
modernized form in the text.

Agnew, J-C. (1986) *Worlds Apart: The Market and the Theater in Anglo-American
    Thought, 1550–1750*, Cambridge, Cambridge University Press
Allen, P. S. and H. M.(1922) *Opus Epistolarum Des. Erasmi Roterodami*, Oxford,
    Clarendon Press
Altman, J. (1978) *The Tudor Play of Mind: Rhetorical Enquiry and the Development
    of Elizabethan Drama*, Berkeley, University of California Press
Amussen, S. (1988) *An Ordered Society*, Oxford, Basil Blackwell
Anglin, S. P. (1985) *The Third University: A Survey of Schools and Schoolmasters in
    the Elizabethan Diocese of London*, Norwood Pa., Norwood Editions
Ascham, Roger (1570) *The Scholemaster*, London, John Daye
Axton, M. (1977) *The Queen's Two Bodies: Drama and the Elizabethan Succession*,
    London, Royal Historical Society
Bacon, Francis (1605) *The Twoo Bookes of Francis Bacon Of the proficience and
    aduancement of Learning, diuine and humane*, London, Henry Tomes
Bacon, Francis (1623) *De Dignitate et Augmentis Scientiarum* (trans. Spedding) in
    The Philosophical Works of Francis Bacon, ed. J. Robertson, Freeport, N.Y.,
    Books for Libraries Press, 1905 (repr. 1970), pp. 413–638
Bald, R. C. (1970) *John Donne: A Life*, Oxford, Clarendon Press
Baldwin, T. W. (1944) *Shakespeare's Small Latine and Lesse Greeke*, Urbana,
    University of Illinois Press, 2 vols

Bale, John (1557) *Scriptorum Illustrium Maioris Brytannie*, Basle, John Oporinus

Barclay, Alexander (1508) *Shyp of Folys*, London, printed by Richard Pynson

Barclay, Alexander (1523) *Mirrour of Good Manners*, London, printed by Richard Pynson

Barish, J. (1981) *The Antitheatrical Prejudice*, Berkeley, University of California Press

Barton, A. (Righter) (1962) *Shakespeare and the Idea of the Play*, London, Chatto and Windus

Bentley, G. E. (1971) *The Profession of Dramatist in Shakespeare's Time 1590–1642*, Princeton, Princeton University Press

Bentley, G. E. (1984) *The Profession of Player in Shakespeare's Time 1590–1642*, Princeton, Princeton University Press

Berry, R. (1988) *Shakespeare and Social Class*, Atlantic Heights, N.J., Humanities Press International Inc.

Bevington, D. (1962) *From Mankind to Marlowe: The Growth of Structure in the Popular Drama of Tudor England*, Cambridge, Mass., Harvard University Press

Bevington, D. (1968) *Tudor Drama and Politics: A Critical Approach to Topical Meaning*, Cambridge, Mass., Harvard University Press

Bland, D. S. (1969) 'Henry VIII's Royal Commission on the Inns of Court', *Journal of the Society of Public Teachers of Law*, n.s.10, 178–94

Boas, F. (1914) *University Drama of the Tudor Age*, New York, Benjamin Blom

Boas, F. (1923) *Shakespeare and the Universities*, Oxford, Basil Blackwell

Bolgar, R. R. (1954) *The Classical Heritage and its Beneficiaries*, Cambridge, Cambridge University Press

Bolgar, R. R. (1973) 'From Humanism to the Humanities', *Twentieth Century Studies* 9, pp. 8–21

Bourdieu, P. (1980) *The Logic of Practice*, translated by R. Nice, Polity Press, Cambridge

Bourdieu, P. (1984) *Distinction: A Social Critique of the Judgement of Taste*, translated by R. Nice, London, Routledge and Kegan Paul

Bourdieu, P. (1991) *Language and Symbolic Power*, ed. J. B. Thompson, translated by G. Raymond and M. Adamson, Polity Press, Cambridge

Bradbrook, M. (1962) *The Rise of the Common Player: A Study of the Actor and Society in Shakespeare's England*, London, Chatto and Windus

Brewer, J. S. (1895) *Calendar of State Papers*, Vol. 14, Part 2, London, H.M.S.O.

Brinsley, John (1612) *Ludus Literarius or, the Grammar Schoole*, London, printed by Thomas Man

Brinsley, John (1622) *A Consolation for ovr Grammar Schooles*, London, printed by Richard Field for Thomas Man

Bristol, M. (1985) *Carnival and Theater: Plebeian Culture and the Structure of Authority in Renaissance England*, London, Routledge

Brodrick, G. C. (1881) 'The Law and Custom of Primogeniture', in *Systems of Land Tenure in Various Countries*, ed. J. W. Probyn, London, Cassell, Petter and Galpin, pp. 93–168

Bruster, D. (1992) *Drama and the Market in the Age of Shakespeare*, Cambridge, Cambridge University Press

Burke, K. (1962) *A Grammar of Motives and A Rhetoric of Motives*, New York, Meridian Books (first published 1945 and 1950 respectively)

Burke, P. (1978) *Popular Culture in Early Modern Europe*, London, Temple Smith

Burke, P. (1995) *The Fortunes of the Courtier: The European Reception of Castiglione's Cortegiano*, Cambridge, Polity Press

Burton, Robert (1621) *The Anatomy of Melancholy*, ed. T. C. Faulkner, N. K. Kiessling and R. L. Blair, Oxford, Clarendon Press, 1989

Butler, M. (1984) *Theatre and Crisis 1632–1642*, Cambridge, Cambridge University Press

Butler, M. (1990) 'Private and Occasional Drama', in *The Cambridge Companion to English Renaissance Drama*, ed. A. Braunmuller and M. Hattaway, Cambridge, Cambridge University Press, pp. 127–59

Campbell L. (ed.) (1938) *The Mirror for Magistrates*, Cambridge, Cambridge University Press

Cane, Andrew (1641) *The Stage-Players Complaint in a pleasant Dialogue between Cane of the* Fortune *and Reed of the* Friers, London, printed by Thomas Bates

Carlisle, N. (1818) *A Concise Description of the Endowed Grammar Schools in England and Wales*, London, Baldwin, Cradock and Joy, 2 vols

Carson, N. (1988) *A Companion to Henslowe's Diary*, Cambridge, Cambridge University Press

Caspari, F. (1954) *Humanism and the Social Order in Tudor England*, Chicago, Chicago University Press

Chambers, E. K. (1903) *The Mediaeval Stage*, Oxford, Clarendon Press, 3 vols

Chambers, E. K. (1923) *The Elizabethan Stage*, Oxford, Clarendon Press, 4 vols

Chapman, George (1609) *Euthymiae Raptus or The Tears of Peace*, in *The Poems of George Chapman*, ed. P. B. Bartlett, New York, Oxford University Press, 1941

Charlton, K. (1965) *Education in Renaissance England*, London, Routledge and Kegan Paul

Chrimes, S. B. (trans. and ed.) (1942) Sir John Fortescue, *De Laudibus Legum Anglie*, London, Cambridge, Cambridge University Press

Cyuile and Vncyuile Life. A discourse very profitable, pleasant, and fit to bee read of all Nobilitie and Gentlemen (1579) London, printed by Richard Jones

Clare, J. (1990) *'Art made tongue-tied by authority': Elizabethan and Jacobean Dramatic Censorship*, Manchester, Manchester University Press

Clarendon, Edward Earl (1842) *Life of Edward Earl of Clarendon, Written by Himself*, Oxford, Oxford University Press (edited from the original manuscripts in 1842, and appended to his *History of the Rebellion and Civil Wars in England*)

Clark, P. and P. Slack (eds) (1976) *English Towns in Transition 1500–1700*, Oxford, Oxford University Press

Clarke, M. L. (1959) *Classical Education in Britain 1500–1900*, Cambridge, Cambridge University Press

Clay, C. G. A. (1984) *Economic Expansion and Social Change: England 1500–1700*, Vol. 1, Cambridge, Cambridge University Press

Clement, Francis (1587) *The Petie Schole*, London, printed by Thomas Vautrollier

Collier, J. P. (1831) *The History of English Dramatic Poetry to the Time of Shakespeare and Annals of the Stage to the Restoration*, London, John Murray

Collinson, P. (1988) *The Birthpangs of Protestant England*, London, Macmillan

Conley, C. (1927) *First English Translators of Classics*, New Haven, Yale University Press

Cook A.-J. (1981) *The Privileged Playgoers of Shakespeare's London, 1576–1642*, Princeton, Princeton University Press

Cooper, J. (1983) *Land, Men and Belief*, London, Hambledon

Cowper, J. (1927) *England in the Reign of Henry the Eighth*, London, *EETS*, e.s.12

Cox, J. and D. Kastan (eds) (1997) *A New History of Early English Drama*, New York, Columbia University Press

Craik, T. W. (1953) 'The Political Interpretation of Two Tudor Interludes', *RES*, n.s. 4, pp. 98–108

Craik, T. W. (1958) *The Tudor Interlude*, London, Leicester University Press

Craik, T. W. (1980) 'The Companies and the Repertory', in *The Revels History of Drama in English Volume II: 1500–1576*, ed. N. Sanders, R. Southern, T. W. Craik and L. Potter, London, Methuen, pp. 103–39

Cressy, D. (1975) *Education in Tudor and Stuart England*, London, Edward Arnold

Cressy, D. (1980) *Literacy and the Social Order: Reading and Writing in Tudor and Stuart England*, Cambridge, Cambridge University Press

Cressy, D. (1989) *Bonfires and Bells: National Memory and the Protestant Calendar in Elizabethan and Stuart England*, London, Weidenfeld and Nicholson

Crosse, Henry (1603) *Vertves Common-wealth or The Highway to Honour*, London, printed for John Newberry

Crowley, R. (1548) *An Informacion and Peticion agaynst the oppressours of the Pore Commons of this Realme*, London, printed by John Day

Cunliffe, J. W. (ed.) (1910) *The Complete Works of George Gascoigne*, Vol. 2, Cambridge, Cambridge University Press

Curtis, M. (1959) *Oxford and Cambridge in Transition 1558–1642*, Oxford, Clarendon Press

Curtis, M. (1962) 'The Alienated Intellectuals of Early Stuart England', *P&P* 23, pp. 25–43

Daniel, Samuel (1599) *Musophilus: Containing a generall defence of learning*, London, printed by P. Short for Simon Waterson

Davis, J. (1967) *The Sons of Ben: Jonsonian Comedy in Caroline England*, Detroit, Wayne State University Press

Dekker, Thomas (1603) *The Wonderfull Yeare*, in *The Non-Dramatic Works of Thomas Dekker*, Vol. 1, ed. A. B. Grosart, New York, Russell and Russell, 1963, 5 vols

Dekker, Thomas (1609) *The Gvls Horne-booke* London, printed for R. S.

De Mause, L. (ed.) (1976) *The History of Childhood: The evolution of parent-child relationships as a factor in history*, London, Souvenir Press

Devereux, W. (1853) *Lives and Letters of the Devereux*, London, John Murray

Discourse of the Common Weal (1581) London, ed. E. Lamond, Cambridge, Cambridge University Press, 1893

Dollimore, J. (1984) *Radical Tragedy: Religion, Ideology and Power in the Drama of Shakespeare and His Contemporaries*, Brighton, Harvester Press

Dollimore, J. and A. Sinfield (eds) (1985) *Political Shakespeare*, Manchester, Manchester University Press

Dryden, John (1672) *The Defence of the Epilogue or, An Essay on the Dramatique Poetry of the Last Age* (attached to *The Conquest of Granada*, II), in *The Works of John Dryden*, (gen. ed. H. T. Swedenberg) Vol. 11, ed. J. Loftis and D. S. Rodes, Berkeley, University of California Press, 1978

Dudley, Edmund (1509) *The Tree of Commonwealth*, ed. D. M. Brodie, Cambridge, Cambridge University Press, 1948

Dugdale, Sir William (1666) *Origines Juridicales*, London, F. and T. Warren

Dutton, R. (1991) *Mastering the Revels: The Regulation and Censorship of English Renaissance Drama*, London, Macmillan

Earle, John (1633) *Microcosmographie*, London, reprinted from 1628 edition by Robert Allot, facsimile, Methuen, 1904

Eccles, M. (1977) 'John Webster', *TLS*, 21 Jan, p. 71

Edgerton, W. L. (1965) *Nicholas Udall*, New York, Twayne

Education of children in learning, The (1588) London, printed by Thomas Orwin for John Porter and Thomas Gubbin

Elliott, J. (1995) 'Plays, Players and Playwrights in Renaissance Oxford', in *From Page to Performance: Essays in Early English Drama*, ed. J. A. Alford, East Lansing, Michigan University Press, pp. 179–94

Elliott, J. (1997) 'Early Staging in Oxford', in Cox and Kastan, pp. 68–76

Ellis, H. (1800) 'Biographical Anecdotes of Richard Mulcaster', *The Gentleman's Magazine . . . for the Year 1800*, May, p. 70

Elton, W. (2000) *Shakespeare's* Troilus and Cressida *and the Inns of Court Revels*, Aldershot, Ashgate

Elyot, Sir Thomas (1531) *The Boke named the Gouernour, deuised by Thomas Elyot Knight*, London, printed by Thomas Berthelet

Elyot, Sir Thomas (1535) *The Education or Bringing Vp of Children, translated out of Plutarche*, London, no date given or printer named in colophon

Esler, A. (1966) *The aspiring mind of the Elizabethan younger generation*, Durham, N.C., Duke University Press

Eutheo, Anglo-phile (1586) (pseud. Anthony Munday) *A second and third blast of retrait from plaies and Theaters*, London, printed by Henrie Denham for William Seres

Feingold, M. (1997) 'The Humanities', in *The History of the University of Oxford*, Vol.4, ed. N. Tyacke, Oxford, Oxford University Press, pp. 211–357

Ferne, Sir John (1586) *The Blazon of Gentrie*, London, printed by John Windet

Feuillerat, A. (1914) 'The Performance of a Tragedy at New College, Oxford, in the Time of Queen Mary', *MLR* 9, pp. 96–7

Finkelpearl, P. (1969) *John Marston of the Middle Temple: An Elizabethan Dramatist in His Social Setting*, Cambridge, Mass. Harvard University Press

Fisher, G. W. (1899) *Annals of Shrewsbury School*, London, Methuen

Fletcher, A. (1994) 'Prescription and Practice: Protestantism and the Upbringing of Children, 1560–1700', in *The Church and Childhood*, ed. D. Wood, Oxford, Basil Blackwell

Fletcher, J. M. (1996) 'The Faculty of Arts', in *The History of the University of Oxford*, ed. J. McConica, Oxford, Clarendon Press

Forshall, F. H. (1884) *Westminster School, Past and Present*, London, Wyman and Sons

Foucault, M. (1980) 'Prison Talk', in *Power/Knowledge*, ed. C. Gordon, Brighton, Harvester Press, pp. 36–54

Furnivall, F. J. (ed.) (1868) *Early English Meals and Manners*, London, *EETS*, o.s. 32

Gardiner, H. (1946) *Mysteries End*, New Haven, Yale University Press

Gee, J. A. (1928) *The Life and Works of Thomas Lupset*, New Haven, Yale University Press

Gent, N. B. (1618) *The Court and Country or A Briefe Discourse betweene the Courtier and the Country-Man; of the Manner, Nature, and condition of their lives*, in Hazlitt, 1868, pp. 171–211

Gent, S. R. (trans.) (1577) *The Covrte of Ciuill Courtesie*, London, Richard Jones

Gibbs, A. M. (1972) *Sir William Davenant: The Shorter Poems and Songs from the Poems and Masques*, Oxford, Clarendon Press

Gilbert, Sir Humphrey (1572) *Queene Elizabethes Achademy*, ed. F. J. Furnivall, London, *EETS*, e.s. 8, 1869

Gildersleeve, V. (1961) *The Government Regulation of the Elizabethan Drama*, New York, Burt Franklin

Golding, A. S. (1984) *Classicistic Acting*, Lanham, M.D., University Press of America

Gosson, Stephen (1579) *The School of Abuse*, London, printed for Thomas Woodcocke

Gosson, Stephen (1582) *Playes Confuted in Five Actions*, London, printed for Thomas Gosson

Grafton, A. and L. Jardine (1986) *From Humanism to the Humanities: Education and the Liberal Arts in Fifteenth and Sixteenth-Century Europe*, London, Duckworth

Graves, F. P. (1912) *Peter Ramus and the Educational Reformation of the Sixteenth Century*, New York, Macmillan

Gray, C. H. (1905) *Lodowick Carliell: His Life, a Discussion of his Plays and 'The Deserving Favourite'*, Chicago, University of Chicago Press

Greenblatt, S. (1980) *Renaissance Self-Fashioning: From More to Shakespeare*, Chicago, University of Chicago Press

Greenblatt, S. (1988) *Shakespearean Negotiations: The Circulation of Social Energy in Renaissance England*, Oxford, Clarendon Press

Greene, Robert (1589) *Menaphon*, London, printed by T.O. for Sampson Clarke

Greene, Robert (1590) *Francesco's Fortunes, Or the Second Part of Neuer too late*, London, printed for N.L. and John Busbie

Greene, Robert (1592) *A Groats-worth of Witte, bought with a million of Repentance*, London, printed for William Wright

Greene, Robert (1592b) *A Quip for an Vpstart Courtier Or, A quaint dispute between Veluet breeches and Clothbreeches*, London, printed by John Wolfe

Grosart, A. B. (ed.) (1885) *The Complete Works in Verse and Prose of Samuel Daniel*, London, Spenser Society

Gurr, A. (1988) *Playgoing in Shakespeare's London*, Cambridge, Cambridge University Press

Gurr, A. (1992) *The Shakespearean Stage 1574–1642*, Cambridge, Cambridge University Press

Gurr, A (1993) 'The General and the Caviar: Learned Audiences in the Early Theatre', *Studies in the Literary Imagination* 26, no. 1, pp. 7–20

Gurr, A. (1996) *The Shakespearian Playing Companies*, Oxford, Clarendon Press

Harbage, A. (1952) *Shakespeare and the Rival Traditions*, Bloomington, Indiana University Press

Harrison, William (1577/1587) *Harrison's Description of England in Shakspere's Youth, being the second and third books of his Description of Britaine and England*, ed. F. J. Furnivall, London, N. Trübner and Co, for the New Shakspere Society, 1877 (collation of 1577 and 1587 editions)

Harvey, Gabriel (1593) *Pierces Supererogation, or A New Prayse of the Old Asse*,
    London, printed by John Wolfe
Hattaway, M. (1982) *Elizabethan Popular Theatre: Plays in Performance*, London,
    Routledge and Kegan Paul
Hazlitt, W. C. (ed.) (1868) *Inedited Tracts Illustrating the Manners, Opinions and
    Occupations of Englishmen During the Sixteenth and Seventeenth Centuries*,
    London, Roxburgh Library
Hazlitt, W. C. (ed.) (repr. 1964) *A Select Collection of Old English Plays Originally
    Published by Robert Dodsley in the Year 1744*, reprinted New York,
    Benjamin Blom
Health to the Gentlemanly Profession of Servingmen, A (1598) in Hazlitt, 1868, pp.
    95–167
Heinemann, M. (1992) '"God help the poor: the rich can shift": The World Upside-
    Down and the Popular Tradition in the Theatre', in *The Politics of
    Tragicomedy*, ed. G. McMullan and J, Hope, London, Routledge, pp. 151–65
Herford, C. H. and P.Simpson (eds) (1925–52) *Ben Jonson* Oxford, Clarendon Press
Heywood, J. (1840) *Collection of Statutes for the University and Colleges of
    Cambridge*, London, William Clowes and Sons
Heywood, Thomas (1612) *An Apology for Actors*, London, printed by Nicholas Okes
Hexter, J. H. (1950) 'The Education of the Aristocracy in the Renaissance', *Journal of
    Modern History* 22, pp. 1–20
Hill, C. (1955) *The English Revolution 1640*, London, Lawrence and Wishart
Hillebrand, H. N. (1964) *The Child Actors*, New York, Russell and Russell
Hoby, Sir Thomas (1561) *The Courtyer of Count Baldessar Castilio, diuided into
    foure bookes*, London, printed by William Seres
Holinshed, Raphael (1577) *Holinshed's Chronicles of England, Scotland and Ireland*,
    Vol. 1, London, ed. J. Johnson et al., 1807
Hosking, G. L. (1952) *The Life and Times of Edward Alleyn: Actor, master of the
    King's Bears, Founder of the College of God's Gift at Dulwich*, London,
    Jonathan Cape
Howard, J. (1986) 'The New Historicism in Renaissance Studies', *ELR* 16, pp. 13–43
Howard, J. (1994) *The Stage and Social Struggle in Early Modern England*, London,
    Routledge
Howard-Hill, T. H. (1996) 'U and Non-U: Class and Discourse Level in *Othello*', in
    *Shakespeare's Universe: Renaissance Essays and Conventions. Essays in
    honour of W. R. Elton*, ed. J. M. Mucciolo, Scolar Press, pp. 175–86
Hughes, P. and Larkin J. (1964) *Tudor Royal Proclamations*, New Haven, Yale
    University Press
Hunter, G. K. (1962) *John Lyly: the Humanist as Courtier*, London, Routledge and
    Kegan Paul
Hunter, G. K. (1997) *English Drama 1586–1642*, Oxford, Clarendon Press
Huntington, J. W. (1996) '"This Ticklish Title": Chapman, Nennio and the Critique of
    Nobility', *ELR* 26, pp. 291–312
Inderwick, F. A. (1896) *A Calendar of the Inner Temple Records*, Vol. 1, London,
    Charles Whittingham and Co.
Institucion of a Gentleman, The (1555) London, printed by Thomas Marshe
James, M. (1974) *Family, Lineage and Civil Society*, Oxford, Clarendon Press
James, M. (1986) *Society, Politics and Culture, Studies in Early Modern England*,
    Cambridge, Cambridge University Press

Jardine, L. (1975) 'Humanism and the Sixteenth-Century Cambridge Arts Course', *History of Education* 4, pp. 16–31

Jardine, L. (1996) *Worldly Goods*, London, Macmillan

Jonson, Ben (1641) *Timber or Discoveries Made Vpon Men And Matter,* in Herford and Simpson, 1925–52, Vol. 8

Jordan, W. K. (1960) *The Charities of London 1480–1660*, London, George Allen and Unwin

Jordan, W. K. (1970) *Edward VI, The Young King*, London, George Allen and Unwin

Kearney, K. (1970) *Scholars and Gentlemen: Universities and Society in Pre-Industrial Britain 1500–1700*, London, Faber and Faber

Kelso, R. (1929) *The Doctrine of the English Gentleman in the Sixteenth Century*, Urbana, University of Illinois Press

Kipling, G. (1977) 'Triumphal Drama: Forms in English Civic Pageantry', *RenD*, n.s.8, pp. 37–56

Knighton, C. S. (ed.) (1992) *State Papers of Edward VI (Calendar of State Papers, Domestic Series, of the Reign of Edward VI: 1547–1553)*, London, H.M.S.O

Knights, L. C. (1937) *Drama and Society in the Age of Jonson*, London, Chatto and Windus

Knox, D. (1991) '*Disciplina*: The Monastic and Clerical Origins of European Civility' in *Renaissance Society and Culture: Essays in Honor of Eugene F. Rice, Jr.*, ed. J. Monfasani and R. G. Musto, Italica Press, New York, pp. 107–35

Kolve, V. A. (1966) *The Play Called Corpus Christi*, Stanford, Stanford University Press

Kristeller, P. O. (1961) *Renaissance Thought: The Classic, Scholastic and Humanist Strains*, New York, Harper and Row

Lancashire, I. (1976) 'The Auspices of *The World and the Child*', *R&R* 12, pp. 95–105

Lancashire, I. (1984) *Dramatic Texts and Records of Britain: A Chronological Topography to 1558*, Toronto, University of Toronto Press

La Perrière, Guillaume de (1598) *The Mirrour of Policie* (translation of *Le miroir politique*) London, printed by Adam Islip

Lawson, J. and Silver, H. (1973, reprinted 1978) *A Social History History of Education*, London, Methuen

Leach, A. F. (ed. and trans.) (1911) *Educational Charters and Documents 598–1909*, Cambridge, Cambridge University Press

Lee, S. (1916) *A Life of William Shakespeare*, London, John Lane

Leggatt, A. (1992) *Jacobean Popular Theatre*, London, Routledge

Legh, Gerard (1562) *Accedens of Armorie*, London, Richard Tottel

Leinwand, T. (1990) 'Negotiation and New Historicism', *PMLA* 105, pp. 477–90

Lenton, Francis (1629) *The Yovng Gallants Whirligigg or Yovths Reakes*, London, printed by M.F. for Robert Bostocke

Ling, Nicholas (1597) *Politeuphuia, Wits Common Wealth*, London, printed by I.R.

Lodge, Thomas (1596) *Wits Miserie and the Worlds Madnesse*, London, printed by Adam Islip

Lovelace, Richard (1906) *Poems of Richard Lovelace*, London, Hutchinson

Lovelace, Richard (1659) *Lucasta: Posthume Poems of Richard Lovelace Esq.*, London, printed by William Godbid for Clement Darby

Macalindon, T. (1973) *Shakespeare and Decorum*, London, Macmillan

McConica, J. (1974) 'Scholars and Commoners in Renaissance Oxford', in *The University in Society: Oxford and Cambridge from the 14th to the Early 19th Century*, ed. L. Stone, Princeton, N.J., Princeton University Press

McConica, J. (ed.) (1986) *The History of the University of Oxford, Volume III: The Collegiate University*, Oxford, Clarendon Press

MacCulloch, D. (1990) *The Later Reformation in England*, London, Macmillan

McDonnell, M. (1977) *The Registers of St Paul's School 1509–1784*, London, privately printed

Macfarlane, A. (1986) *Marriage and Love in England 1300–1840*, Oxford, Basil Blackwell

Machyn, Henry (1563) *The Diary of Henry Machyn*, ed. J. G. Nichols, London, Camden Society/ J. B. Nichols and Son, 1848

McIntosh, M. K. (1978) 'The Fall of a Tudor Gentle Family: The Cookes of Gidea Hall, Essex 1579–1629', *Huntingdon Library Quarterly* 41, no. 3, pp. 279–97

McKerrow, R. B. (1904) *The Works of Thomas Nashe*, London, A. H. Bullen

McLuskie, K. (1985) 'The Patriarchal Bard', in Dollimore and Sinfield, pp. 88–108

McLuskie, K. (1989) *Renaissance Dramatists*, Hemel Hempstead, Harvester Press

McLuskie, K. (1994) *Dekker and Heywood: Professional Dramatists*, London, Macmillan

Mallet, C. (1924–7) *A History of the University of Oxford*, London, Methuen

Manley, L. (ed.) (1986) *London in the Age of Shakespeare: An Anthology*, London, Croom Helm

Marcus, L. (1978) *Childhood and Cultural Despair*, Pittsburgh, University of Pittsburgh Press

Marcus, L. (1986) *The Politics of Mirth: Jonson, Herrick, Milton, Marvell and the Defense of Old Holiday Pastimes*, Chicago, University of Chicago Press

Marston, John (1598) (pseud. W. Kinsayder) *The Scovrge of Villanie*, London, printed by I. R. Mason, J. E. (1935 repr. 1971) *Gentlefolk in the Making*, New York, Octagon

Maxwell Lyte, H. C. (1911) *A History of Eton College*, London, Macmillan

Meredith, P. (1984) '"Farte Pryke in Cule" and Cock-Fighting in *Fulgens and Lucres*', *MET* 6, no. 1, pp. 30–39

Meres, Francis (1598) *Palladis Tamia, Wits Treasury Being the Second part of Wits Commonwealth*, London, printed by P. Short for Cuthbert Burbie

Middleton, Thomas (1604) (pseud. Oliver Hubburd) *Father Hubburd's Tales*, London, printed by T. C. for William Cotton

Mildenberger, K. (1951) 'Robert Greene at Cambridge', *MLN* 66, pp. 546–9

Miles, R. *Ben Jonson: His Life and Work*, London, Routledge and Kegan Paul, 1986

Moryson, Fynes (1617) *An Itinerary* in *Harrison's Description of England in Shakspere's Youth, being the second and third books of his Description of Britaine and England*, ed. F. J. Furnivall, London, N. Trübner and Co, for the New Shakspere Society, 1877

Motter, F. H. V. (1929) *The School Drama in England*, Port Washington, N.Y., Kennikat Press

Mulcaster, Richard (1581) *Positions Wherin those Primitive Circumstances be examined which are necessarie for the training vp of children*, printed by Thomas Vautrollier, London

Mulcaster, Richard (1582) *Elementarie*, ed. E. T. Campagnac, Oxford, Clarendon Press, 1925

Murray, J. T. (1910) *English Dramatic Companies 1558–1642*, London, Constable and Co.

Nashe, Thomas (1589) 'To the Gentlemen Students of Both Universities' (prefacing Greene's *Menaphon*), in McKerrow, Vol. 3, 1904

Nashe, Thomas (1592) *Pierce Penilesse his Supplication to the Diuell Describing the ouer-spreading of Vice, and suppression of Vertue*, in McKerrow, Vol. 1, 1904

Nashe, Thomas (1592b) *Strange Newes of the intercepting Certaine Letters* or *The Four Letters Confuted*, in McKerrow, Vol. 3, 1904

Nashe, Thomas (1596) *Haue with you to Saffron-walden or Gabriell Harueys Hunt is vp*, in McKerrow, Vol. 3, 1904

Neale, J. E. (1949) *The Elizabethan House of Commons*, London, Jonathan Cape

Nelson, A. H. (1994) *Early Cambridge Theatres*, Cambridge, Cambridge University Press

Norland, H. B. (1995) *Drama in Early Tudor Britain 1485–1558*, Lincoln, Nebraska, University of Nebraska Press

Northbrooke, John (1577?) *A Treatise Wherein Dicing, Dauncing, Vaine Playes or Enterludes with other idle pastimes etc commonly used on the Sabboth day, are repreued by the Authoritie of the word of God and auntient writers*, London, printed by H. Bynneman for George Byshop

O'Day, R. (1982) *Education and Society 1500–1800: The Social Foundations of Education in Modern Britain*, London, Longman

Ong, W. (1977) *Interfaces of the Word: Studies in the Evolution of Consciousness and Culture*, Ithaca, Cornell University Press

Orgel, S. (1975) *The Illusion of Power: Political Theatre in the English Renaissance*, Berkeley and Los Angeles, University of California Press

Orme, N. (1989) *Education and Society in Medieval and Renaissance England*, London, Hambledon

Osborn, L. B. (1937) *The Life, Letters and Writings of John Hoskyns 1566–1638*, New Haven, Yale University Press

Padelford, F. M. (1905) *Select Translations from Scaliger's Poetics*, New York, Henry Holt and Co.

Page, W. (ed.) (1907) *Victoria County History: Suffolk*, Vol. 2, London, Archibald Constable and Co.

Palliser, D. (1982) 'Civic Mentality and the Environment in Tudor York', *Northern History* 18, pp. 78–115

Parmiter, G. de C. (1976) *English Popish Recusancy in the Inns of Court*, London, Institute of Historical Research

Parr, J. (1962) 'Robert Greene and his Classmates at Cambridge', *PMLA* 77, pp. 536–43.

Pauck, W. (ed.) (1969) *Melanchthon and Bucer*, London, SCM Press

Peacham, Henry (1622) *The Compleat Gentleman*, London, printed by F. Constable

Penniman, J. (1897) *The War of the Theatres*, Boston, Ginn and Co.

Pettie, G. (trans.) (1581) *The Civile Conuersation of M. Steeuen Guazzo*, London, printed by Richard Watkins

Phythian-Adams, C. (1972) 'Ceremony and the Citizen: The Communal Year at Coventry 1450–1550', in *Crisis and Order in English Towns 1500–1700*, ed P. Clark and P. Slack, London, Routledge, pp. 57–85

Phythian-Adams, C. (1975) *Local History and Folklore: A New Framework*, London, Bedford Square Press

Phythian-Adams, C. (1979) *Desolation of a City: Coventry and the Urban Crisis of the Late Middle Ages*, Cambridge, Cambridge University Press

Pollock, L. (1983) *Forgotten Children: Parent-Child Relations from 1500 to 1900*, Cambridge, Cambridge University Press

Prest, W. R. (1972) *The Inns of Court under Elizabeth I and the Early Stuarts*, London, Longman

Ratseis Ghost Or the Second Part of His Madde Prankes and Robberies (1605) facsimile reprint with introduction by H. B. Charlton, Manchester, Manchester University Press, 1932

REED Cambridge (1989) ed. A. Nelson, Toronto, Toronto University Press

REED Cumberland, Westmoreland, Gloucestershire (1986) ed. A. Douglas and P. Greenfield, Toronto, Toronto University Press

REED York (1979) ed. A. F. Johnson and M. Rogerson, Toronto, Toronto University Press

Rees, E. (1954) *The Tragedies of George Chapman: Renaissance Ethics in Action*, Cambridge, Mass., Harvard University Press

Riggs, D. (1989) *Ben Jonson, A Life*, Cambridge, Mass., Harvard University Press

Roper, William (1626) *The Lyfe of Sir Thomas More*, ed. E. V. Hitchcock, *EETS*, o.s. 197, Oxford, Oxford University Press, 1934 (reprinted 1938)

Rowe, G. (1988) *Distinguishing Jonson: Imitation, Rivalry and the Direction of a Dramatic Career*, Lincoln, University of Nebraska Press

Rowlands, Samuel (1600) *The Letting of Hvmovrs Blood in the Head-Vaine / Epigrams*, London, printed by W. White for W.F.

Rowse, A. L. (1981) *What Shakespeare Read and Thought*, New York, Coward, McCann and Geoghan

Salingar, L. (1991) 'Jacobean Playwrights and "Judicious" Spectators', *RenD*, n.s. 22, pp. 209–34

Sargeaunt, J. (1898) *Annals of Westminster School*, London, Methuen

Schmitt, C. (1997) 'Writing the Nation in Early Modern England: The Case of Rhetoric and Poetics', *Gramma* 5, pp. 183–97

Schoenbaum, S. (1977) *William Shakespeare: A Compact Documentary Life* (revised edition), Oxford, Oxford University Press

Schoole of good manners or A new Schoole of Vertue, The, translated our of French by W F (1595) London, printed by I. Danter for William Jhones

Shakespeare, William (1609) *The Sonnets*, ed. M. Dodsworth, London, J. M. Dent, 1995

Shapiro, M. (1973) 'Audience vs. Dramatist in Jonson's *Epicoene* and Other Plays of the Children's Troupes', *ELR* 3, pp. 400–417

Sharpe, J. A. (1987) *Early Modern England: A Social History 1550–1760*, London, Edward Arnold

Shirley, James (1646) *Poems &c*, London, printed for Humphrey Moseley, reprinted as a Scolar Press facsimile, Menston, 1970

Shuger, D. (1990) *Habits of Thought in the English Renaissance: Religion, Politics and the Dominant Culture*, Berkeley, University of California Press

Sidney, Sir Philip (1595) *An Apologie for Poetrie*, London, printed for Henry Olney

Simon, J. (1966) *Education and Society in Tudor England*, Cambridge, Cambridge University Press

Simpson, R. (1878) *The School of Shakspere*, Vol. 2, New York, J. W. Bouton

Sinfield, A. (1985) 'Power and Ideology: An Outline Theory and Sidney's *Arcadia*', *ELH* 52, pp. 259–77

Skelton, John (1983) *The Complete Poems*, ed. J. Scattergood, New Haven, Yale University Press

Small, R. (1899) *The Stage-Quarrel between Ben Jonson and the So-Called Poetasters*, Breslau, M.and H. Marcus

Smith, B. (1988) *Ancient Scripts and Modern Experience on the English Stage 1500–1700*, Princeton, Princeton University Press

Smith, G. C. M (1923) *College Plays Performed in the University of Cambridge*, Cambridge, Cambridge University Press

Smith, Sir Thomas (1584) *De Republica Anglorum*, London, ed. M. Dewar, Cambridge, Cambridge University Press, 1982

Smuts, M. (1987) *Court Culture and the Origins of a Royalist Tradition in Early Stuart England*, Philadelphia, University of Philadelphia Press

Southern, R. (1973) *The Staging of Plays before Shakespeare*, London, Faber

Spedding, J., R. Ellis and D. Heath (eds) (1868) *The Works of Francis Bacon*, Vol. 11: *The Letters and Life Volume IV*, London, Longmans, Green, Reader and Dyer

Starkey, Thomas (1533–6) *The Dialogue between Cardinal Pole and Thomas Lupset*, London, no printer named

Stevens, M. (1987) *Four Middle English Mystery Cycles: Textual, Contextual and Critical Interpretations*, Princeton, N.J., Princeton University Press

Stone, L. (1964) 'The Educational Revolution in England 1560–1640', *P&P* 28, pp. 41–80

Stone, L. (1965) *The Crisis of the Aristocracy 1558–1640*, Oxford, Clarendon Press

Stone, L. (ed.) (1965b) *Social Change and Revolution in England 1540–1640*, London, Longmans

Stone, L. (1966) 'Social Mobility in England, 1500–1700', *P&P* 33, pp. 16–55

Stone, L. (1972) *The Causes of the English Revolution 1529–1642*, London, Ark Paperbacks

Stone, L. (ed.) (1974) *The University in Society*, Princeton, Princeton University Press, 2 vols

Stone, L. (ed.) (1976) *Schooling and Society*, Baltimore, Johns Hopkins University Press

Stone, L. (1977) *The Family, Sex and Marriage in England 1500–1800*, London, Weidenfeld and Nicholson

Stone, L. (1984) *An Open Elite? England 1540–1880*, Oxford, Clarendon Press

Stowe, J. (1614) *The Annales or Generall Chronicle of England began first by Maister Iohn Stow, and after him continued and augmented with matters forreyne, and domestique, auncient and moderne vnto the ende of this present yeere 1614 by Edmond Howes, gentleman*, London, printed by Thomas Adams

Strype, John (1694) *Memorials of the Most Reverend Father in God, Thomas Cranmer, sometime Lord Archbishop of Canterbury*, London, printed by Richard Chiswell, 3 vols

Sturgess, K. (1987) *Jacobean Private Theatre*, London, Routledge and Kegan Paul

Sweeney, J. G. (1985) *Jonson and the Psychology of the Public Theater*, Princeton, N.J., Princeton University Press

Sweezy, P. et al. (1978) *The Transition from Feudalism to Capitalism*, London, Verso

Sylvester, R. (ed.) (1963) *The Complete Works of Sir Thomas More*, Vol. 2, New Haven, Yale University Press

Taunton, N. 'Biography, a University Education, and Playwriting: Fletcher and Marlowe' *Research Opportunities in Renaissance Drama* 33, 1994, pp. 63–97

Tomkis, Thomas (1617) *Lingua, or The Combat of the Tongue and the fiue Senses for Superiority*, London, printed by Nicholas Okes for Simon Waterson

Udall, Nicholas (1533) *Floures for Latine Spekyng*, London, printed by Thomas Berthelet

Vives, Luis (1531) *On Education (De Tradendis Disciplinis)*, trans. and ed. F. Watson, Cambridge, Cambridge University Press, 1913

Vos, A. (ed.) (1989) *The Letters of Roger Ascham*, trans. M. Hatch and A. Vos, New York, Peter Lang

Walker, G. (1991) *Plays of Persuasion: Drama and Politics at the Court of Henry VIII*, Cambridge, Cambridge University Press

Walker, G. (1998) *The Politics of Performance in Early Renaissance Drama*, Cambridge, Cambridge University Press

Warner, William (1589) *The Second Part of Albion's England*, London, printed by Thomas Orwin for Thomas Cadman

Watson, F. (1908) *The English Grammar Schools to 1660*, Cambridge, Cambridge University Press

Welsford, E. (1968) *The Fool: His Social and Literary History*, London, Faber and Faber

Westfall, S. R. (1990) *Patrons and Performance: Early Tudor Household Revels*, Oxford, Clarendon Press

Wheeler, G. W. (ed.) (1926) *Letters of Sir Thomas Bodley to Thomas James, First Keeper of the Bodleian Library*, Oxford, Oxford University Press

Whibley, C. (ed.) (1904) *The Triumphant Reigne of Henry VIII by Edward Hall*, London, T. C and E. C. Jack, 2 vols

Whigham, F. (1984) *Ambition and Privilege: The Social Tropes of Elizabethan Courtesy Theory*, Berkeley, University of California Press

White, P. W. (1993) *Theatre and Reformation: Protestantism, patronage and playing in Tudor England*, Cambridge, Cambridge University Press.

White, P. W. (1997) 'The Theater and Religious Culture', in Cox and Kastan, pp. 133–51

Whitelocke, Sir James, (1609–32) *Liber Famelicus of Sir James Whitelocke*, ed. J. Bruce, London, Camden Society, 1858

Whytinton, Robert (1534) *The Thre Bookes of Tullyes offyces* (trans. of Cicero's *De Officiis*), London, printed by Wynkyn de Worde

Wickham, G. (1959) *Early English Stages Volume I: 1300–1576*, London, Routledge and Kegan Paul

Wigfall Green, A. (1931) *The Inns of Court and Early English Drama*, New York, Benjamin Blom

Williams, R. (1981) *Culture*, Glasgow, Fontana

Wilson, D. A. (1978) *England in the Age of Thomas More*, St Albans, Granada

Wilson, K. J. (1985) *Incomplete Fictions: the Formation of English Renaissance Dialogues*, Washington D.C., Catholic University of America Press

Wither, George (1613) *Abuses Stript and Whipt, or Satirical Essayes*, London, printed by G. Eld for Francis Burton

Wood, A. à (1796) *The History and Antiquities of the University of Oxford*, Oxford, privately printed.

Wright, L. B. (ed.) (1962) *Advice to a Son*, Ithaca, Cornell University Press

Wright, Thomas (1601) *The Passions of the Minde in Generall* London, printed by V. Simmes for WB

Wright, W. S. (1965) 'Edward Alleyn, Actor and Benefactor 1566–1626', *TN* 20, pp. 155–60

Wrightson, K. (1982) *English Society 1580–1680*, London, Hutchinson

Wrightson, K. (1991) 'Estates, degrees, and sorts: changing perceptions of society in Tudor and Stuart England', in *Language, History and Class*, ed. P. J. Corfield, Oxford, Basil Blackwell, pp. 30–52

Youings, J. (1984) *Sixteenth-Century England*, Harmondsworth, Penguin

Editions of Plays and Revels Discussed or Cited

As the original printed texts of plays have been used in some instances, for the sake of consistency old spelling editions have been used wherever possible in the case of others, except for Shakespeare. For Shirley's plays the edition of the *Dramatic Works* by Gifford and Dyce has been used, except where more recent editions of individual plays using old spelling are available.

Beaumont, Francis *The Woman Hater* (1606), in Bowers, Vol. 1, 1966–94

Beaumont, Francis *The Knight of the Burning Pestle* (1607), in Bowers, Vol. 1, 1966–1994

Brome, Richard *The Novella* (1632), London, printed by Richard Marriott and Thomas Dring, 1653

Brome, Richard *The Love-Sick Court* (1639), in *Dramatic Works*, Vol. 2

Brome, Richard *The New Academy* (1631), in *Dramatic Works*, Vol. 2

Chapman, George *All Fools* (1601), ed. G. Blakemore Evans in Holaday, 1970

Chapman, George *The Gentleman Usher* (1602), ed. R. Ornstein in Holaday, 1970

Chapman, George *A Humourous Day's Mirth* (1598), ed. A. Holaday in Holaday, 1970

Chapman, George *May Day* (1602), ed. R. F. Welsh in Holaday, 1970

Chapman, George *The Memorable Masque* (1613) ed. G. Blakemore Evans in Holaday, 1970

Chapman, George *Monsieur D'Olive* (1605), ed. A. Holaday in Holaday, 1970

Chapman, George *The Revenge of* Bussy *D'Ambois* (1610) ed. R. J. Lordi in Holaday, 1987

Chapman, George *Sir Gyles Goosecappe, Knight* (1602), in Holaday, 1987

Club Law (1599–60) ed. G. C. Moore Smith, Cambridge, Cambridge University Press, 1907

Contention between Liberality and Prodigality, The (1602) Oxford, Malone Society Reprints, 1913

Dekker, Thomas *If It Be Not Good The Diuel Is In It* (1612), in Bowers, Vol. 3, 1953–61

Dekker, Thomas *Patient Grissil* (1600), in Bowers, Vol. 1, 1955

Dekker, Thomas *Satiromastix* (1601), in Bowers, Vol. 1, 1953–61

Dekker, Thomas *The Shoemaker's Holiday* (1599), in Bowers, Vol. 1, 1953–61
Dekker, Thomas *The Whore of Babylon* (1606), in Bowers, Vol. 2, 1955
Edwardes, Richard *Damon and Pithias* (1564–65) ed. D. J. White, New York, Garland
        Publishing Inc., 1980
Englelond (Inglelond), Thomas *The Disobedient Child* (printed c. 1560) ed. J.
        Halliwell, London, Percy Society, 1848
Every Woman in her Humour (1607/8) ed. A. M. Tyson, New York, Garland, 1980
Fletcher, John *The Faithful Shepherdess* (1608?), in Bowers, Vol. 3, 1966–94
Fletcher, John *The Wild Goose Chase* (1621), in Bowers, Vol. 6, 1966–94
Ford, John *The Lover's Melancholy* (1621) ed. R. F. Hill, Manchester, Manchester
        University Press, 1985
Fulwell, Ulpian *Like Will to Like* (c.1568), in Happé, 1972
Gascoigne, George *The Glasse of Government* (1575) in Cunliffe, 1910
Gesta Grayorum, or the History of the High and Mighty Henry Prince of Purpoole
        (1594) ed. D. Bland, Liverpool, Liverpool University Press, 1968
Glapthorne, Henry *Wit in a Constable* (1639), London, printed by John Okes for F.C.,
        1640
Goffe, Thomas *The Careless Shepherdess* (1638), London, printed for Richard Rogers
        and William Ley, 1565
Greene, Robert *The Honorable Historie of Frier Bacon and Frier Bongay* (c.1590) in
        Collins, 1945
Greene, Robert *John of Bordeaux* (c. 1590) ed. B. Cellini, Florence, La Nuova Italia,
        1952
Greene, Robert *The Scottish Historie of Iames the Fovrth* (c. 1591), in Collins, 1945
Heywood, John. *Gentleness and Nobility* (1522–3?) London, printed by John Rastell,
        1525, in Axton, 1979
Heywood, John *Thyestes* (1560), London, printed by Henrye Sutton, 1560
Heywood, Thomas *The Brazen Age* (1613), London, printed by Nicholas Okes
        Hick Scorner (1513–14) in Manly, Vol. 1, 1897
Heteroclitanomalonomia in S. Gossett, and T. L. Berger (eds) *Jacobean
        AcademicPlays*, Oxford, Malone Society Collections 14, 1998
Impatient Poverty (1560) ed. J. Farmer, Tudor Reprinted and Parallel Texts (private
        printing) 1909
Jacob and Esau (1568) in White, 1992
Jonson, Ben, *Bartholemew Fair* (1614) in Herford and Simpson, Vol. 6
Jonson, Ben, *Cynthias Revels* (1600) in Herford and Simpson, Vol. 4
Jonson, Ben *The Case is Altered* 9 (1597) in Herford and Simpson, Vol. 3
Jonson, Ben *Epicoene or The Silent Woman* (1609) in Herford and Simpson Vol. 5
Jonson, Ben *Every Man in His Humour* (1598 and 1616) in Herford and Simpson,
        Vol. 3
Jonson, Ben *Every Man out of His Humour* (1599) in Herford and Simpson, Vol. 3
Jonson, Ben *The Magnetic Lady* (1632) in Herford and Simpson, Vol. 6
Jonson, Ben *The Masque of Queens* (1609) in Herford and Simpson, Vol. 7
Jonson, Ben *The Staple of News* (1626) in Herford and Simpson, Vol. 6
July and Julian (1547–53) Oxford, Malone Society Reprints, 1955
Liberality and Prodigality (1601) (see *Contention between Liberality and Prodigality*)
Love Feigned and Unfeigned (1540–60) (fragment) Oxford, Malone Society
        Collections, Part 1, 1907

Lupton, Thomas *All for Money* (1578) London, printed Roger Ward and Richard Mundee

Lusty Juventus (c.1550) Oxford, Malone Society Reprints, 1966

Lyly, John *Midas* (1590) in Bond, Vol. 3, 1967

Lyly, John *Mother Bombie* (1590) in Bond, Vol. 3, 1967

Lyly, John *Sapho and Phao* (1583) in Bond, Vol. 2, 1902,

Mankind (c. 1470) in Wickham, 1976

Marlowe, Christopher *Doctor Faustus* (1588–89) in Bowers, Vol. 2, 1971

Marston, John *The Dutch Courtesan* (1604), ed. P. Davison, Edinburgh, Oliver and Boyd, 1968

Marston, John *Histrio-mastix, Or The Player Whipt* (1598?, printed 1600), in Wood, Vol. 3, 1939

Marston, John *Jack Drums Entertainment or The Comedie of Pasquill and Katherine* (1601) in Wood, Vol. 3, 1939

Massinger, Philip and John Fletcher *The Elder Brother* (1624/5) in Bowers, Vol. 9, 1966–94

Mayne, Jasper *The City Match* (1637–8), Oxford, printed by Henry Hall, 1658

Medwall, Henry *Fulgens and Lucres* (1497–98?) in Nelson, 1980

Medwall, Henry *Nature* (1490–1500, printed London, John Rastell, c. 1530) in Nelson, 1980

Merbury, Francis *Marriage of Wit and Wisdom* (1571–78) in Wickham, 1976

Middleton, Thomas *A Chaste Maid in Cheapside* (1613) ed. C. Barber, Edinburgh, Oliver and Boyd, 1969

Middleton, Thomas and William Rowley *Wit at Several Weapons* (1613) London, printed for J.T., 1718 (misattributed to Beaumont and Fletcher)

Misogonus (1571) in R. W. Bond, *Early Plays from the Italian*, Oxford, Clarendon Press, 1911

Nabbes, Thomas *Tottenham Court* (1634?), printed by James Roberts and E. Berington, 1718

Nabbes, Thomas *Covent Garden* (1632) London, printed by Richard Oulton for Charles Green,

Nice Wanton (1550) in Manly, Vol. 1, 1967

The Parnassus Trilogy (1600–1601?) in J. B. Leishman (ed.) *The Three Parnassus Plays,* London, Ivor Nicholson and Watson, 1949

Play of Poore, The (fragment, c. 1617/8) ed. D. Carnegie, Malone Society Collections Part 15, 1993

The Prodigal Son (Pater, Filius et Uxor – fragment) (1530) Oxford, Malone Society Collections, Part I, 1907

Prodigal Son, The Comedy of the (printed 1620, possibly performed 1594) in Simpson, 1878

The Puritan, or the Widow of Watling Street (1606) London, printed for J. Tonson, 1734

Randolph, Thomas *Aristippus or The Iouiall Philosopher* (1626) London, printed by Thomas Harper for John Marriott, 1630

Randolph, Thomas (?) *The Drinking Academy* (1623–24?) ed. S. Tannenbaum and H. Rollins, Cambridge, Mass., Harvard University Press, 1930

Randolph, Thomas, *The Muses Looking Glass* (1630) London, printed 1662, no printer named

Rastell, John *Four Elements* (printed 1520) in Axton, 1979

Redford, John *The Marriage of Wit and Science* (c. 1539) in Happé, 1972

Rowley, Samuel *When You See Me, You Know Me Or the famous Chronicle Historie of king Henry the eight, with the birth and vertuous life of Edward, Prince of Wales* (1604) Oxford, Malone Society Reprints, 1952

Shakespeare, William *All's Well that Ends Well* (1602) ed. G. K. Hunter, London, Methuen (Arden), 1959

Shakespeare, William, *As You Like It* (c. 1599) ed. A. Latham, London, Methuen (Arden), 1975

Shakespeare, William *Hamlet* (1601) ed. H. Jenkins, London, Methuen (Arden), 1982

Shakespeare, William, *King Lear* (1605) ed. K. Muir, London, Methuen (Arden), 1964

Shakespeare, William *King Richard II*, ed. P. Ure, London, Methuen, (Arden), 1956

Shakespeare, William *A Midsummer Night's Dream* (c. 1595) ed. H. F. Brooks, London, Methuen (Arden), 1979

Shakespeare, William *Love's Labours Lost*, (1597) ed. R. David, London, Methuen (Arden), 1951, repr. 1983

Shakespeare, William *Troilus and Cressida* (Second Issue 1609), London, printed by G. Eld for R. Bonian and H. Whalley

Shakespeare, William *Twelfth Night* (1601) ed. J. M. Lothian and T. W. Craik, London, Methuen (Arden), 1975

Sharpham, Edward *Cupid's Whirligig* (1607) ed. A. Nicoll, London, Golden Cockerel Press, 1926

Shirley, James *The Ball* (1632) in Gifford and Dyce, Vol. 3, 1833

Shirley, James *A Contention for Honour and Riches* (1631) in Gifford and Dyce, Vol. 6, 1833

Shirley, James *The Gentleman of Venice* of (1639) in Gifford and Dyce, Vol. 5, 1833

Shirley, James *Honoria and Mammon* (1658) in Gifford and Dyce, Vol. 2, 1833

Shirley, James *The Humorous Courtier* (1631) ed. M. Morillo, New York, Garland, 1979

Shirley, James *Hyde Park* (1632) in Gifford and Dyce, Vol. 2, 1833

Shirley, James *The Lady of Pleasure* (1635), ed. M. J. Thorssen, New York, Garland, 1980

Shirley, James *Love Tricks, or The School of Complement* (1625) in Gifford and Dyce, Vol. 1, 1833

Shirley, James *The Sisters* (1642) in Gifford and Dyce, Vol. 5, 1833

Shirley, James *The Triumph of Beauty* (1646) in Gifford and Dyce, Vol. 5, 1833

Skelton, John *Magnificence* (1520–22) ed. P. Neuss, Manchester, Manchester University Press, 1980

Stevenson, William (?) *Gammer Gurton's Needle* (1553) in W. Tydeman, *Four Tudor Comedies*, Harmondsworth, Penguin, 1984

Tomkis, Thomas *Albumazar* (1614), London, printed by Nicholas Okes for Walter Burre, 1615

Trial of Treasure, The (c. 1565) ed. J. O. Halliwell, Percy Society, 1850

Wager, Lewis *The Life and Repentaunce of Marie Magdaleine* (c.1550) in White, 1992

Wager, Lewis *The Longer Thou Livest* (1560–68) London, printed by Wyllyam How for Richarde Johnes

Webster, John *The White Devil* (1612) in *The Complete Works of John Webster*, ed. F.L. Lucas, London, Chatto and Windus, Vol. 1, 1927

Wealth and Health (1553–57) Oxford, Malone Society Reprints, 1907

Wild, Robert *The Benefice* (printed 1639, written earlier) London, printed by R.
    Janeway
Wilson, Robert *The Cobler's Prophecy* (1594) ed. A. C. Wood and W. W. Greg,
    Oxford, Malone Society Reprints, 1914
Wily Beguiled (1602) ed. W. W. Greg, Oxford, Malone Society Reprints, 1913
Wit's Triumvirate (c. 1635) ed. C. A. Wilson, Salzburg, Institut für Englische Sprache
    und Literatur, 1975
The World and the Child (c. 1507) in Manly, Vol. 1, 1897
Youth (1513–29) in Happé, 1972

Anthologies and Collected Editions

Axton, R. (ed.) (1979) *Three Rastell Plays*, Cambridge, D. S. Brewer
Bond, R. W. (ed.) (1967) *The Complete Works of John Lyly*, Oxford, Clarendon Press
Bowers, F. (ed.) (1953–61) *The Dramatic Works of Thomas Dekker*, Cambridge,
    Cambridge University Press, 4 vols
Bowers, F. (1966–94) (gen. ed.) *The Dramatic Works in the Beaumont and Fletcher
    Canon*, London, Cambridge University Press, 10 vols
Bowers, F. (1973) *The Complete Works of Christopher Marlowe*, Cambridge,
    Cambridge University Press
Brome, Richard (no ed.) (1873) *The Dramatic Works of Richard Brome*, London, John
    Pearson, 3 vols
Collins, J. C. (ed.) (1945) *The Plays and Poems of Robert Greene*, Oxford, Clarendon
    Press
Gifford, W. and A. Dyce (eds) (1833) *The Dramatic Works and Poems of James
    Shirley*, London, John Murray, 6 vols
Happé, P. (1972) *Tudor Interludes*, Harmondsworth, Penguin
Holaday, A. (gen. ed.) (1970) *The Plays of George Chapman, Volume 1: The
    Comedies* Urbana, University of Illinois Press
Holaday, A. (gen. ed.) (1987) *The Plays of George Chapman: The Tragedies with* Sir
    Gyles Goosecappe, Cambridge, D. S. Brewer
Lancashire I. (ed.) (1980) *Two Tudor Interludes: The Interlude of Youth, Hick
    Scorner*, Manchester, Manchester University Press
Manly, J. (ed.) (1967) *Specimens of the Pre-Shaksperean Drama*, New York, Biblo
    and Tannen (originally published 1897, Boston, Ginn and Co.)
Nelson A. H. (ed.) (1980) *The Plays of Henry Medwall*, Cambridge, D. S. Brewer
Somerset, J. A. (1974) (ed.) *Four Tudor Interludes*, London, Athlone Press
Wickham, G. (ed.) (1976) *English Moral Interludes*, London, Dent
White, P. W. (1992) *Reformation Biblical Drama in England: The Life and
    Repentaunce of Mary Magdalene and The History of Jacob and Esau*, New
    York, Garland
Wood, H. (ed.) (1939) *The Plays of John Marston*, Edinburgh, Oliver and Boyd

Index